DAILY LIFE IN THE LATE MIDDLE AGES

EDITED BY RICHARD BRITNELL

SUTTON PUBLISHING

First published in 1998 by
Sutton Publishing Limited · Phoenix Mill
Thrupp · Stroud · Gloucestershire · GL5 2BU

British Library Cataloguing in Publication Data
A catalogue record for this book is available from the British Library.

ISBN 0-7509-1587-0

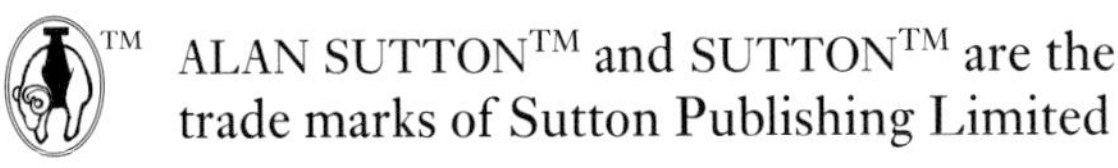

Typeset in 11/12 pt Ehrhardt.
Typesetting and origination by
Sutton Publishing Limited.
Printed in Great Britain by
Butler & Tanner, Frome, Somerset.

Contents

Colour plates appear between pp. 90 and 91.

Britnell, Richard (ed), *Daily Life in the Late Middle Ages*
ISBN 0 7509 1587 0

Errata

Colour plate 9, caption should read, *An illuminated book describing the 'goostly tresoure' built up by the Tailors' fraternity. The master and wardens listed served in 1456–7, but the book was probably compiled* c. *1510. At the Reformation the particulars of indulgences, confraternal links with religious houses and the foundation of a chapel in St. Paul's Cathedral were crossed out. (Guildhall Library, Merchant Taylors' Company, London, Ancient MS Books, vol. 2, f. 17. By permission of the Merchant Taylors' Company, London.)*

Colour plate 10, caption should read, *The Pewterers' charter granted in 1473. (Guildhall Library, MS 8695. By permission of the Worshipful Company of Pewterers, London.)*

p. 129, caption should read, *A list of 112 crafts practised in the City of London in 1422, drawn up by the clerk of the Brewers' Company. (Guildhall Library, MS 5440, f. 11v. By permission of the Worshipful Company of Brewers, London.)*

p. 131, caption should read, *Payments received from various groups for hiring Brewers' Hall in the 1420s, including the sum of 1*s 8d *(20*d*) received 'of þe ffootballpleyers be ii tymes'. (Guildhall Library, MS 5440, f. 84. By permission of the Worshipful Company of Brewers, London.)*

p. 133, caption should read, *A menu for the annual feast held by the Tailors on the Nativity of St John the Baptist in 1429. (Merchant Taylors' Company, London, Accounts, vol. 1, f. 212. By permission of the Merchant Taylors' Company, London.)*

p. 136, caption should read, *Expenses for men and equipment contributed by the Tailors' guild to the force being assembled in 1436 in order to relieve the town of Calais. (Merchant Taylors' Company, London, Accounts, vol. 1, f. 276. By permission of the Merchant Taylors' Company, London.)*

p. 142, caption should read, *A copy of a letter from the master and wardens of the Tailors in November 1492, requesting them to provide 'xxx persones on horssebak' to greet Henry VII on his return from France. (Merchant Taylors' Company, London, Court Minutes, vol. 2, f. 52. By permission of the Merchant Taylors' Company, London.)*

Bristol Record Society, and is currently editing the churchwardens' accounts of St Andrew Hubbard, London.

Professor Richard Britnell, who teaches History at the University of Durham, writes mostly about economic history. His most recent book is *The Closing of the Middle Ages? England 1471–1529*.

ACKNOWLEDGEMENTS

Five chapters in this collection (1, 2, 7–9) were originally prepared for a conference at the University of Kent at Canterbury between 29 and 31 March 1996, organized by Peter and Carolyn Hammond on behalf of the Richard III Society. The remainder were specially written for this volume to improve its range and balance. I am grateful to all the authors for their smooth cooperation in putting the book together. Carole Rawcliffe not only contributed chapter 3 but also gave welcome advice at other points, particularly relating to the choice of illustrations. My thanks, too, to Jan Rhodes for checking the proofs and preparing the index.

Richard Britnell

Introduction

RICHARD BRITNELL

The daily lives of many families in the late Middle Ages of course shared common features, and historians can recover some of this shared knowledge and experience from the rich documentary and archaeological evidence that has survived. For example, they can describe with considerable reliability what sort of house a fifteenth-century tenant farmer in the English Midlands might have lived in, what sort of utensils he used at home, how he dressed, how he spoke, how he ploughed his land, what he sowed, what animals he kept, what sort of levels of productivity he obtained from his labours, what rent he paid and what he ate, how he went about redressing wrongs done to him, what religious doctrines he held, what devout practices were open to him, and how he supported his parish church. All this counts a lot towards understanding his daily life, and variations in many of these details could be compared both between different parts of the country and across time.

There remains a very great deal, nevertheless, that cannot be recovered from any possible source. The conduct of everyday life depends upon a complex set of understandings about how to do things, and this sort of knowledge, learned from infancy till it becomes second nature, is rarely written down. Even with all our modern exposure to other peoples' business, it is not difficult to think of areas of experience where it is impossible to say what is predictable or 'normal'. The impossibility of directly observing medieval ways is not compensated by the kind of written evidence that proliferates in modern times, so that it is impossible to describe the daily life of any fifteenth-century person in detail, even in the case of those (like kings) who attracted considerable personal interest, or those (like monks) who lived by prescribed routines. However much we can reliably say about a Midland tenant farmer, it does not amount to a narrative of his daily life, even for a day when he was out in the fields with a plough or a harrow, and we should be even more exercised to describe a day in the life of his wife, his young children, or his elderly parents. At every point, from the moment the first member of the family was woken up by a baby, a cockerel or the sun, we should have to engage in imaginative invention in order to compile a continuous account of a day in the life of such country folk.

Ignorance creates empty spaces into which unexamined assumptions can worm their way. In the absence of recorded expression of opinion from all but a small minority of fifteenth-century people, it is easy to assume that their beliefs and experiences were much more of a piece than they really were. The idea that medieval people all thought the same is encouraged, of course, by evidence of the remarkable effectiveness of the Roman Church in formalizing large areas of doctrine and unifying its organization to the exclusion of overt dissent. Yet the notion that the Church turned people into peas in a pod is a fiction. It is no more legitimate to suppose that all Christians thought and behaved in the same way then than to conclude that all participants in parliamentary democracy think and behave in the same way now. On questions of ecclesiastical organization there was considerable scope for variety. There was evidently vast room for disagreement among intellectuals about how much reform the Church needed, and where the main effort should be directed. The continuing existence of the Lollard movement, although only as a suppressed minority of the population, shows that there was also disagreement among non-intellectuals. In some matters the Church tolerated considerable diversity of practice. One of these – and one that impinged on debates about reform – was the great issue of what constituted superstition and magic. Between the most sceptical philosopher and the most credulous dupe there were wide differences of opinion both about what was efficacious and about what was permissible within a Christian framework. The ecclesiastical courts aimed to suppress some practices deemed beyond the pale, but they did not tangle with wide areas of belief about which the educated classes differed among themselves.

Many secure generalizations may be made concerning the material conditions of everyday life in the later Middle Ages, simply because we know so much about the level of technical knowledge available and can often picture its implications quite accurately. Of all the different aspects of economic and social history, this is perhaps the most responsive to accurate observation and description. The main difficulty, as in any period of history, is not to say what technical knowledge permitted but to describe how in fact its benefits were distributed. In one aspect of the problem, this means recognizing that in the Middle Ages, as now, the rich were more able than the poor to benefit from particular technologies designed to serve their needs. We know that books were being printed in England from 1476, but it is a different problem to say just who benefited from the change, and how the number and nature of these beneficiaries changed over time. Research in areas like this requires much more than just historical imagination!

Both intellectually and materially, then, the range of daily experience in late medieval England was wide. The number of people in the kingdom was probably below 2 million through most of the period. The best estimates suggest about 2.5 to 3 million in 1377 and about 1.8 to 2.3 million in 1522, but with a prolonged decline in between. Yet this small number of people was hierarchically organized into many different self-conscious strata (both lay and clerical) of differing income and status. These scattered families also supported a complex economy in which there were numerous towns and trading institutions, and in which most families depended to some extent on trade, if only to obtain cash to pay their rent and taxes. A high degree of occupational specialization was characteristic chiefly of the towns, where craft regulations and apprenticeship rules often imply that men were normally expected to work in a single trade. Diversity of occupation was more usual among the population as a whole, either because the nature of work changed with the seasons (as in the case of agricultural work) or because people had to put together a variety of different types of work to earn a living. Many smallholders, for example, combined work on the land with some part-time manufacturing work at home. The diversity of individual experience means that it is inappropriate to think of daily life in the later Middle Ages as some variant of tribal 'organic solidarity'.

The essays in this volume avoid broad generalizations about medieval people that might be historical but so limited as to be not very interesting. They also avoid imaginative constructions of daily life that might be engaging but not very historical. The path between these two pitfalls is by way of evidence that illustrates clearly defined social environments and particular norms of thought and behaviour. Though the collection does not set out to give even the illusion of comprehensiveness, an effort has been made to represent different aspects of late medieval society – rural and urban, male and female, secular and religious, private and public, nationwide and local. Within this variety of coverage, the various soundings of the past intersect, and readers will find that despite their diversity of approach the different papers often come together on particular issues. This approach to the Middle Ages is like getting to know a town by just walking about, sometimes exploring unfamiliar streets, sometimes returning, whether unexpectedly or by design, to central squares and familiar landmarks. For the purposes of daily life, at least, this is the most pleasant and appropriate technique.

CHAPTER 1

Dress and Fashions *c.* 1470

ANNE SUTTON

In the romance of *Partonope de Blois*, written before 1188, the French author spent forty-six rhapsodic lines of verse describing the beauty and the dress of a princess; in the middle of the fifteenth century an English poet made a lively, competent and amusing translation, and this is his rendering of the passage:

> Within awhile come in anon
> A seemly lady, and that a fair one.
> In her person was found no lack:
> Her hair hung tressed at her back,
> Full 'bloye' [= blond], which hung down to her feet.
> Each of her beauties to other was meet,
> And so answering in each degree,
> That she was praised passingly of beauty.
> Her array to rehearse here,
> I needeth not, but in the best manner
> She was arrayed, this fair may.
> But who so lust to hear of her array,
> Let him go to the French book,
> That idle matter I forsake
> To tell it in prose or else in rhyme.
> For me thought it tarried great time,
> And is a matter full needless,
> For each man wot well withouten less,
> A lady that is of high degree
> Arrayed in the best manner must be.
> What needs to speak of her forehead,
> Of her nose, her mouth, her lips red,
> Of her shape, her arms small?
> Of this and more a right great tale
> Mine author maketh, which shall not for me
> Be now rehearsed, but thus that she
> Was helden one of the fairest
> That was alive, and thereto the goodliest
> With to deal that might be
> And Urake for sooth hight she.[1]

Dame Prudence, in the fantasy dress suited to a Virtue, surrounded by princesses all in contemporary, fashionable gowns and tires or atours. *(Yale University, Beinecke Rare Book and Manuscript Library, Beinecke MS 427, f. 16. By permission.)*

Instead of forty-six lines of useful information about female attire in the mid-fifteenth century, we have thirty lines of authorial expostulation. The author's excuses illustrate some of the problems relating to the study of female dress in England in the fifteenth century: texts tell us little and male writers are not interested in women's dress.

This article will focus on the years around 1470, paying particular attention to women's dress; it will, it is hoped, illustrate both the dress of the time effectively, and the wide variety, and often surprising sources to which the historian of English medieval dress is reduced. There is generally a paucity of sources of all kinds for dress in England at this date, in particular the indispensable domestic accounts and inventories; there are few for men and almost none for women, of all ranks.[2] References have to be scoured from wills – again, there are comparatively few for women – and a wide variety of apparently unlikely sources, some of which are illustrated below. Recourse also has to be made to continental sources both written and, especially, pictorial to supply the lack of English illustrative material.[3]

Enormously rich sources for the study of dress in the fifteenth century are the book illustrations and panel paintings produced in the Low Countries and France, but they also present problems. We are indebted to the realism of painters in the tradition of Van Eyck, which ensured that contemporary dress was precisely copied in its style and manufacture as well as in its textiles and decoration; it was also the custom to dress personages of the past – Caesar and Alexander, Guinevere and Arthur – in contemporary and fashionable dress appropriate to their rank. In English manuscripts the realism achieved may have been inadequate, but the Virgin Mary as Queen of Heaven was, for example, consistently dressed in the robes which the queen of England wore on state occasions. From about 1450, however, and with increasing momentum to the end of the century, this changed: artists began to depict characters from the past in exotic and fanciful 'costume' rather than in contemporary dress. The realism of the painters, when applied to the textiles and jewels worn by saints and long-dead kings and queens, thus becomes a snare: increasingly the same realism is not applied to the fashion of the garments. This predilection for fantasy can also be illustrated from an elegant poem, *The Flower and the Leaf*, datable to the 1470s, full of courtly touches and details of dress. It has only one full description of a dress, the one worn by the allegorical character of Lady Temperance:

And furthermore to speak of her array
I shall you tell the manner of her gown:
Of cloth of gold full rich, it is no nay,
The colour blue of a right good fashion,
In tabard wise, the sleeves hanging down;
And what purfile there was and in what wise
So as I can I shall it you devise.

After a sort the collar and the vent,
Like as ermine is made in purfiling,
With great pearls full fine and orient
They were couched all after one working,
With diamonds instead of powdering;
The sleeves and purfiles of assize,
They were made like in everywise;

About her neck a 'serpe' of fair rubies
In white flowers of right fine enamel;
Upon her head set in the freshest wise
A circle with great balas of entail.[4]

The tabard and the long hanging sleeves reveal that the author is not speaking of *fashionable* dress of the 1470s; the jewelled borders of sleeves, hem and neckline, diamonds taking the place of the black tails that usually powdered ermine, are pure fantasy. The poet cannot mislead us so effectively, however, as the painter and by the sixteenth century there is little useful information as regards

The presentation of the book to Duke Philip the Good takes place at the back within the palace; courtiers strut in the courtyard, and in the town street outside the precinct stall-keepers, including some women, are busy. The broad-shouldered, short gowns and the long-toed shoes which came increasingly into vogue in the 1460s are well shown. The bourgeois, and increasingly old-fashioned, hood of the male stall-keepers contrasts with the hats of the other men; the women wear versions of hood and coverchief. (From the Life of Charlemagne, *illustrated by Jan Tavernier, before March 1460. Brussels, Bibliothèque Royale MS 9066, f. 11. Copyright Bibliothèque Royale Albert Ier, Bruxelles. By permission.)*

contemporary dress in the illustrations of books, tapestries or stained glass; everything was fantasy, frequently a fantasy rendering of what was thought to be Greek or Roman dress.

We also have to face up to the problem that most pictorial sources for dress are not dated precisely. We may be able to date the writing of a finely illustrated manuscript and still be misled because the illustrations were done much later. We have to be careful to rely first and foremost on those images that are dated securely. But even that does not save us from the artist who shows us garments which are out of date because he liked the style or had dressed a model in an old garment in his studio.[5] To date dress and to understand dress we need also to see both men and women in a picture, because the dress of men and women changes in different ways and at different speeds. In the later Middle Ages the dress of women changed much more slowly than that of men and it was subject to far less dramatic changes of style, largely because only men could vary the length of their skirts from the very short to the very long.[6] To see men and women together in a picture safeguards us against misunderstanding the scene, particularly as regards date. The student of fashion cannot afford to ignore the dress of one sex because the dress of both is needed to understand and date the dress of each.

Which leads us to a third problem specifically for the student of female dress: as most books were written by men, about men and illustrated by men for men, and women were excluded from most activities described in these books, such as government, administration, councils and warfare – and battles above all were favourite subjects for illustration – women are severely underrepresented in pictures. This applies even to books of history and romances where women were permitted some activities. To give an example, the famous manuscript of the *Life of Charlemagne*, illustrated for Philip the Good by Jan Tavernier, one of the most gifted of the artists employed by Philip in the 1450s, contains a famous and frequently reproduced scene showing the presentation of the book to Philip. This has, in the foreground, some shopkeepers, some women and a few other characters in a narrow street of one of the duke's dominions; every other of the 105 pictures in the book is of a battle.[7] Turning the pages, one suspects that Tavernier's despair was equal to ours.

There are also considerable problems of terminology, a confusion often exacerbated by the failure of historians to use the contemporary terms either at all or with precision and care. Changes in fashion did not necessarily bring about immediate changes in terminology. The clerks on whom we depend for our wording were more concerned with recording the money spent than with fashion, and they tended to use the same blanket terms for a range of closely related garments; often they mention only one garment and fail to specify the equally important accessories. Rarely can we relate a verbal description to a picture; rarely can we match a particular item of clothing to an illustration. Françoise Piponnier correctly observes that the life of the words and the life of the fashions and shapes were more or less autonomous: we have to group words rather than find precise meanings for them.[8] For England there are additional problems. The English never had as many words for fashionable garments and accessories as the French, they frequently borrowed and used the French words and we still have to borrow some French words to fill out the English vocabulary. As soon as the English adopted a French word it began to have its own 'English' meaning. For example, in fifteenth-century England the word 'robe' continued to have its old meaning of a collection of several garments and was used particularly for the royal robe(s) of estate for the king and queen which might comprise three or more garments; in France, however, it came to refer to one garment only, the equivalent of the English 'gown'.[9]

The main elements of male dress in the later fifteenth century in English (and French) were as follows: the shirt (*chemise*); hose (*chausses*), usually of cloth cut on the bias, and lined throughout or half-lined, with feet or without;[10] the doublet (*pourpoint*[11]), a short, under-garment; the gown (*robe*), which could be long, to the knee or mid-leg, or short, and was usually lined; the jacket (*jacquette*), an alternative to the short gown, usually lined, which could be short or longer but not full length; the mantle, cloak or cape (*manteau*, *cape*); hood (*chaperon* and the *cornette*, which was both a new version of the hood developed in the second half of the fifteenth century and the name applied to the long tail of the hood); hat (*chapeau*) and bonnet (*bonnet*), both in many styles and shapes.[12] For women there was the smock (*chemise*);[13] hose (*chausses*), which were always of black woollen cloth; the kirtle (*la cotte*), worn alone inside the house or in warm weather or for work, but usually worn as an undergarment (it was laced and the lacing could be done in a way that revealed the smock below); the gown (*robe*), lined and worn with a train or without; an alternative to the gown was the surcoat (*surcot*), an old-fashioned garment worn to show rank, sleeveless and 'open' (*ouvert*), showing both the sleeves and the sides of the body of the kirtle or 'coat', hence surcoat; girdle (*ceinture*); coverchiefs and kerchiefs, for the head and the neck, and to go over headdresses (*couvrechiefs*, *couvrechiefs à atourner*, *tourets de cols*); mantle, cloak or cape (*manteau*, *cape*); hood (*chaperon*, *cornette*) and bonnet (*bonnet*); and lastly the *atours*, the structures built up on the base of a bonnet,[14] which was usually rendered by 'tire' or 'tires' in the plural (often referred to as a pair).[15] There were other names that denoted fashionable varieties of all these garments, some French, some Italian.

A little more needs to be said about the *atours*, which fascinate the modern observer, but about which remarkably little is known, English sources being especially silent. Insufficient details survive about the styles and the making up of even the designs devised by King René of Anjou for his court ladies.[16] The lack of specific detail, apart from in pictorial sources, is perhaps not surprising because *atours* were ephemeral confections; like ladies' hats in the twentieth century before the 1960s, they were unique to the wearer, soon wore out and were soon out of fashion, their parts re-used for the next creation. In 1466 the inventory of Lady Elizabeth Lewkenor included 'vij pecis of perle set on parchemyn and gold foile made yn levis and for fillettes', which seem to be part of the decoration of a headdress. And more readily understandable: a pair of 'tiris' of silver wire and over gilt with the fillet of the same, weighing 1⅜ oz, valued at 3*s* 4*d*. The fillet may be the long band which surrounds the face.[17] The Howard household books of 1481 record 'a peyer of tyres'.[18]

The main sources for English terminology are wills and inventories, although they rarely go into fashionable details: it is the main garments that are mentioned along with the jewelled accessories, and the terminology remains the same over several decades.[19] Some examples are found in the wills of several reasonably prosperous London widows. Elizabeth Kirkby (née Heron), was a prosperous widow of St Dunstan's in the East, London. In her will of 1488 she left her sister, Margaret Strother, her best gown of violet in grain furred with grey and her narrow girdle of red with a long harness of silver and a pair of coral beads with gauds of gold; her next sister, Katherine, received her second-best gown of violet in grain furred with grey, another narrow red girdle with a long harness of silver and a pair of beads of unspecified material with gauds of silver gilt; her third sister, Isabel, was left a gown of russet furred with shanks, another narrow girdle (no colour given) harnessed with silver and a pair of beads of mother-of-pearl with gauds of silver gilt. The sisters appear to be listed and rewarded according to their married status, and perhaps also by their age. A niece receives her gown of murrey in grain furred with grey and a girdle called a 'dimyseut', and to another goes a gown of blue furred with white and a violet girdle with a broad harness. A cousin, presumably a poor relation, receives one of her 'worst' girdles, among other things. She also leaves her 'son in law' (stepson), Richard Kirkby, a murrey gown in grain furred with marten that had belonged to his father. She has an impressive number of gowns to leave, several of the same colour and/or cloth, several expensive ones in grain, others more workaday in russet. The furred ones are obviously of greater value both for status and for warmth: she wears grey, that is the back fur of the grey squirrel; the white is probably lamb rather than the old-fashioned miniver, the white belly fur of the squirrel, which she would probably have specified. She leaves no more expensive furs of her own although her late husband had had a gown of murrey in grain furred with marten, a much more luxurious fur. The jewellery mentioned consists mainly of a variety of prayer-beads, attractive if hung at the waist, and girdles. But she also left her 'best table dyamound' to Lewis Bonvice, a merchant of Lucca; a small pair of amber beads to an Elizabeth Elderton with one of her 'tablets' of gold 'to hang aboute hyr nek'; a ring of gold with a 'poynted dyamound enamelyd aboute' to Katherine, wife of her brother, John Heron, mercer of London; her girdle harnessed with gold, presumably her best, to Our Lady of Walsingham; an ouche of gold 'with ij lyons sett with stone and perle' to Our Lady of Hull, where she had been born; and a cross of gold set with emeralds to Our Lady of Doncaster.[20] Elizabeth's will is about as expressive as we can hope for as regards clothes.[21]

Another will of a London widow, Margaret Agmondesham, possibly a mercer or silkwoman in her own right, left several bequests in 1493, including her two 'tukking' girdles (girdles through which the gown or kirtle was drawn until the skirt reached the desired length),[22] her 'bonett of velvet with all my frountelettys longing therto' and her tippet of silk.[23] The velvet bonnet and frontlet (the long lappet or band, often also of velvet, which surrounded the face) was worn by women in different styles and shapes from the 1470s onwards.[24] The 'tippet' was ubiquitous in accounts and wills and worn by men and women at the end of the fifteenth century; at this date it was worn round the neck and shoulders for warmth.[25] Some wills give a brief image of a particular gown in use: Joan Alford, widow of Peter, mercer of London, in 1492 left to Margaret, her servant, 'my blacke gowne that I sytt in the parlour furred at the making of this my said testament'.[26]

Enough has been said to indicate that 'fashion' is the most elusive element of the study of dress before the modern period, but something, nevertheless, can be revealed of the 'fashions' of northern France, the Low Countries and England round about 1470. England cannot be treated in isolation because England lacks the pictorial sources from which to work.[27]

The late 1450s and 1460s witnessed a marked fashion change and caused such a furore that a variety of commentators rushed to put their thoughts into writing. An unknown Burgundian chronicler decided to put in his chronicle an account of the changes he had witnessed in fashionable dress under the events of the year 1467. The account was certainly not original to him but he and his source had at least seen and experienced the changes of fashion they recorded.

> In this year [1467] ladies and young gentlewomen (*demoiselles*) put aside the trains they wore on their gowns, and instead they wore (*mirent*) borders on their gowns of grey, lettice[28] and marten, of velvet and other fabrics, as wide and as valuable as they could afford *velours de hault* or more. And they wore headdresses (*boureles*)[29] in the shape of a round bonnet which narrowed above, some to a height of half an ell or three quarters and some lower; with delicate (*deliez*) coverchiefs over them, some hanging down at the back to the ground

Two ladies gardening in plain gowns (kirtles beneath) with warm tippets about their necks. One wears a fashionable bonnet with coverchief, the other, probably of lower status, has her hair concealed in a simple coverchief, the ends pinned up while she is working. The style would have recommended itself to the Lady of the Vision of Edmund Leversedge. *(From a Dutch version of Christine de Pizan,* Cité des Dames, *copied 1475, BL, Additional MS 20,698, f. 17. By permission of the British Library.)*

and others not so long. And they took to wearing their girdles of silk much wider than they were used to do with much more lavish buckles, and collars of gold round their necks in a different way and much more elegantly than they were used to, and in various styles.

And at this time also the men took to wearing clothes shorter than they had ever done, to such a degree that one could see the shape of their buttocks and genitals, in the same way as people usually dress monkeys, which was

The two ladies again; the one of lower social status reveals the back of her gown and wears a lower bonnet than the other. (From a Dutch version of Christine de Pizan, Cité des Dames, *copied 1475, BL, Additional MS 20,698, f. 14. By permission of the British Library.)*

ungentlemanly (*mal honneste*) and very immodest. And they made slits in the sleeves of their gowns and doublets (*robes*; *pourpoints*) in order to show off their fine, large, white shirts; they also wore their hair so long that their faces were hidden, even their eyes. And on their heads they wore bonnets of cloth as tall as a quarter [ell] or more; both knights and esquires also wore most sumptuous chains of gold without difference of rank. Even yeomen (*vallets*) wore doublets of silk, of satin and velvet, and almost everyone, especially those in the courts of princes, had shoes with long pikes a quarter [ell] long, and indeed even longer. They also wore in their doublets great bolsters (*mahoitres*)[30] on their shoulders to show that they were broad shouldered which is very vain and probably hateful to God; and those who wore short dress one day wore long clothes to the ground the next day; and this was so common that there was no fellow, however lowly, who did not want to wear the fashions of the great and rich, be it long or short, without thinking of the cost and expenditure or whether it was fitting to his rank.[31]

In England, one poem, among several with the same theme, castigated various elements in society that the author thought were contributing to the country's ruin:

Ye proud gallants heartless,
With your high caps witless,
And your short gowns thriftless,
Have brought this land in great heaviness.

With your long peaked shoon,
Therfore your thrift is almost done,
And with your long hair into your eyen,
Have brought this land to great pain.[32]

These pronounced changes in dress also figured in specifically moralizing and didactic works, because they could so easily be classified under the sin of pride.[33] Peter Idley, in his *Instructions to his Son*, finished before his death in 1473–4, updates his text and sources on the sin of pride with an introductory castigation of contemporary excesses of dress by gallants and the aping of the higher ranks by their social inferiors, while deploring the long hair and fringes and the tendency of hose to part from the over-short doublet! As a past royal official he is well aware of the new sumptuary laws of the 1460s.[34]

The new fashions were also a main theme in an account of a man's vision of his future punishment in purgatory: the *Vision of Edmund Leversedge* of Frome, Somerset,[35] is the story of the repentance of a man for indulging in the 'principal sin' of proud English gallants in May 1465, at the height of the fashion furore. He is taught his lesson during a frightening visit to the Otherworld under the guidance of his good angel and is allowed by the Lady to recover from his sickness on condition that he lives a virtuous and soberly dressed life. The text contains some interesting particulars on the dress of his fellow gallants and a little on that

An animated court scene of 1469 showing the full extravagance of the prevailing fashions. Dido kisses Ascaniud. (From a copy of the Histoire de Troie, *written by Jacques de Lespluc, 1469, now Geneva, Collection Bodmer, MS 160, f. 225.)*

of women. Edmund's soul is claimed by devils dressed in the very clothes which he had loved to wear: short gowns and doublets, tight hose, long hair 'upon their brows', pikes on their shoes a foot or more in length and 'high bonnets as I myself sometime used'. They claim Leversedge as their rightful prey for his vicious living, but 'principally the inordinate and shameful array' he had worn. They showed 'a similitude and shapes of the fashion of my pikes, bolsters, stuffed doublets, short gowns, high bonnets, long hair and of all the inordinate array that ever I used, and shook it and shoved it' before the Lady to make their point. The Lady orders him to put all these things aside:

> ordain thee a plain doublet without stuffing and bolsters . . . a plain set gown, to the middle of thy leg and no shorter, of black colour, price a yard 2*s* 6*d* or 2*s* 7*d*. . . . Cut thy hair short and show thy face and let it be cut round with the over part of the ear. . . . Ordain thee a round cap and use to draw it down about thy head. Also I charge thee never use more close hose, but . . . a pair of long hose with linen cloth, and usen never other.[36] . . . Ordain thee shoes without pikes, with a little stopping before.

Leversedge agrees and, once he is reclothed, soon convinces himself that the new 'gear' is, in fact, more becoming to him. Such touches of detail add a distinct element of humour to this otherwise serious and alarming tale, of which another glimmer is his small victory over the Lady when she also commands him to give up kissing women. This he argues, and manages to prove, is the custom of England – as Erasmus noted many years later. She gives way, but lays down that any such kissing should be pure in intent.[37]

The clothes-conscious Leversedge also takes detailed notes of the Lady's own apparel, which he likens to that of a vowess (a widow who has taken a vow of chastity and chooses to wear certain clothes). On her head she wears 'a fair white kerchief' under her crown. She has a long black mantle which covers her feet, hands and shape entirely, 'with a standing collar closed straight till her neck', the mantle being 'much like unto those mantles of those ladies that have taken the mantle and the ring wearen' except it was longer and the colour 'higher'. There was 'no blasing of kerchiefs nor showing of her breasts . . . but all was close . . . She had no tires to exalt up her head but was and is content with one single kerchief, whereof two ends were pinned or else knit up, and two other ends come down over her shoulders'.[38]

What the Burgundian chronicler, under 1467, the anonymous poet and Peter Idley in the 1460s and Edmund Leversedge in 1465 are all voicing is the outrage felt by men used to the older fashions of short hair and bulky, longer gowns worn in the 1440s and 1450s. It was undoubtedly a spectacular change for contemporaries – which is not so vivid 500 years later – and a comparison with the pronounced changes which occurred in fashion from the 1950s to the later 1960s may be useful. Fashions, then as now, went in cycles of approximately ten years, the period that it takes for the average person to recognize, without much effort, that a certain item of clothing is out of date.

If we turn to more precisely datable records of this fashion furore, we find complaints against short male clothes, the inordinate stuffing or bolstering of garments and the long-toed shoes had been current some years before the date given for their emergence by the Burgundian chronicler.[39] Regulations against all these practices had been incorporated into the English sumptuary legislation of 1463: short clothes were not to be worn by men of a lesser rank than gentleman, the wearer was to be fined £1 and the tailor who made them forfeited the goods. The ordinances of the London Mercers' Company had already forbidden their younger members to wear long pointed shoes and stuffed garments in 1462. And in November 1462 even the aldermen of London added a rider that the 'bolsters' and the pleats, the rolls of the hoods and the length of the shoes should all be moderate when ordaining the provision of their own gowns and cloaks of scarlet and violet for the Christmas season.[40] In the English sumptuary acts of 1463 there was the usual and overriding concern that men should not, by refinements of dress, attempt to pretend to a higher station in life than was theirs by birth.[41] This was exactly in keeping with the Burgundian chronicler's and Peter Idley's outbursts. It was reinforced in regulations and oaths of office other than those of the London companies: for example, in 1465 the Sacristan of St Mary's, Warwick, took an oath of office which included a promise not to wear 'bolsters in my clothing ne pikes on my shoes . . . but I shall array me like a clerk'. According to the so-called Gregory's Chronicle of London, the Pope in 1468 forbade the wearing of shoes with pikes of more than two inches. 'Gregory' was probably in fact thinking of parliament's general sumptuary act of 1463, which included a clause against the long-toed shoes, and of the act of 1464, which set out specifically to control the makers of long-toed shoes. He recorded that some Londoners 'said they would wear long pikes whether the pope will or nill'. In other words no sumptuary legislation in England, at least, could ensure that young men gave up a popular fashion.[42] It is clear that the attempt by chroniclers to tie down the appearance of fashions to a precise date is fairly meaningless – it merely suggests the decade and gives an idea of what were seen by contemporaries as the high points of current fashions.

Having set the scene, let us finally turn to a specific manuscript made *c.* 1470. It is something of an oddity and exemplifies another problem for the historian of dress: the text and the pictures contradict each other both in spirit and in date. The text describes lavish court dress of the 1440s and the pictures portray average fashions of *c.* 1470. *Clériadus et Méliadice* is one of two surviving romances which may have belonged to Edward IV or a member of his family.[43] It is a courtly romance written in French prose, probably 1440–4.[44]

It is the story of a perfect knight: it teaches young men the benefit of having an irreproachable lifestyle, courtly manners and honourable behaviour, as well as skill at arms and courage; such a young man may win a kingdom for himself and rule it with justice and in peace. It is also an entertaining love story: it describes to perfection the dress, games, chivalry and manners of a fifteenth-century court. The author goes out of his way to describe the dress of the participants, male and female. As a text, therefore, it is of extreme interest for the dress of the 1440s, and particularly for the headdresses of women.

The manuscript has twenty-eight illustrations, of which only the first is a large one across two columns;[45] fourteen include women. At first glance these paintings are unexciting: details are sparse and they convey little of the splendid courtly luxuries described in the text. The person who chose the subjects for the pictures had a distressing tendency to prefer a messenger delivering a letter – a lot of letter-writing and carrying of messages takes place in the story – to one of the more interesting events of the story. The artist used a limited palette of colours,[46] but when studied merely as pictures of clothes his work proves to be of great interest: he was competent and could draw figures, faces and gestures well, he had no predeliction for display, despite the persuasions of the text, and did plain scenes in keeping with the small space available to him, either on his own initiative or because his exemplar had already done the same. He was drawing the

Clériadus is in a short gown or jacket with neat shoes, the same size as his foot – no long-pointed styles. All the gowns or jackets of the men are broad in the shoulders, with well-defined pleats where they are drawn into the waist, the fashion of the later 1460s and early 1470s. All of the men could be of any well-to-do class, but the ladies' dress indicates this is a court scene. They wear the tall attenuated bonnets associated with ladies of status; these are worn to the back of the head with no frontlets, the hair taken well off the face, the tiny loop of black velvet worn centre-forehead is visible and over all is the long, transparent coverchief extending forward over the face to below the eyes. Their gowns are full-skirted, nipped into broad belts immediately below the bosom; the gown's opening is worn wide across the shoulders, trimmed with fur, revealing a v-shaped section of the kirtle beneath; the sleeves are long and tight, and have long cuffs all worn turned back in this picture. (From Clériadus and Méliadice, *BL, Royal MS 20 C ii, f. 15. By permission of the British Library.)*

dress of his own time, aimed at an unadorned realism and had no interest in creating a fantasy world. He was also very consistent: most of his characters appear in the same basic gowns, shoes and headwear throughout the book, in the fashions of *c.* 1470, when the excesses of the early 1460s were over. He also gave brief glimpses of styles coming into fashion and others going out. In other words, he was aware of the clothes which were really being worn around him at the time.

A brief narrative of the story, picking out some of the descriptions of dress, the meanings and importance attached to colours and courtly games and court festivities will illustrate its delights and its value to the court and dress historian of the 1440s – the dress of the text is that of the Devonshire tapestries at the Victoria and Albert Museum. Most of the terminology used, however, is the same as that used in the 1470s, and sometimes the circumstances of the story aid an understanding of the status and use of the garment. Most importantly for the present survey, the author refers in detail to the dress of women. The courtly games described are also still entirely relevant to the Yorkist court of thirty years later. The manuscript pictures included here, and described in the captions, show the fashions of the late 1460s to early 1470s.

The large black plumes on the four executioners' white hats seem frivolous, given that poor Méliadice is pleading for her life in the forest. These round hats with feathers, often straight white tufts sticking up at the back of the head, otherwise curled like these, but white, are very common in the 1470s and 1480s and became even more extravagant in the 1490s. The painter has seized on a new fashion for four villains who turn out to have good hearts – he cannot give them white plumes in the circumstances so he makes them black. Two of them are wearing what appear to be the usual short jackets common to men of their rank, and one wears leg armour. The other two may be wearing brigandines (a defensive jacket padded and reinforced with metal plates), especially as both are also wearing some leg and arm armour. The black collars may be the collars of their doublets underneath. Méliadice is only in her kirtle with a plain round neckline and long tight sleeves; if she had been wearing her gown only a v-shaped portion of the kirtle's bodice would have been visible. (From Clériadus and Méliadice, *BL, MS Royal 20 C ii, f. 82. By permission of the British Library.)*

The story is set in England during the reign of the aged King Phillipon, who has only one, fifteen-year-old and very beautiful daughter, Méliadice, to succeed him. He decides to call in the Count of Asturies to govern the kingdom in his name, passing over his own half-brother, the Duke of l'Angarde. The Count of Asturies has a young son of twenty-two called Clériadus who falls in love with Méliadice at first sight and swears he will make himself a knight without equal in order to be worthy of her. At their first meeting Clériadus is described as dressed in a white satin gown furred with marten and a hood of scarlet covered with goldsmith's work: the *cornette* bears a clasp worth one hundred bezants. The princess is clothed 'in very elegant fashion (*moult gentement*) in a fitted kirtle or *cotte* (*coste juste*) of cloth of gold with a train and winged tabard sleeves (*d'ailles de tabar*) furred with ermine, and with a very rich collar (*petrail*) over her shoulders; her hair was bound at the back (*liez par derriere*) and was as fair as gold thread, on her forehead was a chaplet of gold (*chapeau d'or*)'.[47] Clériadus soon shows that he excels all the young men of the court at dancing and singing and at all the other accomplishments of leisure, and he soon has a chance to prove himself in battle defending a disputed right of the old king. He is wounded but victorious. Méliadice visits the wounded hero in great distress, the young man declares his love and she responds. They decide that their love will remain chaste, faithful and secret.

One day the King of Spain sends a messenger to seek the hand of the sister of Clériadus in marriage and the Count of Asturies agrees. Clériadus leaves to attend the marriage magnificently attired in bright red (*vermeille*), and she takes to wearing grey during his absence, colours which they have together secretly agreed and vowed to wear for each other.[48]

Clériadus has many adventures in what may be termed his 'red period', on his way to Spain and back. On the return journey he and Méliadice meet again secretly. For his next enterprise Méliadice selects green to be the colour worn by him; grey, which was her first choice, might link him too obviously with her as she is still wearing it for him. She gives him a gold chain of love-knots to wear over his armour, and he gives her a clasp (*fermillet*).[49] The new enterprise is a joust for all comers. Many details are given of the preparations of his equipment, clothes and the liveries for all: everything is in green embroidered with the leaves and flowers of sage, the herb of goodness (*de toute bonne*). The youngest of six maidens carries his challenge to the court, dressed in flowered green satin with a girdle of pearls, a purse (*aumonière*) and a chaplet of evergreen or sage leaves on her head,[50] riding on a white palfrey harnessed in the same fashion, and accompanied by six esquires. For thirty days a daily joust will be held and the Green Knight of the Flower (*Chevalier Vert à la Fleur*) challenges all comers.[51] Clériadus is victorious over all knights, and treats the court to a feast, distributing gowns of green cloth of gold furred with marten to all his prisoners. Later Méliadice gives rich gowns of crimson satin furred with miniver to the six maidens and her own gown of cloth of gold to the lady of the house where the festivities had taken place.[52]

While Clériadus is away on his next adventure, betrayal (*forfait*) is being prepared: Thomas l'Angarde, the uncle of Méliadice, accuses her and Clériadus of treason. The king, her father, delivers his daughter to the executioners. In the forest Méliadice persuades her would-be murderers not to kill her on condition that she goes into exile; she rewards them with her kirtle (*cotte*) and a chain of gold with a rich clasp (*fermillet*) hanging from it and is left stranded in her smock (*chemise*).[53] The court and realm are dismayed to learn of her death and Thomas l'Angarde installs himself as ruler. Méliadice travels to Asturies in the service of a woman wool merchant, first as a pack-bearer and then as her chambermaid (*chambrière*), taking the name of Ladirée. Her employer provides her with a new smock (*chemise*), a simple kirtle (*cotte simple*), a purse (*bourse*)[54] and a cloak (*peleton*), as well as a hood (*chapperon*), hose and shoes (*chausses et solliers*).[55] Later she makes coifs and purses (*coeffes et bourses*) for another female employer to sell and these are so beautiful[56] that they bring her to the attention of the King and Queen of Asturies. Faithful to her word she does not reveal her identity.

When Clériadus arrives back in England he learns of the death of Méliadice and it takes all the skill of his friends to ensure that he does not kill himself. By a subterfuge Thomas l'Angarde is captured and confesses his crimes. Clériadus leaves England brokenhearted and gives up the life of a knight; he becomes a pilgrim and goes home to his own country of Asturies. Overcome with grief when he arrives in the familiar place he sits down by the very fountain where Méliadice is accustomed to fetch water every day at that time. She takes pity on the pilgrim

The ceremony of the vows of the peacock at the feast. The artist has carefully drawn the pleating pulled into the centre of the back of the jacket of the powerfully built young man in the centre-front, and the line of the collar shows how it joins on to the body. His hairstyle is the usual one given to young men by this artist, neat, sometimes with a little fringe, and no sign of the long hairstyles that the moralists so disliked. The kirtles and headdresses of the two damsels at the front are different from the gowns and tall bonnets worn by the other ladies in this manuscript and by Méliadice in this picture. Both gowns are entirely plain with round necklines and long tight sleeves with fur cuffs, exactly like the kirtle which Méliadice was wearing in the forest. It is worn with a plain bonnet into which all the hair has been packed, with the customary little loop on the forehead; they have no coverchiefs. The artist appears to allow a glimpse of a comparatively new fashion which would be more important in the later 1470s. The young women or damsels of the court probably wore smaller, plain, uncovered bonnets long before any older woman or lady of high rank. (From Clériadus and Méliadice, *BL, MS Royal 20 C ii, f. 119. By permission of the British Library.)*

and asks him his trouble, promptly fainting as soon as she recognizes him. Messages are busily exchanged to explain everything to everyone.[57] Méliadice lavishly rewards the women who have befriended her with money to buy rents – so that they can give up the menial activity of trade – and she gives the ladies of the court gowns of satin and velvet, furred with grey and miniver, and girdles, and to the Count and Countess of Asturies collars of gold. Dressed in a gown of white cloth of gold, with a collar of gold round her neck and a gold chaplet (*chappeau*)[58] on her head she leaves for England with Clériadus.[59] They go via France where they are sumptuously entertained in Paris for a month: the first feast is marked by the ceremony of vows of the peacock,[60] the king swearing to hold jousts for all comers for the love of Méliadice on the next day and everyone taking an oath in the same spirit, Méliadice swearing to reward the victor with the coronet she is wearing, and her lover managing to swear in such a way as to ensure that he can joust incognito. The clothes of all are described. Méliadice wears a gown of white satin covered with gold roses, a crimson girdle, her hair is dressed in the style of her own country of England with 'a gold chaplet above', and her ladies are in the same except that their roses were of silver.[61] The jousts are won by Clériadus as the White Knight, dressed in white powdered with wreaths of leaves (*chappeaulx de fueillage*). The dress for the following supper and dancing by torchlight is equally eleborate. Méliadice is in green velvet with long trailing sleeves to the ground, bordered with jewels and a chain of gold leaves (*de fueillage*) over her shoulders and reaching to the ground, and on her head a chaplet of gold.[62] This chaplet is to be the reward of the White Knight and she receives in recompense a 'fine green headdress of beautiful marjoram' (*beau bourrelet tout vert de belle marioulaine*) from the king and queen.[63] In the subsequent courtly games she asks for and receives a special chaplet of roses made of white *floquart* from Clériadus who also presents white gowns decorated with goldsmiths' work to certain courtiers.[64] By this time the clues of the colours and the exchange of gifts has allowed the love between the two to be guessed by the court. At length it is announced to Méliadice that she must return to England.

Méliadice enters London in triumph, having declared she will marry none but Clériadus. At the palace Méliadice's father throws himself at his daughter's feet and grants both his daughter and his crown to Clériadus. The marriage is planned for thirty days hence, the festivities are elaborate and clothes receive due attention. At the feast and dance two *ensembles* are described for Méliadice. First she wears a tight-fitting kirtle (*corset*) of cloth of gold with a train and large sleeves lined with ermine trailing behind her for at least an ell. Her head is dressed in the English style (*etait atournée à la guise d'Angleterre*) – a chaplet (*chappeau*) of red roses confined within a circle or net of gold sewn with pearls and gems visible above the roses beneath (*bouté dedens une raye d'or qui bien seoit à veoir par dessus les roses qui desoubz estoient*) – and there is a jewel at her neck. She then puts off the close-fitting kirtle and her headdress (*de son atour*) and changes into 'a gown (*hoppelande*) of crimson satin entirely covered with large pearls and gems and so covered with gold that with a thousand pains one could discover the value'. She has 'a white girdle which she ties above', and is wearing a headdress *à templettes* and crown on her head.[65] For their marriage Clériadus wears his royal

Clériadus and Méliadice, now King and Queen, watch the dancing that precedes their marriage. Trumpeters are energetically blowing behind the hero's head. Particularly well drawn are the pleats and shapely fronts of the two leading male dancers. The long gown of the man on the left is a mix of new and old fashions: bag-sleeves with two vents for the arms were not only convenient but also showed off the rich linings and a handsome sleeve of an undergarment, in this case a tight-fitting doublet. This sleeve fashion had had a long history back to the early 1400s and had at times been very extravagant. The gown is pleated into the waist by a narrow belt; the pleats tend to be placed mainly at the centre front (and back), which was usual, and the waistline drops in a rather elegant u-line at the centre front. This suits the masculine figure which inclines to put on weight here, but it also forms a slightly pouter-pigeon look which became increasingly fashionable through the 1470s. A more elegant version adorns a courtier attending on Margaret of York in a miniature painted in 1475 (Bodleian Library, Douce MS 365, f. 115). By 1475 the fashion was more developed, and in the manuscript of Clériadus and Méliadice, *we seem to be seeing an early rendering of a new fashion. Note how the ladies hold up their skirts and show their kirtles; they keep their eyes down while the men look ahead. (From* Clériadus and Méliadice, *BL, MS Royal 20 C ii, f. 159. By permission of the British Library.)*

The man in the long gown is the feature of interest here: the collar of gold shows his rank; the gown is fashionably pleated in such a way as to produce the bow-shaped front; a novelty are the narrower sleeves which are split at the back over the elbow so that the white linen shirt can show through, especially when the arm is bent. This is another version of the affectation complained of by the Burgundian chronicler and it became increasingly fashionable into the 1480s. In the 1490s this fashion reached ridiculous levels in the dress of the fashionable young and hardly any seam was fully joined. Again the artist of Clériadus and Méliadice *is showing us, once only, a new, up-and-coming fashion. (From* Clériadus and Méliadice, *BL, MS Royal 20 C ii, f. 197. By permission of the British Library.)*

robes and Méliadice a simple cotte of white cloth of gold with a mantle of the same furred with ermine and a long train and a mantle lace (*atache*) of gold with a great clasp (*fermeil*) holding it on her breast. Her hair is 'curled and braided with two gold clasps at the end of the braids';[66] she also has a girdle, a purse (*bourse*), a crown, and wears all her jewels.[67] Two months of festivities follow; 800 knights take part in deeds of chivalry and courtesy but Clériadus is indisputably the master of all.

After their coronation Clériadus and Méliadice base their rule on justice and love of their neighbours and are rewarded with peace and prosperity.

This Flemish manuscript of *Clériadus et Méliadice* is a good example of the pleasures and the problems of the historian of English medieval dress. There is a profusion of descriptions, but most of the dress described in the text of the romance – datable to the 1440s – is that of the very rich, setting out to be as extravagant and whimsical as their money allowed. Some of the descriptions, particularly of the ladies' headdresses, are of great interest for their rarity. Only the garments allotted the destitute heroine are those necessary for comfort. In complete contrast are the far less pretentious pictures of the manuscript, which do not interpret the text, but capture the dress of *c.* 1470 without the

Apart from the man in entirely parti-coloured clothes – even his hat is in two colours – it is the headdresses of the ladies which come as a surprise. All the other details of their attire correspond to the dress usually given to ladies in this book, but here they are given an entirely new look by the black frontlets to their bonnets. Frontlets were usually of velvet and were a fashion which at first continued alongside and then increasingly replaced the severer style of transparent coverchiefs; it is a style particularly associated with Margaret of York. As the atour *became shorter and shorter, the frontlet and a plain bonnet became the usual headdress of late fifteenth-century women and then developed into another severe style, the Tudor gable. (From* Apollonius of Tyre, *illustrated by the same artist as* Clériadus and Méliadice, *BL, MS Royal 20 C ii, f. 217v. By permission of the British Library.)*

exaggerations of high fashion, except for the tall bonnets of the ladies, and reveal the repetitious nature of average and everyday clothing. It is the very unpretentious realism of the pictures which makes them important. The painter's budget did not allow him time, space or the necessary colours for courtly extravagance, so he painted what he saw every day and only occasionally added in a new trend – whether a bow-fronted gown or a frontlet – which was to become a new fashion worn by everyone. He cut his cloth to suit his pocket, but he did not take the easy way out used by the English translator of *Partonope de Blois* and say the matter was needless or in 'the French book'. Dress was important, both as a social indicator, as so many of the hostile critics of the 1460s show, and as a necessary part of everyday life.

CHAPTER 2

Townswomen and their Households

JENNIFER WARD

Historians studying women and towns in fifteenth-century England immediately become aware of the enormous variety in their investigations. Towns ranged from the small market towns of a few hundred people, with close connections with the surrounding villages, to the 'provincial capitals' like York, Bristol and Norwich with populations of several thousand. London as capital of the realm was in a pre-eminent place of its own. Many towns were subject to fluctuations of fortune, which had considerable impact on the lives of their inhabitants. Within the towns, the studies which have been done on urban society emphasize the social hierarchy based on wealth, rank and occupation. In addition, social difference has to be seen at the various stages of life; position and expectations varied between childhood, adolescence, married life and old age. Within these categories, women may be seen as being at a disadvantage; their lack of standing in the eyes of the law, unless they were widows or 'single women' (*femmes soles*), and their absence from office-holding and public life mean that historians hear more about their fathers, husbands and sons than about the women themselves.

Yet in the face of all these differences, the household stands as a unifying factor. Membership of a household was common to the great majority of townswomen at all stages of their lives. The definition of household in late medieval England was essentially flexible. At its centre was usually the husband of the family with his wife and children, but dependent kinsmen, servants and apprentices were all integral members, even if they belonged to a particular household for only a short time. On the death of the husband, the widow took his place as the head of the household; if she remarried, she and her children became members of the new husband's household, possibly in association with the children of his former marriage or marriages. Thus the size and type of the household were subject to constant change, both for these demographic reasons, and also according to the economic circumstances of the family and its changing levels of prosperity or poverty. The variety in the nature and size of the household is apparent in Coventry in the early sixteenth century where it has been found that while

75.6 per cent of households contained couples, 12.1 per cent were headed by widows; size varied according to numbers of children and servants.[1] Admittedly, by the time the Coventry censuses were drawn up in the 1520s, the city was in serious decline, but the household as a constantly changing entity existed in fifteenth-century England and before, and women would have become accustomed to changes at various points in their lives, as children, servants and apprentices came and went.

The household was more than the place where the woman lived. It was through the household that she gained her identity, status and security, whatever her household role. It was inevitable, given the ideas universally held in medieval society, that she would be known as the wife, widow, child, servant or apprentice of a townsman, but this gave her an element of protection not available to women living on their own. The household was the focal point of a woman's life. Unable to undertake a public role in the town's councils, courts and guilds, she made use of the household as the centre of much of her work, her charitable activity and her social network.

Many women had their first experience of town life as servants, migrating from the country in order to find work in the town.[2] Occupational opportunities opened up for women not only as a result of the great drop in population levels caused by plague and epidemics, but also with the expansion of many of the larger towns in the later fourteenth century. By the Yorkist period, employment opportunities for women were becoming more limited, and in the sixteenth century preference was given to male workers.[3] However, it has to be borne in mind that employment of servants was not restricted to wealthy households. Even in the lowest rental category (of 1–6*s*) in early sixteenth-century Coventry, 13.4 per cent of households had servants, rising to just under half of the households in the 13–18*s* group. As might be expected, between 85 and 91 per cent of the households in the rental categories over 30*s* had servants.[4]

It is likely that these immigrant servants found greater independence in the town; many were probably teenagers, anxious to earn money for a dowry and to acquire skills which would enable them to continue to earn money when they were married. A few girls were apprenticed, but far more found work as servants, an element of stability being provided by the legal requirement that engagements had to be for a year.[5] Supervision by master and mistress took the place of parents, and the servant was regarded as an integral member of the household, for whom the head of the household was responsible.

The servant was probably expected to do both domestic and occupational work, according to the trade or craft of the household; no demarcation line would be drawn between different kinds of work. The mid-fifteenth-century poem, *The Servant Girl's Holiday*, speaks of spinning and weaving, sweeping the floor and lighting the fire, milking the cow and making bread.[6] Holidays and the opportunity to go out with a boyfriend were eagerly anticipated. Masters and mistresses varied, as did servants; corporal punishment of the servant, as of wife and child, was universally accepted, and the servant girl in the poem dreaded telling her mistress that she was pregnant. In 1403 Joan Potter of Nottingham complained that her master, John Lorimer, had struck her on the head and beaten

A late medieval marriage scene. The bride and groom are holding hands in the presence of the priest and witnesses. The groom holds his cap in his other hand. (From the Seven Sacraments font at Badingham, Suffolk, c. *1500.)*

her all over; John admitted that he had done this, but said that Joan had answered him back. Although Joan did not pursue the case, John was condemned for drawing blood.[7] In another Nottingham case five years later, John de Bothall alleged that his servant Margaret Pope had made various keys for the doors in his house, opened the wine tavern and taken out and distributed thirty gallons of wine to neighbours without his knowledge; the jury however found Margaret not guilty.[8]

Some wills show a sense of responsibility and gratitude to one's servants, a desire to provide for a girl's marriage, and possibly to contribute some capital for business. Thomas Wood, draper and alderman of Hull, left a bequest of Spanish iron to his maidservant in 1491.[9] Joan Candell of York, twelve years earlier, described in detail the goods which she was leaving to her servant, Cristian Forman, including white hangings painted with the seven works of mercy, bed linen, including two pillows embroidered in black silk and two in white thread, latten candlesticks, a brass pot and vessels of pewter.[10] Small sums of money were frequently left to servants, as by Matilda Botyller of Barking in Essex in 1451.[11]

Time in service introduced a girl to mixed adolescent as well as adult society and gave her skills and the opportunity to collect a dowry. She thus laid the basis for her married life, and Jeremy Goldberg's studies of the York cause paper evidence point to partners marrying in their mid-twenties and making their own decisions as to whom they were going to marry.[12] However, it is likely in the case of wealthier girls that their parents had a say in who they were to marry, and care was taken to avoid social disparagement.[13] Fathers were concerned to provide for their daughters' dowries, as when, in the mid-fifteenth century, Thomas Baldwin, citizen and tailor of London, bequeathed £20 sterling to his daughter Joan for her marriage.[14] Wealthy wives were in demand and ambitious townsmen were on the look-out for them, as is apparent in the case of George Cely's marriage to the childless widow Margery Rygon; Margery's first husband had been a London draper and she brought George a considerable dowry.[15] Such a dowry provided the husband with valuable capital.

Both husband and wife were regarded as contributing to the formation of the new household by way of money and skills, and these formed the basis of their future life. The wife was usually expected to provide the household goods. In some places the wife could bring to her husband the status of freeman; at Canterbury a man who married a freeman's daughter secured the freedom of the city, giving a boost to his future activities.[16] Many marriages were probably rooted in affection, as well as having an eye to economic provision. Once marriage had taken place, it was expected to last for life; divorce or separation was rare. Evidence on the nature of family relationships, however, whether between husbands and wives or parents and children, tends to be formal and legalistic. Many households must have undergone changes in fortune, either as a result of urban decline, or because of extravagance, inefficiency or carelessness by the couple or by the husband or wife. Moreover, with the wife's property being legally in the hands of her husband, it would be possible for him to waste her inheritance. Medieval courts tried to provide some safeguard against this by examining the wife on her own when alienations of property were made, but this was not a foolproof guarantee.[17]

In the circumstances, it is likely that there was great variety in the relations of husbands and wives. Evidence from wills in particular points in many cases to a working partnership between husband and wife. This evidence is only available for wealthier townspeople, although it may well reflect attitudes further down the social scale. Moreover, the majority of wills were made by men and it is unusual to find wills made by a married woman, who had to have her husband's consent. Wills rarely give an indication of the degree of affection or dislike between husband and wife; burial beside each other may point to affection but could equally well be the result of social convention. Often, however, wills point to trust between husband and wife, particularly when, as was frequently the practice, the wife was appointed executor; such an appointment presupposed that the wife was familiar with the husband's affairs. Execution of wills involved considerable work and might well lead to litigation.[18]

Partnership and joint concerns sometimes become apparent when the wills of both husband and wife survive. Thomas Baldwin, citizen and tailor of London, made his will in April 1454. He wanted to be buried in the parish church of St Mary Abchurch, and laid down detailed arrangements for his funeral. He wanted masses to be celebrated in the church by an honest priest for three years after his death, for the benefit of his own soul and those of his parents and of the faithful departed. His mother Denise was to receive £1 a year, and his daughter Joan the sum of £20 for her marriage. His wife Joan was the executrix.[19] She died the following August.[20] She wished to be buried next to her husband and like him bequeathed 6*s* 8*d* to the church fabric for having her burial there. She wanted a year to be added to the requiem masses for the benefit of her soul and Thomas' and all the faithful departed, if her goods would stretch to this. Most of the family silver was left to her daughter Joan, with one piece bequeathed to her son Thomas, but Joan was only to receive her share if she married with the approval of her mother's executors. The wills give the impression that there had been collaboration between husband and wife as to what they wanted to happen after their deaths; the impression is probably heightened by the fact that the deaths took place within a few months of each other.

In other cases, trust and partnership simply did not exist, and problems within marriage are illuminated by the proceedings of the church courts, which detail accusations of adultery and cruelty. In late fifteenth-century London John Wren was accused of wounding his pregnant wife so as to bring on a miscarriage, and the baby died.[21] Matilda Beke spread the story that Robert and Margaret Bedill had been expelled from Romford because of Margaret's adultery with John Jacson; Margaret retaliated by calling Matilda a whore.[22] Occasionally, cases with more circumstantial detail are found. In the mid-fifteenth century John Neuport of Colchester and his wife Alice brought a case in Chancery, claiming property which had been left to Alice for life by her former husband, William Prentys. In the course of the case, it was alleged that, according to rumour, John and Alice had connived at William's death. According to the verdict of a Colchester jury, William Prentys died intestate, because his time was too short for him to make a will; it was usual for a man to draw up his will when he was on his death-bed. John was in William's house the night he died. Before his death, William was reported to have said that Alice should have none of his goods if she married John Neuport. No will was found after William died, but later John brought a paper will to the scrivener John Spaldinge, asking him to write it up on parchment. The scrivener pointed out that the writing had an old date, but was in a new hand. Later, John Neuport and another scrivener, Simon Langton, confessed to worthy persons in Colchester that Simon wrote the will; Simon was a well-known forger in the town.[23] It looks as if things went badly wrong in the marriage of William Prentys and Alice.

Both Alice Prentys and Joan Baldwin survived their husbands, and this was in fact true of many women. At the time of the death of their husbands, women were again faced with a major change in their lives, and their households had to be adapted to meet changing circumstances. For many, the change came suddenly and unexpectedly and left them with diminished resources with which they often

The sacrament of extreme unction; the wife stands at the foot of the bed, while the priest anoints the dying man. (From the Seven Sacraments font at Badingham, Suffolk, c. *1500.)*

had to bring up their families. In 1416 the mayor of King's Lynn, Thomas Hunte, was trying to ensure that the goods of the sailor, Robert Furneys, would be passed on to his widow Agnes, who had two young daughters. Robert had died in Lisbon; his money, amounting to £11 10*s* 0*d*, came into the hands of another sailor, and when the ship reached Drogheda in Ireland it was handed over to a local merchant for Agnes' use.[24]

Every widow was entitled to dower from her husband's property. If she was an heiress, control of her inheritance came into her hands and she was also entitled to property which had been held jointly by husband and wife. As a widow she counted as a *femme sole*, entitled to administer her own property, take responsibility for business and for her own debts, and plead in the courts as

A priest baptises a baby in the font. The godfather and godmother stand to the left and the right of the panel. (From the Seven Sacraments font at Badingham, Suffolk, c. *1500.)*

necessary.[25] Dower, according to common law, amounted to one-third of the husband's property, which the widow was entitled to hold for life. In London, and some other towns, the widow received a share of her husband's goods and his dwelling-house, but she lost the latter if she remarried.[26] The division of property was sometimes made explicit in wills, as when William Smyth of Colchester in 1486 divided his lands, merchandise, debts and household goods equally between his wife and son.[27] The arrangements made by John Dalton of Hull in 1487 were typical of many testators; he provided that after his debts were paid his goods were to be divided into three, with one part for his wife, one for his children and the third to be disposed of by his executors for the good of his soul.[28] Even for wealthier women, such provision might well lead to household contraction, while poor widows would find themselves in real need.

It was in such circumstances that a number of women remarried. This was supposed to be a matter of individual choice, although there are indications that advice was sometimes sought and quite possibly pressure brought to bear. Much must have depended on individual circumstances, and poorer women may have found the option of remarriage unavailable. In London remarriage was more common among widows with young children.[29] Such women may well have felt vulnerable on their own, and wanted help with business and property as well as

A confirmation. The woman is holding a small child in her arms. (From the Seven Sacraments font at Badingham, Suffolk, c. *1500.)*

with their children. The desire for affection and companionship was probably widespread. Young widows might well be physically attractive, and the importance of the lure of wealth and status, as well as the significance of family and mercantile alliances, should not be underestimated. Remarriage might take place within the town, or the widow might move elsewhere. On the death of the shearman John Sayer of Colchester, his widow Lucy was left comfortably off and was guided by her husband's executors in the choice of her second and third husbands: the second was Thomas Halke, a man of substance and reputation and one of the aldermen of Colchester, and two years after his death she married Thomas Profete of Nayland in Suffolk, a man of substance and thrift.[30] The close links between Hull and York were epitomized when the widow of John Dalton of Hull took as her later husbands John Whitfield of Hull and Sir Richard York of York.[31] The merchants of Hull, as of numerous other towns, were extensively interrelated.[32]

The relationship between husband and wife was central to the household, and so too were the relationships between parents and children. It was assumed when a marriage took place that the birth of children would follow. Families with property especially looked forward to passing property on to an heir. However, in view of the high mortality in towns, and a relatively late age for marriage, families might well be small and be further reduced by infant mortality. Moreover, very little is known of women's varying experiences in pregnancy and childbirth. Margery Kempe's description of post-natal depression following the birth of her first child is virtually unique.[33] Characteristically, families were small in the late Middle Ages. Margaret and John Croke of London may have had twelve children altogether, of whom five sons and two daughters grew up, but this was larger than most families.[34] An examination of the size of families recorded in London wills between 1288 and 1527 revealed that at no time did the average number of male heirs per family reach two, and a large proportion of men left no sons. An analysis of the number of sons mentioned by male testators in the archdeaconry of Essex points to an increase from 0.54 between 1420 and 1435 to 1.1 between 1480 and 1492.[35] Still, since one reason for small families was a high rate of infant and child mortality, many townswomen must have spent much of their married lives bearing and nursing children, and their responsibility for children was an important part of their lives. In the event of widowhood, mothers were often named as guardians, although in London guardianship was supervised by the city authorities. Mothers' responsibilities would be greatest while the children were young; many teenagers would move away from home into apprenticeship and service, and many mothers would then find that they were responsible for adolescents from other families. Both wives and widows could take on apprentices,[36] and wives were bequeathed apprentices by their husbands. Thomas Austyn, citizen and mercer of London, in his will of 1391, left the custody of his three children and the remaining terms of his apprentices to his wife Alice. In her own will four years later, Alice had to provide for the family house and shop to be looked after until her son Thomas completed his apprenticeship and could take over.[37]

The relationship between mother and child, and parents and stepchildren, is an area of which relatively little is known, although some details come to light as a result of legal disputes and bequests in wills. The problem with legal material is that there is often no way of telling whether charges were justified, and bequests, such as provision of prayers for one's mother, could be motivated by a variety of considerations.[38] When making her will with the consent of her husband in 1466, Matilda Mogge of Barking was well aware of possible problems. She arranged for land to be held by her husband for eight years and then to pass to her son John Hacche (presumably her son by a previous marriage), on the condition that John was of good rule, conversation and governance during the eight years.[39] Allegations of parental neglect were made by Katherine Sayer of Colchester. Her father John arranged in his will for his two children to be provided for by his wife until they grew up. Lucy, his wife, asserted that she did this, setting them to crafts at her cost and labour. The son John died, but the daughter Katherine grew up and married. Katherine however alleged that after her brother's death her mother refused to keep her in meat, drink and clothing, and never set her to a craft.[40]

To judge by surviving wills, and bearing in mind that they did not necessarily refer to all the children of the family, it appears that on the whole fathers and mothers were concerned to ensure that each child, male and female, received money, property or goods as a basis for their future livelihood. Rose Thorne of St Albans, in her will of 1479, distributed her personal and household effects among her sons, daughters and daughter-in-law.[41] Eight years earlier Denise,

Paycocke's House, Coggeshall (Essex), c. *1500, built for Thomas Paycocke, the clothier (who died in 1518) and his wife, Margaret Horrold. The house was formerly three-storeyed.*

widow of John Holme of Beverley in Yorkshire, specified in detail what she wanted her children to receive. The sum of £66 13*s* 4*d* (100 marks) together with plate was left to each son, Henry and Nicholas, plate and a crimson gown to her daughter Alice, and a gown to her daughter Denise. Another daughter, Joan, received a piece of silver and a crimson gown, while her husband, William Eland, received £20 for counselling the executors. Grandchildren were not forgotten: each of William's and Joan's six children received a piece of silver, while Alice's daughter was left 10 marks towards her marriage, a piece of plate, a primer and an embroidered and gilt girdle of tawny silk.[42] Denise's own daughters did not receive sums of money, but these would have been paid by their parents as dowry when they married.

Pregnancy and child rearing would take up much of the townswoman's time, whatever her status. It was also her responsibility to run the household; this domestic side of her tasks has not received much emphasis from recent historians, but must have involved much labour and time. Even the larger houses must have been crowded with family, servants, apprentices and visitors, with the hall acting as the focus of household life. An analysis of surviving housing at King's Lynn has emphasized the prevalence of the three-roomed house of the lesser merchants and well-off shopkeepers and craftsmen where, in addition to the hall and shop or

A former shop-front at Lavenham (Suffolk), c. *1500.*

workshop, there would be one room for the head of the household.[43] For other members of the household privacy would be at a premium. Contracts for the building of similar timber-framed houses survive for London and Canterbury.[44] Archaeology has brought to light some of the activities which went on within the house, as in the excavation of three craftsmen's tenements at Worcester.[45] Larger houses existed in London and the principal provincial towns, but they were only for the wealthy élite. Whatever the size of the house and household, its smooth running necessitated careful thought, planning and hard work on the part of the housewife.

In an age which attached importance to outward splendour and display, the house and its possessions had to be shown off to best advantage. This is reflected in wills which give detailed descriptions of goods, indicating the housewife's pride in her possessions and her desire in some cases for them to be treated as family heirlooms. Isabel Wilton of Hull in 1487 described in detail the rosary, the violet gown and hood, the scarlet kirtle and the best spruce chest which she bequeathed to her daughter Marion, and she also left her best girdle, which had been a present to Isabel from her husband, Marion's father.[46] Margaret Alestre of

Nottingham in 1491 described many of her pieces of silver individually in the codicil of her will as she arranged for them to be divided among members of her family and others; her daughter Cecily received a standing maser with a gilt foot and a gilt cover, and Margaret Bingham a piece with a cover which had the names of the Three Kings of Cologne on it.[47]

The multitudinous duties of the housewife are brought out in the late fourteenth-century book that the so-called Menagier of Paris (*menagier* meaning 'householder') wrote for the instruction of his young wife. He stressed the need to make her husband comfortable, to give him clean clothes, good food and drink and a comfortable and clean bed. Three things, he said, drove a husband from home – a leaking roof, a smoking chimney and a scolding woman. He urged his wife to look after children and stepchildren with the same care as she looked after her husband. She should also keep good order among her servants and guard their morals. The Menagier provided a section of recipes and advice on shopping, listing the various markets in Paris and the amount of meat consumed in the households of various members of the royal family. He went into great detail over particular household tasks, for instance, providing six ways of getting rid of fleas, the best being to fold up the infested robes and coverlets and press them hard, so that the fleas lacked light and air and would immediately perish. The Menagier's book makes clear that housekeeping was extremely time-consuming, even if the household employed servants.[48]

It was taken for granted in the fifteenth century that work within the household would include helping in the husband's craft or trade. This is implied in the guild ordinances which allowed the master to teach his craft to his wife, children and apprentices, and in the assumption that the widow could take over her husband's craft. The use of family labour was widespread, even if its female components are often invisible in the records.[49] Wives were employed on the sales side as well as in manufacture; the Chester court records show that women served in the shop and made purchases and deliveries.[50] Similarly, husbands and wives collaborated in running inns, as with John and Agnes Wigmore at Westminster in 1398.[51]

The women who worked with their husbands belonged to craft and shopkeeping families. Other women, both wealthier and poorer, worked independently, probably fitting in their work with their household and family commitments. Such wives and working widows can often be described as *femmes soles*, who were responsible for their own business and their own debts. Levels of wealth and status among the *femmes soles* varied, and it must not be assumed that prosperous women did not engage in working for money. Some of these women worked from the household and achieved business success, for example, Alice Claver and Beatrice Fyler, silkwomen of London.[52] Alice served her apprenticeship in London as a silkwoman, married the mercer Richard Claver and practised her trade during her marriage and after her husband's death, supplying silk to both Edward IV and Richard III. Alice Claver's good fortune may be contrasted with Margery Kempe's failure to succeed in her business ventures into brewing and corn-milling.[53]

Many widows who carried on their husbands' businesses probably worked from the household. Several of these women had the skill needed for the management of affairs, but only remained in business for a short time, winding up their husbands' affairs and facilitating the takeover by a son or other member of the family. Businesses ranged from shops and crafts to involvement in overseas trade. Agnes Aleyn of St Albans referred to a shop and stallage in her will of 1475, and Emmot Pannall of York in 1458 to her saddler's workshop.[54] Margaret Rowley of Bristol was named as shipping wine and woad from Bordeaux in 1479, immediately after the death of her husband Thomas.[55] Agnes Kyte of Bristol in 1488 left her son all the merchandise beyond the sea which was already in his governance; presumably she had been left the business by her husband, but had involved her son in it before her death.[56] Similarly, women merchants recorded in the Hull customs accounts mainly operated over a short period. Denise Holme shipped out wool and wool-fells between 1465 and 1470, from the time of her husband's death until shortly before her own. Marion Kent of York seems to have withdrawn from business as her children grew up; she exported cloth and lead in 1471–3, importing a wide range of merchandise, and was exceptional among the *femmes soles* in serving on the council of the York mercers' guild in 1474–5.[57]

Such women were indeed exceptional, and it was far more usual to find women working as hucksters, petty traders and stallholders, and appearing in the court records as forestallers and regraters.[58] The prevalence of these occupations indicates that for many people the household was not the workplace. Many Chester *femmes soles* were hucksters, and for some this occupation was combined with running noisy alehouses in the city's cellars; however, most of the women who kept taverns were married, and their husbands were generally middling craftsmen.[59] Chester was not the only place to have disorderly taverns run by women; in both Durham and Nottingham, women were accused over the night-time activities at their inns.[60] Hucksters were common in Bristol and Nottingham, and women were referred to as running stalls at Colchester.[61] At Bristol, tapsters, hucksters and retail traders in victuals had the special status of portmen and portwomen, although it was decided in 1470–1 that no more were to be created. The York chamberlains' accounts of the 1460s and 1470s give yearly rents for stallage, which list a number of women, some of whose trades are given, such as chapwoman and breadseller. Several of the women listed as freemen of York were described as huckster and chapwoman.[62] Women were prominent as retailers at Westminster.[63] Goods sold often comprised foodstuffs and ale, and women's association with brewing is well documented. It was the richer women who engaged in the actual brewing, within their households, while the less well-off sold ale and ran alehouses. The growth of beer-making in the fifteenth century, however, may well have undermined this activity.[64]

Apart from retailing, many women took up work as unskilled labourers, or jobs in the crafts, making use of skills learned in their early life at home, or in service or apprenticeship. Again, they were working outside their own households. They are found in a wide variety of occupations. Only a few jobs were gender-specific, such as midwives and washerwomen, along with certain processes in the cloth industry, such as washing wool and spinning. Work such as spinning only brought in a low wage, and men and women working in a number of processes in the cloth industry might easily be exploited. This explains why the ordinances of the merchant guild at Worcester in 1467 laid down that employment in the cloth industry was to be given to men and women of the city, for the benefit of the poor commonalty, and that all workers were to be paid in money, not in goods.[65]

It is likely that it was the women relying on wage labour who were most affected by decreasing employment opportunities in the later fifteenth century when many of the larger towns went into decline. Circumstances varied from town to town, and local conditions obviously have to be taken into account. The weavers' ordinance at Bristol in 1461 referred to some weavers who used their wives, daughters and maids to work on their own looms or to be employed by another weaver. As a result, many men, who were fit to do the king service in his wars and in the defence of the land, and who were skilled in the craft, were living as vagrants. The use of female labour was therefore to stop, except in the case of the weaver's present wife, who was to be allowed to work for her husband as long as she lived.[66]

Throughout urban society, therefore, women were engaged in contributing to the family income; they did not necessarily work in their husbands' trades, nor were they restricted to working within their husbands' households. It is likely that many, especially poorer, women engaged in retailing and wage-labour part-time, fitting work in between pregnancies and household duties, taking advantage of the employment opportunities available and making money where they could.

The time would come, however, when the widow retired from business, possibly because of old age, or when children or possibly apprentices grew up and took over the business. In some cases, retirement might be forced on the widow as a result of a second marriage. Certain guilds were wary of second husbands and suspected a lack of proper training. According to the York textwriters' and illuminators' ordinances of 1487, an apprentice might continue with his master's widow as long as she remained unmarried. The York butchers' ordinances of 1498 laid down that a man of another occupation who married a butcher's widow was to have nothing to do with butchering until he had come to an arrangement with the city chamber and the guild.[67] The weavers' guild of Shrewsbury in 1448 laid down that a weaver's widow was only to carry on the craft for three months after the death of her husband so that she could finish off any of her husband's work left unwrought.[68]

Once a widow was no longer concerned with business, and her family had grown up, her household would necessarily contract. Some women would become isolated as their children moved away, or in some cases died, and this may well explain the networks of female friends which are found in some wills and the bequests to trusted servants. Margaret Cappes of Hornchurch, Essex, decided to move to London after the death of her second husband; her daughters were married and settled in London and in Maldon and Stondon Massey in Essex.[69] The women named in the will of Emma Boteler of St Albans in 1471–2 were probably close friends; furnishings, clothes and money were left to Margaret and Eleanor Stepeneth, the wife of Richard Dell, and Joan, the wife of Edward Bonage, as well as to her servant Alice.[70]

Lack of family as well as piety may explain the close connection between some widows and the Church. Sometimes the household took on a religious tinge when a widow took a vow of chastity after the death of her husband, although no religious rule of life was specified for the vowess. Although feelings of piety motivated some widows to take the vow, secular considerations were also present; some husbands laid down that property was only to be held by the widow for as long as she remained unmarried, and some widows may have wished to run their lives without the pressure to remarry.[71] The role of the household in the dispensing of charity was always regarded as important;[72] feeding and clothing the poor were regarded as an essential part of the housewife's duties, and it is significant that many depictions of the Seven Works of Mercy show them being performed by a woman. The giving of charity may have intensified in the houses of some older and more wealthy widows and is to be seen in bequests in wills. At Barking in Essex, in 1430, Alice Ewer wanted property to be sold by her executors and the money to be used for requiem masses, almsgiving, road repair and works of charity, as they thought best for the salvation of her and her husband's souls.[73]

In many wills, as in this one, charitable gifts were set alongside gifts to the Church, and, quite apart from the concern to help the passage of the soul through purgatory, it is possible that widows found that the Church provided social contact as well as religious comfort. The son of Agnes Fylour of Bristol was a mercer in London and not best pleased when he found after Agnes' death in 1467 that she had left a dwelling-house to All Saints' Church; the vicar was said to have prevailed on Alice to do this, and payment for writing and sealing the will is entered in the All Saints' Church book. Agnes was well off and decided to use her resources in this way.[74]

Many poor widows had to give up their households in old age. Some were cared for by their families, as was Margaret Bentley of St Albans.[75] Some found refuge in other households: Alice Claver took Katherine Hardman into her household in the 1480s.[76] For others there was the possibility of entering an almshouse; the York city chamberlains made a regular payment of £1 a year to the poor women of the *maison Dieu* on Ouse Bridge.[77] Alternatively, they might be dependent on casual charity and bequests; in the will of Agnes Mayr of St Albans in 1484, the account survives of the men and women who received shirts and smocks.[78] All these women were vulnerable because of poverty and because they no longer had the protection of and identity with a household of their own.

The importance of the household in providing security, identity, respectability and status is further underlined by the fact that it was the women outside a household who were marginalized in urban society, and this tendency towards marginalization was increasing in the later fifteenth century. The Coventry Leet Book in 1492 forbade single women who were strong and healthy and under the age of fifty to rent houses or rooms, but instead laid down that they were to go into service. Women of evil reputation were to be evicted by their landlords. Prostitutes were to be reported and then expelled from Leicester in 1467. Fifteen year later, York decreed that common women were to live in the suburbs.[79] The most notorious stews, and those about which a considerable amount is known, were in Southwark. A fifteenth-century custumal laid down detailed regulations concerning the owners of the brothels and the prostitutes themselves. They were to wear distinctive dress, rules were laid down over soliciting, they were not allowed to have their own partners, or their own brothels, they had to leave Southwark on holy days and they were to be evicted if they were found to be pregnant. No married or religious women were supposed to be prostitutes.[80] These regulations indicate how vulnerable they were. They were suspected by the authorities of causing disorder, but it is likely that in many cases they were forced into prostitution by poverty; women on their own lacked the male relatives and household support to vouch for their identity and good behaviour.

The household provided a safe basis for townswomen of every age and status. It was both home and workplace for husband and wife, children, apprentices and servants. Its size and nature changed constantly over time; the household of a young family would be very different from that of a widow. Belonging to a household gave men and women an element of protection and security in urban society; it was those who lacked this stake in the town who were regarded as potentially threatening in an age when the fear of disorder was widespread. Women within the household lived full and often hard lives, but their place within the town was recognized. The household unit was an integral part of the neighbourhood, the parish and the town itself. It gave women a base for participation in the life of the town, sharing with their husbands in the religious and social activities of the guilds and making their house the setting for entertainment, recreation and charity. By looking at townswomen in the context of the household, we can see them in all their variety, from childhood to old age.

I would like to thank those present at the conference for their questions and comments, which have enabled me to extend the scope of this paper. I would also like to thank Kay Lacey, with whom I have discussed a number of points.

CHAPTER 3

Hospital Nurses and their Work

CAROLE RAWCLIFFE

> You will be called upon . . . to attend the sick day and night, often to assist them to rise, to tolerate their infirmities, their filth and their vermin, to endure harsh words and answer them gently; you will often have to fast, often confess that you are at fault and be harshly admonished, and you will have to bear this with grace and without rancour and suffer for the love of God. . . . You will have to get up when you want to sleep, rise when you are exhausted and want to rest, work when you long for recreation. (*Statutes of the Hospital of St Nicholas du Bruille, Tournai, 1460*)

At some point during the third quarter of the fifteenth century, Jehan Henry, a senior official of the parlement of Paris and canon of the Cathedral of Notre Dame, composed a book for the guidance of the sisters of the city's largest hospital, the Hôtel Dieu. These religious women, professed sisters of the Augustinian order, had chosen to pursue the active rather than the contemplative life: they followed Martha rather than Mary, devoting themselves to the service of the sick poor.[1] Henry's output had previously included three substantial works on Christian mysticism and two manuals designed to raise levels of spirituality and discipline in female monastic communities. Years of experience as supervisor of the Hôtel Dieu had convinced him that this institution also needed reform, while none the less sharpening his appreciation of the qualities demonstrated by women who cared on a daily basis for the least favoured members of society.[2] In 1482, when he assumed office for a second time, the female staff comprised some thirty-seven sisters, eighteen novices (known as *filles blanches*) and a number of female servants, including a midwife and her assistant.[3] With four wards and a lying-in room, the hospital could accommodate over 870 patients at once, although it rarely sheltered more than 500. Even so, the demands made upon the nurses were extremely onerous. The work was menial as well as exhausting, each novice being first sent to serve in one of the two laundries, where upwards of 900 sheets and the clothes of the new patients were washed every week. Promotion came slowly, with the result that senior members of the nursing staff were extremely experienced.[4]

Henry's *Livre de Vie Active* (Book of the Active Life) is dedicated to the sub-prioress, sister Perrenelle Alaine, towards whom he expressed more than conventional admiration:

> In this house and island of hospitality lives this devout and charitable servant, to whom I feel constrained under the terms of our community of faith to entrust whatever spiritual merit my own soul may acquire, with the aid of grace, in the hazardous pursuit of the active life. Indeed, it seems to me, I could find no better way of protecting my precious gift than to place it in the hands of one who must surely command a great share of the [heavenly] reward earned by the spiritual fraternity there; and who, through the works of mercy she herself has performed in this house of God, has contributed so signally to His precious gift, whereby others are able to benefit from the hospital's treasury of merit.[5]

In short, the almsdeeds performed by the sisters constituted a celestial bank account, upon which the house's benefactors and patrons could draw to pay their way out of Purgatory.

Yet, to Henry, the Hôtel Dieu was far more than an institution for the care of the sick poor, or even a deposit box for the purchase of Paradise. It also possessed a symbolic value, as an earthly representation of the Church, the human soul or even the Kingdom of Heaven. Understandably, in view of his intended readership, his choice of metaphors drew upon the quotidian round of the nursing sister, and is thus unusual, not simply because of the intimate picture of hospital life which emerges from the 123 folios of text, but also on account of his manifest respect (on paper at least) for women whose contribution to society generally went unremarked by his contemporaries.[6] As if to atone for this omission, he employed unusually fulsome language. The dormitory where the sisters slept after their physical exertions was, for example, compared by him to 'the high house of God triumphant, which is the final resting place of they who have laboured virtuously and faithfully in the Hôtel Dieu'. Elsewhere he championed the women who 'through charity offer their goods and hard physical labour in the service of their neighbour', promising them a place in Heaven 'above the confessors and the martyrs'.[7]

At least one other celebrated mystic had shared Henry's respect for the sisters of this Parisian hospital. In 1406 the reformer, Jean Gerson, had preached before the King of France on behalf of the staff and inmates, drawing attention, albeit in less extravagant terms, to the demanding and all too often thankless work of the nurses. In winter, he reported, the honest widows and virgins who had pledged themselves to a life of chastity might be found up to their knees in the icy mud of the Seine, washing sheets; and throughout the year, day and night, they undertook to care for hundreds of sick paupers, bathing them, putting them to bed, feeding them, attending to all their bodily needs and offering constant solace.[8] Like Gerson, Henry made much of the way in which the sisters performed the Seven Comfortable or Corporal Works of Mercy, which constituted the bedrock of Christian charity and were a prerequisite of salvation.[9] No English medieval hospital was even half the size of the Hôtel Dieu, nor did any possess a salaried medical staff before the sixteenth century, but all shared this common purpose. And in England, too, the nurse, a figure so far 'hidden from history' as to be almost invisible, played a vital role in transforming the wishes of pious benefactors into real physical care.[10]

The term 'hospital' covers such a wide range of institutions – from houses specializing in the care of lepers, the blind or the insane to night-shelters, and from corporate bodies like the Hôtel Dieu, which maintained a steady turnover of acute cases, to tiny rural almshouses accommodating only three or four residents – that generalizations tend to mislead rather than illuminate.[11] Most were relatively poor, and not even the richest emerged unaffected by the economic, social and demographic upheavals of the fourteenth century. Statistics about English hospitals remain impressionistic, as do attempts to categorize them, although historians generally agree that a distinct shift in provision occurred during the later Middle Ages, from the monastic or quasi-monastic model, with its open-ward infirmary and comparatively large staff, to the small, selective almshouse for respectable elderly paupers. The gradual disappearance of leprosy meant that many of the 350 or so refuges endowed for the reception and isolation of sufferers either closed or were converted into almshouses. Not many more than a hundred hospitals of the first type, offering sustained care, bed and board to other categories of the sick poor, have been documented in the towns and cities of pre-Reformation England. The two largest (St Leonard's, York, and St Mary's Bishopsgate, in London) could accommodate up to 206 and 180 patients respectively, but most were far more modest with a potential capacity of fewer than forty or fifty beds, albeit often shared.[12] Together they provide most of the available evidence about nursing in later medieval England, which, as this essay reveals, differed little in essence from the work of professed sisters in comparative continental institutions.

As King Henry VII acknowledged when drawing up his will in 1509, he and other wealthy men could gain spiritual health 'by meanes of keping, susteynyng and maynteynyng of commune hospitallis' where most of the Comfortable Works could be discharged on a daily basis.[13] The obligation to visit the sick, shelter the homeless, provide the poor with clothes and sustenance and prepare the dead for burial could there be delegated to the hospital nurse (who might herself appear a worthy recipient of charitable relief). So too could at least four of the seven corresponding Spiritual Works, it being incumbent upon her to comfort and pray for the afflicted, while accepting and forgiving difficult, sometimes physically violent patients.[14] That nurses should console the sick with uplifting assurances of the constancy of God's love was generally expected, if, perhaps, less often achieved. St Elizabeth of Hungary served as an exemplar to all nursing sisters because her charity towards the sick poor had been accompanied by a remarkable outpouring of personal piety. Her hospital at Marburg was noted throughout Europe as much for her concern about the diseased souls of the patients as it was for her own personal involvement in every aspect of physical care, however distasteful. Thomas, Lord Berkeley's bequest of a psalter, a set of church vestments and an English translation of *The Golden Legend* (which included a life

The endowment of a hospital or almshouse promised salvation through the performance of the Seven Comfortable Works. On his deathbed, the wealthy mercer, Richard Whittington (d. 1423), instructs his executors to take the necessary steps, while the poor and crippled bedesmen stand ready to pray for his soul, rosaries in hand. (1442 copy of The Ordinances of Whittington's Almshouse, *reproduced by courtesy of the Mercers' Company, London.)*

St Elizabeth of Hungary tends the sick poor in the hospital she herself built at Marburg. To the right a servant discharges two more of the Seven Comfortable Works by providing loaves of bread and water in a jug. (St Elizabeth window, Church of St Elizabeth, Marburg. Photograph, Private Collection.)

of St Elizabeth) to the sisters of the hospital of St Mary Magdalen near Bristol was thus especially appropriate, although they no doubt welcomed his gift of £5 in cash with equal enthusiasm, as their house was small and underfunded.[15]

Some nursing sisters with a talent for healing undoubtedly assumed an important and personally fulfilling role as spiritual intermediaries, freed by good works from the yoke of priestly authority. Nor, unlike those religious women whose piety assumed more exuberant and idiosyncratic forms, did they inspire unease in the male clerical establishment.[16] But their position in the ecclesiastical hierarchy still remained subservient. Just as spiritual almsdeeds appeared infinitely superior to corporal ones, so the nurse ranked some way below the priest, who was aptly described as a physician of souls. The statutes of the Savoy Hospital, founded by King Henry VII shortly before his death, clearly enunciated a scale of priorities which had defined and dictated the role of the hospital in the Christian west for over a millennium:

> Whereas sickness takes two forms – namely of the body and of the soul – it is necessary that each should be provided with health-giving medicines. And these should be principally for the health of the soul which is more honourable, more dignified and more excellent than the body.[17]

In some English hospitals, such as St Leonard's, York, one of the sisters' principal tasks was to fetch a chaplain if the patients wished to confess their sins, or seemed close to death.[18] In this context, at least, the nurse was a handmaiden and had to comport herself with due deference.

Hospitals like St Leonard's, which followed the Augustinian rule, allowed a degree of freedom from religious observance to those engaged in charitable activities, but still imposed strict discipline. Whatever their choice of rule, most founders insisted upon regular (often weekly) chapter meetings, where faults were investigated, corrected and, if necessary, punished. Nurses had to take the customary monastic vows of poverty, chastity and obedience, dressing in a seemly – often precisely circumscribed – fashion, and behaving with humility at all times.[19] These feminine virtues which, in the perfect nurse, were accompanied by penitence and compassion, figured prominently among the attributes of the Virgin Mary.[20] As assistant to her son, *Christus Medicus*, she represented the most influential of all role models for those who tended the sick.[21] Although English hospital regulations reveal comparatively little about patient care before the sixteenth century, they (and the reports made by the episcopal visitors who tried to enforce them) frequently expressed concern about the appearance and demeanour of nursing staff. Undue familiarity with male brethren was, for example, a charge levelled against the Augustinian sisters of St Thomas' Hospital, Southwark, a house dogged by disciplinary problems throughout the later Middle Ages.[22]

Whereas a nun retreated into the cloister to lead a secluded, inaccessible life and was thus able to retain a measure of female sensuality (albeit carefully channelled in the direction of Christian mysticism), the nursing sister was denied the luxury of such 'private space'. Since so many of her tasks were performed in intimate proximity to members of the opposite sex she had, like the priest, to be manifestly asexual.[23] It was no coincidence that newly professed sisters at the Hôtel Dieu spent their first years in the laundry, far away from the eyes of male patients, or that Walter Suffield, founder of St Giles' Hospital, Norwich, insisted that the nurses should be aged fifty or thereabouts. Medieval physicians warned against the dangers posed to the sick by menstruating women, but Suffield's primary concern was almost certainly for the souls rather than the bodies of patients and clergy.[24] Even at the Savoy, where nurses ranked as salaried employees and could leave if they wished to marry, all recruits had to be over thirty-six and either virgins or (in the absence of suitable applicants) respectable widows. Their conditions of service were essentially monastic and may well have been far stricter in terms of conduct, dress and hard physical labour than was the case in some hospitals following a religious rule.[25]

When they were not under constant scrutiny in the wards, hospital sisters preserved their chastity (and that of the priests and lay brothers with whom they worked) by avoiding all but essential contact with men. Sexual misdemeanours undermined discipline, deterred wealthy patrons and, most important of all, created a miasma of sin which threatened the spiritual health of staff and patients alike. A visitation of St Bartholomew's Hospital, conducted in 1316 by Bishop Segrave of London, revealed general laxity, neglect of patients and insubordination. His response to the situation was to recommend that stricter segregation be enforced by 'a man of exemplary moral character' acting as doorkeeper to the sisters' quarters. Only the master could authorize male visitors, but he too was evidently susceptible to temptation, being later accused of sexual incontinence with one of the nurses.[26] At St Leonard's, York, the sisters not only occupied 'an honest place' to the west of the hospital church (the two sexes commonly sat apart in most medieval European churches), but had their own doorway into the nave, which was forbidden to the brothers and priests unless processions were being staged. This arrangement not only maintained the customary decencies, but kept the women away from the consecrated space of the chancel.[27]

In many respects the nurse's duties were directly analogous to those of the priest, since she worked alongside him in a parallel, secular dimension. To a certain degree, this division of labour reflected the widespread – but not invariably pejorative – assumption that women had more in common with corporeal matter, while men commanded greater intellectual, rational and spiritual authority. If 'physical, tangible humanity might be symbolized or understood as female', women were demonstrably better equipped to minister to its most vulnerable members.[28] Conventional depictions of medieval hospitals, such as that of the Hôtel Dieu, Paris, *c.* 1500, underscore the distinction between care of the body and the soul, one fed by the nurse, the other by the priest. The burial of the dead, a seventh work of mercy added by medieval theologians to the six itemized by Christ in St Matthew's Gospel (Matt. 25: 32–6), was in a very real sense shared between them, the priest attending to the welfare of the deceased's immortal soul, while the nurse prepared the corpse for commitment.[29] The grim, but routine, task of 'winding' the dead in shrouds or sheets generally fell to women, and it must have provided the hospital nurse with regular employment.[30] In 1546, for example, the master of the Eastbridge Hospital, Canterbury, claimed additional expenses for 'the sokking sheets and the burying of poor people that dy within the said hospital, the which of late hath been very chargeable and like to increase'.[31] Sisters at the Savoy were specifically instructed to arrange for the burial of patients, and, as a matter of course, to perform the other Comfortable Works as well.[32]

Founded at a time when humanist reformers, such as Sir Thomas More, were promoting schemes for the improvement of hospitals, and heavily influenced by developments in Italy, the Savoy put into effect a number of practical measures to contain potential sources of infection.[33] The sisters were instructed 'not only to purify the dormitory and cleanse it of all putrefaction, faeces, filth, corrupt matter and any other impurity, dirt and cobwebs, but also of anything whatsoever which smells bad and savours strongly, or may generate an evil or unhealthy stench'.[34] Medieval men and women had long recognized and feared the enormous risks faced by individuals who spent their lives in close proximity to the dead and dying. The idea that disease was spread by foul or contaminated air

Care of the body accompanies that of the soul. Sisters at the Hôtel Dieu, Paris, provide meals and prepare the dead for burial, while the priest celebrates holy communion, or possibly administers the last rites. In the centre of the picture, novices are received into the hospital, while the King of France himself hopes to gain merit from the good works performed through his patronage. (Bibliothèque Nationale, Paris, MS Ea res.)

made them nervous of anything or anyone likely to give off unpleasant odours.[35] One of the saintly attributes of Louis IX of France was his apparent indifference to the dangerous miasmas hovering in the hospital wards he so often visited. His eagerness to minister to the sick poor in the most intimate and potentially life-threatening situations, and even to help prepare their bodies for interment, horrified his entourage, while at the same time establishing his reputation for sanctity.[36] Yet this was the daily lot of the hospital nurse.

Sin, of course, constituted an even more lethal source of infection, liable to immediate punishment through earthly suffering and disease. Just as the priest was called upon to make a spiritual diagnosis of his parishioners, so the nurse had to be able to recognize dangerous symptoms, such as those of leprosy, which most non-specialist hospitals viewed with alarm.[37] In larger institutions, including the Savoy and the Heilig Geist Spital in Nuremberg (founded 1393), admissions were carefully scrutinized by a senior nursing sister to make sure that no infectious or otherwise disruptive patients were accepted.[38] Those who passed scrutiny were then made welcome and directed to their beds. A writer of contemplative literature, like Jehan Henry, could appreciate the close correspondence between physical and spiritual care, using it to hearten and guide his readers. Drawing

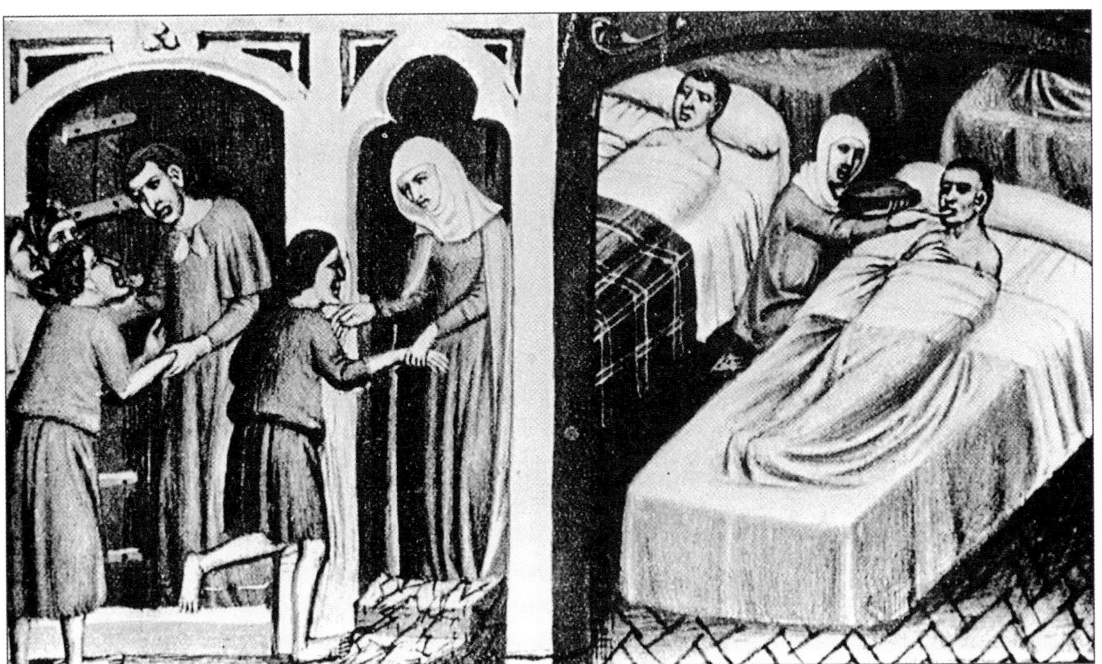

Welcoming the sick poor at the Hôtel Dieu, Paris, in the name of Christ, but also making sure that none of them suffer from dangerous diseases. Once they have passed scrutiny they are given a bed and nourishing food. (Bibliothèque Nationale, Paris, MS Latin 8846, f. 106r.)

upon the analogy between church and hospital, he explained how sick and battered souls were likewise set upon the journey to health by a female porter:

> Those who are afflicted with a mortal disease are sent by her to the low beds of Humility in the infirmary . . . where the sick may recuperate, and be brought from a condition of spiritual illness to the healthy state of grace through the ministry of the chatelaine, Penitence, accompanied by the sisters Contrition, Confession and Satisfaction. They . . . administer drugs acquired in the pharmacy of Grace to the sick, restoring them to spiritual health. . . . Confession administers purgative medicines by mouth, and Satisfaction gives the comforting and restorative electuaries [medicinal drinks] of fasting, prayer, almsdeeds and other such virtuous and testing works.[39]

Medieval hospital patients were generally expected to confess their sins on arrival, a process sometimes accompanied by the removal of filthy, verminous clothing and the provision of partial or complete baths. Regulations drawn up for the sisters at the Hospital of St Nicolas du Bruille (Tournai) in 1460 introduced a stringent examination in weekly chapter meetings so that any failings with regard to the spiritual as well as the physical hygiene of their charges would come to light:

> Has she [the nurse] failed to care for the poor and the sick, to feed them on time, to see they have confessed and to arrange for them to receive the sacraments? Has she neglected to make their beds or renew their sheets, to bathe them, to wash those in need and cleanse their wounds? Has she omitted to give them what they need or would like to have, so far as the resources of the hospital allow? Has she replied harshly to them?[40]

The correspondence between spiritual and physical cleansing appealed to authors throughout the Middle Ages and beyond. A few decades later, the Italian theologian, Giovanni Vivaldi, described contrition as 'the sweetest bath by which the physician of our souls beneficially cures the unwholesome diseases of the human heart'.[41] Jehan Henry was thus able to tap a rich and familiar reserve of metaphors when he came to discuss the treatment of the repentant soul:

> At the entrance to the Hôtel Dieu stand two ladies, Sacred Prayer and Oblation through the Almsbox, who help the sick on their way to the room of Penitence. And Examination of Conscience, the ladies' servant, draws the water of tears from the deep wells of the heart, and with his broom, which records all diseases, sweeps up all the filthy refuse to be thrown out of the hospital. . . . In the stripping room, Displeasure . . . hands over the sheets of the bed of Affection, where the sick have sought rest in their illness, to Compunction, mistress of the great laundry, to be cleansed in the wash of scalding tears mixed with the ashes of remembrance of death.[42]

The ubiquity of medical metaphors in late medieval religious writing amply supports the view that, although it came some way behind the soul, care of the body remained a high priority. John Mirfeld (d. 1407), a clerk who occupied rooms at St Bartholomew's Hospital, London, for over forty years, produced two major compilations, one of medical texts and the other of sacred writings. His *Breviarium Bartholomei* concentrates on the attainment and preservation of physical health and contains a prayer of thanks for the divine gift of medicine, 'that thy servants, by whatever disease they may be troubled, may, by means of the healing here set forth, attain to recovery'.[43] The *Breviarium* was drawn from a variety of standard medical authorities for the benefit of those without access to a suitable library and provides a digest of information (including a list of signs of approaching death) which would have proved useful in the neighbouring infirmary.[44] Although Mirfeld reserved his most scathing censure for negligent and avaricious priests rather than physicians, his remarks about the cost and inaccessibility of professional medical services help to explain why they were not a regular feature of life at St Bartholomew's.

The almost complete absence of documentary evidence for the presence of either physicians or surgeons in English hospitals before the sixteenth century has perplexed many historians, who have tried, with little success, to make the most of a handful of rather tenuous connections.[45] Few would agree with the extreme and essentially anachronistic view that medieval hospitals in general were 'poorly equipped facilities which reflected little careful thought for the comfort, cleanliness, or, ironically, the health of their patients'.[46] But it is generally assumed that no more than rudimentary physical care, in the way of rest, food, warmth and security can have been available to the average medieval English patient, or indeed to the sick poor who found refuge in the smaller institutions of continental Europe. Since these men and women may well have been malnourished, exhausted or homeless, such a basic level of support would alone have been of incalculable benefit and, in almshouses catering for the elderly or handicapped, would often have stretched resources to the limit. The value placed upon a welcoming and safe environment should not be underestimated. A descriptive list of London churches and monasteries, preserved in a mid-fifteenth-century commonplace book, contains favourable comments about four of the larger city hospitals. St Bartholomew's was described as being 'of grete comforte to poore men as for hyr loggyng and yn specyalle unto yong wymmen that have mysse done that ben wythe chylde', while St Thomas', Southwark, earned similar praise for its hospitality and maternity services. The insane in the Hospital of St Mary Bethlehem were reputedly kept 'full honestely' and sometimes restored to their wits, and the work of the sisters of St Thomas', Southwark, in tending 'the beddys for pore men that come to that place' was also noted.[47] When reading such comments, it is important to remember that, to contemporaries of whatever social status, care equated cure, the two being often indistinguishable.[48]

Other important factors need to be borne in mind so far as the question of medical treatment and its availability in medieval hospitals is concerned. In the first place, only a relatively small proportion of the population could ever afford the services of a university-trained or licensed practitioner, while the rest had always relied heavily on female healers whose activities are almost as poorly documented as those of the English hospital nurse. That remedies would be provided by unlettered women in the home or local community was taken for granted, and thus rarely mentioned.[49] The same is undoubtedly true of nurses: hospital statutes requiring them simply to 'tend the sick' did no more than state the obvious and needed no further elaboration. Female empirics who overstepped the mark by resorting to dubious practices or setting up in direct competition to men attracted attention, but nursing sisters were unlikely to invite censure on this score and thus went about their work in decent obscurity.

The appearance of salaried physicians and surgeons in European hospitals generally followed the introduction of local or national legislation against unlicensed empirics, many of whom were female. Attempts to impose a medical monopoly had little effect in England before the second decade of the sixteenth century. It is thus hardly surprising that English hospitals lagged behind the Continent so far as the introduction of professional services was concerned, or that Henry VII turned to Italy when he wanted a different model for his new foundation.[50] But the gradual trend towards medicalization did not always bring improvements. Medieval hospital patients were spared the unnecessary suffering caused by the aggressive and often painful types of treatment favoured by highly qualified practitioners. Domestic medicine drew heavily upon ingredients from the larder and garden, which may not always have proved beneficial, but at least had the merit of causing less damage than some items in the medieval pharmacopoeia, such as raw arsenic.[51] Flour, wax, honey, animal fat and herbs, the essential components of poultices and pills, were readily available in the hospital kitchen, while rudimentary surgical skills, including phlebotomy (bloodletting), could be passed on in exactly the same way as the barber trained his apprentice: by empirical observation. Ointments and plasters were widely used, especially in the treatment of skin diseases, which were endemic among the sick poor. Jehan Henry speaks of 'the ointment of Mercy, which Pity carries closed in the box of her heart',[52] and John Mirfeld provided his readers with many useful recipes. Some demanded expensive and esoteric ingredients, but most, including his 'plaster of Bartholomew', an all-purpose cure for ulcers, fistulae, wounds and sores, required no more than parsley, plantain, cornflour and honey, which were blended over an open fire.[53]

A further consideration concerns the nature of medieval medicine itself. Following the classical tradition which loomed so large in all areas of practice, physicians favoured a holistic approach to healing. In a pre-Cartesian world, the idea of treating the body or its component parts without reference to the living conditions and emotions of the patient seemed as alien as the thought of divorcing the self-same body from the soul. By the later Middle Ages, these theories found coherent expression in a series of guidelines, known as the *Regimen Sanitatis*, or regimen of health, which themselves derived from a variety of popular texts attributed to the medical school at Salerno.[54] Affluent patients could commission their own, personally customized, *regimina* at great expense from a physician, but vernacular literature describing the fundamental principles of the genre circulated widely and was easy to understand. Particular emphasis was placed upon the proper management of six 'non-naturals' (diet, rest and exercise, evacuation and repletion, sleep, environment and state of mind), in order to maintain the body's equilibrium. The possibility that health could be preserved or regained in this way proved immensely attractive in an age when neither medication nor surgery could offer much hope of success.[55] In theory, if less often in practice, the precisely regulated environment of the medieval hospital lent itself especially well to the implementation of a system which integrated earthly and spiritual medicine in a carefully balanced way. It was, perhaps, for this reason that John Mirfeld chose to reproduce the passages on the *regimen sanitatis* which had originally appeared in his *Breviarium* in the collection of religious texts made by him towards the end of his life (known as the *Florarium Bartholomei*).[56] Since the regimen could not succeed without a measure of self-control on the part of the patient, preachers and the authors of pastoral literature often referred to it when they wished to illustrate the virtues of spiritual discipline.[57]

While recognizing that, in the long term, illness was often a punishment for wrongdoing, medieval men and women sought a more immediate, physiological explanation for disease. Good health, they believed, depended upon maintaining a careful balance between the four bodily humours, which were generated through a cooking process in the stomach. Any of the non-naturals listed above could affect this balance, but inadequate or unsuitable food had an immediate and potentially lethal impact. Diet, 'the first instrument of medicine', thus came to

The nurse, here quite probably a paid servant rather than a professed sister, stands by ready to feed the patient once his spiritual wants have been met. (Wellcome Iconographic Collection, Wellcome Institute, London, woodcut, French, c. *1524.)*

Women played a notable part in medical treatment at home (where all but the poorest patients were treated), administering food in accordance with an appropriate regimen. Here the invalid is being given barley soup, which was believed to stimulate the production of bile and was thus considered beneficial for individuals whose temperament was too hot. (National Library of Vienna, Tacuinum Sanitatis, *Codex 2466, f. 44v.)*

play a vital role in both the prevention and cure of sickness, and was the principal agent through which the physician applied his remedies. It was also a type of treatment which women were especially well qualified to prepare and administer. Notwithstanding the idea that paupers might be tempted into vice and gluttony if they were fed too well, the founders of hospitals and those who implemented their wishes tried to provide nourishing and appropriate fare.[58]

At the Hospital of St Just, Narbonne, a small house with about thirty-two beds (only twelve of which were in regular use) and a staff of six nurses, diet assumed overwhelming importance. Once the souls of the sick poor had been fed with the sacraments of the Church, their bodies were to be sustained as effectively as possible. The sisters' first duty was to prepare food for the patients, putting their needs before any other items of hospital business. Could such a modest institution have fulfilled the requirements of the town council by providing nutritious vegetarian meals for those whose condition forbade the consumption of meat and wine? And would it have been possible to supply poultry (considered an ideal food for invalids) each day to convalescents?[59] The distance between ideal and reality was often great, but whatever the resources of such hospitals, it was evidently understood that the nurses would have sufficient grasp of humoral theory to devise an effective *regimen sanitatis*. Information was probably passed on (as in lay society) by word of mouth and example. Nurses may also have been instructed by members of the clerical staff, who, in larger hospitals, were often graduates familiar with the academic medical syllabus.

Louis IX was in the habit of feeding delicacies to the sick poor in the *maison Dieu* he founded at Vernon, but only after he had asked the sisters 'what was wrong with them, if they could eat meat and other things, and what was good and healthy for their meals'.[60] At the Hospital of St Nicholas de Bruille, where all the care was provided by six Augustinian sisters and a few novices, the rules likewise specified that

> before the sisters take their food, the said sick patients shall be fed in accordance with their infirmities and their wishes, so far as can be arranged and so long as nothing is harmful to their health. As funds allow, they will be diligently supplied with their needs until they regain their health. And so that nobody who has recovered should fall ill again because they are forced to leave too soon, if they wish they may [then] be succoured for two or three days or more, if the prioress considers it necessary.[61]

The lay brothers of St Leonard's Hospital, York, who helped the sisters to care for the sick by performing heavy manual tasks, were accustomed 'to ask the cellarer at any reasonable hour for special foods from the cellar for those in their charge', which suggests that care was indeed taken to provide each patient with an appropriate diet.[62]

The significance of food to medieval women and the notable part it played in their charitable activities have been examined by a number of writers.[63] Caroline Walker Bynum has chronicled the heroic austerities of holy women who devoted their lives to the welfare of the sick poor while relentlessly mortifying their own flesh. This aspect of their role clearly enabled some nurses to identify closely with Christ and his mother, and bestowed considerable spiritual power upon them.[64] Yet it also brought dangerous temptations. The sisters at Bruille, for example, were warned to avoid harmful and excessive periods of fasting, which was intended 'not to destroy the body but to extirpate vices and eliminate sin'.[65] They were expected to set a good example by putting the sensible counsels of the regimen into practice.

Concern lest the brothers and sisters might indulge themselves at the expense of the sick poor weighed far more heavily with the founders of medieval hospitals. Staff at St John's, Nottingham, were warned 'to be chaste and sober . . . moderate in diet, faithfully converting the goods of the house and the alms they receive to the necessities of the poor and infirm', an admonition frequently encountered in surviving charters and statutes.[66] In small, cloistered communities, where meals tended to dominate the day, staff often complained about the poor quality of their food and drink. Visitation reports drew attention to the 'insipid and inadequate' diet provided at St Thomas' Hospital, Southwark (for patients), and St Bartholomew's, London (for nurses), but not all houses were so frugal.[67] Both

St Leonard's, York, and St Giles', Norwich, which are comparatively well documented, provided staff and patients with meat, fish, dairy produce, pulses, eggs, plentiful supplies of bread (baked on the premises) and ale (also brewed there).[68] Recent archaeological research on water management in hospitals suggests, too, that by medieval standards the larger houses were efficiently supplied with fresh water and carefully planned drainage and sewage systems. Hospitals were almost invariably sited on, or near, rivers, which provided water for cooking, drinking, sanitation and, possibly, purification rituals associated with healing.[69] As Jehan Henry made clear, the washing of diseased bodies and dirty linen offered many symbolic meanings.

With 100 beds, each fully appointed with a feather mattress, two pairs of blankets, three pairs of sheets, a coverlet and embroidered counterpane (emblazoned with the Tudor rose), the Savoy was far from typical. The fine linen sheets were to be freshly laundered for each patient, who enjoyed the luxury of sleeping alone. Any bedding which became 'soiled or defiled with blood, urine or faeces, or infested with vermin, or in any way torn or damaged' was to be removed at once by the sisters, 'so that each and every bed may be properly equipped and perfectly clean, by day and by night'.[70] Although the importance of both spiritual and physical cleanliness was acknowledged, few medieval English hospitals could aspire to this ideal. Yet many had wooden beds with sheets, pillows and blankets, often provided by pious benefactors, who also donated food and fuel. Besides running the laundry, nurses were often required to keep lamps burning at the patients' bedsides, which must have provided comfort in large, dark infirmary halls.[71] Beds, generally occupied by two or even three individuals of the same sex, were ranged near the walls, allowing plenty of space for the circulation of fresh air and access to nurses and priests. Whatever health hazards a shared bed may have posed, it at least had the benefit of generating heat.[72] It is now impossible to tell what proportion of the large quantities of kindling used by some hospitals was actually allocated to the infirmary, but fires were customarily lit to keep the patients warm. In winter, nurses at the Savoy were supposed to have them burning every evening and by about five in the morning, and at St Giles', Norwich, paupers in receipt of free food, as well as the poor in the hospital itself, were able to take their meals by a blazing hearth.[73] Among the most serious charges of mismanagement levelled in 1403 against the keeper of the Hospital of St Mary Bethlehem in London was that of failing to heat the wards and removing wood for his own use.[74]

Historians of the medieval English hospital have rarely appreciated the essential role played by gardens, which not only supplied fuel, food and medicinal herbs but also contributed in less immediately obvious ways to the holistic therapy characteristic of the time. During the twelfth century, the garden of the Hospital of St John the Baptist at Castle Donington, Leicestershire, had, indeed, produced such 'powerful herbs and roots' that a local physician had gone there to seek a cure for his own tertian fever.[75] Following a practice discernible at all levels of society, from the peasantry to the baronage, the cultivation of many hospital gardens appears to have been undertaken by women. Since it was such a large and affluent institution, the Savoy could afford to retain a gardener, who took his orders from the matron, as well as the physician and surgeon. He grew herbs, fruits and other plants 'for the relief and refreshment of the poor who flock to this hospital'. These were used in cooking, for the preparation of medicines and medicinal baths and for other 'health-giving purposes', which probably included the production of scented candles and fumigants for dispelling the miasmas of disease.[76] John Mirfeld, who wrote to 'delight the hearts' of his readers, 'just as the flowers of roses do give forth a sweet odour', recommended a variety of unguents using oils extracted from the roots and petals of plants.[77] Sweet-smelling herbs, such as rosemary, were carried at funerals as well as being wrapped by women around the corpse as a means of purifying the air in an age before the widespread use of coffins.[78]

Herbal baths, the ingredients carefully selected in accordance with the patient's malady, played an important part in the medieval *regimen sanitatis*, not least because they offered a rare promise of relief from pain. The nurses at Henry VII's hospital were expected to bathe each of their charges in warm water on arrival, either washing the feet and legs alone or, when necessary, immersing the whole body. This was, indeed, a traditional act of Christian piety, intended to reassure the poor (and those who cared for them) of their elevated status in the eyes of God, but it had more than ritual significance.[79] The statutes of the Savoy assumed that newcomers would be filthy, bloodstained, ulcerated and verminous, so the demand for soothing and sweet-smelling preparations must have been considerable. It is worth noting that an oven was also provided for delousing patients' clothes.[80]

In smaller houses, such as St Giles' Hospital, Norwich, the sisters themselves grew and processed whatever plants might be needed. Their walled garden, with its thatched pentice, was but one of several green spaces in the precinct, which included the master's ornamental garden, a great garden where trees and vegetables were cultivated, a pond yard, a piggery and a kitchen garden. During the fourteenth century surplus apples, pears, onions and leeks were sold on the open market as a cash crop; other produce included saffron, garlic, hemp and henbane, each of which featured prominently in the medieval pharmacopoeia. The hospital precincts also incorporated a great meadow, with its prelapsarian 'paradyse garden'.[81] The thirteenth-century encyclopaedist, Bartholomeus Anglicus, had waxed lyrical upon the health-giving properties of open lawns. Scattered with 'herbes and gras and flowers of dyuers kynde', they appeared to laugh with pleasure, promoting a sense of well-being in the beholder.[82] They too were a valuable source of medicinal plants. At St Giles', the watermeadows provided rushes and flowers to be strewn in the church at the east end of the infirmary, as well as grazing for the cattle which supplied the house with fresh milk, butter, cheese and meat.[83] It should be noted that aromatic preparations, which were used in great quantities, especially during times of plague, were believed to work more quickly on the body's vital spirits than anything taken by mouth, and some nurses may have administered them.[84] On the other hand, as Erasmus famously complained, the English habit of leaving filthy rushes to moulder for months at a time on unswept floors constituted a dangerous health hazard, to be avoided at all costs in a hospital.[85]

St Elizabeth of Hungary bathes two leprous women, an act at once beneficial to her spiritual health and their physical wellbeing. This altarpiece of c. *1500 shows a servant providing poultry, in the best traditions of the regimen. (Altarpiece from the Collegiate Church of Laufen, near Basel. Photograph, Private Collection.)*

The use of alcohol-based herbal potions to deaden pain during surgical procedures was common in later medieval England. A number of vernacular remedy books contain recipes for drinks such as 'dwale', which combined a powerful – and potentially lethal – mix of henbane, hemlock and opium with natural laxatives to render the patient insensible for a limited period. Hospital and infirmary gardens clearly furnished the vegetable ingredients necessary for these and other analgesics. Recent excavation on the site of the Augustinian hospital at Soutra in Mid-Lothian suggests that soporifics may regularly have been deployed in the care of patients, along with a remarkable range of herbal cures. Not all archaeologists are, however, convinced by the evidence, which remains controversial because of the sampling methods used. Another means of soothing pain, through the use of prayers and Christian charms, was an even more traditional staple of the female healer, which would have found a natural place in the religious ambience of the hospital ward. However, the herbal skills of the nurse should not be underestimated: women, as the fourteenth-century botanist, Henry Daniel, acknowledged, might possess rare accomplishments in this regard.[86]

Gardens must also have provided nursing sisters with a rare opportunity for individual privacy and rest after their labours. At the London hospital of St Mary Bishopsgate the sisters lodged in segregated quarters to the north of the infirmary in a stone-built range with a refectory and dorter, which gave access to their own garden.[87] Elderly corrodians, such as Joan Lunde, who lived in a 'celle sett yn the sauthe part of the [in]ffermory' of St Giles' Hospital, Beverley, were anxious to secure such a source of 'greate yerthely comfort'. In 1500–1 she complained to the Court of Chancery that, notwithstanding the money she had spent on maintaining the garden which formed part of her corrody, it had been given to another sister, 'to here greate troble vexacion and also uttere confusion'.[88] As strictly segregated in death as they were in life, the sisters and bedeswomen of the Hospital of St Katherine by the Tower had a separate walled cemetery in their close, which lay, along with their quarters, to the south of the hospital church. The brothers, clerks and choristers lived at a safe distance around a cloister on the north side.[89] The fitter and more mobile residents of English almshouses, such as those at Ewelme and Arundel, were expected to weed and tidy precinct gardens, but we have little evidence of their use by convalescent patients.[90] At the leper hospital run by St Albans Abbey inmates who had been phlebotomized were permitted to rest in a private garden, but many of them appear to have been Benedictines, already accustomed to the prophylactic regimen of the monastic infirmary.[91]

Although, in accordance with the regimen, the medieval hospital aimed to provide a calm and restful atmosphere in which the patient could recover both physical and spiritual health, it must often have been a noisy, bustling place where sleep proved elusive. The great fourteenth-century physician, Bernard Gordon, began consultations by asking his patients if they were disturbed by such irritations as barking dogs, which did, indeed, constitute a major problem in some houses.[92] At the Hospital of St Mary in the Newarke, Leicester, for example, the master not only protested about the packs of hounds and birds of prey which accompanied the patron's retainers to church, but also objected to the bear-baiting, 'May games' and 'common spectacles' staged there by this ill-governed crew.[93] The patients (and possibly their nurses) may have welcomed pageants about Robin Hood as a pleasant change from the solemn liturgical round, but other disturbances, such as the clamour and smell of the industrial processes which were a common feature of life in the precincts of several London hospitals, had nothing to recommend them.[94]

In all but the smallest institutions, the *opus Dei*, which comprised seven or eight services beginning at first light, was observed daily. At the Savoy, the great bell began ringing at five in the morning to rouse the house for matins and tolled intermittently from then onwards.[95] Some hospitals, such as St Giles', Norwich, actually incorporated a parish church, where weddings, baptisms and funerals regularly took place. This meant that parishioners were constantly coming and going next to the infirmary, which was separated from the nave by no more than a screen. Such close proximity appealed to local benefactors, who often required the sick poor 'lying in their beds' and nurses to join in prayers for their salvation. St Giles' ran a large choir and staff of chaplains, whose duties involved the regular celebration of requiem masses and obits for deceased patrons. Music, an accepted part of the *regimen sanitatis*, was generally deemed to possess curative powers over both mind and body. The sight of the Host, with its promise of spiritual regeneration, and the melodious, repetitive round of services (which in larger hospitals were observed with great splendour) provided intensive care for the soul, and may often have promoted a sense of physical well-being too.[96]

This was certainly the intention. Following a venerable medical tradition, which dated back to pre-Hippocratic times, medieval writers on medicine placed great importance upon the psychological state of the patient. Books on surgical practice, such as one composed by the fourteenth-century English surgeon, John of Arderne, stressed the desirability of a calm, confident and encouraging demeanour. 'It spedeth that a leche kunne talke of gode tales and of honest that may make the pacientes to laugh', he advised, 'and any other thingis . . . to . . . make or induce a light hert.'[97] Hospital sisters were likewise urged to avoid any form of behaviour which might intimidate or depress their charges, but to make even the most despised among them feel as welcome as a lord entering his inheritance. A 'patient and friendly manner' was expected of the matron at the Heilig Geist Spital in Munich, while the statutes of the Savoy elaborated at some length the virtues of assiduousness, diligence and a cheerful disposition.[98] Nurses at the Hospital of St Nicholas du Bruille were warned against the snares of depression, 'which is the cause of all evil and often of both bodily and spiritual death'. The exhortation that they should learn to 'live joyfully in Our Lord', serving Christ through the poor, as symbols of his earthly suffering, was one with which most nurses were familiar.[99] Yet not all took it to heart.

By the fourteenth century, if not before, a two-tier organization had developed in some English hospitals. The routine task of caring for the sick was assigned to female servants or corrodians of relatively humble status, while the professed sisters undertook other, less physically demanding work. A visitation report of 1364 criticized the sisters of St Leonard's Hospital, York, for wearing long overtunics and mantles which interfered with their duties, and, implicitly, for allowing servants to care for the patients while they sought paid employment in the city. (Much to the irritation of the prioress, patrons of the Hôtel Dieu, Paris, expected the nurses to tend them at home when they fell ill, and the practice of making 'house calls' may have been common.)[100] Conventional depictions of the medieval midwife show her with bare arms and tied-up sleeves, a style of dress essential for those who laboured in a hospital laundry or helped to bathe patients, but less pleasing to women of rank.[101] In his will of 1408, the poet, John Gower, left 3*s* 4*d* to every professed sister at St Thomas' Hospital, Southwark, at St Mary's, Westminster, and at two London hospitals, and 1*s* 8*d* to each of the servants or handmaids (*ancillae*) who looked after the sick, which suggests that the practice of hiring nurses had by then become widespread.[102] Some institutions were, in any event, reluctant to engage individuals who had little taste for the harsh realities of the active life. Revised statutes of the Hospital of St John, Bridgwater, promulgated in 1457, instructed the master to find

> two or three women, not noble but suitable and of good conversation and report, who are willing and able to serve the infirm poor . . . and they are to stay by themselves in a cell or chamber in the infirmary near the needy and poor, and sleep there, and be maintained as the master and brethren shall see fit. They are to be watchful and ready, night and day to help the infirm and to minister to them in all things, and they are not to turn aside to other acts or services, except the prayers which are due.[103]

A combination of financial pressures and changing functions led some hospitals to replace professed sisters with female servants as an economy measure. Once an increasing number of quasi-monastic houses of moderate size began to function primarily as collegiate foundations dedicated to the commemoration of the dead, care of the living became a less urgent priority. At St John's Hospital, Oxford, two laywomen had by 1390 taken over the nursing duties previously assigned to six sisters, although their claims to have been kept hard at work supervising the patients suggest that there was still plenty for them to do.[104] Some institutions responded to social, demographic and religious change by converting open-ward infirmaries into private chambers for a few carefully chosen almsmen or women, such as the above-mentioned Joan Lunde, while others adopted the practice of selling corrodies (that is board and lodging for life) at reduced rates to honest, respectable women who would be prepared to nurse the sick until they, in turn, grew incapacitated. Certainly, by the close of the Middle Ages, the distinction between patient and carer is not always easy to make. Nor can any significant conclusions be drawn from the apparently wide divergence in ratios between the two, which appear misleadingly low where servants were employed, and high when many of the sisters were pensioners.[105] At St John's Hospital, Winchester, a small but steady stream of sick paupers and wayfarers appear to have been tended by some of the female corrodians or almswomen, who received a basic fee for their work.[106] Such arrangements were common throughout Europe: at the Hospital of St Just in Narbonne, for example, the nurses could expect to be supported in their old age; and certain Florentine institutions regarded the employment of single poor women as an act of charity.[107]

St Paul's Hospital, Norwich, had originally maintained a sizeable number of lay brothers and sisters dedicated to the care of twenty sick paupers and an unspecified number of impoverished wayfarers. After the Black Death it became a home to twenty-four almswomen, some of whom helped to nurse a modest (but still significant) number of 'pore straungers, vagrantes [and] syck and impotent persons', while others, who had themselves benefited from a good education, taught local children to read.[108] The same trend is apparent in the city's largest hospital, St Giles', where female corrodians continued to tend the sick until the Reformation. The generosity shown by testators to the sisters and sick poor of both houses throughout this period confirms that such changes had not apparently been accompanied by a fall in standards or commitment among the nursing staff. A bequest made in 1528 by a patient on his death bed at St Giles' not only left money to the sister (and her servant) who had tended him, but also entrusted her with the task of executing his will as she thought best 'with laude and prayse of almyghty God' for the salvation of his soul.[109] It would be hard to imagine a more complete expression of trust.

Initially seen as a valuable means of harnessing female spirituality, which might otherwise have been drawn into subversive channels, nursing the sick poor had become less of an overtly religious vocation in late medieval England. As the focus of care for the needy moved from the hospital soup-kitchen and infirmary to the almshouse and parish, women found other ways of dispensing charity and identifying with the poor of Christ. Yet the nurse, whether lay or religious, continued to perform an important role, which was more fully recognized and delineated in the statutes of English hospitals refounded after the Reformation.[110] The citizens of Norwich and London, who gave careful thought to the medicalization of their hospitals in the brave new Protestant world of the later sixteenth century, would have found Jehan Henry's lengthy disquisition on the intercessionary powers of the hospital sister profoundly uncongenial. The idea of administrators and patrons as passengers in a humble barge, attached to the sisters' ship, Religious Profession, by the slender rope of Mercy, would have seemed heretical and impious to men who had abandoned the idea of Purgatory. But they would surely have responded more favourably to another of his images: the hospital as a verdant island in a troubled sea, where the trees of charity never lost 'the leaves of help and service which are my daughters'. If, in practice, the sheltered isle proved less than idyllic, it is gratifying to observe that some of its most valued occupants were female.[111]

I would like to thank Professor Gilchrist for the many occasions on which we have discussed the ideas developed in this paper and Dr Philippa Maddern for her valuable comments on it.

CHAPTER 4

Religion and the Paston Family

GILLIAN PRITCHARD

The Church influenced the everyday lives of fifteenth-century people in three main ways. It provided a perceptual and expressive framework within which they lived. It influenced the events of their lives by demanding submission and worship. Individuals in turn contributed to the operation of the established Church through their patronage and support of various religious institutions. For these reasons, religion occupied a vital and integral role in fifteenth-century communities. I have chosen to examine these aspects of lay religion by looking at the beliefs and practices of one particular, and well-documented, landowning family, the Pastons, who lived in Norfolk. For the purposes of medieval historians, interest in the family begins with William I (1378–1444) and ends with his grandchildren. This is not because of events in the Pastons' lives during these three generations, but rather because of their surviving letters from this period. No other collection from this time is as large or covers such diverse subjects. They provide a unique perspective of the fifteenth century, particularly because of their evidence relating to the thoughts of Paston family members.[1]

The Pastons' religious beliefs implied acceptance of the institutional Church, whose teaching inculcated a perceptual framework widely shared in their community. Their understanding of Christianity was complemented by habits of expression which assumed an everyday familiarity with religious values and teachings. Even in secular business, for example, the institutional Church introduced and perpetuated divisions of time and space that were used as standards of reference for dating and locating transactions, decisions and documents. Seasons, days and even hours were defined according to their position in an elaborate calendar that allowed any moment to be located by reference to some liturgical event.[2] The normal later medieval convention of using church festivals to date events and documents is widespread throughout the *Paston Letters* and the majority of letters end with a reference to a holy day.[3] If the current day was not a religious festival then it was located in relation to the closest appropriate festival. Such references occur frequently throughout the letters.

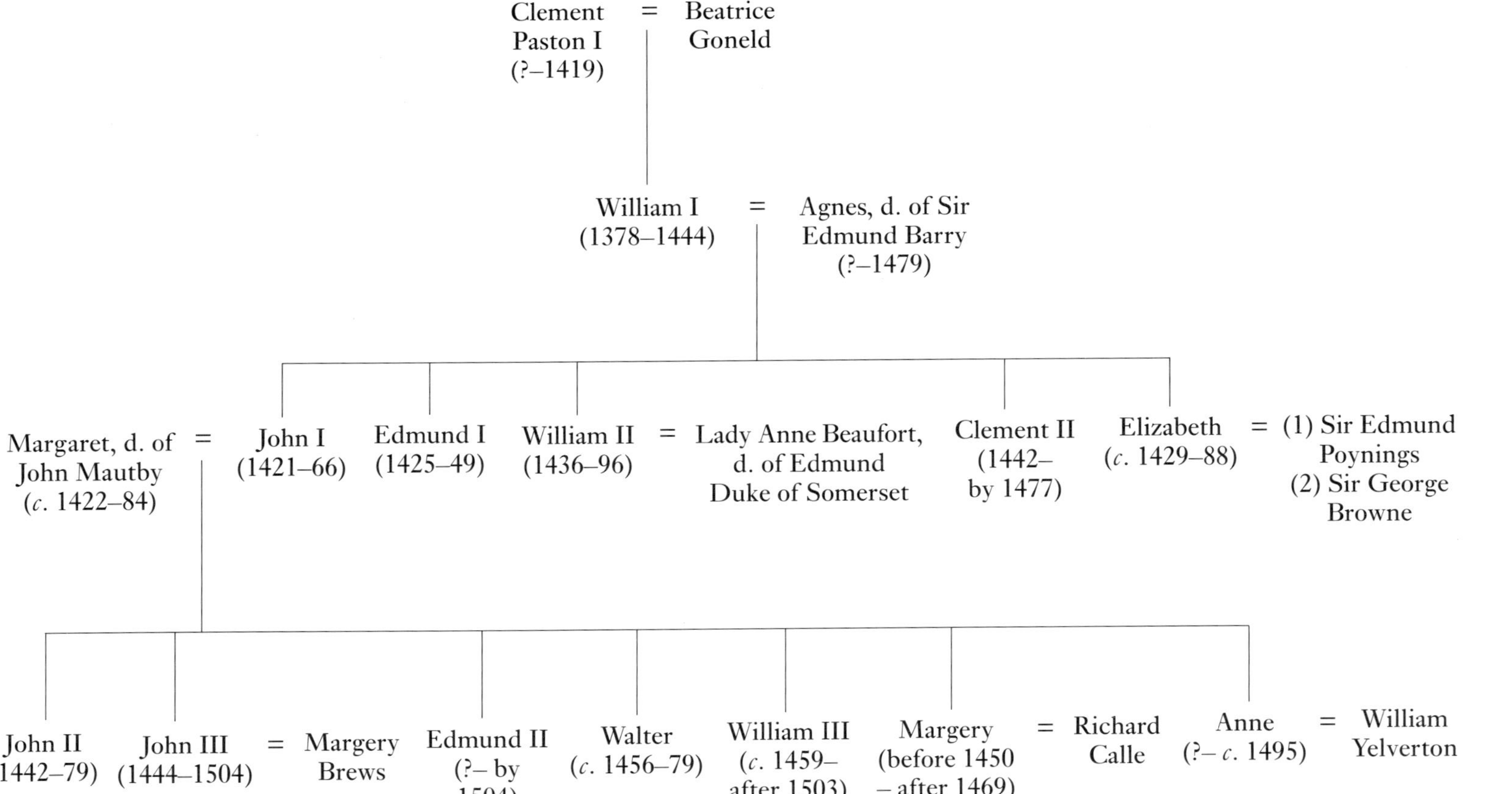

The Paston Family.

Agnes Paston reported in a letter of 'the Thorsdaie aftir Candelmasse Daie' in 1445 that a dispute over a road had been settled 'in Lenttyn laste'. In a letter written 'the Tewysday next before Seynt Thomas Day' (probably 1451), Margaret Paston wrote that she expected wood and hay to be cheapest 'be-twyx this and Seynt Margretys masse'. John Paston II reported from London 'on Mychellmesse Euyn' in 1471 that Elizabeth Browne had given birth to a son 'wyth-in ij day afftre Seynt Bertelmew'.[4] Robert Repps, writing to John Paston I in 1440, provides an example of the older style of giving the time of day when he records that his letter was written 'at the feast of All Saints between Mass and matins' (*in le fest de toutz seynts, entre messe et mateyns*).[5] New influences were gradually emerging and reshaping people's perspectives of time, influencing different aspects of perception and different individuals at different rates. Occasionally, a few writers used the secular calendar to date their letters; John Paston II, who provides the clearest example of this, abandoned liturgically perceived time and adopted instead a secular style of dating.[6] Clock time had virtually replaced religious services as the main manner in which periods of a day were perceived. But this transition had proceeded much further in identifying times of day than in dating days in the year, and James Gresham demonstrates the temporal perspective which was the norm for the Pastons when he wrote 'wretyn at ix on the clokke at euyn the Moneday nex to-fore Seint Gregory Day'.[7]

In a similar manner, the Pastons perceived much of the space in which they lived in religious terms. Churches or parishes were often used to locate and distinguish properties, or as the equivalent of a modern postal address. Margaret reported to John Paston I, that 'ther is a fayre plase to sell in Seynt Laveransis parysch, and stant nere the chirche', and Sir John Fastolf wrote of his 'tenement by Seynt Olof chyrch'.[8] Agnes used a parish reference to direct a letter: 'To Meye Barkere of Synt Clementys parys, in Norwych'.[9] The parish church itself occupied a central place in the activity of the Pastons and their community. Rather than being a building devoted solely to religion, removed from everyday concerns, the church responded to the needs of the community, thereby reinforcing the interdependence of secular and religious perceptions of space. Churches might be used as meeting places for the negotiation of secular business, particularly controversial matters. In the middle of a dispute over the manor of Cotton in Suffolk, for example, John Pampyng met with the Pastons' adversaries in St Laurence's Church in Ipswich.[10]

Religious language, phrases and appeals are a common feature of the *Paston Letters* in a wide variety of forms. They demonstrate the Pastons' understanding of religious themes and the universal familiarity of those ideas. Many of the letters are almost a tripartite conversation between the author, the recipient and God. John II invoked God's assistance for his brother Edmond II: 'God sende yow som good warde off hys.'[11] The majority of letters end with a valediction in the form of a prayer to protect the recipient from harm. God, Jesus, the Holy Ghost, or all three as the Holy Trinity,[12] were commonly invoked in phrases which ranged from the short 'God kepe yow' to the more elaborate 'the blissyd Trynyté haue yow in hys kepyng and sende yow helthe and good spede in all yowre materris'.[13] Such clauses were formulaic, but might be either elaborated or condensed,

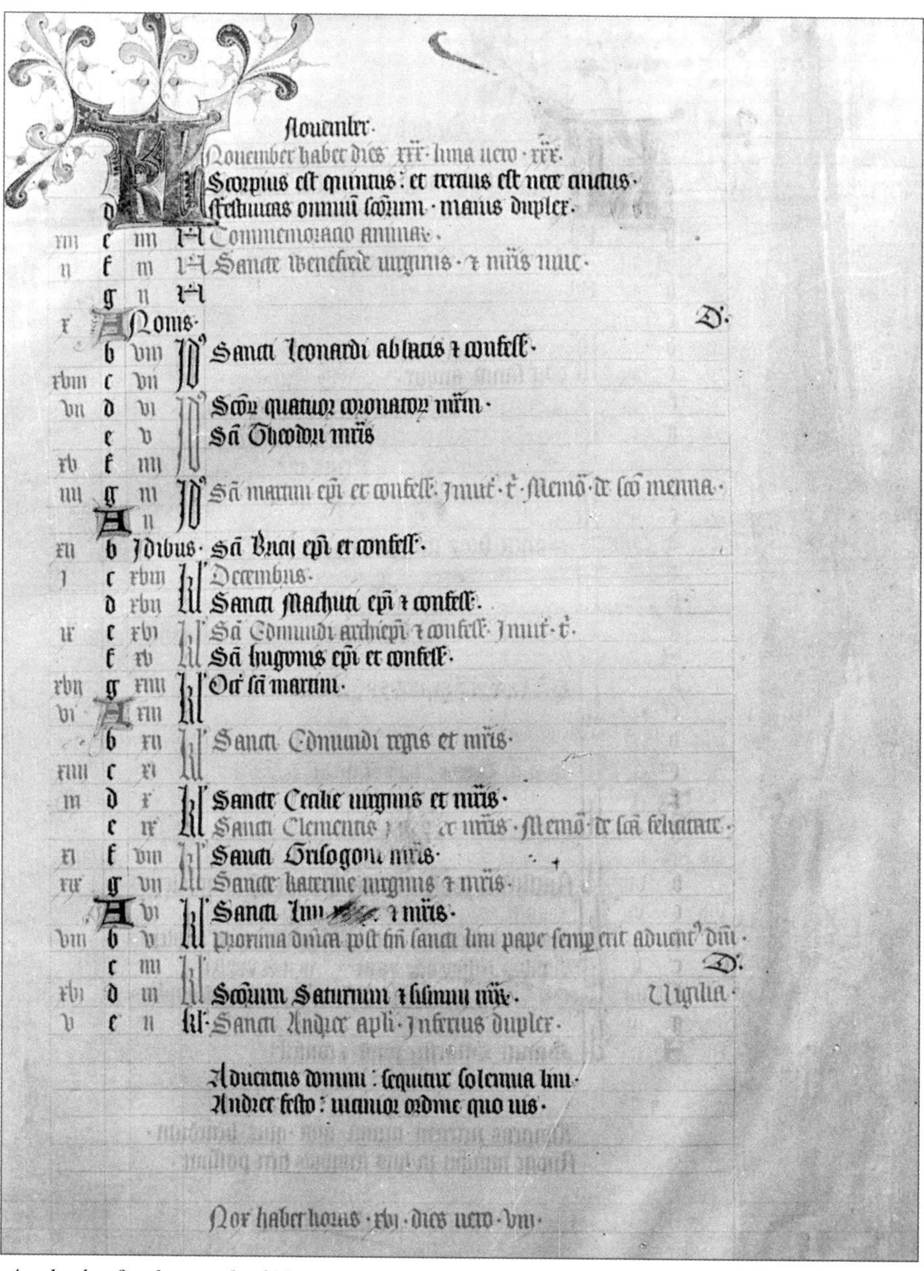
Nouembr.
Nouember habet dies xxx. luna uero xxx.
Scorpius est quintus: et tercius est nece cinctus.
Festiuitas omnium sanctorum · maius duplex.
Nonis.
Sancti leonardi abbatis et confessoris.
Idibus.
Decembris.
Sancti Edmundi regis et martiris.
Aduentus domini: sequitur solemnia lini.
Andree festo: uicinior ordine quo uis.

A calendar for the month of November, from a psalter of the early fifteenth century once used at the Abbey of Bury St Edmunds. The chief focus is on events of the liturgical year, including many saints' festivals, and the only secular dating system is that of the Roman calendar, in which days were related to the Nones, Ides and Kalends of each month. This calendar, from a psalter preserved at King Edward VI Grammar School, Bury St Edmunds, shows, among other feast days, that of St Edmund on 16 November (XVI Kal. Dec.). (The Conway Library, the Courtauld Institute of Art.)

probably according to the circumstances in which a letter was written. In the secular matter of the letters, references to biblical characters were made easily and familiarly. Thomas Denys wrote to Margaret and urged hasty action in a dispute because 'on the aduersarie parte Judas slepith not'.[14] Just as Judas Iscariot was an archetypal traitor, King Herod was an archetypal tyrant. In describing to John Paston II how the Duke of Suffolk behaved high-handedly at Hellesden in Whitweek 1478, a correspondent observed that 'ther was neuer no man that playd Herrod in Corpus Crysty play better and more agreable to hys pageaunt than he dud'.[15] Meanwhile numerous formulae of clerical origin were prominent in the concepts of sin, repentance, retribution and virtue that were constantly used in the rhetorical presentation of everyday issues.[16]

The religious component of the Pastons' thought was an inherited tradition, disseminated throughout society in a variety of ways and absorbed by individuals as a cultural norm. But the *Paston Letters* provide little indication as to the means by which this information was transmitted. Religious instruction was passed on by the clergy – through sermons, festivals such as the Corpus Christi celebrations and ecclesiastical art – and within families. The letters only provide incidental references to such traditions, suggesting that patterns of instruction were established and assumed. A sermon preserved among the *Paston Letters* illustrates the didactic nature of preaching, with its instructions about the proper method of prayer: 'How that ye shuld prayn to God and askyn I taught you on Estern Day. Therfore ye shall pray God be good werkyng, right full levyng, and in good dedes perseueryng.'[17] The impact of ceremonies such as the Corpus Christi plays was great, and references to the plays occurred in everyday language. Eamon Duffy explains that such performances exercised 'enormous didactic and imaginative effectiveness' to the extent that they were rarely forgotten.[18] Personal prompting within the family may also be directly observed from time to time. Margaret makes several comments to her husband and sons, providing religious advice and indicating an ongoing habit of spiritual discussion within the family. On one occasion she made her farewell with the words, 'God have you in hys kepyng and make yow a good man, and gyf yow grace to do as well as I wold ye shuld do'.[19]

Religious language and perceptions occupied such a fundamental place because they stemmed from the essential beliefs shared by most Christians. However, a distinction must be made between the general acceptance of fifteenth-century intellectual conventions and the varying degrees of conviction and patterns of action which could develop from them. An elementary education in the articles of faith did not necessarily develop into effective acceptance of the Church's teaching that one's actions would influence one's eternal fate, and the consequent behavioural decisions which stemmed from that conviction. This distinction helps explain the various levels of piety which existed within the all-encompassing Christian nature of fifteenth-century England. Since it has recently been argued that the religion of the English gentry was lacking in vitality in the pre-Reformation period,[20] it is desirable to examine the Pastons from this point of view.

For those who held that their actions would have an impact on their chances of salvation death was an important focus for their thinking. Agnes demonstrated this view in a letter to John I, where she observed that, 'this worlde is but a thorugh-

The tomb of John Baret (d. 1467) in the church of St Mary, Bury St Edmunds. It belongs to a category known as cadaver tombs, because they show the deceased as a decaying corpse. To ensure that the point is not overlooked, this example has some verses, concluding:

For lych as I am right so schal ye all be
Now God on my sowle have mercy and pite. Amen.

(The Conway Library, the Courtauld Institute of Art.)

fare and ful of woo, and whan we departe ther-fro, rigth nougght bere wyth vs but oure good dedys and ylle'. Furthermore, Agnes believed that the unpredictability of one's death meant that every day should be lived with it in mind, and that this should govern one's behaviour: 'And ther knoweth no man how soon God woll clepe hym, and ther-for it is good for euery creature to be redy.'[21] Such uncertainty troubled even the most pious among them, because it heightened the fear of dying unprepared, in a state of sin. In particular, the prevalence of the plague prompted much concern for their own safety and for the safety of relatives and friends, and considerable effort was expended in attempts to avoid the disease. In 1479 John II remarked that, because of the plague, he feared for his life in London, while, in 1471, Margaret wrote that 'we lewyn in fere'.[22]

Belief in the inevitability of judgement may be discerned in the reactions of the Pastons to the deaths of members of their family, though these often supply only very formal expressions of pious concern. Edmond II wrote to John III, 'Suere dydyngys arn com to Norwyche that my grandam is dyssessyd, whom God assoyle'. In the same letter Edmond II mentioned the death of his brother Walter ('whom God assoyle') and of his sister's new-born baby: 'My syster is delyuerd, and the chyld passyd to God, who send vus hys grace.'[23] Such absence of explicit emotion does not necessarily demonstrate a lack of sensitivity or concern. It may suggest that there were emotions that did not need to be written about. I suspect that news of this type was often considered too personal to be delivered in a written form and that the death of family members and friends might be more significant than the reserved statements preserved in the letters indicate. Elizabeth Browne's letter to her brother John III indicates that family members were often present or expected to be present at another relative's deathbed.[24] Occasionally a more personal statement was made. Informing John I of the death of John Estgate in 1465, Margaret wrote that 'Maister Estgade ys passyd to God on Thursday last passyd, whos sawle God assoyle; wherof in gode fayth I am ryght sory, for I fond hym ryght faythfull to you'.[25] However, concern for the deceased inevitably diminished according to emotional distance, and some reports were strikingly matter-of-fact. This is illustrated by Margaret's comment to John III in 1471 concerning the deaths of John Berney of Witchingham and others: 'As fore the tydyngys here, ywre cosyn Barney of Wychshynggam ys passyd to Gode, hwm Gode asoyle. Veylys wyfe and Londonys wyfe and Pycard the bacar of Twmlond ben gon also.'[26] The concern expressed in such letters was often more concerned with the worldly goods of the departed than with the welfare of their souls. Reporting the death of Henry Inglose in 1451 ('hoys sowle God asoyll'), Margaret instructed John I, 'if ye desyer to bey any of hys stuff I pray you send me word ther-of in hast, and I shall speke to Robert Inglose and to Wychyngham ther-of. I suppose thei ben executorys'.[27] In 1473 (probably) she said she was sorry if reports of John Daye's death were true, 'for I know not howe to comme by my mony that he oweith me'.[28] Concerns about the disposal of property might lead to a surprising degree of apparent indifference to the last wishes of even close relatives. When William Paston died in London in 1444, his son waited a week before leaving Norfolk, and then proceeded to disregard his father's wish for a perpetual chantry to be endowed out of his estate. John II and John III were to display a similar reluctance to provide a lasting memorial for their father. Were the Pastons in the vanguard of those gentry who, albeit shamefacedly, ignored their dead?[29]

Religious faith manifested itself as practice in two main ways. The first mode involved dependence upon the Church as the source of spiritual authority, submitting to its teaching and participating in its ceremonies. The second mode involved activities that implied the dependence of churchmen on lay patronage. Both the manner of the Pastons' spiritual observances and their opportunities for exercising patronage over clergy and ecclesiastical institutions were heavily influenced by their wealth and status, and so changed with the family's rise in society. This was well indicated by the choice of burial location. Clement I, William I's father, provides evidence of the Paston family's humble ancestry through his choice of the parish church of Paston.[30] The contrast with his son is striking: William advertised the improved position of the Paston family and their higher standards of worship by being buried in the Lady Chapel in Norwich Cathedral.[31] When John Paston I died in London in 1466, his body was carried back to Norwich with great solemnity and then taken for interment at Bromholm Priory with unnecessarily ostentatious ceremonial and hospitality.[32] Such extravagance and concern with status put the Pastons unambiguously in the camp of those untainted either by Lollardy or other traditions of self-denying piety.[33]

The Pastons' submission to the teachings of the Church entailed a diversity of activities whose devotional significance varied. These ranged from the essential duties of religious observance, centred on the sacraments, through the imposed requirements of canon law, to secondary and less obligatory practices, such as pilgrimage. The Pastons' commitment to these various practices, particularly the subsidiary and less prescribed activities, should provide a scale against which the style of their devotion can be assessed.

The sacraments, the means by which an individual could receive the grace of God, were indispensable to the medieval Christian faith. For the laity, these were baptism, confirmation, marriage, confession, the Mass (at which lay people only occasionally received the consecrated host) and extreme unction (the last rites). The Church's instructions on these subjects were accepted as an integral part of the Christian faith. Sporadic references to different sacraments occur in the letters, mostly incidentally. Those that served as rites of passage (baptism, confirmation, marriage, extreme unction) were all unique events in the course of a lifetime and were all governed by tight social convention, so that participation in them offered little guide to piety of either individuals or families, even in the extreme case of heretics who doubted or rejected their necessity or validity.[34] John III's comments on baptism – on the occasion of the baptism of the daughter of the Duchess of Norfolk – illustrate the social importance of this sacrament. Beforehand, John III advised John II to attend the service because 'it shall cause you gret thank, and a gret fordell in your mater'.[35] His subsequent description of the service mentioned that the Bishop of Winchester baptized the baby and was her godfather.[36] Godparents were responsible for bringing a child up in a Christian community, but also assumed secular responsibilities, because becoming a godparent was a practice which could cement a social and political tie between the parties involved.[37] As a result of these dual obligations, the social aspects of the ceremony received as much attention as the spiritual event.[38] The sacrament of marriage was even more heavily influenced by social factors. The impression given by the Pastons' correspondence is of an event which was part financial transaction, part romance, part confirmation of social status and part religious ceremony.[39] John II describes the proposed marriage of John III and Margery Brews as 'welthy and convenyent' and cites Margery's youth, personality, family background, her likely virtue and her love for John III as reasons to endorse the union, thereby illustrating some of the factors considered important by medieval families.[40] In contrast, Margery Paston's socially unsuitable marriage to the Paston's head bailiff, Richard Calle, caused a family scandal and was condemned by all. The family's wrath reached such heights that they had the Bishop of Norwich examine Margery and Richard Calle to determine whether or not the marriage was valid.[41] Theologically, a marriage could be lawfully carried out without the involvement of the Church. Any couple who exchanged 'words of present consent' were lawfully married and the only need for a priest was to perform the, optional, nuptial Mass, though the laity, for social and legal reasons, encouraged church weddings.[42] When Margery repeated the promise she had made to Calle, despite the family's objections, her vows fulfilled the requirements of Church law.[43] Little is recorded in the *Paston Letters* about extreme unction, but it must be supposed to have been taken for granted. William I's death at St Bride's in London suggests that he would have received extreme unction, but no mention is made of it in a letter by his daughter which tells of William's last days.[44]

Confession and attendance at Mass, which could be frequently repeated, allowed people to vary in their standards of formal piety, but there is little in the *Paston Letters* to suggest that family members treated them as other than matters of routine. The Church required the laity to attend Mass on Sundays and holy days; on all other occasions attendance was optional.[45] A direct reference to the importance of attending Mass comes from Margaret who admonished John I: 'I pray yw hertyly here masse and other servys that ye arn bwn to here wyth a devwt hert.'[46] The Pastons' church attendance was taken for granted. When J. Whetley delivered a subpoena on behalf of John II, he reported that he did so 'on Trenité Sondaye in hys parych cherch at matens tyme be-for the substans of the parych'.[47] Agnes Paston's casual reference to the Mass in her description of a local incident 'on Fryday after sakeryng' suggests that attendance was a usual part of her lifestyle.[48] She expressed no surprise that Sir John Heveningham had gone to church and heard three Masses on a Tuesday.[49] Other services mentioned include matins, evensong, and ceremonies at Easter.[50] Confession in Holy Week and attendance at Mass at Easter were Christian duties, and for most people this was the only occasion in the year when they received communion, rather than just hearing and seeing the liturgy. A suitor appealed to Elizabeth Clere, one Easter Eve, 'for his sake that I had receyved that day', and William Worcester swore by 'the blissed Sacrament that I receyued at Pasch'.[51] The sacrament of penance was not discussed. The only reference to confession is made within the narration of a case of rape by John I, who reports the victim had told her confessor she would never marry the assailant.[52]

Many aspects of daily life under the authority of the Church were governed by canon law. This was the law administered in ecclesiastical courts by which the Church imposed its definition of aspects of religious belief and practice.[53] Orthodoxy was equally enforced by the community, and dissidents faced social censure, so that comprehensive dissidence was rare. Certainly the Pastons took the authority of the Church for granted in this respect, whether they needed pardon for past behaviour or some privilege, exempting them from future restrictions. A pardon was required when Margaret and her sons were at fault for the speedy action they took in distributing the goods of John I, Margaret's late husband. She wrote that 'we ben all a-cursed that we haue thus mynystred the dedes godes wyth-ought licence or auctorité' and she begged John II to remedy the situation. The only option for a remedy was to obtain a licence from the Archbishop of Canterbury 'in dischargyng of my conscyens and yowres'.[54]

Alternatively, conscience could be discharged in advance, so to speak, by securing a dispensation from some particular ruling of canon law. Late in 1471 Margaret acquired such a dispensation for one year from the Bishop of Norwich to allow her to receive the Eucharist in her private chapel at Mautby, and she subsequently sought renewals of the licence. Her determination is clear from her letter to John III: 'For all maner of casweltés of me and myn I wold hauyt grauntyd yf I myth.' Margaret asserted that she needed the dispensation because the parish church was far from her home, she was sickly and the parson was unreliable.[55] Margaret's urgent desire for the dispensation was prompted, in part, by the social status attached to ecclesiastical privileges, even if such privileges were perceived to permit the recipient to lead a 'fuller spiritual life'.[56]

Margaret's attempt to obtain this privilege illustrates the existence of a hierarchy of ecclesiastical authority, which was supported by canon law and which had to be known and understood by anyone wanting to get things done. A licence granted by the Archbishop of Canterbury, being 'most swyr for all plas', carried more weight than one from the Bishop of Norwich.[57] Similarly, the ecclesiastical hierarchy worked to permit each higher level of authority to dispense with sins of greater seriousness. When John II reversed his promise to marry Anne Hault, the only course of action open to him was to obtain a dispensation from Rome. In a letter to his brother, John III, he illustrates the supreme position of the Court of Rome. The curia was 'the welle off grace' and the 'salve sufficiaunt fore suche a soore'; only a pardon from Rome would suffice 'that I may be dyspencyd wyth'.[58] John II made an interesting observation on the enforcement of canon law in 1477. He refused to grant his brother property which he was going to inherit after Margaret's death, but would allow John III and his wife to live there. He compared his approach to that of the Pope. 'The Pope will suffre a thyng to be vsyd,' he asserted, 'but he will nott lycence nor grant it to be vsyd ner don.'[59] John II's comments refer to the surprising tolerance which the Papacy, in practice, displayed towards many aspects of English statute law which challenged or contradicted canon law. One example is the fourteenth-century Statute of Praemunire, which prohibited individuals from appealing to the Roman court to settle a dispute over a presentation to a benefice.[60]

'Sacramental religion affected only part of the people's religious attention', and the same may be said of legal obligation.[61] Many practices encouraged by the Church were essentially optional, although frequently they were closely associated with sacramental theology. One of the difficulties of assessing the significance of such apparent piety as a guide to inner motivation is that so many of them were governed as much by social convention as by the hope of salvation. Charitable donations, for example, sometimes followed from strong religious conviction, but such munificence was so bound up with social expectations that it could be a matter of routine, or even self-serving. Church teaching promoted the Corporal Works of Mercy (feeding the hungry, giving drink to the thirsty, clothing the naked, visiting the sick, relieving the prisoner, housing the stranger and burying the dead), and alms-deeds were a recognized form of penance.[62] In fact, little trace of such everyday charity to the needy appears in the *Paston Letters*, except that John I gave 7*s* in 1458 'to divers poor people of Norwich for relief of their charge'.[63] Predictably, there is more substantial evidence of a concern for the poor in Paston wills, as in that of Margaret Paston (1482), which makes a number of such bequests to impoverished families among her tenants as well as to others in Norwich and Ipswich.[64] Such negligible evidence of charitable giving as a regular concern may mean that for the Pastons such giving was a symbolic activity 'appended to funerary and commemorative occasions'.[65] Alternatively, the Pastons may have exercised charity so much as a routine, in keeping with ecclesiastical and social expectations, that their acts did not warrant comment in a letter. Neither the magnitude of their contributions nor the relative degrees of routine and spontaneity can be assessed.

A similar problem arises in the cases of guild membership. Though many Pastons belonged to the guild of St George in Norwich, 'the chief, the most prosperous and the longest lived' guild there, the *Paston Letters* do not refer to allegiance to any religious guilds.[66] There is no evidence, in fact, that the Pastons ever took an active part in any guild, and they appear to illustrate Colin Richmond's contention that such participation was generally uncharacteristic of the gentry.[67] It is likely that the Pastons valued a passive membership of the guild of St George more for the social connections it implied than for any of its spiritual benefits.

Away from the home, pilgrimage was one of the major manifestations of the religious conviction that one's actions influenced one's chances of salvation. The Pastons and others planned and made pilgrimages to Walsingham (quite near home), Canterbury and occasionally to places in Europe, illustrating for Colin Richmond 'the resilience of late medieval religion'.[68] Pilgrimage was a national pastime. 'As for tydyngys,' wrote John II, 'the Kyng and the Qwyen and moche other pepell ar ryden and goon to Canterbury, neuyr so moche peple seyn in pylgrymage her-to-foor at ones, as men seye.'[69] References to pilgrimages by people outside the Paston family, and particularly major political figures, are common.[70] In many cases, pilgrimage was a type of prayer for the mediation of saints, particularly for recovery from disease.[71] This was demonstrated by Margaret and Agnes when John I became ill around 1443. Agnes promised an image of wax of the weight of John I to the chapel of Our Lady of Walsingham and gave four nobles to the four orders of Friars at Norwich to pray for John I's health; Margaret promised to go on pilgrimage to Walsingham and St Leonard's Priory.[72] These displays of faith were not limited to times of crisis. John III later urged Margaret to visit religious sites while she was in London, convinced of the spiritual benefits of this devotion, but not without a sense of humour. 'I pray yow vysyt the Rood of Northedor, and Seynt Sauyour at Barmonsey,' he wrote. 'And let my sustyr Margery goo wyth yow to prey to them that sche may haue a good hosbond or sche com hom ayen.'[73] These pieties are further evidence that the Pastons were firmly in the ranks of the orthodox, rather than among those affected by the teachings of the Lollards, who considered pilgrimages to be spiritually valueless.[74]

The extent to which Christian symbolism, and perhaps devotion, extended beyond liturgical contexts and reflected differences of wealth and status was demonstrated by the lay ownership of religious objects. Both John II and Agnes owned several religious books: the former's inventory of books (mostly secular)

St George, from the early fifteenth-century painted screen at Ranworth (Norfolk). St George was widely venerated in medieval Christendom for his knightly valour and for his powers of endurance in the face of very extreme and extraordinary sufferings as a Christian martyr. His cult grew in line with the development of English nationalism in the later Middle Ages, especially following Edward III's establishment of the knightly Order of St George (later known more commonly as the Order of the Garter) in 1348. (The Conway Library, the Courtauld Institute of Art.)

lists a compilation of texts including 'the Medis off the Masse', and 'a Preyer to the Vernycle', and the latter's will bequeaths two books of prayers.[75] The will of Elizabeth Browne abounds with ecclesiastical items: a holy water stoup of silver, an Agnus with the image of St Anthony, a tablet depicting the Salutation of Our Lady and the three Kings of Cologne (the Magi), a 'pece of the Holy Crosse, crossewise made, bordured with silver aboute', a paxboard and numerous albs, stoles, vestments and altar cloths.[76]

The ownership of a private chapel, though a formal manifestation of piety among the laity, was also an unmistakable status symbol. That the Pastons had one is illustrated by several references to chapels in their letters from the time of William Paston in the 1430s. In 1445 Agnes referred to 'the chapelle at Paston'.[77] Margaret Paston's enthusiasm for this particular manifestation of gentle status has already been discussed. In this respect, again, the religious history of the Paston family illustrates how a religious tradition common to families of all levels of wealth was nevertheless diffracted by sharp social distinctions of wealth and prestige.

Private ownership of a chapel has been interpreted as a withdrawal from the parish community,[78] but the evidence from the *Paston Letters* does not substantiate this claim, and the Paston family attended their parish churches. In addition, outside their own household they exercised ecclesiastical patronage by presenting clerics to benefices, though inevitably their superior social status was again explicit here, since this form of participation in the life of the Church depended upon wealth and rank rather than any particular piety. The Pastons were committed to a group of clerics who were, in turn, politically and spiritually indebted to members of the family. Some presentations to benefices give the impression that social and political considerations were paramount. John II nominated John Yotton to the free chapel in Caister 'at the speciall request of the Qwen and othere especiall good lordes of myn', instead of giving the chapel to his own nominee.[79] This type of presentation is not the only kind mentioned in the *Paston Letters*, however. Margaret reveals an attitude which was more concerned with the welfare of the parishioners. When filling a vacancy at the parish church of Mautby, she suggested Thomas Lyndis, 'for he is rit a prystly man and vertusly dysposyd'. Margaret's reasons for choosing Lyndis demonstrate the diversity of factors involved in choosing a candidate and they centred on the upkeep of the benefice. Lyndis, wrote Margaret, was brother of the 'good parsone' of St Michael's whom John 'lovyd ryght well', and he would reside in the benefice and repair the property, improvements greatly needed.[80] William II wrote what was virtually an advertisement for the living at Oxnead in 1478, providing a more pragmatic view of the desires of the clergy. He described the property and assets of the benefice and listed the financial obligations of the incumbent, while stressing that the spiritual obligations were minimal.[81]

Although William II's persuasive memorandum gives the impression that candidates for benefices could be difficult to find, perhaps implying that benefices could be a burden, later letters clearly demonstrate the importance to patrons of having benefices to bestow. In October 1478 William II wrote to the Bishop of Norwich's brother, complaining that the clerk his mother had presented to

The Holy Trinity, as represented in a Book of Hours preserved in Swaffham parish church. God the Father supports his crucified Son. A small dove beside his neck represents the Holy Ghost. Books of hours were collections of prayers that were widely used among the wealthier and more literate laity, and the illustrations they contained were important as aids to meditation and prayer. (The Conway Library, the Courtauld Institute of Art.)

Oxnead had not been admitted. He explained, that although 'the benyfys is small and of lytill valew, yet myn moder wolde be full loth to lose here ryght'.[82] John I and Margaret were so keen to gain the patronage of a living that they bought the advowson of St Peter's Hungate in Norwich in 1458.[83] The desire to maintain and obtain the gift of benefices might lead to fierce disputes and arbitration by courts.[84] Only William I indicated that the patronage of a benefice was anything other than an asset. Ralph, the parson of Cressingham, wrote to William to arrange a meeting with him and complained about William's neglect of the parsonage.[85] William I's lack of interest contrasts greatly with the efforts made by his descendants to maintain and acquire benefices. Agnes, Margaret and John I were much more aware of the social and political benefits which this form of patronage provided. This shift in perspective illustrates the Paston family's improving socio-political position and the new aspirations and ambitions which resulted from their improved status.

Presenting to a benefice was only one of several ways in which the Pastons exercised patronage toward churches. Frequently, members of the family spent considerable amounts of money on the repair or beautification of churches and religious institutions.[86] John I employed a glazier to work at the Priory of Bromholm and for the Austin Friars in South Town, Yarmouth, and paid for repairs at the parish church of Gresham.[87] William II accepted the work of Vyall, a painter, at the White Friars, in lieu of payment for part of the £5 which he had lent Vyall.[88] The rewards of such patronage varied. Most of these institutions had close links with the Paston family and so their generosity was as much maintenance of their status as it was a manifestation of piety. While paying for glazing at the Bromholm Priory was an act of charity, it also strengthened the ties between the priory and the Pastons.[89]

Appeals made to the Pastons, usually for financial aid, demonstrate the implied benefits of patronage. These were primarily represented in terms of spiritual welfare (although perhaps political advantage was not considered an appropriate object with which to bargain). Henry Berry, a monk of St Augustine's Abbey, Canterbury, wrote to John I in a desperate plea for financial aid. The monastery had never before been in such misery, wrote Henry, and he appealed to John to 'do your allmesse and charité'. The reward: 'hitt schall cause you to be prayed for, and all your kynne, as longe as the chirche stantt'.[90] As such appeals for aid demonstrate, religious patronage was motivated by a desire for political and spiritual loyalty. In this context, the most reliable form of patronage was the direct employment of priests as personal chaplains. Money was expended, in the form of a stipend, for the purpose of worship, but the Pastons retained a much higher level of control than they could with any other expenditure. In this sense, the employment of personal chaplains was similar to the acquirement of religious possessions. John I listed as one of his expenses in 1458 the stipend for Henry Bolte, chaplain, with amounts of 13*s* 4*d* and £1 6*s* 8*d*.[91]

As this implies, the Pastons' relations with the clergy cannot be analysed simply in terms of a contrast between laymen and clergy because issues of rank were also involved. The social gradations among the clergy were almost as wide and complex as those among the laity, and the Pastons clearly regarded some clergy as of lower and dependent status. Such considerations were particularly dominant in the handling of purely secular business in which clergy were involved. Lay interaction with the Church in the *Paston Letters* takes place in a variety of ways, not all religious. The letters demonstrate how churchmen often operated outside the spiritual sphere because of the responsibilities they acquired for secular administration or for the management of property. Heavy involvement in secular affairs was particularly common among the highest ranks of the clergy, since many bishops held high-ranking positions in government.[92] The clergy were as fully involved in politics and local affairs, according to their status, as lay members of society, and at each level there was corresponding interaction between clergy and laity in purely secular matters.[93] This type of interaction with the clergy was not perceived by the Pastons, or those around them, as having any specifically religious significance.

The picture of medieval lay religion provided by the *Paston Letters* is vivid but incomplete. It shows a piety with many predictable features, but it would be unwise to conclude that there was nothing to the Pastons' religion but lip service. As Christine Carpenter has observed, the fact that the religion of fifteenth-century gentry families was 'utterly conventional' does not mean that they did not mean what they said.[94] The fact that the family did not produce religious enthusiasts does not imply that religion was intellectually and emotionally unimportant to its members. In this respect the letters reveal themselves to have limitations. They are not the sort of source where absence can be as revealing as presence, since the omission of a topic from discussion does not necessarily mean the absence of that subject from the Pastons' lives. Colin Richmond pointed out that 'one did not then waste precious paper, time and energy in discussing such familiar or personal matters as the Mass, the Sacrament of penance, or our Lord's Passion'.[95] In many examples the urgent need to communicate overrode constraints of time, but the resultant letter was concise and often ended 'wretyn in hast'.[96] This was not an atmosphere conducive to personal reflection on the significance of attending Mass at the parish church. Remarks about religion were restricted to incidental details and occasional encouragement to devotion. As Roger Virgoe comments, 'the letters are not and were not intended to be, very revealing of opinions, emotions and character'.[97] The use of scribes to write many of the letters introduces a further unknown and imponderable influence over the form and content of dictated letters. Margaret Paston's 124 surviving letters were written by approximately 29 different scribes, ranging from family members to friends and employees.[98] Margaret's letter to John II describing the interrogation of Margery by the Bishop of Norwich over her unsuitable marriage, a particularly personal and sensitive letter, was written by her son Edmond II.[99] This contrasts with the equally urgent, but more businesslike letter written the following day by James Gloys, the Paston chaplain, and suggests that the Pastons were aware of the intrusion of the scribes into the letter-writing process and were keen to protect their privacy. Awareness of the unpredictable nature of the composition of the letters reinforces the importance of not overestimating the significance of silence.

However, these silences are not without interest, especially when the letters are set against the writings of fifteenth-century people whose religious commitment

A knight at prayer, from stained glass in the parish church of Bardwell (Suffolk). He probably represents Sir William de Bardwell who died in 1421. (The Conway Library, the Courtauld Institute of Art.)

was nearer the surface. It is difficult to imagine Margaret Paston at home with those other late medieval Norfolk women, Julian of Norwich (*c.* 1342–*c.* 1420) and Margery Kempe (*c.* 1373–*c.* 1439), both famous for their (very different) manifestations of piety. However devoutly held their religious beliefs may have been, the Pastons and their correspondents managed to say an impressive amount to one another without bringing religious belief and precept into account in any way. This is a point of some interest as an observation concerning their daily lives.

CHAPTER 5

Peasants in Arden

ANDREW WATKINS

Rodney Hilton has argued that there is 'perhaps no darker century in the history of English rural society than the fifteenth', and despite much subsequent research it remains dimly illuminated. The darkness stems from a decline in both the quality and quantity of surviving sources and is all the more profound because of the almost universal pessimism which surrounds those features that can be discerned. It differs from both the preceding and following periods of agrarian history, as it is not usually associated with any degree of economic expansion or innovation. Many landlords experienced continuing reductions in their incomes, causing them finally to abandon the direct exploitation of their estates and to lease out their demesnes for rent, while arrears piled up on many estates. In the countryside there were many social and economic problems. Arable land no longer required to feed the smaller population fell out of use, strips were put down to grass and land everywhere reverted to pasture. On some estates it became impossible for lords to find new tenants, and some holdings remained vacant for many years. Others were abandoned as their tenants died or moved away, and some villages contracted in size. There was abandonment and dilapidation of rural property, and often only grassy tofts, or the mounds left by collapsed buildings, remained after their structures crumbled and fell down, while in extreme instances settlements became deserted.[1]

To compound this contraction, the internal market in grains was reduced, and prices, especially those of cereals and livestock, declined, causing a particularly severe depression between the 1440s and 1470s. Towards the end of the fifteenth century the profitability of pastoral farming, particularly sheep-grazing, and the relative ease of acquiring rural land meant that both the encloser and the engrosser presented threats in many villages. Where either could establish themselves they could significantly alter the social order of the village, ultimately resulting in the social tension which was so manifest in the early sixteenth century.[2] It is possible to emphasize the more positive features of the century: A.R. Bridbury has argued that it was a period of great economic vitality and growth, while more cautiously, others have stressed improving tenurial conditions, the advance of pastoral farming and the strong position of the labourer as real wages increased, while the quality of the diet was improving for all elements in society.[3]

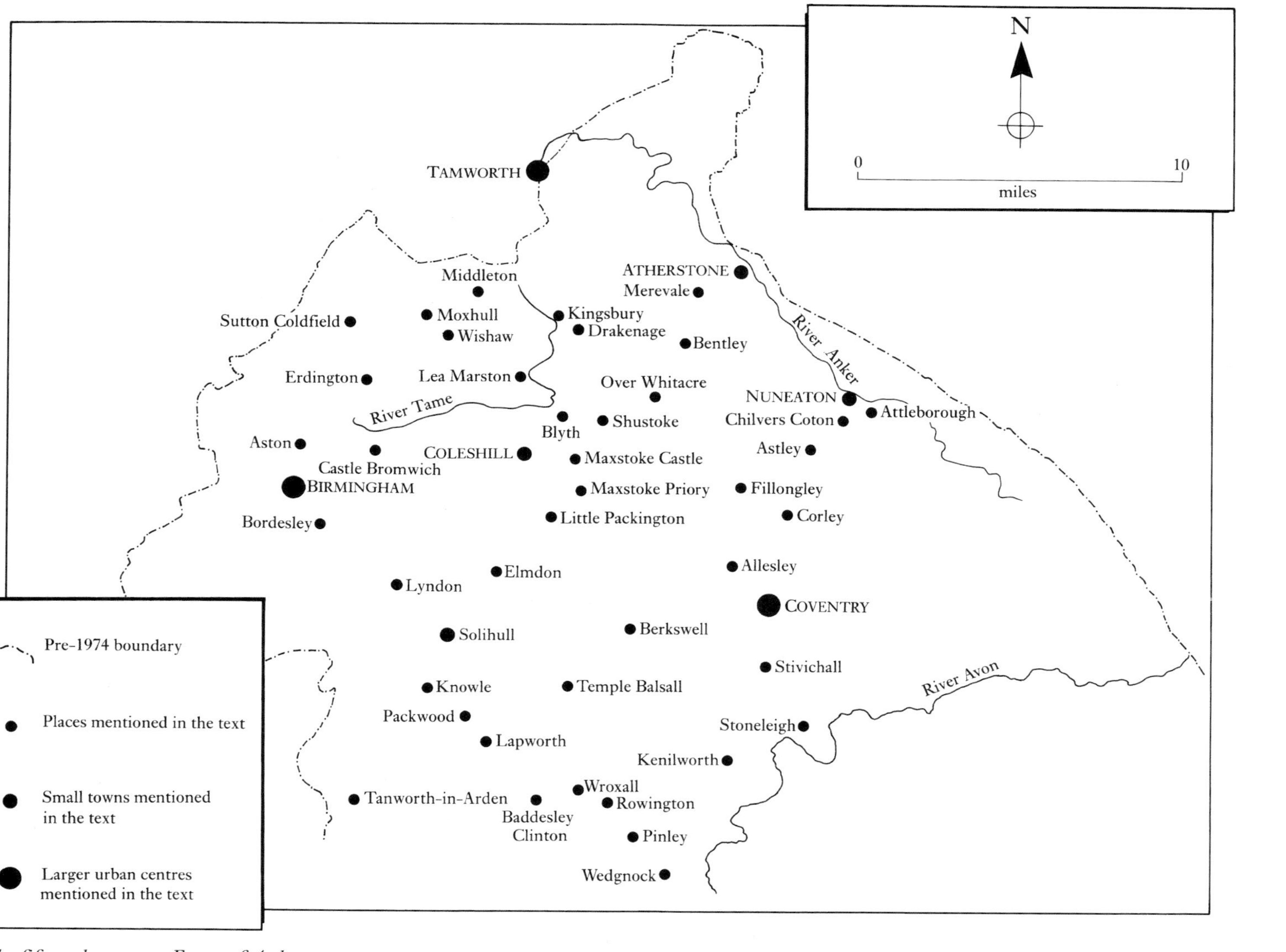

The fifteenth-century Forest of Arden

A contrast and complement to these views can be provided by focusing upon an area which lay outside the heavily feudalized, champion regions of England. The Forest of Arden lies in Warwickshire to the north of the River Avon. It is largely coterminous with the Birmingham Plateau and formed a well-defined *pays*, or countryside, during the later Middle Ages. It is mainly broken, hilly ground, much of it over 400 ft, and it is characterized by damp, heavy soils, fit only for heath and rough pasture. By the fifteenth century, if not earlier, it was a heavily enclosed landscape of woodland and pasture, where the main economic activities were cattle-grazing and various industries associated with its woodland resources. Most of the resident landlords retained some form of direct demesne agriculture. This often implied the utilization of a home farm to provide food, but on other estates there was commercial specialization, such as cattle-grazing, horse-breeding, the exploitation of woodland resources and industrial activities.[4] The economic robustness of the area in the fifteenth century is shown by the 1525 lay subsidy assessment, which, when compared to the distribution of taxable wealth in Edward III's reign, reveals the Arden to have become relatively more prosperous and populous than the Feldon region of south Warwickshire during the intervening period. The growing prosperity of the area is further reflected in the quantity of church-building at this time and the comparative rarity of deserted villages when compared to the Feldon.[5] Even so, the area was not immune from rural decay. As holdings were abandoned their buildings became ruined and were replaced by tofts. Seigniorial accounts reveal a rapid decline in rents, with arrears mounting up, particularly in the mid-century, and the dilapidation of demesne assets such as mills and barns. Arable land no longer needed for cereals was falling out of use, and in extreme cases it became overgrown with weeds, brambles and, eventually, more substantial shrubs. Land also lapsed into rough pasture within the common fields, with grassy leys and baulks interspersed with ploughed strips.[6]

It is difficult to establish the precise chronology of agricultural changes in Arden. As with other parts of the country the old order of demesne agriculture enjoyed its 'Indian Summer' during the late fourteenth century, continuing until the early fifteenth century, when some demesnes and their assets were put out to farm. On others the old system was adapted to create home farms and specialized cattle ranches, and a number of these had emerged by the 1430s and 1440s. Some could be quite short-lived, only lasting a few years, but many endured until the end of the century. One of the most significant developments was the conversion of arable land into pasture, which account rolls and the land transactions recorded in final concords suggest was most pronounced in the 1440s. Even during the great slump of the mid-fifteenth century there is little evidence of the agrarian depression experienced elsewhere: home farms continued to function unabated, the values of leased pasture and meadow held up well and some entrepreneurial peasants were at their most dynamic during this time. From the 1470s onwards there appears to have been greater pressure on land; livestock stints were imposed on common grazing, and peasants resorted to ploughing up land that lay outside the cultivated area. These problems seem to have been particularly acute in the 1490s.[7]

Two faces, which could be of later medieval Arden peasants, stare out on either side of a wyvern (a two-legged dragon) on a misericord in Astley church. (Photograph, Private Collection.)

The social framework of fifteenth-century Arden had been influenced by the comparatively late colonization of the area in the twelfth and thirteenth centuries and was characterized by generally weak feudalism and a less servile peasantry. The Hundred Rolls of 1279 reveal that almost half the tenants in the Arden Hundred of Stoneleigh enjoyed freehold, whereas only about a fifth were freeholders in the Kineton Hundred of south Warwickshire. Labour services in the Arden were lighter and less onerous than those in the Feldon. Social controls in the Arden were weak, but on some estates, usually those owned by larger religious institutions, there was a keen awareness of feudal rights, as by the Abbot of Westminster on his manor of Knowle, the Abbot of Stoneleigh, and the Abbot of Bec on his estate at Atherstone, where, even in 1387, he was trying to enforce suit of oven. Although as late as 1502 the Abbot of Westminster was still allowing lessees at Knowle to call upon customary labour services, this was an anachronism; by the fifteenth century nearly all such trappings had disappeared from Arden court and account rolls.[8]

The later Middle Ages saw many changes in the peasant land market of the Arden. As in other parts of the country there were adjustments in tenurial status, notably the evolution of tenancy-at-will and copyhold from customary tenure, but also the decline in family inheritance and the contraction and enlargement of holdings by short-term leases of land, often to accommodate changes in the size of the family. The emergence of tenancy-at-will from villein tenure was widespread by the mid-fourteenth century, and the development of leasehold placed large amounts of land on the market on much more advantageous terms for the peasant cultivator. This greater fluidity, combined with the diminishing importance of family inheritance, allowed some peasants to build up large holdings, composed of a mixture of free and unfree, so that 'yeoman' and 'husbandman' became far more important designations of status than those connected with tenures, such as 'villein' and 'free man'.[9] Within Warwickshire many who had been either landless or the possessors of smallholdings before the epidemics of the mid-fourteenth century were able to acquire the lands of more substantial villagers who had perished. Only in a few instances were Arden peasants able to acquire sufficient land to dominate a particular village, such as the Slades of Maxstoke. They rose from humble origins to create a sufficiently large holding to have it recognized as a sub-manor by the end of the fifteenth century, by which time they were acknowledged as members of the gentry.[10]

In other parts of the country some of the most dynamic elements within rural society were those who leased seigniorial assets. As we have seen many of those in the Arden were retained and adapted at various times by their lords, but where a resident lord was absent they were usually leased. By the early fifteenth century a number had converted entirely to pasture, as at Aston, Bordesley and Maxstoke Castle, while on others the proportion of grazing land increased as the century progressed. Butcher graziers were in the forefront of those taking up leases of entire demesnes, as happened at Tanworth-in-Arden, Berkswell, Lea Marston, and Wedgnock Park.[11] On other estates it was more usual for the demesne land to be leased piecemeal to local peasants, and as a consequence it was unusual for any to incorporate the entire resources of a demesne into their holding. It was more usual for those peasants who were able to build up large holdings to have their lands distributed over a number of neighbouring manors. Some were engrossers, building up their holdings by taking on the lands of others, such as the Deys of Drakenage, who ultimately amassed sufficient land and wealth to enter the ranks of the lesser gentry. As with a number of other entrepreneurial peasant families, their wealth was based on cattle-grazing, and by 1472 they possessed an estate of pasture and meadow land scattered over nine manors. Another family, the Chattocks, from Castle Bromwich, held lands in at least seven other manors by the mid-fifteenth century. The land market allowed for considerable social mobility. The Deys, Chattocks and Slades all came from obscure origins, while even those who had held their land by servile tenure, or had the personal status of serfs, could assemble holdings of considerable size composed of land of mixed tenurial status. John Spooner of Allesley, for example, who had bought manumission for himself and his two sons by the early fifteenth century, possessed a holding composed of a mixture of free and unfree land, including two messuages, three cottages, half a virgate, nearly 19 acres of arable land, an acre of wood and a large pasture called Honysiche Field.[12]

One of the most important influences on the nature of peasant agriculture in the Arden was the peculiar characteristics of communal agriculture, particularly the operation of the field systems and the weakness of manorial control. In the 1530s Leland asserted that 'the grownde in Arden is muche enclosyd', and this landscape feature can be traced back in rentals, deeds and court rolls to the previous century, if not before. Although changes in the rural economy had placed a stronger emphasis on pastoral farming, cereal production remained important, even if the amount of land devoted to this was declining. The acreage under communal control was significantly less than in the Feldon. The irregular nature of the open-field system has long been appreciated.[13] Instead of two or three open fields containing winter and spring crops, with a field left as fallow, which was more typical of a champion village, most Arden settlements had many cropping units. At Knowle there were some seventy individual elements within the open fields, at Middleton there were sixty and at Erdington some eighty-seven separate fields came under communal control. A multiplicity of settlements within the large woodland parishes of the Arden added another dimension to a fragmented and complicated landscape. In Coleshill, a parish of about 6,000 acres, there were five settlements, each with its own communal land, so that fifteen open fields existed within the parish, and similarities can be seen in many others.[14] The open-field land represented the extent of woodland cleared before the dynamic colonization of the Arden, while those assarted subsequently resulted in closes in severalty. In some instances these enclosures were incorporated into the field system. In 1495 at Moxhull tenants were instructed to let common crofts lie open with the common fields, while in 1505 a croft called Newland was described as being in the tenure of John Cheshire and 'it was sometimes kept in severalty and sometimes common as cornfields are and like as a certain croft . . . called Hog Hill is kept with the fields aforesaid', while similar examples occur elsewhere, at Lea Marston, Maxstoke, Kingsbury and Middleton.[15]

Throughout the Arden peasants were trying to break free from communal control by enclosing parcels within arable fields. They wished to gain greater freedom of choice over their husbandry, and the results formed an important and beneficial step in the development of the reorganization and rationalization of peasant holdings. Enclosure increased the value of the land and was especially advantageous for those keeping livestock, as hedges, fences and ditches kept animals together and allowed greater control over their breeding, while for those engaged in arable farming there was greater choice over their crops. They were also trying to enclose open land for their own use and denying access to it as common pasture so that they could crop it more frequently. This seems to have been particularly pronounced at Middleton between 1395 and 1397 and at Lea Marston in the 1470s, where villagers were cultivating fields that should have been fallow, or enclosing crofts which should have been thrown open.[16] Peasants at Kingsbury refused to let their crofts, which some neighbours regarded as part of the open fields, lie open. Others were more obviously trying to rationalize their holdings. The Domesday of Enclosures of 1517 reveals a number of Arden peasant families, such as the Hollyers of Bentley and the Lekes of Fillongley, enclosing holdings of around 30 acres (in other words about a yardland), the

Although this scene comes from a French book of hours, it presents scenes immediately recognizable to an inhabitant of the fifteenth-century Forest of Arden. An amiable-looking bull is at pasture next to a stand of oak trees, while a well-dressed peasant makes off with a green branch, probably to feed it to his cattle as browse. (The Bodleian Library, Oxford, MS Auct. D. inf. 2.11, f. 4r.)

standard size of holding for a well-to-do peasant. In 1422 Thomas Mollesley made a new enclosure of 6 acres at Middleton, while in 1450 William Fox of Lea Marston was fined for enclosing land next to his house. John Hall of Kenilworth incurred a penalty in 1478 for enclosing land belonging to the Abbot of Kenilworth.[17] Others tried to increase their lands by encroaching on land subject to communal rights. At Nuneaton in 1399 John Hallend ploughed part of the common, while enclosing highways is mentioned at Attleborough and Nuneaton. In 1427 Reginald Reynard, a forerunner of the early modern squatter, built a house on the common in Nuneaton.[18] In most instances such actions only came to light when the enclosure caused friction within the peasant community, as at Erdington in 1467, when two neighbours disputed the line of a new fence. Occasionally enclosure was actively encouraged by the landlord, as by the late Duke of Clarence's officials at Berkswell in 1479, or by the Prioress of Wroxall, who in 1416 stipulated that her tenant John Saunders had to enclose land with fences and ditches and keep it in severalty. Peasants could be inconvenienced, and outraged, by landlords arbitrarily enclosing lands that were regarded as being open, as in 1447 when the Prioress of Nuneaton enclosed Horestonfield, provoking the freeholders of Nuneaton to tear down the fences in 1448 in order to reclaim their common rights. Undeterred, the prioress replaced the enclosures and in 1453 was claiming the right to impound any cattle found grazing there. By the 1490s there was renewed demand for land for arable cultivation, when land that had not been cultivated for many years was once again being brought under cultivation.[19]

It is not clear exactly how much communal control was exerted by the Arden communities over cultivation, but peasant cultivators probably enjoyed greater freedom of action than in some other areas. The typical woodland settlement landscape, with the absence of compact settlements, the rarity of parishes coterminous with manors, the multiplicity of cropping units, and the shifting distribution between common and several land must have limited the scope for complete communal control. The volume of bylaws and presentments in Arden manorial courts show communities trying to impose their collective will over the management of the open fields, to determine their crop rotations and when they were to be ploughed, sowed, harvested, gleaned and fallowed. A village community could try to dictate when they should be enclosed and when they should be thrown open for common grazing, as well as other agricultural practices and communal concerns, such as the good repair of highways and bridges, and limiting the activities of those whose behaviour threatened the communal good.[20] Many bylaws sought to curtail unsupervised grazing and consequent destruction of crops, meadow land and woodland. Pigs were ordered to be ringed and yoked, and courts agreed when animals could be folded onto the stubble of the harvested field. Detailed arrangements for tethering horses and colts within fields were set out at Lea Marston and Shustoke, and cattle, horses and geese were excluded from meadows at Kingsbury.[21] Officials, such as haywards and herdsmen, enforced ordinances about enclosures and the trespassing of beasts, placing impounded beasts in the pinfold. Many communities throughout the Arden were concerned to the point of obsession with the unblocking and scouring of ditches and water courses. In many instances

Four generations of a family tree, from the staid great-grandparents, the mature parents, the older children to the babies in the cradle, all in dress and colours suited to their age and rank. (From Jehan Boutillier, La Somme rural, *a book of the customs of northern France; copied by Jean Paradis at Bruges in 1471 for Louis de Gruthuuse, and illuminated by Loyset Liédet: Bibliothèque nationale, MS fr. 202, f. 9. By permission.)*

A novice, dressed in white, disembarks on the isle of hospitality (the Hôtel Dieu) from the ship, Religious Profession, *accompanied by chastity, poverty and obedience. She presents herself at the door of contemplation, but the arrival of the patient in a stretcher at the gate of the active life suggests that she will have a busy time ahead. So too does the scene to the right, showing the sisters at work in the laundry. (Musée de l'Assistance, Paris, Jehan Henry,* Livre de Vie Active, *frontispiece.)*

*Sick but penitent souls in the infirmary of the Church encounter the four professed sisters, Prudence, Temperance, Fortitude and Justice (with the appropriate symbols: rod, bridle, tower and scales), who, with a retinue of postulants, will help them to recover. As was customary in a hospital ward, the patients sleep naked, two to a bed. (*Musée de l'Assistance, Paris, Jehan Henry, *Livre de Vie Active.)*

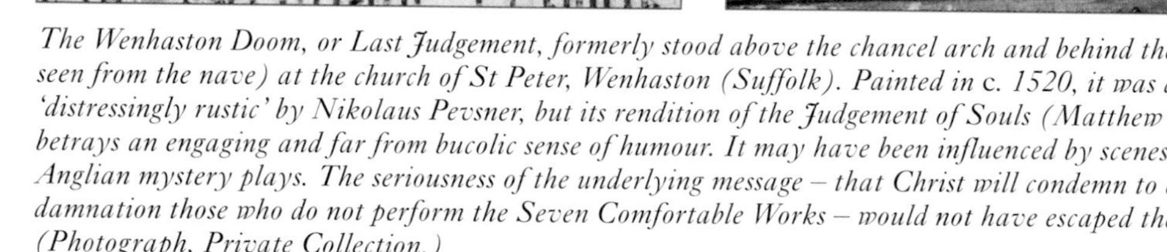

The Wenhaston Doom, or Last Judgement, formerly stood above the chancel arch and behind the rood (when seen from the nave) at the church of St Peter, Wenhaston (Suffolk). Painted in c. *1520, it was described as 'distressingly rustic' by Nikolaus Pevsner, but its rendition of the Judgement of Souls (Matthew 25: 31–46) betrays an engaging and far from bucolic sense of humour. It may have been influenced by scenes from East Anglian mystery plays. The seriousness of the underlying message – that Christ will condemn to everlasting damnation those who do not perform the Seven Comfortable Works – would not have escaped the congregation. (Photograph, Private Collection.)*

A double bench-end at the parish church of St Mary, Ufford (Suffolk), depicting two of the most popular female saints of later medieval England, separated by an elaborately carved poppyhead characteristic of the region. St Katherine (left) sits with a wheel that symbolizes her martyrdom. St Margaret (right), having sprung triumpantly from the belly of a dragon, despatches her diabolical adversary with a sword. Both saints were role models for women and were believed to offer them special protection; both were invoked during the pains of childbirth. It is appropriate that their images should appear in the nave, where women sat, rather than in the exclusively male preserve of the chancel. (Photograph, Private Collection.)

A countryman digging. The drawing decorates the margin of a manuscript of the C text of William Langland's Piers Plowman, *copied in 1427. (The Bodleian Library, Oxford, MS Douce 104, f. 39.)*

*The central tower, Durham Cathedral. Durham Cathedral was the mother church of the Durham diocese but also the monastic church of Durham Priory. There were six other monastic cathedrals of this type in England, at Canterbury, Ely, Norwich, Rochester, Winchester and Worcester. Most of the church at Durham dates from the twelfth century, but the tower had to be rebuilt in the fifteenth century after an earlier one was damaged by lightning. The lower stage (*c. *1465–83) has tall two-light windows with simple Perpendicular tracery. The upper stage (*c. *1483–90) has similar but shorter windows. (Photograph, Private Collection.)*

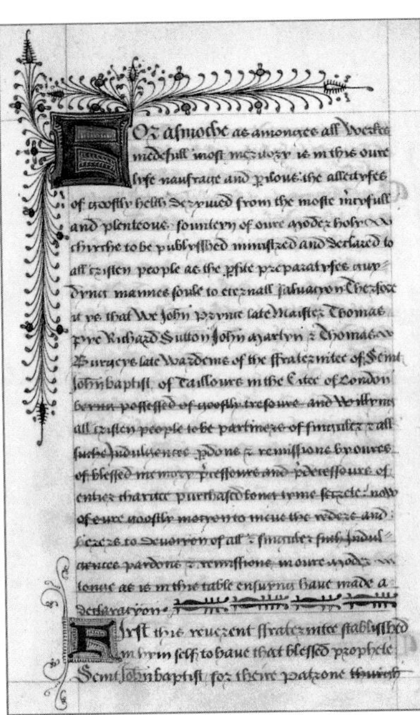

For asmoche as amonges all werkes
nedefull most meritory is in this oure
lyfe naufraucte and perlous the allectyfes
of goostly helth deryued from the moste mercyfull
and plentevous fountayn of oure moder holy
chirche to be publysshed ministred and declared to
all cristen people as the prise preparatyfes unto
dyuer mannes soule to eternall saluacyon Therfore
it ys that we John Pervnte late Maister Thomas
Frye Richard Sutton John Martyn & Thomas
Burgeys late wardeyns of the fraternitee of Seint
John baptist of Taillours in the Citee of London
beyng possessed of goostly tresoure and willyng
all cristen people to be partyners of suche & all
suche indulgences pardons & remissions by oures
of blessed memory predecessours and predecessours of
entier charitee purchased somtyme seculer now
of oure goostly mocyon to meue the reders and
herers to devocyon of all & singuler such indul
gences pardons & remissions in oure moder [illegible]
lonne as is in this table ensuyng haue made a
declaracyon

First this reuerent fraternitee stablisshed
in hym self to haue that blessed prophete
Seint John baptist for theire patrone which

The Pewterers' charter granted in 1473. (Guildhall Library, MS 8695. By permission of the Worshipful Company of Pewterers, London.)

A copy of a letter from the mayor to the master and wardens of the Tailors in November 1492, requesting them to provide 'xxx persones on horssebak' to greet Henry VII on his return from France. (Merchant Taylors' Company, London, Court Minutes, vol. 2, f. 52. By permission of the Merchant Taylors' Company, London.)

Barley Hall in Coffee Yard, off Stonegate, York. York Archaeological Trust has recreated this property, from derelict remains, to illustrate how it may have looked in 1483, when it was leased by William Snawsell, goldsmith and alderman of York, from Nostell Priory. The hospice occupied by Snawsell had a central great hall flanked by two residential wings. (York Archaeological Trust.)

The buttery at Barley Hall, reconstructed by York Archaeological Trust to its probable fifteenth-century appearance. The word 'buttery' has nothing to do with butter, but there is disagreement among etymologists about whether the root derives from the Old French bouteille *(bottle) or from the medieval Latin* butta *(butt, cask). It was the place in the household from which drink was served, together with bread and some other food. (York Archaeological Trust.)*

The high table at Barley Hall, reconstructed with facsimile textiles, vessels and utensils by York Archaeological Trust. A good deal of the decorated pottery used in late medieval England was imported and the handsome blue and white jug is copied from Dutch majolica of the period. (York Archaeological Trust.)

these appear to be communal actions to chide peasants for a lack of diligence; however, in some cases they may conceal something more deliberate. In the 1490s at Nuneaton two men were presented for obstructing a water course near the tithe barn, while a subsequent court reveals that they had constructed a 'dyke' across the stream. Similarly, the Prior of Arbury was presented for building a dyke in a stream in another part of the manor. In neither instance is it made explicit why the obstructions were made, but perhaps they were building a fish pond, or deliberately diverting the water to fill a pond for some other purpose. The community could also act against the antisocial, such as the woman who put lime into a pond where horses drank at Atherstone in 1420, or the peasant whose dog worried sheep at Sutton Coldfield in 1421. Although an abundance of ordinances concerning agricultural practices survive for the Arden, their very frequency and constant repetition suggests that they were often ignored. The relentless nagging of the court at Middleton concerning the maintenance of ditches suggests that such orders often fell onto deaf ears, while it seems that some peasants felt that the benefits of individualistic behaviour far outweighed any communal censure.[22]

Although he was writing in the 1530s, Leland neatly encapsulated the relative unimportance of arable cultivation in the fifteenth-century Arden when he wrote that the ground within the Arden was 'plentiful of gres, but no great plenty of corne'. Although the peasant economy within the Arden was very diverse, many cultivated a wide variety of cereals and industrial crops, both in the open fields and in enclosures. The quantity of crops harvested on Arden demesnes during this time suggests that wheat and peas and beans were the most significant, composing some 36 per cent and 29 per cent respectively, while oats accounted for 13 per cent, with barley, rye, pulse and drage (a mixture of barley and oats) forming the remainder. The evidence for crops grown by peasants is conflicting. Tithe grain at Lea Marston in the late fourteenth century shows that 62 per cent of it was wheat, the remainder being barley, but such a high ratio of wheat appears unusual. Oats were common on many holdings, such as that of John Kent of Stivichall in 1481, where oats composed almost half his crop, the remainder comprising rye, drage and barley. Occasionally other references are made to the crops cultivated by peasants. In 1407 Laurence Scott of Middleton was arrested and in his barn were found peas and beans, oats, drage and hay. Another Middleton man, John Gammel, had his wheat, barley, peas and beans destroyed by straying animals in 1423. Increasingly in the fifteenth century large acreages were given over to peas and beans, mainly because of their value as fodder crops, while recorded allegations of trespass suggests that wheat, barley and drage were common on peasant holdings. Although many were reducing their sown acreages in the fifteenth century to make greater use of pasture, probably at least a third of their holding was still arable.[23]

What were the practices of peasant cultivation? Some settlements tried to dictate a two-field rotation of winter and spring crops, usually sowing wheat for the former and barley for the latter, but as we have seen many tried to break free from this system, enclosing parcels of land and omitting fallow years to try to crop more frequently. Peasants worked hard to maintain and improve the fertility of the soil. The manor courts dictated a regime of folding cattle and sheep onto the fallow fields, and the ownership of the marl pits among the peasantry is well recorded.[24] The large numbers of animals in the Arden contributed to generous quantities of manure, the ownership of 'mukkehilloks' being particularly well recorded on the Stoneleigh Abbey estates. Peasants made agreements to supply one another with manure, and occasionally, when the contract was breached, the dispute is recorded, such as that between Richard Stonley of Stoneleigh and William Stockton. The former accused the latter of selling manure that he was supposed to have used 'for the improvement of the . . . land'.[25] Furthermore, the large acreages given over to legumes must also have provided a beneficial effect on soil quality. Unfortunately, the yield of only one peasant holding in the fifteenth-century Arden is known, that of the aforementioned John Kent. He possessed a holding of about 50 acres, and when he died in 1481, having agreed to reconstruct a burnt-out building, his harvested crops were used by the lord to pay for the repairs. The bailiff accounted for the sale of 47½ quarters of rye, barley, drage and oats, with oats contributing just over 23 quarters to the total. If Kent's holding was cultivated on a three-course rotation, and if a third of it was fallowed each year, this would represent an overall yield of about 11½ bushels an acre. At first sight this hardly seems impressive, but if we consider that the harvest of 1481 was bad, and that oats, which comprised about half the total crop by volume, yielded less well than other crops, his arable farming may be judged quite successful. It would be unwise to generalize from such a slender piece of evidence, but it would seem that he enjoyed a return from his land superior to those recorded on many demesnes.

Although cereal cultivation among the peasantry was mainly for subsistence, some also sold their grains and legumes. Disputes over debts in the courts of Atherstone and Nuneaton suggest that there was considerable traffic in these commodities in the small towns of the area. Household accounts reveal the Mountfords of Coleshill, the Willoughbys of Middleton and Maxstoke Priory buying grains and legumes from local peasants, in some instances from their own tenants, such as Henry Porter, who between 1448 and 1450 supplied the canons of Maxstoke with over 28 quarters of wheat and 20 quarters of barley, as well as selling 17*s* worth of hay to the household of the Duke of Buckingham in 1453.[26] The large numbers of animals within the area meant that there was a great demand for oats, hay, peas and beans for fodder, and straw for bedding. During the 1440s and 1450s the Buckingham household regularly spent between £14 and £18 a year on hay purchased from local peasants, as during 1454 and 1455 when they bought 300 cartloads of hay, 32 cartloads of straw and over 140 quarters of oats. Even in the previous year when demand was less, some twenty-seven peasants received between them £9 19*s* 5½*d* for oats, barley and straw.[27]

Animal husbandry played an important part in the peasant economy of the Arden. It was less labour intensive than arable, and if the latter was largely for subsistence, the products of animals, their meat, fleeces, dairy produce, horn, hides and tallow, were more obviously destined for the market. The large towns of Birmingham, Coventry and Warwick, as well as the proximity of long-distance droving routes, meant a well-developed commercial network existed for cattle, and with a profit margin of about a third of the purchase price, beef production was clearly an attractive proposition for both landlord and peasant.[28] Complaints

Cattle played an important role in maintaining the economic buoyancy of the Forest of Arden in the later Middle Ages. Large livestock markets, often for the sale of Welsh beasts, were held at Birmingham, Coventry and Warwick, as well as in smaller towns of the area. In this market scene, a stockman drags a steer across a pen by a rope around its horns, while his assistant twists its tail. (The Bodleian Library, Oxford, MS Gough Liturg. 7, f. 10r.)

of trespass in court rolls suggest that peasant herds of between ten and thirty were common, and larger ones of up to sixty beasts not exceptional. The active involvement of a number of demesnes in cattle-grazing had a beneficial impact on the local economy, as demesne managers not only visited markets and fairs in search of stock, but also bought animals from peasants. In the 1490s agents of Merevale Abbey regularly toured surrounding villages buying up calves and steers from peasants, such as the ten store beasts bought for £3 6*s* 2*d* from Richard Hebbe in 1500. Others specialized in dairying, such as Robert Campyon, who leased a bull and forty cows from the Abbot of Westminster at Knowle in the early fifteenth century.[29] By the middle of the century, particularly from the 1470s onwards, there was a crescendo of complaints against overstocking common lands, and the imposition of stints by courts suggests that livestock numbers were becoming too large to be sustained on the existing resources.[30] Sheep are most associated with such restrictions, but it is difficult to assess their importance within the Arden as it was not a major wool-producing area and sheep flocks appear to have rarely been kept on fifteenth-century demesnes. However, many hundreds grazed within the pastures of the Arden. Sheep flocks were recorded in over two-thirds of the earliest probate records of the 1540s, and it is reasonable to assume that they had similar prominence in the previous century. A flock of sixty is recorded at Nuneaton in 1473, while stints at Moxhull allowed each tenant to place up to sixty sheep on the commons, and at Nuneaton in 1466 each yardlander could graze forty.[31] Some peasants, too, reared poultry commercially. In 1398 a Nuneaton peasant was amerced for trespassing with twenty-four geese, while later in the same year another was presented for trespassing with a gaggle of thirty. In 1434 John Raves supplied the Mountford household at Coleshill with thirty-four hens for 2*s* 10½*d*, while the wife of John Baggeslowe of Blyth sold the same household sixty geese for 10*s*.[32]

The garden of the Arden peasant's holding was an important, if poorly documented, resource. Apple, cherry, plum and pear trees seem to have been common on many holdings, as in 1463 at Erdington, where nearly all peasant holdings contained orchards. The range of crops cultivated on the peasant's curtilage is poorly recorded, but the garden of Richard Sharpmore of Erdington was probably typical. In 1380 trespassing pigs ruined his vegetables, grass, beans and peas. Some peasants grew industrial crops such as flax, hemp and osiers. They could gather from the wild turves, furze and heath and broom for their own use.[33]

Many peasant households produced prepared foodstuffs both for their own consumption and for retail, some brewing ale, while others baked bread. The development of inns during the later Middle Ages is most often seen in an urban context, yet within Arden at least one rural inn, The George at Middleton, had developed by the early fifteenth century. Butchery is often associated with the entrepreneurial butcher grazier from the larger town, but butchers of a more modest scale lived within the Arden, many selling their meat in the small towns of Atherstone and Nuneaton. Simon Hayne of Attleborough was amerced for selling meat in every surviving frankpledge court roll for Nuneaton between 1389 until 1409.[34]

Some supplemented their income through taking up leases of fishponds and fisheries on rivers. At Knowle in the first half of the fifteenth century two men were leasing a 'fishtrap called a wear on the river Blythe'. Some supplied seigniorial households, some sold their catch to fishmongers, while others stocked seigniorial fisheries. John Summerlane of Castle Bromwich supplied 80 couples of bream at 4*d* a couple, 100 couples of bream at 1½*d*, and 20 couples of tench to the Erdingtons to restock one of their demesne fishponds. Similarly, when John Brome refurbished his fishpond next to the gatehouse at Baddesley Clinton, he paid £7 5*s* 10½*d* to men from surrounding villages for bream, tench, roach and eels. Other lords hired the services of men to catch fish for their table, such as the Warwick household, who in 1453 paid 8*s* to John Burbage and William Lempe of Sutton Coldfield to catch six bream in the pools within Sutton Chase; these were baked with flour, spices, pepper, saffron, cloves and cinnamon and then carried by Thomas Harris of Sutton Coldfield to the earl at Middleham in Yorkshire.[35]

The woodland nature of the area also allowed peasants to raise cash from game. Bows and arrows, snares and nets were owned by many peasants, while others possessed hunting animals. The use of ferrets to hunt rabbits within the park was outlawed at Sutton Coldfield in 1467, when four common hunters were amerced for selling rabbits, while households such as the Mountfords, Willoughbys and Maxstoke Priory bought pheasants, woodcock, teal, partridges, rabbits and conies from peasant hunters. Other local residents took out leases of rabbit warrens and hunting rights. Merevale Abbey leased two of its warrens in 1499 for £16 and £14 respectively, and in 1432 Maxstoke Priory also leased out rights to hunt small game in some of its woodlands, agreeing that the lessee could take, between Christmas and Easter, pheasants, partridges, woodcock and wild duck.[36] Some people generated income from selling what they could collect and gather from within woodlands, such as acorns and mast, used as fodder for pigs, which was being sold at Sutton Coldfield in 1425. Woodland also yielded apples, crab apples, pears, cherries, damsons, sloes and plums, hazelnuts and a variety of berries. Although much picking of fruit went unrecorded, Henry Harries was fined in 1416 for collecting fruit in demesne woods at Sutton Coldfield and selling it at Coleshill. Many peasants owned hives on their own holdings and swarms of bees reported as straying into lordships were rapidly acquired by peasants. Others gathered wild honey and wax from the woodlands, and household accounts, such as those for the Mountfords and Maxstoke Priory, suggest a ready market existed for honey.[37]

The peasant's economy of the Arden was not purely based upon agriculture, and many were involved in woodcrafts, often as a sideline occupation to their agricultural activities. By the fifteenth century woodland was a carefully managed asset, largely confined to enclosed seigniorial woodlands, hunting parks and peasant groves. The mature oaks and ashes yielded great timber, used as building materials, while underwood was used in a wide variety of processes. There is abundant evidence of Arden peasants taking on leases of both great timber and underwood, either for specific number of trees (126 at Coleshill in 1481, 73 at Maxstoke in 1441), or for tracts of underwood by the acre. Some leases were for large quantities of timber or underwood and could often commit the peasant financially for many years, as when Simon Grove of Packwood leased woodland on the Earl of Warwick's demesne at Tanworth in Arden for £40 in 1414, or when Stephen Rowlone took out a lease of all underwood except oak, ash, maple, holly, crabtree and fallen timber on the same demesne for twenty years from 1463. The collier (charcoal-burner) Henry Avery of Elmdon took on a lease of Beltesley Wood in Coleshill in 1402, paying £60 13*s* 4*d* over four years.[38] The Arden was an important area for the manufacture of wood-based fuels, and nearby Coventry, with its great demand for fuel for both industrial and domestic purposes, provided a ready and thriving market. Demesne woodlands were leased for the manufacture of charcoal at Elmdon, Middleton, Coleshill, Lea Marston, Fillongley, Nuneaton, Maxstoke, Packwood and Solihull, while charcoal production is indicated by the place name Sutton Coldfield.[39]

Although there have been coal workings in the eastern fringe of the Arden since Roman times, those on the Nuneaton Priory estate seem to have been abandoned by the fifteenth century, possibly because the outcropping seams had become exhausted. Some peasants trespassed and took coal, such as John de Allesworth who dug the prioress's soil at le Haunch in 1354, or the three men who were digging coals in the High Wood in 1355. Other coalpits did exist within the Arden, such as at Merevale Abbey in the 1490s, but no details survive as to how they were exploited.[40] Faggots (or 'kids') were another important source of wood-based fuels. Their manufacture was comparatively easy, as they were made

Woodland resources were prudently and effectively exploited throughout the Arden. Here two peasants cut branches from pollarded trees, while a woman ties them into a bundle. Another climbs a ladder to prune a sapling which is growing against the side of the stone building. (The Bodleian Library, Oxford, MS Gough Liturg. 7, f. 2r.)

from bundles of branches and rods, and many of those peasants leasing acres of underwood were involved in their making. Seigniorial households bought faggots in large quantities, such as the 1,000 made by Roger Cooke at Baddesley Clinton in 1447, or the 500 bought by Maxstoke Priory in 1451 from Ranulph Jolif. Smaller branches were bound as kindling or used in making brooms and baskets. Other peasants made fencing and hurdles from underwood (uses recorded at Lea Marston, Middleton, Erdington and Minworth), and it also provided the infill for the walls of timber-framed buildings. Although the wealthier and more specialized workers in wood might lease timber and underwood from landlords, other peasants plundered seigniorial woodlands. The Yate brothers of Lea Marston made off with two oaks, two ashes and six cartloads of underwood from Hams park, and on a more modest scale William Bryan of Lyndon took 'whypstokkes and wylstaves' in 1464. Similar incidences are recorded throughout the Arden. On many demesnes men were employed to produce dressed timber, such as laths, spars, shingles and boards, and when new buildings were constructed or older ones refurbished, it was usually to local carpenters that the demesne managers turned.[41]

The Forest of Arden supplied other building materials, and many were involved in their manufacture. Merevale Abbey and Maxstoke Priory owned quarries, and others are mentioned at Allesley, Attleborough, Corley, Rowington, Shawbury and Sutton Coldfield. The Prioress of Nuneaton owned a number of quarries and most of these were leased out in the later Middle Ages, as in 1386 when John Cook of Attleborough and Roger Tysoe leased a rod of stone of 24 ft for three years in 'Attleboroughquerer', paying £1 7*s* 4*d* a year. The demand for sandstone in the mid-fifteenth century was sufficient to persuade John Brome to refurbish and reopen the quarry at Baddesley Clinton. This produced large numbers of ashlars and burial stones for masons from all over the Arden.[42] Many peasants produced pottery, tiles and bricks, often combining this with an agricultural holding. This industry was particularly concentrated around Chilvers Coton, near Nuneaton, but peasants firing clay to supply seigniorial households are also recorded at Temple Balsall, Baddesley Clinton, Packwood and Solihull. The manufacture of tiles and bricks explains reports in court rolls of men being amerced for digging seigniorial soil, such as several peasants at Lode Heath in Solihull in 1421, or the man fined for digging the lady's 'clay' at Nuneaton in 1490. Some produced on a large scale. When a barn at Knowle was repaired between 1434 and 1435, Richard Breybown of Packwood supplied some 2,000 tiles, and Thomas Tyler furnished two dozen gutters and twenty crests.[43] Buildings accounts for Arden demesnes, and those for the guild of the Holy Cross at Stratford-upon-Avon, show that lime and plaster were produced within the forest. Other industrial processes are occasionally mentioned, such as rope-making, ash-burning for the manufacture of glass and the collection of bark to be used in tanning. Ironworkers had appeared in the western parts of the Arden by the end of the thirteenth century, and occupational designations in fifteenth-century documents suggest that a number of peasants were still involved in producing metal goods, although it was not until the sixteenth and seventeenth centuries that the area developed an iron industry of more than local importance. As in other parts of the country, notably where concentrations of industry existed, in Cornwall, Devon, Wiltshire and the West Riding of Yorkshire, the agrarian sector of the Arden peasant economy was bolstered by a strong demand for foodstuffs, created by both the proximity of a large population centre at Coventry and also the growing numbers of craftsmen within the Arden who were not involved in producing their own food.[44]

The continued active exploitation of many estates by resident landlords further helped the local economy, through the purchase of livestock, fodder, grains, foodstuffs, fuels and building materials, through the employment of craftsmen and through cash spent on wage labour. Although many manors employed a few full-time waged employees, usually specialist stockmen or woodwards, far more were employed on a casual basis, allowing some peasants to combine their own husbandry with wage labour.[45] When Sir Henry Willoughby revived demesne farming at Middleton in the late 1440s, the ploughing, harrowing, harvesting, carting, threshing and winnowing were performed by wage-labourers. Some forty-six peasants received payment. Some were specialized building craftsmen from outside the manor. The majority, however, were tenants of the Willoughbys, employed for cereal cultivation, mowing of meadow land, cutting and dressing timber, repairing and making enclosures and building work, such as basic carpentry, winding the walls and daubing.

Some employees were from the highest ranks of the peasantry, such as Richard of the Lee, who was frequently a juror and an affeerer of the manor court of Middleton, and whose father had been the Freville's bailiff. The family holding was a messuage near the church worth £1 annually, and they had expanded their holding further by leasing demesne pastures. Richard was hired by the Willoughbys almost as a subcontractor, using his cart to transport tiles, stone, timber, clay, bricks and grains, and providing ploughs and harrows to cultivate the demesne arable. He swelled his income by selling grains and livestock to the Willoughbys. Other peasants who owned carts, ploughs and harrows were also employed by the Willoughbys. Similarly, demesnes at Baddesley Clinton, Knowle, Maxstoke Priory and Coleshill hired the services of those who possessed wagons and ploughs, probably drawn from the higher ranks of peasant society. It is clear therefore that although some wage-earners may have been from the margins of society, among the landless or smallholders, wage-labour was not their exclusive preserve; it was also undertaken by the well-to-do, office-holding peasant élite. Wages could furnish a good cash income for some peasants. Nicholas Baggeley leased a messuage in Middleton worth 10*s* in 1454 and regularly appeared throughout the 1450s and 1460s as a peasant office-holder in the court rolls of the manor. He performed most of the fencing and hedging work on the Willoughby estate, receiving 3½*d* a day, or about 1½*d* for a rod of fencing. The volume of work he undertook brought him in large sums of money. During 1450 he and another peasant, Edmund Bryde, were employed for hedging and fencing around various compartments within the park at Middleton, repairing the park gates, as well as cutting underwood, making pales, mowing grass and harvesting grains. In this year he was paid £3 15*s* 8½*d* for all his labours, a sum which suggests he was employed for nearly ten months of the year, while Bryde received £3 6*s* ¾*d* and must have spent a similar amount of time working on the demesne.[46]

Historians of the sixteenth century have long appreciated the regional characteristics and specialization of the agrarian economy of different parts of the country. Medievalists have generally exhibited a reluctance to pursue this line of investigation, instead preferring to follow the long tradition of examining either a single manor or the estates of greater lords or religious institutions, often scattered over several counties and a variety of *pays*, only connected by common lordship. In many ways it is difficult to generalize from the former studies, as the economy of such *pays* could be very localized and very sensitive to short-term financial trends, as on the vaccaries of the FitzHugh estate by the Rivers Lune and Tees during the late 1430s, or on the Derbyshire pastures of the Duchy of Lancaster.[47] However, despite these limitations, insufficient attention has previously been paid to the distinctive economic development of such *pays*, and how they contribute to our broader appreciation and understanding of the later medieval economy.[48]

The experiences of one such *pays*, the Forest of Arden, clearly lends support to the view that woodland areas retained their vitality in the fifteenth and early sixteenth centuries rather better than some others. As in other parts of England, there was clearly rural decay. Some settlements contracted in size, demesne assets and peasant buildings fell into disuse and disrepair and lords often had difficulty

The Arden was an important area for the manufacture of wood-based fuels. In this scene, a peasant standing on a ladder cuts off branches, while two others bind these into a faggot. Along with charcoal, these were an important source of fuel. They gave a short, hot blaze and were used in some industrial processes as well as for heating and cooking. (Two Peasants Binding Faggots, *by Pieter Breughel the Younger, The Barber Institute of Fine Arts, The University of Birmingham.*)

Although much modernized and modified, Woodbine Cottage at Maxstoke is a rare surviving example of a later medieval peasant's dwelling in the Forest of Arden. It was constructed in the fifteenth or early sixteenth century and originally consisted of a large open hall with three cells. Cruck-built houses such as this were widely owned in the area during the fifteenth century and indicate both the good quality of peasant housing and the expertise of those engaged in their construction.

in finding tenants to take on abandoned holdings. The value of rents and land therefore remained low, and the increasing arrears, particularly in the mid-century, show that many were finding it difficult to generate the money to pay. Furthermore, the generally low prices for producers, even for some animal products, meant low incomes for many. However, the abundance of resources allowed for economic diversity among the peasantry of the Arden, and weak social controls afforded the opportunity for economic individualism. There was a multiplicity of economic activities that were supportive of and interdependent on one another. In contrast to the general subsistence nature of Arden demesne production during the fifteenth century, the peasant economy of the area was much more commercialized and geared towards the generating of cash from sales. It is difficult to overstate the importance of beef animals, which strengthened the rural economy of the Arden, in contrast to sheep-grazing, which was frequently a source of weakness. As the price of wool sank during the great slump of the fifteenth century, the sustained and continued demand for beef meant that its price generally held up well, even during this most pronounced of national depressions, and even rose slightly from the 1450s onwards. This in turn influenced the variety and quantity of crops cultivated, keeping many areas in cultivation. Woodlands were an important resource and the degree of their utilization so varied that all elements within Arden society could benefit from them. Woodcrafts and by-occupations flourished, while even those who were totally devoid of any woodworking skills could make faggots, collect branches and twigs and gather honey, fruits and holly for cattle feed. The continued functioning of many demesnes, albeit in a modified form, also helped to stimulate the local economy through purchases of stock and grains and, perhaps more importantly, through the amount of money acquired by the peasantry through payments to wage labourers, who as we have seen were not all from the margins of society but rather resembled modern agricultural contractors, employed to perform specific, skilled tasks on the estate.[49]

Undeniably, for many rural people some periods of the fifteenth century were times of trial and tribulation, economic hardship and social misery, but it was not so for everyone all the time. Although the Arden exhibited many signs of rural decay, for many it was neither depressed nor declining, but vital and full of enterprise, affording opportunity for the acquisition of land, wealth and prosperity. Only other detailed studies of other local *pays*, especially those that lay in more marginal areas where cereal cultivation was not necessarily the main economic function, such as those that supported concentrations of industry, or were upland pasture, wetland, coastline, as well as woodland, will determine how typical were the experiences of the Forest of Arden during this time. It may be through such enterprises that the darkness enshrouding and obscuring the fifteenth-century rural economy may be illuminated.

As ever I am extremely grateful for the kind and generous help of Chris Dyer, Rodney Hilton and Jean Birrell. Mr and Mrs F.W. Follett kindly allowed a picture of their house to be included, and the Reverend John Philpott gave permission for the misericords in Astley Church to be photographed. Rex Darby of Classic Images, Coleshill, provided enormous help and advice with the original photography. Ben Henry efficiently and patiently transferred the evolving text onto disk.

CHAPTER 6

A Priory and its Tenants

RICHARD LOMAS

Nearly forty years ago, when assessing the condition of rural England at the end of the fourteenth century, May McKisack observed that

> the demarcation of the agricultural population into the three main categories – freeholders, tenant-farmers, and landless, or nearly landless, labourers – which was to form the characteristic pattern of English rural society until the end of the eighteenth century, is already clearly foreshadowed. By and large, the great landlords had delegated their responsibilities as farmers to their tenants; henceforward, their main interest in their estates would be financial and administrative.[1]

The purpose of this paper is to test the validity of this assertion for one great landlord, and then to examine in detail how this new landlord–tenant relationship actually functioned on his estate. The landlord in question is the bursar of the Cathedral Priory of Durham, and the opportunity for this close scrutiny is the detailed rent book which has survived for the financial year 1495/6 (from Michaelmas 1495 to Michaelmas 1496).[2] This comprises two paper quires, originally of forty-four and fifty-eight leaves and measuring 220 mm by 150 mm, bound in a contemporary cover of stiff parchment.[3] The document was prepared before the start of the financial year by a clerk who listed, in most cases four per page, the names of the tenants and the rent each owed.[4] The generous spaces left between the entries were subsequently used by another clerk to record the individual rent payments as they were made. Most of these entries were very detailed and, although untidily written, they provide revealing evidence of how, when, where, by whom and in what form rents were paid.

At the outset it must be said that the properties administered by the bursar were far from comprising the whole of the priory's estate. In addition to the mother house, the priory had cells, each endowed with property sufficient to sustain its life and function. Originally there were nine cells, but in 1462 the Durham monks abandoned their struggle to retain control of the cell at Coldingham in Berwickshire in the face of the ambition of the Scottish kings and the Home family.[5] In so doing they lost property which, in the 1290s, had been worth almost £600 a year.[6] The other cells were in England at Holy Island and on

The places shown opposite are those where the bursar had real property from which he drew rent. Those in bold are the townships and/or manorial farms which formed the core elements of his estate. Not shown are Shoreswood, Cornhill, Ellingham, Harbottle and Warkworth in north Northumberland, and Woodhall in the East Riding of Yorkshire.

1 Cramlington
2 Newcastle-upon-Tyne
3 Prudhoe
4 Gateshead
5 Jarrow
6 **Willington**
7 **Wallsend**
8 **Heworth (Over & Nether)**
9 Felling
10 Follingsby
11 **Hebburn**
12 **Monkton**
13 **Hedworth**
14 **Preston and Simonside**
15 **Harton**
16 **Westoe**
17 **South Shields**
18 **Monkwearmouth**
19 **Fulwell**
20 **Southwick**
21 Silksworth
22 **West Rainton**
23 **East Rainton**
24 Cocken
25 Ravensflat
26 **N. Pittington**
27 **S. Pittington**
28 **Moorsley**
29 Ludworth
30 **Dalton-le-Dale**
31 Hawton
32 Thorpe
33 **Monk Hesledon**
34 Hardwick
35 Castle Eden
36 Hulham
37 Hutton Henry
38 Fishburn
39 Hartlepool
40 Claxton
41 **Billingham**
42 **Cowpen Bewley**
43 **Wolviston**
44 **Newton Bewley**
45 Blakiston
46 Ponteys
47 Sadberge
48 Burdon
49 Barmpton
50 Skerningham
51 Coatham Mundeville
52 Summerhouse
53 Cleatlam
54 Newsham and Winston
55 Osmundcroft
56 Barford
57 Staindrop
58 Heighington
59 Coatsay Moor
60 **Aycliffe**
61 Newhouse
62 Greystones
63 **Newton Ketton**
64 Woodham
65 Nunstainton
66 Mainsforth
67 **Kirk Merrington**
68 **Middlestone**
69 **Westerton**
70 **Great Chilton**
71 **Ferryhill**
72 **Hett**
73 **Spennymoor**
74 Bishop Auckland
75 Hunwick
76 Hamsterley
77 Woodifield
78 Hunstanworth
79 **Edmundbyers**
80 **Muggleswick**
81 Healeyfield
82 Fordhouse
83 **Bearpark**
84 **Aldingrange**
85 Broom
86 **Relley**
87 **Houghall**
88 Durham City
89 Northallerton
90 Brompton
91 N. Otterington

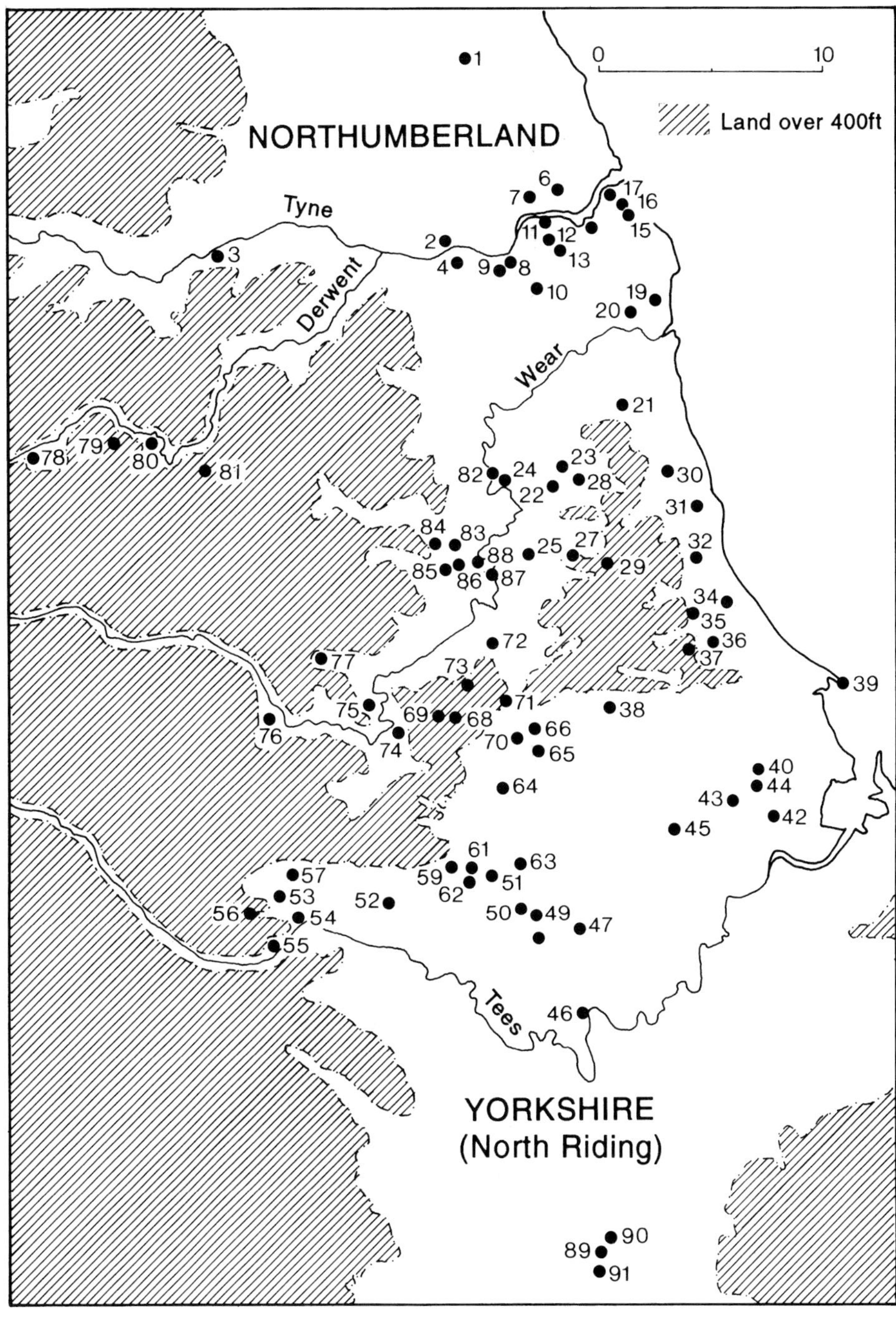

The estate of the bursar of Durham Priory. The places shown are those where the bursar had real property from which he drew rent. The places listed in bold are the townships and/or manorial farms that formed the core elements of his estate. Not shown are Shoreswood, Cornhill, Ellingham, Harbottle and Warkworth (all in north Northumberland) and Woodhall (in the East Riding of Yorkshire).

the Inner Farne in Northumberland, at Jarrow, Monkwearmouth and Finchale in County Durham, at Lytham in Lancashire, at Stamford in Lincolnshire and at Oxford, where the priory's own college was fully established in 1381. In the later fifteenth century the aggregate annual value of these cells was probably in the region of £700.[7]

The administrative arrangements on the priory's main estate were equally complex. As far as can be seen, the Durham monks never organized it as an entity run by a single manager or management team with all income flowing into a central treasury. Instead, it was divided into two main parts: roughly two-thirds of the whole was controlled by the bursar with the help of the terrar and the prior's lay steward,[8] and the remaining third was divided between five other obedientaries, each of whom was responsible for managing the properties assigned to his office and expending the income he drew from them on his particular responsibilities. In the last decade of the fifteenth century these five monks handled income amounting to around £650 (the sacrist £187, the hostillar £163, the commoner £116, the chamberlain £94, and the almoner £90). Moreover, the distribution of property between these six obediences appears highly and unnecessarily complicated in that each had properties in town and country, in County Durham and further afield, and of both a temporal and a spiritual nature.[9]

Perhaps the most evident feature of these properties is their geographical dispersion between the Tweed in the north and the Humber in the south. The bulk of them were located between the Rivers Tyne and Tees, or 'between the waters' (*infra aquas*) as the monks often described County Durham. Of the remainder, those in Northumberland were more important than those in Yorkshire. The other distinctive feature is the combination of temporal and spiritual property. The bulk of the bursar's spiritual income derived from the tithes of fourteen appropriated parishes, eight in County Durham, four in Northumberland and two in Yorkshire, the last two groups being classified collectively as 'beyond the waters' (*extra aquas*). Of the Durham parishes, two, Jarrow and Monkwearmouth, were special in that it was from them that, in 1083, Bishop William of St Calais brought the monks to form the new Benedictine chapter of his cathedral. Thereafter, the two churches were priory cells and had no beneficed parochial incumbencies. The priory was therefore able to collect all of the spiritual income. Not all of it came to the bursar, however. At Jarrow, the grain tithes of Jarrow and Hedworth and all the lesser tithes and altarage were always reserved to the cell, and by 1495 the tithes of Simonside and Wardley Manor had been converted into rent charges which were merged with the temporal rents. The situation at Monkwearmouth was very similar.[10] In 1495 the cell there received all the spiritual income save the grain tithes of Southwick, although this had not always been the arrangement: until about 1400 the tithes of Fulwell and Monkwearmouth, and until 1430 those of Hylton, were paid to the bursar.[11]

Five of the remaining Durham parishes – Pittington, Hesleden, Billingham, Aycliffe and Merrington – were elements of the priory's original endowment, while the sixth, Heighington, to which there is no reference before 1196, may have been created about that time by a division of Aycliffe. All of them were

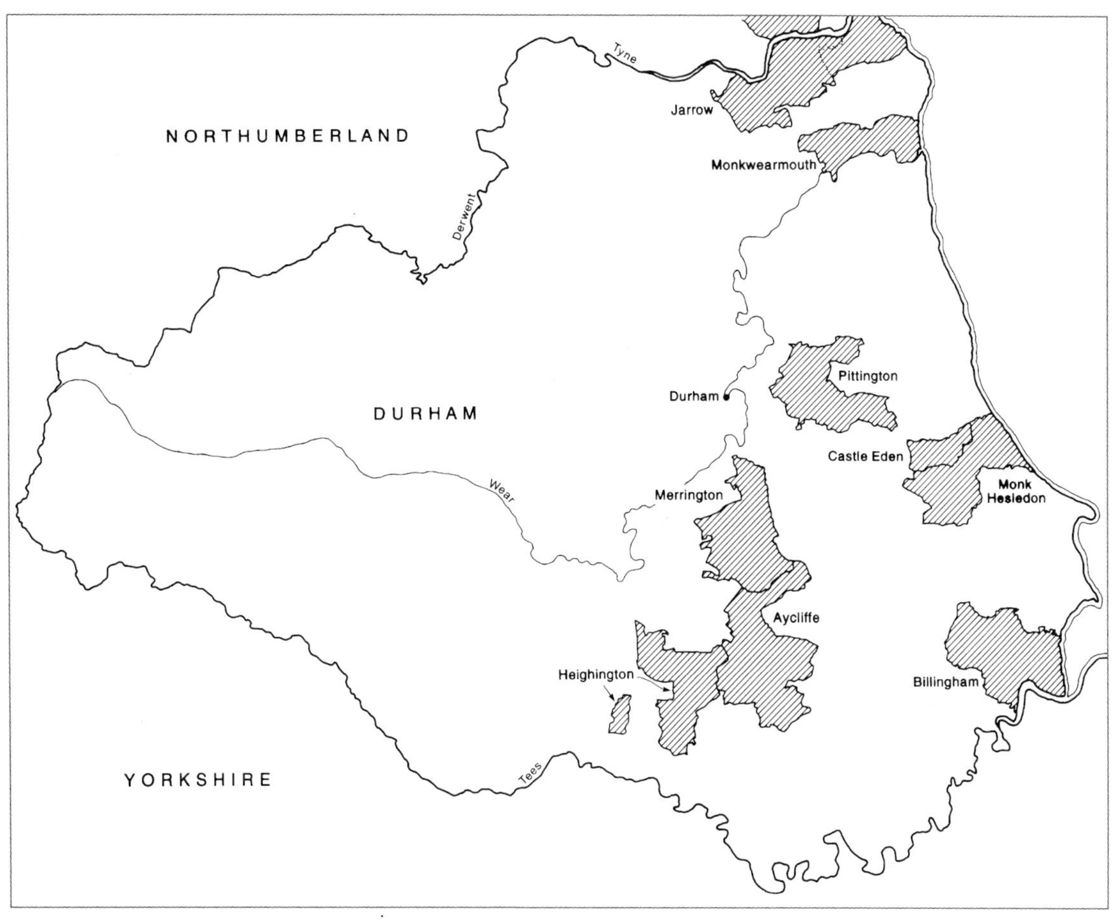

The appropriated parishes of the bursar of Durham Priory.

appropriated, although in several cases after considerable delay and difficulty, between 1150 and 1250.[12] And all were furnished with endowed vicarages, with the result that the bursar, *qua* rector, received only the grain tithes. Throughout the period for which there is an extant administrative record, that is, from the 1290s, the normal practice was for the grain tithes of most of the constituent townships of these parishes to be sold for cash prior to collection, in effect, leased. However, aside from a few years at the very end of the fourteenth century, the grain tithes of a few townships were retained 'in the lord's hand' (*in manu domini*), that is, they were collected, threshed and winnowed and the resulting grain handed over to the priory's granator. In 1495/6 six townships and one manorial farm were in hand. Five of this group were in Billingham parish (Billingham, Wolviston, Cowpen Bewley, Newton Bewley and Bewley Manor), in fact the entire parish except for Bellasis Manor. This arrangement had been in operation since 1449, and prior to that date, as far back as the beginning of the century, the entire parish had been in the lord's hand. The other townships in hand were Heighington and Walworth in Heighington parish.

The bursar's income from grain tithes was also adversely affected by the retreat from arable farming. Archdeacon Newton, a village in Heighington parish, ceased to grow grain after 1330/1, and soon after disappeared from the records, almost certainly because it had become deserted. Likewise, Newton near Hylton in Monkwearmouth parish disengaged from cereal farming after 1368/9, while the farms known as Ravensflatt and Warknoll in Pittington followed suit in 1397/8 and 1435/6 respectively. The worst affected parish was Aycliffe, where the farmers at Grindon abandoned cereals after 1380, as did those of Woodham after 1426/7. Also in this parish, the tithes of the farm called Newhouse were converted into a fixed charge and added to the rent, doubling it from £1 6*s* 8*d* to £2 13*s* 4*d*.[13]

Of the Northumberland parishes that of Holy Island closely resembled Jarrow and Monkwearmouth. It was one of the priory's original endowments, it became one of its cells, no endowed benefice was established and the parochial income was divided between the bursar and the monks living at the cell. The neighbouring parish of Norham was also an original possession, but it remained unappropriated until the 1170s. No cell was created there, but neither was an endowed vicarage; the vicar and the chaplain at the chapel of ease at Cornhill were stipendiary priests, receiving respectively £20 and £5 6*s* 8*d* a year throughout the fifteenth century.[14] The other two Northumberland parishes, Ellingham and Branxton, were gifted to the priory in the twelfth century, the latter occasioning a dispute with the Augustinian priory of Kirkham, and were appropriated before 1275.[15] The bursar had also received the tithes of Bedlington until 1358, when they were transferred to the sacrist's office to which they had originally been appropriated in the mid-thirteenth century. South of the Tees the church at Northallerton was gifted to the monks by King William II in 1091 or 1092 and appropriated by 1167. Brompton was at this date a separate church, but it was united with Northallerton by 1234 and was thereafter one of that parish's constituent townships. The other Yorkshire parish, Eastrington, was in the East Riding. Originally a chapel of Howden, it was appropriated when that church was converted to collegiate status around 1266.[16] Finally, it should be noted that in earlier times the bursar also received tithe income from three Scottish churches acquired in the early twelfth century, namely Edrom, Ednam and Earlston, but like the cell at Coldingham they became casualties of the war with Scotland. Before the battle of Bannockburn in 1314, the bursar's income from these churches was a handsome £150 a year, but this fell to no more than about £20 in the middle decades of the fourteenth century, and ceased altogether after 1377.[17]

Of lesser importance financially were the pensions received from six institutions. Two were paid by parochial incumbents. That from Holtby was a rectorial pension of obscure origin, perhaps predating 1146, while that from

Heighington was paid by the vicar to the sacrist until 1423, when it was exchanged for the rents and profits in Durham and Crossgate boroughs. A third pension was equally recent: from 1426 the hostillar was contracted to pay an annual sum for the cart-horses' hay and fodder (*pro feno et prebenda equorum pro carectis per convencionem*). The remaining pensions were owed by three monasteries as the consequence of their appropriation of five Northumberland churches: by Hexham Priory for Ovingham and Alston appropriated in 1378 and 1379; by Newminster in respect of Stannington and Kirk Whelpington appropriated in 1333 and 1350; and by Tynemouth for Haltwhistle appropriated in 1385. The bursar had also received a pension from Balliol College, Oxford, arising out of its appropriation of Long Benton, but this was reassigned to the priory's college at Oxford in 1423.[18]

The bursar's temporalities were even more complicated, although with a very similar geographical pattern. In all they were located in eighty-four townships. Seven were in Northumberland, including the borough of Newcastle. Not included in this group, however, are the townships of Wallsend and Willington, which, although on the north bank of the Tyne, were historically members of the ancient estate centred on Jarrow on the south bank. For our purposes they are best seen as part of the estate in County Durham. South of the Tees the bursar had property in only four Yorkshire townships: Northallerton, Brompton and North Otterington in the North Riding and Woodhall in the East Riding. The remaining seventy-three townships were in County Durham.

These eighty-four townships fall into two broad categories. By far the more important were thirty-eight which were fully under the priory's direct control. One of them, Shoreswood, was in Northumberland close to Norham and less than three miles south of the Tweed, while two, Elvet and Crossgate, adjacent to Durham, had borough status. The other thirty-five were rural townships distributed in six clusters across the eastern and central parts of County Durham. Together they constituted the core of the bursar's estate. In the other forty-six townships the priory's interest was either confined to a single, and in many cases very small, holding; or, in complete contrast, comprised the entire township or farm but, because of the freehold condition, the monks had little or no control over them and received from them a small, and in real terms diminishing, rent which they were powerless to increase. This group included four properties in Northumberland and four in Yorkshire, and tenements in the boroughs of Newcastle, Gateshead, Hartlepool and Bishop Auckland. In Durham they had holdings in Gilesgate and elsewhere, including the Bailey, the area enclosed by the original town wall where the castle and cathedral were situated, which was burghal in character though not in constitution.

It is clear from earlier rentals and other administrative documents that the bursar's estate was never completely static and that properties were lost and gained from time to time. The tenement in Boston, which had been acquired around 1200 as a necessary base during the bursar's visits to St Botolph's Fair, was transferred to the cell at Stamford in 1387 or 1388. By that time the bursar no longer attended the fair but sold his wool to Newcastle merchants and bought the imported goods he needed from them. Similarly, in the early fifteenth century the

A typical Durham County village green at Westerton. Most Durham villages comprised two rows of farmsteads abutting a rectangular or half-elliptical green. The intrusive building at the centre of the picture is an eighteenth-century observatory built by Thomas Wright. (Photograph, Private Collection.)

rents from the township of Edmundbyers in Derwentdale, the two nearby farms known as Healeyfield and White Hall, and a small tenement in Woodifield some 12 miles away, were moved from the bursar's account to that of the stock-keeper as part of a reorganization of the priory's pastoral farming arrangements. Other losses, however, were involuntary and stemmed from the priory's inability to control or coerce powerful tenants who proved unwilling to pay rent. One solution was to arrange mutually convenient exchanges of property. Thus, in 1428, despairing of ever securing the £1 6*s* 8*d* owed by their tenant in Ludworth, the monks agreed to swap his holding there for tenements in Elvet borough and Westerton which were part of the core estate.[19] Also in the fifteenth century, Hawthorn disappeared from the records for the same reason: in the inventory of the estate drawn up in 1446 the bursar admitted that his office had been unable to extract the rent of 4*s* from the Lumley family for twenty years and more.[20]

There were gains, however. In 1459, an 8-acre holding was acquired in Fishburn, and thirty years later equally insignificant properties were obtained in Thorpe near Easington and in Hamsterley. Three years earlier, in 1486, the priory completed its recovery of the Tyneside township of Simonside, which had slipped from its control in the twelfth century. Unfortunately, by this date the township was virtually deserted, and in 1489 its land was let for grazing to the tenantry of the surrounding townships. The aquisition of new property continued in the sixteenth century with small gains at Mainsforth in 1514 and at Sadberge five years later.[21]

Within and as part of the core townships were a variety of properties over which the priory exercised lordship. By far the most valuable were the 'manors', the term used in north-east England to describe demesne farms. In 1495/6 the bursar controlled nine such farms, all of them leased – Wardley, Pittington, Eden, Hesleden, Bellasis, Bewley, Ketton, Aldin Grange and Houghall. This, however, was less than half the number the bursars of the previous century had possessed. No fewer than nine other manors had disappeared as a result, not solely of the abandonment of direct exploitation, but also of the merging of their land with that of the customary tenants. The result was the enlargement of tenant holdings and the elimination of the distinction between tenant land and demesne land.[22] Two farms, Muggleswick in Derwentdale and Saltholme near the mouth of the Tees, were still in hand, but were now run as pastoral enterprises by the stock-keeper, not the bursar. Another manor still in hand, and therefore missing from the rent book, was that known as Beaurepaire or Bearpark. It was located within the very large park of that name situated on the western outskirts of Durham, at the heart of which was a substantial manor house where in the later Middle Ages the recreational periods known as the *ludi* were most frequently held.[23] Farming there had never been on a large scale and had been abandoned earlier in the century; it was restarted, but only in a minor way, after 1450.

Next in importance were the mills, of which the bursar had fourteen in 1495/6 – Nether Heworth, Hedworth, Westoe, East Rainton, Pittington Hesleden, Wolviston, Billingham, Aycliffe (two), Kirk Merrington, Crossgate and Elvet. As with manors, this was a smaller number than in the previous century. The mills at Moorsley, Dalton, Wallsend, Ketton and Muggleswick had disappeared, almost certainly because of the contraction of both population and cereal cultivation, while the the mill known as Skaltok in Elvet was abandoned in 1462 as the result of the River Wear changing course.[24] The mill at Elvet mentioned in the rent book was a minor replacement, most of the milling burden having been transferred to the mill in Crossgate. Other assets included eight yares (fish traps made of wicker panels attached to wooden stakes driven in the river bed) at Westoe, Hebburn and Gateshead on the Tyne. Two others functioned at Jarrow, but they were assigned to the cell there, while the four at the mouth of the Wear belonged to the cell at Monkwearmouth.[25] Also on the banks of the Tyne were four saltpans at South Shields and a quarry for the production of grindstones at Nether Heworth. Common ovens also appear, but only in the townships of Billingham, Cowpen Bewley, Aycliffe, Ferryhill and Kirk Merrington and in Elvet borough, probably because only in those places was the population large enough to support such a facility.

Other than those still in hand, the bursar's properties were let to about 500 tenants. The precise number cannot be computed with certainty because some properties were let to groups of unnamed tenants, some freeholds were described merely as being in the hands of the heirs of deceased tenants, while the occasional occurrence of the same name in neighbouring townships raises uncertainty as to whether or not it was the same person. Of the total, nearly 350 were in the thirty-five core rural townships and seventy-eight were in the boroughs. As regards legal status, there were two classes, freeholders and leaseholders. Of the former there were possibly seventy-five in possession of eighty-three tenements, and these fall into three clearly distinct groups. Twenty-eight were holdings comprising the whole or part of townships in which the bursar had no other interest. By far the largest of these was the multiple estate known as Staindropshire which was held by the senior branch of the Neville family. At the other end of the scale was the messuage and 12 acres in Hulam in Hesleden parish. Many of these freeholds were owned by members of Durham gentry families: Surtees (Felling and Dinsdale), Hylton (Follingsby), Claxton (Eden, Hulam, Claxton), Blakiston (Blakiston), Esh (Barmpton, Skirningham), Bowes (Newsham, Osmundcroft, Cleatlam, Barforth), Eure (Bishop Auckland). A further twelve were in four of the boroughs – Gateshead, Hartlepool and Crossgate (in each of which there were two), and Elvet (where there were six). The largest group comprised forty-three tenements in twelve of the townships of the core estate, with over half being in Wolviston, Aycliffe and Ferryhill. Most of the holdings belonged to obscure people, although six were in the hands of some of the bursar's fellow obedientaries: the commoner at Hebburn, Monkton, West Rainton and Wolviston, the almoner at Great Burdon, and the sacrist at Kirk Merrington. A further six belonged to gentry families: Hedworth (Hedworth, Monkton, Southwick), Conyers (Wolviston), Fulthorp (Ferryhill) and Eure (Ferryhill). This number, although substantial, was in fact the residue of a much larger cohort which had been reduced in the course of the fourteenth and fifteenth centuries by the deliberate policy of buying back freehold tenements. This policy could have been hindered by the mortmain legislation of Edward I that was supposed to restrict the capacity of churches to acquire new properties, but in fact this proved to be no great obstacle since virtually every Bishop of Durham, the licensing authority in the palatinate, granted licences to his chapter to sidestep the prohibition. As a result, the priory was able to eliminate freehold land entirely from East Rainton, Hesleden, Cowpen Bewley, Middlestone and Westerton and to reduce it substantially in other townships. In all, the licences indicate the recovery of over 2,500 acres, about half of which were in Wolviston, Billingham and Ferryhill.[26]

These recovered freeholds and all other tenements were leaseholds, held in almost all cases for terms of three, six or nine years, and normally renewable. This situation, like all others on the estate, was the product of a slow evolutionary process, the underlying impetus for which was the decline in population initiated by the plague of 1349.[27] In the hundred years after that catastrophic event, in which it is probable that about half the priory's tenants died, three fundamental changes ocurred in the landlord–tenant relationship. The earliest was the disappearence of labour services of both the bondmen, whose rent was entirely in the form of services, and of other sorts of tenant, whose rents were a mixture of cash and work. This process was complete by 1383/4,[28] and was followed by the adoption of the short lease. This form of tenure was introduced in the 1360s, but it did not begin to be widely adopted until the 1390s. In the next four decades, however, it rapidly became the norm in all townships, except the fishing village of South Shields. It replaced two earlier forms of tenure. The more precarious of the two, tenure at the lord's will (*ad voluntatem domini*), was specifically associated with the condition of neifty. By the mid-fourteenth century it occurs infrequently, essentially because the number of neifs was small. What proportion of the tenant-farmer population had ever been neifs cannot be estimated, but the inquest held into the whereabouts of neifs in 1386 revealed the existence of only twenty-nine families in ten townships with seventy-eight members, many of whom were living off the estate and thus effectively emancipated. Their number continued to decline, so that in 1469, the last known occasion when an enquiry was held, there were only eight families of neifs with thirty-two members (seven living off the estate), all belonging to the four townships of Billinghamshire, namely Billingham, Wolviston, Cowpen Bewley and Newton Bewley.[29] The alternative to this form of tenure, which was much more widespread in the fourteenth century, was tenure for life (*pro vita sua*). This involved the payment of an entry fine (*gresuma*), which does not appear to have been related to the size of the holding and carried with it the privilege of widow right and family inheritance.

With the adoption of short leases went the practice of engrossing, made necessary by the fall in the number of available tenants in the thirty-five core townships. Without this the bursar would have been unable to keep all of his holdings tenanted. Together these two developments created a very volatile land market, which continued until the 1430s, when permanent conglomerate holdings, some exceeding 200 acres, gradually coalesced. The initiative for this freedom to deal in land probably came from the tenants, or at least the more enterprising among them, for it made it possible for them to become substantial farmers. However, these conglomerates did not last: gradually they were replaced by syndicates – probably a landlord initiative – wherein the entire land of a township except the freeholds was leased to a group of tenants, each of whom paid an equal portion of a single rent. In 1495 this change was still in progress and it was not to be complete until 1524, when the syndicate was formed at Cowpen Bewley. The only place where this solution was not applicable was the fishing village of South Shields.[30]

In addition to the leaseholders in the core rural townships, there were sixty-six in eight boroughs: Newcastle (1), Gateshead (5), Hartlepool (4), Gilesgate (18), Crossgate (13), Elvet (9) and Durham Bailey (16). Finally, there were twenty miscellaneous tenements in fourteen townships, including four in Northumberland and two in Yorkshire. This group included the glebes of Cornhill chapel and Ellingham church, the surviving assarts on Spennymoor, the large tract of waste north-east of Bishop Auckland, which had been subject to extensive assarting in the late thirteenth and early fourteenth centuries,[31] and a large field next to South Shields called Shieldsheugh, which was enclosed in 1489.[32]

Before looking in more detail at the relationship between these tenants and the bursar and his managerial colleagues, two further points need to be made. The first is to highlight the marked contrast in size between the townships in the north and the south of the county. Although every township had a unique structure, there was a marked contrast between places such as Over Heworth on Tyneside, with nineteen tenements, and the Teesside township of Wolviston with eighty-one; or between the Wearside township of Monkwearmouth, which, like Over Heworth, had only nineteen tenements, and Aycliffe, 5 miles north of Darlington, where the total was forty-nine. These figures are taken from the rentals of the 1340s, but that of 1495/6 shows the same discrepancy: Over Heworth and Monkwearmouth were down to nine and four tenements respectively, but Wolviston and Aycliffe, although reduced, were still much larger with forty-five and thirty-four.[33] The priory's administrative records do not provide an explanation of these differences, which may well have had their roots in the distant past. Secondly, it is worth pausing to note just how accurate May McKisack's assessment was. Certainly the picture presented by the 1495/6 rent book and other contemporary records fully confirms the presence of freeholders and tenant farmers; and given the size of many of their farms the existence of landless labourers cannot be doubted. She was also wise in entering a qualifying 'by and large' when dismissing great landowners as direct exploiters of the soil. Although the bursar's farming activities were reduced to the small enterprise at Beaurepaire, he had continued to farm one of his largest manors, Pittington, until 1456.[34] Moreover, scutiny of the records of his fellow obedientiaries reveals that the hostillar continued to work the farm at Elvethall without a break until the end of the priory's existence; the sacrist, having ceased farming in 1410 or 1411, restarted between 1425 and 1438;[35] and the cellarer worked his manor at Relley together with several closes in the park at Beaurepaire and in the vicinity of Durham.[36]

Nevertheless, the bursar was essentially a *rentier*, and therefore the arrangements he put in place for collecting his rents must be considered. The bursar's accounts and the halmote court rolls indicate that rents were to be paid in cash and in two half-yearly instalments at Whitsun and Michaelmas. With such a large and far-flung estate, a rent-collecting organization was necessary. For the properties, both spiritual and temporal, in north Northumberland there was a local officer, known as the proctor of Norham, who collected the rents, out of which he paid the stipends of the vicar of Norham and the chaplain of Cornhill, and then forwarded the residue of his receipt to the bursar at Durham. Originally, his office had been performed by one of the monks based at the Holy Island cell, or occasionally by the vicar of Norham, but from 1440 the proctor was always a member of a local family named Sanderson.[37] In the thirty-five core townships in County Durham, the halmote court rolls reveal the existence of elected township officers, one of whom was styled the collector of rents. The implication of his title was that he collected the rents of his fellow tenants. In fact, as a number of surviving indentures between bursar and collectors from the 1430s indicate, his function was not so much to collect rents as to ensure that other members of his community paid them. All in all, the accounts and court records suggest a well-ordered and smoothly running system.

The 1495/6 rent book shows that this was far from the truth. Two basic facts stand out. One is that, although rents were recorded in cash, many were paid in

Durham Cathedral Close, known as The College. The bursar's exchequer, now demolished, was on the far right of the picture in the angle between the refectory with its large seventeenth-century windows and the entrance to the passage leading to the south cloister. The cellarer's exchequer, also demolished, was on the far left of the picture in front of the large south window of the monastic dormitory. Part of the dormitory undercroft was the cellarer's store room. (Photograph, Private Collection.)

whole or in part by other means. The other is that relatively few tenants paid their rent in two half-yearly instalments, and that most met their obligations in a much more ad hoc and haphazard way. The book also reveals more of the bursar's rent-collecting organization. He had his own exchequer in the cathedral, close to the passage under the eastern end of the refectory leading to to the southern and eastern cloisters, and, perhaps significantly, close to the prior's hall.[38] Based there was an officer with the title of the 'exchequer courier' (*cursor scaccarii*) and an annual fee of £1 6*s* 8*d*. The holder of this office in 1495/6 was a Richard Wren. His appearences in the rent book, which total 146, show that, while he spent much of his time in the exchequer, his role was also peripatetic, as his title suggests. Moreover, his work was sufficient for him to warrant the services of a servant, a certain W. Sandy. The bursar's accounts also reveal the existence of a clerk of the exchequer with a fee of £1; presumably it was this man who entered the details of rents in the rent book as they were paid. If a rent was paid in full, that fact was normally indicated by the addition of the letters *qt* (= *quietus*, meaning 'quit') in the left-hand margin, and also, although less regularly, for the entry to be closed with the phrase *Et sic quietus* ('And so he is quit'). Where the rent was not fully paid, a cross was entered in the left-hand margin. In theory it is possible to calculate very rapidly how many rents were fully paid and how many were not. In practice, however, this does not give an accurate result since in a number of instances the wrong symbol was added or no symbol at all. Nor does this system of signs distinguish between the partially paid and totally unpaid rents.

As regards the temporalities, some 595 rents were owed. Of these 437 were marked with the 'quit' symbol, to which a further 11 can be added, making a total of 448 or 75 per cent. Of the 92 townships and farms involved, only 37 were recorded as having paid all their rents, while in Ferryhill as few as 54 per cent were paid in full. However, no particular significance appears to attach to these discrepancies. At the other end of the scale were 66 rents for which nothing was paid, thus effectively reducing the rent roll to 529. For this there are several explanations. In one case in South Shields the reason was explicit, namely the death and non-replacement of a tenant.[39] Elsewhere, notably in the boroughs, several tenements were described as 'waste', while in other cases the culprit was a fellow obedientary, the implication here being that non-payment was by mutual agreement. Possibly, war was the reason in one case in the border township of Shoreswood, and its influence may have been felt as far south as Billingham on the Tees, where one rent was paid 'in time of war' by the tenant's wife, presumably because he was away on active service.[40] In several other cases, however, the rent was effectively dead in that it was never paid, and the bursar had no means of enforcing payment. This was certainly so with the Northumberland tenements at Harbottle and Cramlington and those in Yorkshire at North Otterington and Woodhall. The uncollectable rents in Durham were in townships where the priory had no other interest, and in most cases where the tenant was of gentry status.The worst offenders in this respect were the Claxton family, who paid nothing for their holdings in Claxton, Hulam and Castle Eden. The Bowes family paid the rent for Osmundcroft, but not for their lands in Newsham, Cleatlam and Barforth. Recently it has been argued that during the economic depression of the late 1430s the bishop tacitly waived the rent of his gentry tenants in the interests of social and political stability.[41] This does not seem to have been a consideration with the priory: the inventory drawn up in 1446 clearly states in several instances that no rent had been paid for twenty years and more and that nothing would be forthcoming without recourse to law.[42] Even had such moves succeeded, the ill will they would have engendered would have far outweighed the financial gain. Significantly, this refusal to pay did not extend to the nobility. The Earl of Northumberland paid his rent for a small holding in Warkworth, and the Earl of Westmorland for the much more substantial properties of Staindropshire and Summerhouse.The total loss of rent income from this group of rents was £27 0*s* 4½*d*. A slightly greater loss of £30 1*s* 10*d* was sustained by the failure of a larger group of tenants – eighty-nine in twenty-nine townships – to pay their rents in full. In most of these cases the reason would seem to be inability to raise the total rent or dilatoriness, not resistance or refusal.

Whether these shortfalls were made good in the next or later years cannot be determined. Thus it would seem that there was a total loss of income amounting to £57 2*s* 2½*d*. In fact, this was partly offset by over-payments: some thirty-five tenants in eighteen townships paid an excess amounting to £9 9*s* 6½*d*. To five men the bursar made an instant reimbursement, which reduced the excess to £9 6*s* 10*d*, but the others were given a credit 'for the following year' (*pro anno futuro*). As a result of these complications net income loss was reduced to £47 15*s* 4½*d*.

Most rent took the form of cash. In all, 226 rents were paid entirely in cash and a further 165 partly in cash and partly by other means. A total of 984 cash payments were made. In most cases this has to be assumed, since only the sum of money was noted. In 172 instances, however, payments were were said to be in coin (*in pecunia*), while 15 others were in silver (*in argento*) and 5 in gold (*in auro*). It may safely be assumed that payments other than those in gold were made in the five silver coins then in use – groat, half-groat, penny, half-penny and farthing – and that therefore there was no difference between 'in coin' and 'in silver'. And four of the five payments in gold (one of £4, one of £1, one of 6*s* 8*d*, and one of 5*s*) would almost certainly have been made in either the older denominations of 6*s* 8*d* or 3*s* 4*d*, or in the recently introduced ryal (10*s*), half-ryal (5*s*) or quarter-ryal (2*s* 6*d*). The fifth payment, however, was 8*s* 8*d* which could not be achieved by any combination of these coins.[43]

Where payments were made is in most instances not specified, but sufficient detail was recorded to give a very clear idea of the range of options available and used. In forty-seven cases the location was 'in the bursar's exchequer' (*in scaccario bursarii*), indicating that the tenant had made a special journey to pay his rent, or that he had come to Durham for some other reason. Payments were also on occasions received at the exchequers of the terrar and the commoner. More convenient, however, were the sessions of the prior's halmote court, suit of which was a tenurial obligation of all leasehold and many small freehold tenants. It met three times a year at three of the prior's manor houses – those used in 1495/6 were Aycliffe, Bewley and Pittington. In 120 cases the venue was specified or it was stated that the payment was made at the first, second or third tourn of the court. In many others payment was simply described as having been made 'at the court' (*ad curiam*), but there is no reason to doubt that this was intended to indicate a session of the halmote court. Also mentioned as places of payment, but without reference to this court, were the halls of manor houses at Jarrow, Monkwearmouth, Bewley, Pittington and Beaurepaire, the churches of Jarrow, Merrington and Aycliffe, and the chapels at Heworth and Ferryhill. All of these places were public or quasi-public buildings, but it is equally evident that payments were also made in private houses, as is indicated by such phases as 'at the table' (*ad mensam*) and 'in the house' (*in domo*), and occasionally in the open air, as at Monkton when one of the tenants, John Oxenhird, paid 8*s* 'at the plough' (*ad aratrum*).[44]

It was noted that this payment was made before the Master of Jarrow (*coram Magistro de Jarow*), and in very many other instances the names of a witness or witnesses to payments were recorded, clearly to safeguard both the tenant and the bursar's staff. It seems clear that whenever possible office-holders were used,

The church of St John the Baptist, Kirk Merrington, which was one of several where tenants paid their rents. The present building (erected in 1850) is a faithful replica of the twelfth-century original, using much of the old materials. (Photograph, Private Collection.)

since such men as manorial bailiffs, local clergy and members of the priory's administration frequently acted in this capacity. In most cases silence suggests that tenants paid in person, but there were also numerous occasions when it was explicitly stated that payment was made by relations, neighbours and, in the case of the well-to-do, servants.

Although cash was the most important rent element, 138 rents were paid entirely, and 165 partly, in produce or by other means. By far the most important of these was grain. In all, some 115 tenants in twenty-five places, including the manors, paid all or part of the rent in grain, and the apparent regularity of the arrangements indicates that that this was not accidental or haphazard but an agreed scheme mutually convenient to both the priory and its tenants. Payment in grain was not found throughout the estate, however. In particular, it was confined to the thirty-five core townships in County Durham, and within that group there was a heavy bias towards the southern region: none of the Tyneside townships and only two of those on Wearside were involved in the scheme. Essentially, it was from the townships south of the Wear that grain rents came, and there only from those tenants with substantial farms. In total, 428 quarters of wheat, 733 quarters of barley and 311 quarters of oats were acquired by these means, and these quantities covered virtually all of the priory's cereal needs for the year. But when the bursar came to make up his annual account (which he was required to present to the chapter for audit on the Monday after Ascension Day), he represented this process in a convoluted accounting device. In the 'receipt' section of his account he recorded all the income from tenants as though it had been paid entirely in cash. In the later 'expenditure' section, however, he recorded an apparent expenditure of cash on the purchase of grain. Thus what had been in reality a direct payment in kind became a fictitious two-stage process involving the receipt and expenditure of cash. The bursar's accounts, which are virtually complete for the years after 1360, indicate that this practice was well established by 1380. In most places barley was the predominant grain, but in Hesleden, Cowpen Bewley and Aycliffe wheat was rendered in greater quantities. The extent to which the various differences reflected differences in the agrarian potential of different parts of the county, or whether they were merely the outcome of an unrelated administrative arrangement, is impossible to determine from the rent book.

In an equal number of places rents were paid in livestock. The number of tenants involved, ninety-one, was smaller than those paying in grain, but they were more widely distributed. Also, in contrast to payments made in grain, those made in livestock appear to have been more occasional and, in some instances, may have stemmed from a lack of cash. They also extended into Northumberland. Indeed, all the rent payments by the Shoreswood tenants were in the form of animals, which suggests a marked leaning towards pastoral farming in the border country. Too much should not be read into this, however, since in Shoreswood, and indeed in all other townships in Norham and Holy Island parishes grain-growing is amply demonstrated by the tithe record. A similar inclination towards the pastoral could also be inferred for Tyneside in that seven tenants in Over Heworth and the lessee of Wardley Manor paid their rents in animals, but here too the grain-tithe evidence demonstrates an equal commitment to cereals. The two tenants in Crossgate borough who each paid a calf and the Gilesgate tenant who rendered five pullets may be evidence of small-scale urban milk and egg businesses. The total number of animals received cannot be calculated, but it was at least 479. The largest contingents were 199 sheep, 115 cattle and 104 items of poultry.

The next category of payment in kind, fish, was naturally more restricted in its distribution. Curiously, from the bursar's retained yares in the township bordering the Tyne, 54 per cent of the rent was paid in cash and only 26 per cent in fish. In contrast, virtually all the tenants in South Shields paid all of their rents in fish, while fish were rendered as part payment by nineteen other tenants in Nether Heworth, Hebburn, Harton and Westoe on the Tyne, Southwick, Fulwell and Monkwearmouth on the Wear, Cowpen Bewley and Billingham on the Tees, and Hesleden and Hartlepool on the coast, although the payments from the last two look to be occasional and not part of an organized scheme. As regards quantities, the bulk came from South Shields, which is not surprising given that it was a fishing village without any farm land. In all, South Shields supplied the priory with 28,000 red herring, 8 barrels of white herring and over 600 dogdraff (almost certainly cod). The total haul from elsewhere was much smaller: over 1,500 red herring, 300 dogdraff, 6 barrels of fish oil and small quantities of sprats from Billingham, and cockles and mussels from Cowpen Bewley. Finally, five tenants in three townships (Harton and Westoe on the Tyne and Southwick on the Wear) paid in salmon, mostly salted, but some fresh (*calor*).

The composition of the final category of food item is hard to identify with certainty. Some forty-four tenants in thirteen townships in central and southern Durham made small payments 'into the cellarer's book' (*in libro cellerarii*). What these were is not stated, but the evidence in the caterer's accounts suggest that such things as dairy produce and poultry were prominent. In addition, there were small quantities of two chemicals. In Cowpen Bewley, nine tenants paid rent in the form of salt, in total 306 bushels. As they also paid part of their rent in grain it is evident that salt-making was not their full-time occupation. Curiously, the lessees of the saltpans the bursar had retained in hand in Cowpen and South Shields paid their rents in cash and fish, not in salt. The other chemical was lime, which was rendered by two tenants, one in North Pittington, the other in Aycliffe. In total they furnished the priory with 16 chalders and 3 'cartloads' (*plaustrate*), the latter probably amounting to 60 bushels. The final tangible item paid by the tenants was cloth. Sixteen were involved, eleven of whom, not surprisingly, were in the boroughs of Crossgate, Elvet and the Bailey. In all, these rents yielded 235½ ells of cloth: 139½ ells of hardyn (coarse linen), 61 ells of linen (*pannus lineus*), 27 ells of white 'wayn' cloth (*pannus albus wayn*) and 12 ells of white cloth (*pannus albus*). Although the exact meaning to some of these terms is unclear, it is certain that the cloth was of a low grade since the bursar bought quality material for the monastic habits from Leeds.[45]

The remaining rents were paid in intangibles. Some sixty-one tenants in fourteen places made 105 payments in the form of labour. Fourteen of them were in the boroughs of Crossgate, Gilesgate, Elvet and the Bailey, and were probably craftsmen able to discharge some or all of their rent obligation in repair work. Almost all of the rest were in the very populous southern townships of Billingham, Wolviston, Aycliffe, Ferryhill and Kirk Merrington. Those in the last two were concerned almost exclusively with the pulling and carting of rushes. Several of those in Billingham and Wolviston were involved in the collecting and processing of tithe grain from the five places in the parish which were in the lord's hand, and there was sheep-shearing, presumably at the farm at Saltholme, and hay-making at a large meadow in Billingham called Frognell. In addition, a further twenty-seven tenants paid in the form of allowances from sums owed to them by the priory. In many cases the reason for the allowance is not clear, but in nine it was in lieu of some fee. Among this group was the important figure of John Raket, a member of a well-entrenched Durham administrative family, who was clerk of the exchequer and free court and prior's attorney at an annual fee of £6 13*s* 4*d*, which was paid by halving the rent of £13 6*s* 8*d* he owed for the lease of Houghall manor. Other priory officers so paid included Richard Conset, the

The former monastic granary in Durham Cathedral Close. The walls are medieval, but the windows and doorway belong to the conversion of the building to house the canon of the eighth stall in the post-Reformation secular cathedral. (Photograph, Private Collection.)

bailiff of Billingham, the priory's brewer, John Wynter, and the foresters of Aycliffe and Haining (Heworth). In all, these nine men were owed £13 18*s* 4*d* in stipends, of which all but £2 10*s* 0*d* was discharged by means of rent allowances.[46]

It was noted above that the bursar was unable to collect all his temporal rents. There was also a discrepancy between expected and realized grain-tithe income. Interestingly, the problem of shortfall lay largely in the parishes near at hand in County Durham, not in the more distant parishes 'beyond the waters'. Of the latter, those in Northumberland were sold for £69 6*s* 2*d* and realized all but 2*s*, while from those in Yorkshire the receipt of £59 3*s* 2*d* was greater by £1 16*s* 6*d* than the expected £57 6*s* 8*d*. In all, the parishes outwith the Tyne-Tees region realized £128 7*s* 4*d* as against an expectation of £126 12*s* 10*d*. In contrast, the value of the grain tithes 'between the waters' was £128 10*s* 5*d*, which was only 87 per cent of the expected sum of £147 17*s* 6*d*. This shortfall, however, was not uniformly distributed. Income from two parishes, Monkwearmouth and Aycliffe, actually exceeded expectation, but this was more than counterbalanced by deficits in Heighington and Merrington. Overall, tithe revenue, which should have been £274 10*s* 4*d*, was actually £247 5*s* 9*d*.

As regards the forms of payment, the parishes 'beyond the waters' paid exclusively in cash; only in County Durham was there any deviation. From parishes in Durham, £99 10*s* 0*d* was received in cash and £29 0*s* 5*d* in other items. Of the 173 payments made, 144 were in cash and only 29 in kind. Of these, sheep and cattle were the most valuable, realizing £11 4*s* 0*d* and £6 8*s* 8*d* respectively, while only £3 5*s* 2*d* worth of grain was taken. Thus, paradoxically, the bursar had so ordered his estate that many rents for land were paid in grain while what should have been grain rents were paid in cash. There can be no doubt that this was no accident, but there is no obvious explanation for it.

In discussing the lessees it is important to recognize that, even in the County Durham parishes, only seventeen of the twenty-six townships owing grain tithes were owned by the priory as landlord. This had serious implications in that, while the monks could, up to a point at least, dictate the farming policies of their own tenants, they had no influence over other landlords and their tenants. This they had recognized much earlier in the century when seeking to explain why there had been such a marked decline in their tithe income since the last decade of the thirteenth century.[47] Eight of the townships they did control were in Jarrow parish and another in Monkwearmouth, and there the grain tithes were leased to the tenants. In other words, the grain-tithe burden had been converted into a rent charge. By contrast, in Billingham, the other parish where priory control was complete, the tithes of all but one place were collected for the priory's use. In other places the priory's tenants figure, but not exclusively. Thus, at North Pittington, the tithes were leased by Thomas Bee, the largest tenant of the township, but at neighbouring South Pittington, which was rented to one man, John Henryson, the grain tithes were not leased to him but to a Thomas Riop who, though a tenant, held only an orchard in the Bailey. Henryson, however, did lease the tithes of the episcopal township of South Sherburn.[48] The one other point that needs to be made is that the same names occur over many years in the bursar's accounts, making it clear that some men were very actively engaged in getting a livelihood out of leasing tithes.

The arrangements in Northumberland were markedly different in two respects. Firstly, of the thirty-six townships in the four parishes whose tithes were owed to the bursar, only one, Shoreswood, was also a member of the temporal estate. There, grain tithes had been leased to the Sanderson family, the chief tenants of the township, since the 1430s.[49] Elsewhere the lessees were members of the local gentry. Most notable were Sir Robert Manners of Etal and Berrington and Sir Thomas Grey of Chillingham. The latter, who had leased the tithes of Norham, Norham Castle Mains, Horncliffe, Twizel and Felkington, was the cousin of the newly appointed bishop, Richard Fox, and held the offices of sheriff and keeper of Norham. Without doubt, he was the most powerful man in the district.[50] The use of such dignitaries suggests that the bursar had adopted the realistic policy of reaching an accommodation with local men who were willing to buy the tithe rights from him and who had the power to ensure that their bargains were profitable. The same policy is visible at Northallerton, where the grain tithe of the entire parish was leased to William Mountford (Meniforth in the rent book), who was the bishop's receiver in Allertonshire and therefore a man of local standing and authority.[51]

It is important to note that the income recorded in the rent book does not include that received in kind from the four townships and the farm in Billingham parish and the two townships in Heighington parish. These yielded 153 quarters 6 bushels of wheat, 133 quarters 2 bushels of barley, 44 quarters 4 bushels of oats, 8 quarters 7 bushels of rye and 46 quarters of peas and beans. In 1495/6 values were on the low side: wheat and rye 4*s* a quarter, barley 3*s* a quarter, oats 1*s* 3*d* a quarter, and peas and beans 2*s* a quarter, but even so the value of the tithes 'in the lord's hands' was £66 10*s* 7½*d*, and it would have been greater had not 77 quarters of oats and peas been retained at source 'for expenses of horse fodder' (*pro expensis prebendi equorum*).[52]

The remaining spiritual income came from the seven pensions and amounted to £32 18*s* 4*d*, of which £27 came from the the bursar's colleague, the hostillar. All seven entries were awarded the 'quit' sign in the left-hand margin, but the absence of any payment details in three cases, including that of the hostillar, raises doubt as to whether they were paid. If these doubts are suppressed, however, the total income from spiritual sources rises to £367 12*s* 9½*d*, and it would have been £394 16*s* 4½*d* had there not been a shortfall in tithe income.

The total would have risen by £74 19*s* 11½*d* to £1263 16*s* 10¼*d* had all income been collected. Nevertheless, the bursar had succeeded in securing 94 per cent of his charge, a not inconsiderable achievement. And the absence of this income does not seriously distort the significant fact that only 57 per cent receipts were in cash, the remaining 43 per cent being in goods of one sort or another (Table 6.1). The final question, therefore, is whether this was a desired arrangement, or a situation into which he had been forced by the conditions of the time. In favour of the latter is the severe shortage of bullion in the middle decades of the century, resulting in an under-provision of coin by the government. Although the currency situation improved towards the end of the century, the output of the mints, which included that of the Bishop in Durham, may still have been

Table 6.1

The bursar of Durham Priory's total income from rents, 1495/6

	temporal rights			*spiritual rights*			*total*		
	£	*s*	*d*	£	*s*	*d*	£	*s*	*d*
cash	402	1	5¼	280	4	1	682	5	6¼
grain	316	16	10	3	5	2	320	2	0
animals	75	13	10½	19	9	4	95	3	2½
fish	31	13	7	1	6	3	32	19	10
'into the cellarer's book'	13	18	1	0	4	0	14	2	1
lime	1	7	10	1	16	8	3	4	6
salt	6	8	10	0	0	0	6	8	10
cloth	3	14	7	0	0	0	3	14	7
labour	14	9	6	0	4	0	14	13	6
deducted from fees	11	10	2	4	12	8	16	2	10
total	**887**	**14**	**8¾**	**301**	**2**	**2**	**1188**	**16**	**10¾**

insufficient for the needs of the economy.[53] If so, then it is possible that some tenants at least would have been hard pushed to guarantee to meet their rent obligation entirely in cash. In this situation the alternative was payment in kind. There are hints in the rent book that this was indeed the case.

Against this argument, however, are the many tenants who paid entirely in cash, notably those in the Tyneside townships, where it would be difficult to argue that coin was more abundant or more easily come by than elsewhere in the region. The same reasoning applies to the majority of the lessees of grain tithes. Moreover, it has to be recognized that for the bursar, payment in kind meant that he was able to acquire much or all he needed of certain basic commodities by a direct one-stage transaction that was inherently more efficient than the two-stage process of collecting cash rent and then having to resort to what may have been an uncertain and unmanageable market. This explanation rings true as regards fish, lime and salt; and as regards grain it is rendered almost certain by the evidence that the bursars began the practice of obtaining most of their cereal requirements from their tenants as far back as the 1380s: the arrangements visible in the 1495/6 rent book far from being novel were deeply traditional.[54] Consequently, while currency shortage may occasionally have made it necessary for some tenants to pay in kind, it will not serve as a simple and general explanation of the rent system the bursar of Durham operated in 1495/6.

CHAPTER 7

Artisans, Guilds and Government in London

MATTHEW DAVIES

On 27 June 1477 the London mercers met to discuss the events surrounding the arrival of the ambassadors of France and Scotland in the capital earlier that month. While not as significant an event as the celebrated royal entries of Henry V after his victory at Agincourt, or that of Henry VI following his coronation in France in 1432, the importance of the diplomatic process underway in 1477 made it just as vital for the city to put on a splendid show for its guests.[1] As a result it was decided to summon a 'gretter wache', or guard of honour, to be made up of representatives of the city's crafts (selected by their wardens), who were to line the processional route wearing specially commissioned livery robes of 'oon suet of pluncket blew', a similar colour to that chosen in 1445 for the reception of Margaret of Anjou. Unfortunately, not all the crafts were prepared to cooperate in this show of civic unity, for, according to the mercers, instead of the blue robes specified by the mayor 'the Tayllours had made them Jackettes of cremysyn'.[2] The tailors could scarcely have made themselves more distinctive on such an occasion, and the fact that their actions were discussed by the mercers' court shows the seriousness with which this breach of protocol was viewed in some quarters. It is possible that the tailors' choice of dress formed part of some sort of protest, perhaps against an ordinance passed by the city government, or alternatively it may have been designed to upstage one or more of the other crafts.

The promotion of private grievances and rivalries within the context of civic ceremonial was of course nothing new in late medieval England and often threatened to undermine the social cohesion aspired to by the urban authorities who organized the colourful processions and rituals on feast days and other occasions.[3] Tensions between groups of artisans and merchants were especially common and derived much of their bitterness from a merging of purely economic concerns, such as arguments over the precise boundaries between occupations, with less tangible issues of social status and political influence within the urban community. In late fifteenth- and early sixteenth-century London there were disputes over precedence between a number of the city's crafts, including the mercers and grocers, who in 1477 squabbled over standing places along the processional route near St Paul's Cathedral. Other disagreements took place between the shearmen and dyers, whose longstanding rivalry stemmed from the close relationship between their trades, and between the salters and ironmongers, who argued over the relative positions each should occupy in London's increasingly rigid craft hierarchy.[4] These disputes were, of course, not simply between loosely defined groups of citizens, for by this time the vast majority of London's crafts or 'misteries' were headed by guilds, formal associations of the most prosperous artisans and merchants within each craft. Involvement in civic ceremonial, such as the annual processions accompanying the election of the mayor and sheriffs, or a special occasion such as a royal entry into the city, was generally the preserve of members of these élite groups, dressed in their livery robes and hoods, rather than the wider body of citizens. Nevertheless, the tensions which emerged during these events often reflected the ways in which the guilds were able to 'represent' the interests and aspirations of those who were not members, employing their impressive resources in pursuit of their objectives. It is the intention here to look at several aspects of the development and composition of these organizations in the fifteenth century and to examine their relationship with the city authorities, both in terms of their functions as valuable tools of urban government, and as vehicles for the expression of economic and other concerns which, in many cases, sprang from the day-to-day experiences of those who made and sold their goods in the capital.

The growth of what would later be known as the London livery companies has been well documented by George Unwin and others, as well as in numerous histories of individual companies, antiquarian and modern. The trail was blazed by those crafts which later came to make up the bulk of the Great Twelve livery companies, a group headed by the mercers and grocers and completed by the rise of the haberdashers in the second half of the fifteenth century and the incorporation of the fullers and shearmen as the Clothworkers' Company in 1528.[5] Organization within many of these trades had its origins in the thirteenth century and was probably encouraged by the formalizing of the city's custom whereby the freedom could only be obtained through one of the recognized misteries. Elspeth Veale has emphasized the variety of the early associations set up by the craftsmen of London: some, for instance, began as parish fraternities which were dominated by the more successful practitioners of particular crafts, and which were subsequently able to take on regulatory responsibility for the craft as a whole. Among these was the skinners' fraternity, dedicated to the feast of Corpus Christi, whose membership expanded during the course of the fourteenth century to include all prominent London skinners, not just those who lived in the Walbrook and Budge Row areas of the city.[6] Other fraternities were founded by the goldsmiths and by the tailors, whose Guild of St John the Baptist was perhaps the most successful of these organizations. By 1400 the tailors had acquired two royal charters, a hall with a chapel and a second chapel in St Paul's Cathedral, and they had confraternal relations with several religious houses in and around London. Their activities were founded on extensive property holdings in the city which, by the mid-fifteenth century, made up more than two-thirds of a corporate income now well in excess of £200 per annum.

As a consequence of these institutional developments, and the perceived social and spiritual benefits of affiliation, the fifteenth century saw the acquisition of a large and influential membership from outside the tailoring craft, a feature of several other guilds including those founded by the brewers and skinners. This was taken to extremes by the tailors, and between 1398 and 1470 more than 1,200 non-tailors joined on payment of a 20*s* entry fee. The membership included prominent clergy, noblemen and women, well-connected gentry such as Sir John Fastolf and John Paston, as well as members of other London crafts who sought to share in the abundant 'goostly tresoure' built up over the years. Members among the aristocracy and royal family were often recruited for political reasons: Humphrey, Duke of Gloucester, for instance, assisted the tailors during a bitter dispute with the drapers in the 1430s. Likewise, after the accession of Edward IV, membership of the fraternity was granted to George, Duke of Clarence, and Richard, Duke of Gloucester. This paved the way for the grant of a fourth charter to the guild in 1464.[7]

The uniqueness of the association created by the London tailors should not obscure the fact that by 1400 a pattern had emerged as far as the essentials of organization within the city's crafts were concerned, and the principles upon which they were based. Heading many of the misteries by this time were exclusive associations of the more successful artisans or merchants, whose wardens had long exercised a wider authority over their respective crafts on behalf of the city's government. Members of these associations often wore livery gowns and hoods on ceremonial occasions and in due course were known as the 'liverymen' of their crafts, a status which often provided a stepping-stone to office within the craft or in the city administration. Outside these groups lay the great majority of freemen, of whom only a small number were destined to become liverymen. As we have seen, the status of a liveryman was often synonymous with membership of a formally constituted fraternity, such as the goldsmiths' Fraternity of St Dunstan, or the tailors' Fraternity of St John the Baptist, whose activities were often sanctioned by royal letters patent. In other cases, most notably the vintners, ironmongers and mercers, those freemen who wore the livery, though never formally identified as a fraternity, were nevertheless clearly distinct from the rest of the freemen, and as such also acquired letters patent and often exercised similar social and religious functions, including the administration of chantries, the provision of charity to liverymen and their families, and the employment of chaplains, activities usually funded out of large property endowments.[8] Indeed, by the fifteenth century the similarities in structure and ethos between many of these organizations were much more apparent than the differences of emphasis which had been a concomitant part of their development from the mid-thirteenth century.

The fifteenth century itself saw two further important organizational developments within London's crafts, which also served to emphasize the extent to which guilds such as those of the skinners, tailors, grocers and goldsmiths were providing a model for the rest to follow. First, there was a growing trend towards the creation of formal organizations for those freemen outside the livery, such as

Admissions to the Tailors' fraternity of St John the Baptist in 1444–5. Prominent individuals named here include Sir Thomas Hoo, Sir John Fastolf and the Abbot of Bermondsey, as well as a number of London merchants and artisans. (Guildhall Library, Merchant Taylors' Company, London, Accounts, vol. 1, f. 388. By permission of the Merchant Taylors' Company, London.)

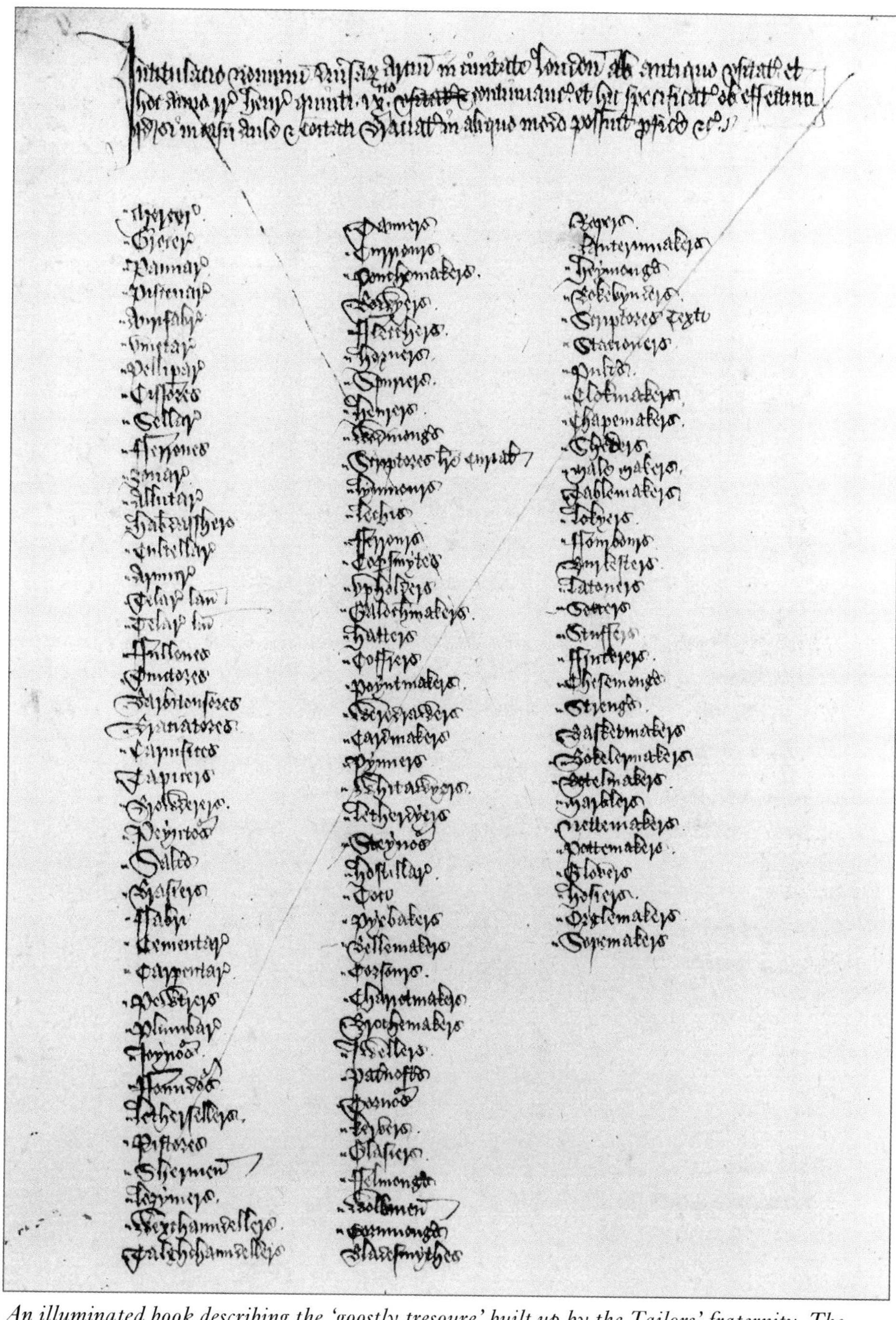

An illuminated book describing the 'goostly tresoure' built up by the Tailors' fraternity. The master and wardens listed served in 1456–7, but the book was probably compiled c. *1510. At the Reformation the particulars of indulgences, confraternal links with religious houses and the foundation of a chapel in St Paul's Cathedral were crossed out. (Guildhall Library, Merchant Taylors' Company, London, Ancient MS Books, vol. 2, f. 17. By permission of the Merchant Taylors' Company, London.)*

the Fraternity of the Assumption which was founded by the skinners as an association for the majority of freemen who were not members of the Corpus Christi Fraternity. Principles of association among the lesser freemen of the crafts were nothing new, although in the late fourteenth century the reputation of such groups was tarnished by the subversive activities of servants and journeymen of the saddlers, cordwainers and other crafts who strove to force up wages through collective action.[9] Incidents such as these were partly responsible for the governmental inquiry of 1388–9 into the activities of guilds and fraternities, an exercise which prompted several of London's craft organizations to acquire letters patent in order to protect their positions. Against this background it was unlikely that fraternities of 'yeomen' or 'bachelors' could expect recognition by the craft or city authorities. Yet by the early fifteenth century hostility to these 'illegal' associations had more or less abated, and the process of assimilation into London's craft structure began in earnest. When, in 1417, some yeomen of the tailors caused disturbances in the Garlickhithe area of the city, they were not disowned by the elders of the guild, who in fact contributed £2 13*s* 4*d* for their supplication to the mayor and aldermen (*lour supplicacion direct as mair et aldermanis*). This enlightened approach probably stemmed from the common ground that existed between the yeomen tailors, many of whom were shop-holders in their own right, and members of the senior guild, to whose status they increasingly aspired. In other crafts, however, yeomen were still predominantly wage-labourers and hence attracted less sympathy: in 1441 the bakers' guild took action against 'the company of the servantes Bakeres' who were alleged to have met together in a 'revelyng hall' as part of a campaign to achieve shorter working hours and higher wages.[10] Nevertheless, the growing respectability of the majority of these groups meant that by the sixteenth century the typical livery company was normally made up of two bodies: a livery and a dependent association for the rest of the freemen. Office-holding within the latter became an important part of the *cursus honorum* for an aspirant artisan or merchant and was often a precursor to admission as a liveryman.[11] A second structural development was the emergence of formal Courts of Assistants, made up of the most influential liverymen, which acted as governing bodies for both the livery and for the mistery as a whole. Their origins lay in the groups of senior artisans and merchants who, from at least the early fourteenth century, were appointed by the city to assist the wardens of the crafts in their 'searches' for defective workmanship.[12] By the fifteenth century their status was formalized among some of the greater guilds, such as those of the mercers and grocers, and the principle was subsequently taken up by the lesser crafts, such as the shearmen, who had such a body by 1452. The tailors' court was in existence by 1435 when the sixteen assistants listed in a book of ordinances included nine who had already held the office of master of the fraternity. By the 1480s it had grown to a body of twenty-four and meetings were held at least once a week for the purpose of enrolling apprentices, drawing up ordinances and resolving disputes between craftsmen.[13]

These further refinements took place at a time when an increasing number of the lesser misteries also began to develop formal hierarchies and to embrace the concept of a 'livery' for the most prominent men and a 'yeomanry' for the other

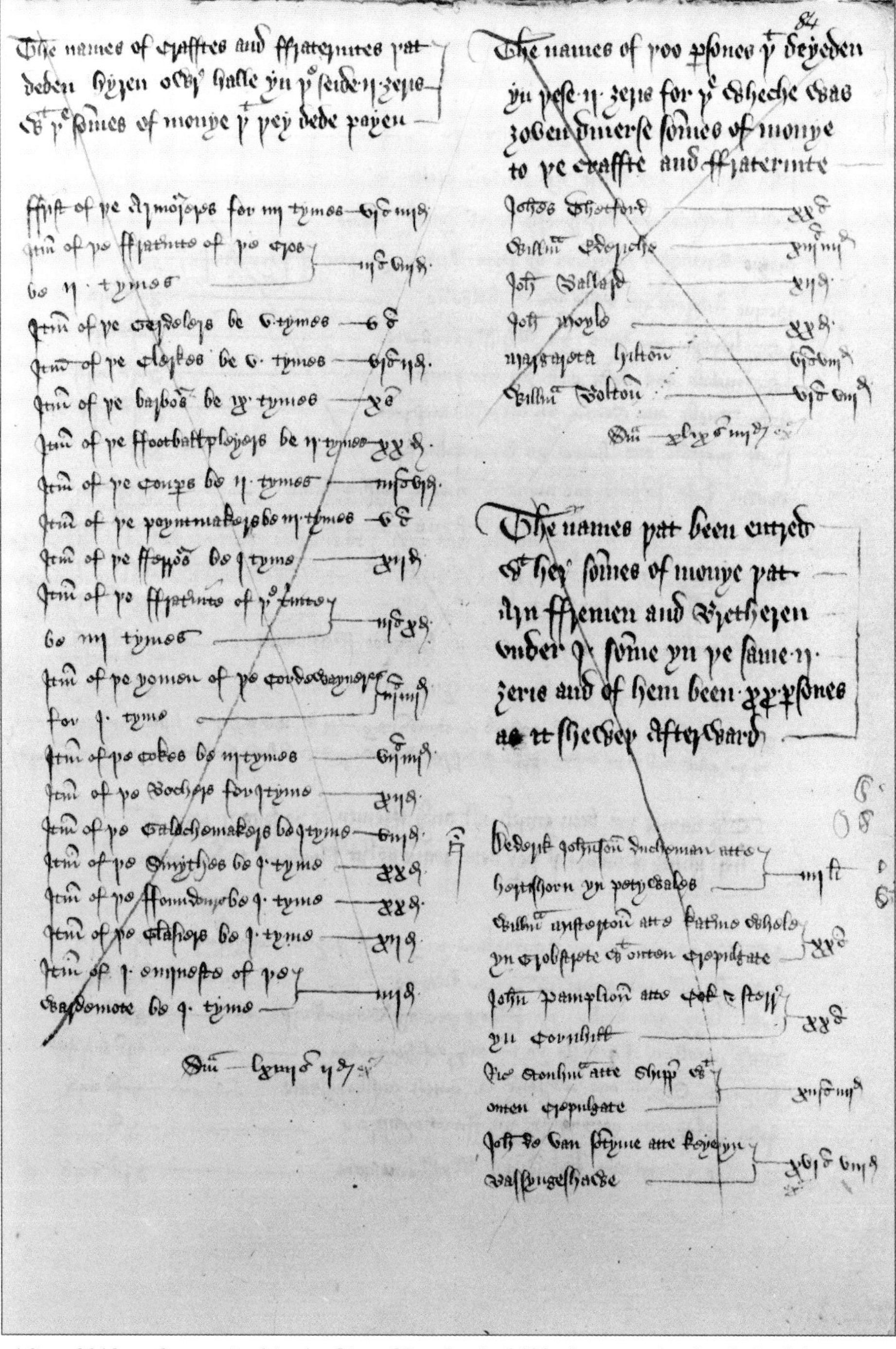

A list of 112 crafts practised in the City of London in 1422, drawn up by the clerk of the Brewers' Company. (Guildhall Library, MS 5440, f. 11v. By permission of the Worshipful Company of Brewers, London.)

freemen. In the absence of medieval records for many of these companies, this movement is not always easy to trace: contemporary lists of the city's crafts, such as the 112 misteries named by the brewers' clerk in 1422, certainly demonstrate the diversity of economic life in the capital, but are poor guides to the development of internal structures within trades as diverse as the fellmongers and the soapmakers. On the other hand, the brewers' accounts also show that groups of artisans, including the girdlers, barbers and coopers, were using their hall as a meeting place in the 1420s, suggesting that these may have been guilds which had not yet acquired halls of their own or the accoutrements of their more prosperous counterparts.[14] The records of the city government can prove similarly frustrating, concentrating as they do upon the economic regulation of the crafts rather than their internal organization, which, as far as possible, guilds tried to keep to themselves. Following an Act of Parliament of 1437, for instance, more than thirty crafts submitted their ordinances to the mayor for ratification. However, in only a few cases is it known whether the wardens who presented them exercised authority as officers of a formal craft association as well as the authority over the mistery as a whole which they discharged on behalf of the mayor.[15]

Occasionally, the level of organization within a craft is revealed by the city's intervention in internal debates: in 1466 the annual election of the wardens of the butchers was disputed by some of the freemen, and so in September that year the mayor and aldermen ruled that only those who wore the livery of the craft were to participate in such elections. The masons, on the other hand, allowed all their freemen to participate in the election of officials, although their petition reveals that they also had a separate livery.[16] Even regulations concerning trade practices could sometimes touch on such matters. In December 1482 ordinances presented by the brewers contained a requirement that new liveries were to be bought every three years and that liverymen were each to be given a sample of cloth which they were to take to their local cloth merchant in order to get the exact shade required.[17] More tangible information arises from the efforts of craft organizations to get external sanction for their activities, particularly in the form of royal charters. In the first half of the century these were acquired only by well-established guilds, such as those of the grocers, drapers and tailors, for whom these were confirmations of existing grants, but in the reigns of Edward IV, Richard III and Henry VII guilds within less prominent crafts, such as the tallow-chandlers, bakers, pewterers, dyers, fullers, cutlers and cooks, gained their first charters, confirming their jurisdiction over their crafts and formally permitting them to hold land, raise revenues from their members and enjoy the other benefits of corporate existence within the City of London. Needless to say, many of these guilds had in fact been in existence, albeit without such formal approval, for many years and so, however celebrated these events were at the time or since, they are rarely an accurate guide to the origins of a particular livery company.[18]

The fortunes of these guilds varied greatly. While some were able to follow in the footsteps of the drapers, tailors and the like, others were unable to establish themselves in the face of changing economic conditions, increasing immigration into the city, as well as the ever-present rivalries between the crafts. The effects of recession prompted the horners and bottlemakers to petition the Court of

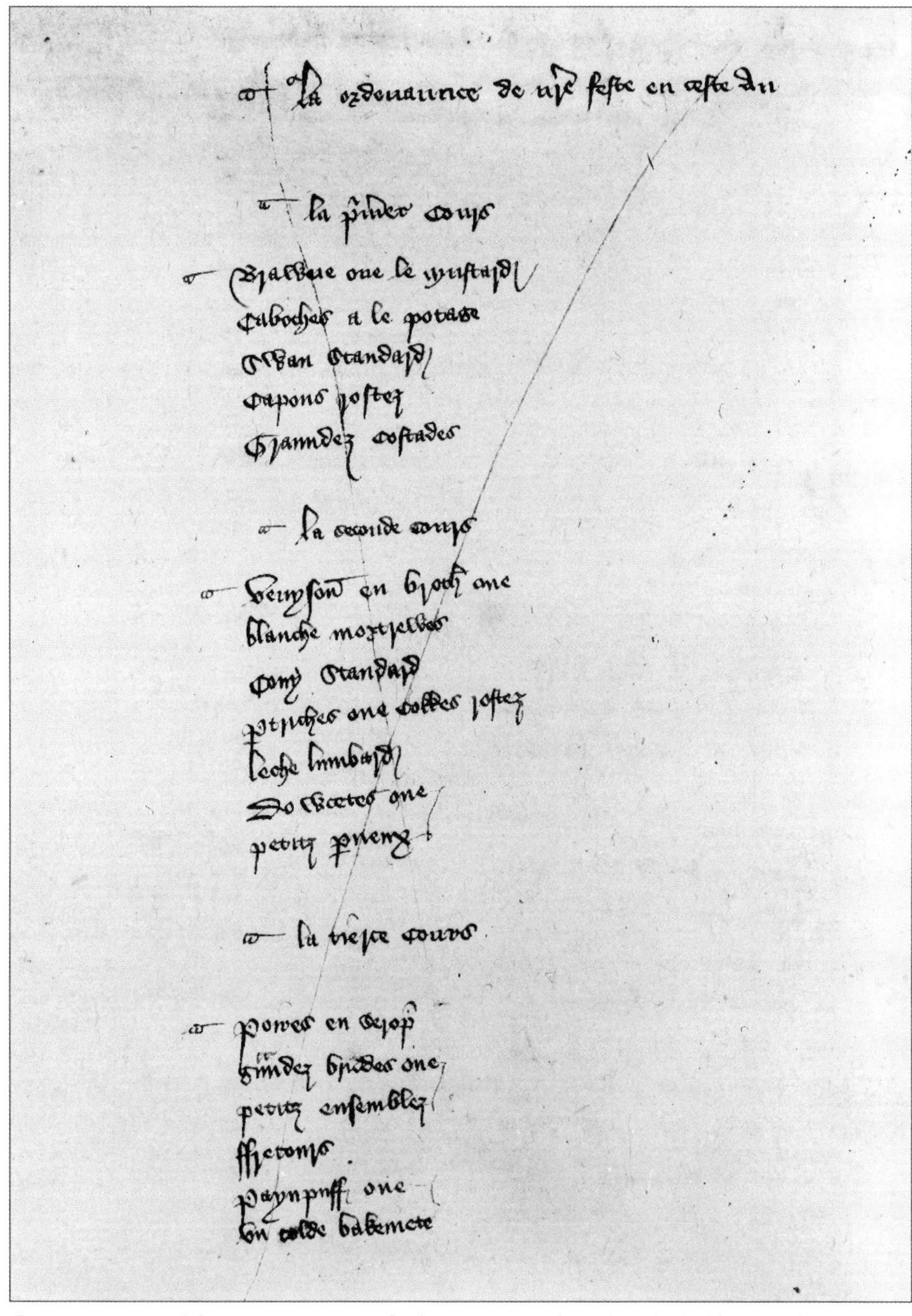
La ordenaunce de une feste en cestre an

La primer cours

Brawne oue le mustard
Caboches a le potage
Swan standard
Capons rostez
Chawndez custades

La seconde cours

Venyson en broth oue
blanche mortrelles
Cony standard
Perches oue cokkes rostez
Leche lumbard
Doucettes oue
petitz pernez

La tierce cours

Powes en dorre
Sindez briddes oue
petitz ensemblez
ffretours
Paynpuff oue
un colde bakemete

*Payments received from various groups for hiring Brewers' Hall in the 1420s, including the sum of 1*s *8*d *(20*d*) received 'of þe ffootballpleyers be ii tymes'. (Guildhall Library, MS 5440, f. 84. By permission of the Worshipful Company of Brewers, London.)*

Aldermen in March 1476, protesting that they were unable to meet their financial obligations to the city and so should be permitted to combine as one mistery.[19] This period witnessed several similar mergers between crafts: in 1479, for instance, the wiredrawers and chapemakers joined together to form the wiremongers, and in 1497 the wiremongers themselves were forced to merge with the pinners to form a new mistery to be known as the wiresellers.[20] In some cases these changes were a recognition that the distinctions between certain crafts had become eroded over time: the realities of the urban economy meant that there was inevitably some conflict between occupations which employed similar skills and materials, or those whose members were actively seeking to expand their activities into closely related areas of production. Economic changes also meant that those crafts which were doing well were able to take advantage of the relative weakness of others. The most dramatic instance of this was the rise of the haberdashers who, during their journey towards membership of the Great Twelve, swallowed up both the hatters and the cappers, whose guilds had been at loggerheads for many years.[21] On the other hand, most guilds managed to protect their positions at the head of their crafts, despite the threats posed by ambitious rivals, and distinctions between them were further reinforced by numerous instances of citizens who sought formally to 'translate' their freedoms from one craft to another. The decisions of three fifteenth-century tailors to translate their freedoms to the drapers probably reflected increasing involvement by many tailors in the cloth trade, as well as a certain amount of social ambition.[22]

By the mid-fifteenth century membership of a guild within a craft was becoming increasingly recognized, not merely as an indication of wealth and standing within one's own mistery, but also as a means by which involvement in the wider affairs of the city could be regulated. An ordinance passed by the Court of Aldermen in September 1475 established that the annual election of the mayor and sheriffs was to be attended by the masters and wardens of the city's misteries and by the 'good men of the same', who, for the first time, were defined as those who were liverymen of their respective crafts. This ordinance superseded one of 1467 which did not refer to liverymen directly, but merely to 'other good men specially summoned'.[23] This was one of several measures promulgated by the city in the later fifteenth century in an attempt to clarify methods of election of officials and thereby define more clearly the social and political bases of the government of the metropolis. Other towns and cities in England were engaged in a similar process: part of the problem for many urban administrations was the very lack of formal rules and definitions of what constituted 'political society', and consequently of who was entitled to a role in government.[24] English towns in the fourteenth and fifteenth centuries witnessed several instances when competing definitions of 'worthies' (*probi homines*) resulted in conflict, often centred on elections. Reforms to the electoral process in late fifteenth-century Leicester, for instance, narrowed the elective body to just forty-eight of the most substantial commoners, to be chosen by the ruling council. This, it was argued, would prevent the frequent disturbances caused by the attendance of large numbers of people at elections. However, the effect of this constitutional change was to provoke the unofficial election of a rival candidate for the mayoralty by those now excluded from the political process.[25] London was beset by similar debates: much of the political instability of the capital in the fourteenth and fifteenth centuries was related in some way to the vagueness of its constitution, which could be exploited by ambitious groups and individuals. As Sylvia Thrupp noted, the legacy of the thirteenth century was a constitutional framework which 'was little better than a confused accumulation of ambiguous precedent and privilege'. For instance, while citizens were recognized as a distinct group within London, with the right to appoint their mayor and sheriffs, the charters granted to the city never defined the methods of election.[26] Before the later fifteenth century the right of attendance at city elections in London had generally been allowed to the 'more sufficient' men of the city, whose definition was never formally settled and hence became a focus for discontent among the wider body of freemen.[27] The bitter conflict between the drapers and tailors in the 1430s began as a trade dispute, but escalated into a wider political movement led by prominent artisans who felt unjustly excluded from governmental processes by the predominantly mercantile oligarchy.[28] From the second half of the fifteenth century onwards some important constitutional changes took place which, as Ian Archer has shown, laid the foundations for the relative stability of London's government in the later sixteenth century. Election procedures were clarified and came to reflect a balance between the perceived rights and duties of the élite, with participation by the more substantial citizens in mayoral elections and by all freemen in vestry meetings and wardmotes. The Common Council grew in size from a body of 96 in the later fourteenth century to 187 by 1460 and 212 by the reign of Elizabeth.[29] The ordinance of 1475 therefore reflected the extent to which guild membership, at whatever level, had become a widespread and important signifier of status, both within the community of the craft and in the city as a whole; the movement towards organization within the crafts, which began in the thirteenth century, had, at last, become integrated into the capital's formal governmental mechanisms. It perhaps also went some way towards involving artisans from lesser crafts in the political process, for apart from two periods in the late fourteenth century the Common Council had always been made up of prominent inhabitants of the wards (who were generally members of the wealthiest guilds), rather than men from the broader economic spectrum represented by the misteries, as was the case in some other towns and cities.[30]

Membership of the livery of a craft brought with it both privileges and obligations in the public as well as the private sphere and as such was normally highly prized by ambitious craftsmen and merchants. Any assessment of the role of these exclusive bodies must take account of the social and economic characteristics of those who were admitted to them in our period and of the policies introduced by the guilds to determine the nature of their memberships. Most evident from the records of the guilds are financial criteria for admission as a liveryman. This in part reflected the fact that the obligations of membership were not to be taken lightly: a liveryman was typically required to buy a livery gown and hood, sometimes every year, make quarterly alms payments and contribute to levies for civic projects, loans to the Crown, or to building projects, such as the growing number of halls, chapels and almshouses that were being

A menu for the annual feast held by the Tailors on the Nativity of St John the Baptist in 1429. (Merchant Taylors' Company, London, Accounts, vol. 1, f. 212. By permission of the Merchant Taylors' Company, London.)

built in fifteenth-century London.[31] Beyond this, attendance at feasts, memorial Masses and processions was often obligatory, with fines levied on those who failed to appear. In 1445 thirty-nine liverymen of the tailors, as well as ninety-four yeomen, were fined for failing to turn up to welcome Margaret of Anjou to London.[32] Occasionally liverymen sought relief from the burdens of membership because of their straitened circumstances: one tailor, John Baynard, paid his guild 3*s* 4*d* 'to be excused of the maistres clothyng thys yer'. Such leniency was balanced by a strict approach to recruitment, which led the mercers to impose a £10 fine on those men, deemed to be eligible, who refused to join the livery.[33] In the light of these obligations it is perhaps not surprising that men who had obtained the freedom by redemption (through the payment of several pounds to the City Chamber) were much more likely to become liverymen than those who had served an apprenticeship. More than a third of the redemptioners whose freedoms are recorded in the fifteenth-century accounts of the tailors went on to join the Guild of St John the Baptist, whereas no more than 15 or 20 per cent of newly qualified apprentices could ever expect to wear the livery of their craft.[34] Wealth was clearly an important criterion for admission, and one which frequently had to be articulated formally. Just as the government of the city was starting to clarify its constitution in the second half of the fifteenth century, so too did many guilds begin to be more specific about the standing of their members. Both the fullers and the carpenters of London, by no means the wealthiest of crafts, introduced property qualifications of £13 6*s* 8*d* (20 marks) for admission to the livery.[35]

Other admissions policies introduced by guilds included hereditary preference, often proposed because of concern at the influx and employment of cheap labour from areas outside London. In September 1459, for instance, the mercers introduced a lower charge of 2*s* for the sons of their freemen who wished to be admitted to the freedom.[36] Yet despite the visibility of a few wealthy families it is clear that such connections never came to dominate London's guilds. Sylvia Thrupp demonstrated that the overwhelming trend among the sons of aldermen was to follow an occupation other than that of their fathers, and indeed London as a whole showed none of the dynastic tendencies of Italian cities such as Florence; there were certainly few 'aldermanic families' in London.[37] Jean Imray's analysis of the membership of the Mercers' Company during this period showed that only 155 out of 1,047 freemen shared a surname with a fellow freeman. Admission to the freedom by patrimony accounted for very few of the mercers' freemen and was itself in decline in the city as a whole from the mid-fourteenth century as apprenticeship gained in popularity as a route to the freedom.[38] Although the sons of lesser merchants and artisans probably had fewer opportunities to choose an alternative occupation to that of their fathers, evidence from other guilds, such as the tailors, suggests that they too chose other paths, and that consequently any informal policy that did exist to keep sons in the trade had only a marginal impact upon the composition of London's crafts.[39]

In so far as connections played a part in admission to the livery of a craft in fifteenth-century London, it was the bond between master and apprentice that was by far the most important. In particular, it is clear that the status of one's master was crucial to the chances of an apprentice making any progress within the craft. In the case of the tailors, for instance, surviving records for apprenticeship enrolments and admissions to the livery demonstrate that former apprentices of liverymen appear to have enjoyed a distinct, and increasing, advantage over their peers, at each stage in their occupational careers (see Table 1). As a result, more than three-quarters of the sixty-one apprentices who eventually entered the Fraternity of St John the Baptist had originally been enrolled by liverymen.

Table 7.1

The 'sponsored mobility' of tailors' apprentices, 1425–45, 1453–8

	number enrolled	*future masters*	*future liverymen*
apprentices of liverymen	893 (57%)	139 (69%)	47 (77%)
apprentices of other freemen	666 (43%)	63 (31%)	14 (23%)
totals	**1559** (100%)	**202** (100%)	**61** (100%)

Source: Merchant Taylors' Company, London, Accounts, vols 1–2. Table 1 also demonstrates the high drop-out rates among the fifteenth-century apprentices of the Tailors, for which see Davies, 'The Tailors of London and their Guild', pp. 181–205.

This pattern of 'sponsored mobility' is by no means surprising, though data of this kind are rarely forthcoming from the records of English craft guilds in this period. For a start, young men apprenticed to liverymen often owed their placement to the influence of well-connected parents who could often afford to make a significant financial contribution to their training. Likewise, liverymen were inherently more likely to possess the resources to set their former apprentices up in business, whether through the advancement of loans, or the provision of sub-contracted work and other paid employment when times were hard. There was an in-built tendency for the well-connected to succeed, but this was as much a product of economic realities as any predisposition on the part of the guilds themselves. Unlike the ties of family, however, the impact of these bonds could often last for more than one generation. The controversial alderman, Ralph Holland, leader of the radical artisan movement of the 1430s, presented Robert Colwich as his apprentice in 1440. Colwich went on to have a distinguished career: he was elected master of the tailors' guild in 1460 and served as city chamberlain from 1463 until 1474, when he too was chosen as an alderman. Colwich's own apprentice, Walter Povy, became master of the guild in 1492 after a successful career during which he became one of an increasing number of members of the livery to engage in overseas trade. For Povy and Colwich, therefore, the status and wealth of their masters were probably vital ingredients in their subsequent success. In his will, proved in 1503, Povy asked to be buried in the church of St Mary Aldermary, close to the tomb of Ralph Holland, whom he evidently regarded as a kind of 'occupational grandfather'.[40]

As Table 1 shows, the status of a liveryman was something to which very few newly enrolled apprentices could aspire. Admission to a guild within one of London's crafts was a jealously guarded privilege, and guild authorities frequently felt it necessary to tighten their criteria for entry when necessary. In the case of the grocers, Pamela Nightingale has argued that the effects of economic recession in the early 1460s prompted the guild to implement a series of measures to safeguard the status of liverymen and to restrict the numbers of apprentices taken on by freemen. Worries of this kind were not confined to the predominantly mercantile crafts: in 1490 the tailors' court complained that some of those admitted to the fraternity were not 'in substaunce of goods as it hath bene supposed whereby they have lytely fallen into the almes of this fraternity'.[41] In fact the Fraternity of St John the Baptist was, in numerical terms, already a far more exclusive body in 1490 than it had been in the early years of the century. Admissions to the livery remained relatively static throughout the period, at about eight men per annum, despite a significant expansion of the craft as a whole in London, which saw the number of tailors taking on apprentices rise from forty-two each year in 1425 to well over a hundred in the early 1460s. The consequences of this trend towards greater exclusiveness depended on both the size and structure of particular crafts, and also on the extent to which the distinction between those in the livery and those outside it reflected differences in economic activity. Some predominantly artisan occupations, for instance, came to be headed by a natural oligarchy of merchants who supplied raw materials to the rest of the freemen. This would appear to have been the case with the London skinners in the fifteenth century: Elspeth Veale has argued for the dependent relationship between artisan skinners (few of whom were members of the senior guild) and the merchant skinners, who dominated the Corpus Christi Fraternity. Guild policies were geared towards the interests of the merchants, in particular to ensure that artisan skinners bought their furs from them rather than from itinerant dealers.[42] Elsewhere, however, the distinction in terms of economic function between members of the ruling guild and those outside was much less clear, despite apparent similarities in size and structure. Although many members of the tailors' guild were becoming more active in the cloth trade by the 1480s, sources of supply in London were too many and varied for them to achieve any kind of monopoly in the provision of raw materials to the large numbers of artisans engaged in the manufacture of clothing. Furthermore, the relatively low capital costs incurred in setting up and running a tailoring shop meant that a high proportion of the freemen as a whole were able to establish successful businesses, whereas artisans within the metal-working trades would often have to invest sizeable sums of money in order to buy the necessary equipment. As a result, it is likely that a higher proportion of freemen in such crafts were forced to work as wage labourers than was the case with the tailors or skinners. For an ironmonger or a founder the acquisition of a business was doubtless a significant achievement, which for many, if not most, may have led to admission to the guild.[43]

Such variations in the size and structure of London's crafts need to be borne in mind when considering the functions performed by the guilds, and the nature of their evolving relationship with the city government. For instance, were the many petitions submitted to the Court of Aldermen by craft officials in the fifteenth century merely the self-interested demands of liverymen or did they in fact represent the wider concerns of artisans working in those industries? Essential to our understanding of this representative role is the recognition that guilds were not merely vehicles of civic policy, but possessed a certain amount of autonomy within the overall framework of urban government.[44] While the city government, like all municipal authorities, sought to establish a degree of control over trade and industry, it necessarily had to delegate to officials within each craft who, in many cases, were as keen to put forward grievances from below as to enforce rules and regulations from above. The quasi-independent position occupied by the guilds had been achieved over a long period of time, and was in many respects an admission by the city authorities that they were powerless to control the development of guilds within the crafts, a reality exemplified by the numbers of guilds turning to the Crown in order to get external sanction for their activities in the form of letters patent. Although the activities of guild officials continued to be liable to regular scrutiny by the mayor, attempts to tighten up the degree of regulation were, by the fifteenth century, introduced infrequently and were often inconsistently and spasmodically enforced. The ratification by the city government of craft ordinances and elections of guild officials reached a peak in the fourteenth century, a period when the number of formal craft associations appears to have expanded dramatically. Thereafter, lists of senior craftsmen were recorded only infrequently in the city journals and letter books.[45] The statute of 1437 which required guilds to have their ordinances ratified by the local justices of the peace (the mayor in the case of London) had only a short-term impact: the same year, four saddlers were required to bring into the Court of Aldermen 'the book of the fraternity', and their charter of 1424 was examined to see if it contravened the liberties of the city.[46] Charters granted to the drapers and the tailors (in 1438 and 1439 respectively) were also part of the short-lived reaction to this legislation, and in the aftermath of the furore caused by the tailors' letters patent it is not surprising that the Court of Aldermen took the unusual step of recording the names of the masters and wardens of the guild on several occasions in the 1440s and 1450s.[47]

On the other hand, there were several spheres of urban life in which the city government was increasingly able to harness the impressive resources at the disposal of the guilds. The raising of revenue was normally carried out through the assessment of citizens ward by ward, but occasionally the mayor and aldermen were able to take advantage of the mechanisms for raising levies which had been established by the guilds over many years, particularly by the Great Twelve, who had long been accustomed to raising large sums for their own purposes. In 1487–8, for instance, all the crafts were required to contribute £4,000 for a loan to Henry VII. The mercers, grocers and drapers were to pay £1,615 between them, the goldsmiths, fishmongers and tailors £946 13*s* 4*d* and an unspecified number of other guilds were to provide the remaining £1,438 6*s* 8*d*.[48] The crafts were also drawn upon in the key areas of public works and defence, and they were once again categorized according to their wealth and size. In 1476–7 the mayor, Ralph Joscelyn, required each craft to undertake the task of repairing a section of the city wall. His own company, the drapers, managed to complete the section from All Hallows London Wall to Bishopsgate before the project lapsed under Joscelyn's successor.[49] When the city prepared its defences against the forces of Henry Tudor in 1485, 3,178 men were drawn from 73 crafts. The tailors, mercers and drapers each provided 200 men, and the grocers raised 220.[50] The city also used the guilds as a convenient means to recruit armed contingents to be sent abroad in the king's service. In 1435, for instance, the mayor and aldermen received an appeal for help from their counterparts in the besieged city of Calais.[51] By July the following year an expeditionary force led by Humphrey, Duke of Gloucester, was being organized, and writs were sent to the sheriffs of London requesting them to make proclamations concerning the provision of weapons and food for the army.[52] Meanwhile, 'by the good a-vyse and consent of craftys', the mayor agreed to send contingents of soldiers to join the force, which was to assemble at Sandwich at the end of July.[53] The tailors' part in the expedition is recorded in their accounts which, in 1435–6, noted expenses incurred 'for writyng of indentures and obligacions to Caleys', and then payments for the soldiers at Calais (*les paiements pur les soudyers a Caleys*) which amounted to £28 6*s* 7*d*. These included payments to ten tailors, six of whom were designated as archers, for sixty days' service at a rate of 1*s* 4*d* a day.[54] The surviving grocers' accounts show that they made a contribution of £14 1*s* 8*d* 'for the sauf kepyng of Caleys yeinst the seege of the fals pretendyng Duke of Burgoyne'.[55] In time of great need the Crown itself appealed directly to the guilds. In 1459, just after the rout at Blore Heath, Henry VI ordered the wardens of the gunners, armourers, bowyers, fletchers, mercers, haberdashers, joiners, tailors and upholders, as well as representatives of the Venetian and Florentine communities, to come to Guildhall to hear his commands. Presumably the choice of these groups was based on the king's need for finance and for vital supplies of arms, armour and clothing for the escalating conflict with the Duke of York.[56]

Despite the useful functions they performed in these areas, it is clear that the relationships between guilds and municipal authorities were essentially a series of dialogues rather than merely an exercise in state control. The growing number of petitions submitted by London's guilds to the Court of Aldermen in the fifteenth century testifies to the extent to which these organizations sought to articulate the concerns of artisans and merchants. Most frequent were petitions arising from disputes between the crafts, many of which had to be submitted to the arbitration of the mayor and aldermen following the failure of negotiations conducted by representatives of their respective guilds. These quarrels frequently centred on areas of overlap between occupations: in 1408, for instance, a settlement was reached between the shearmen and the drapers over the price to be paid for shearing various kinds of cloth. The same year the cutlers were involved in jurisdictional disputes with the sheathers and bladesmiths concerning the joint searches of the shops of members of these closely related crafts.[57] Rivalry between the city's artisan skinners and tailors may likewise have been deepened by the

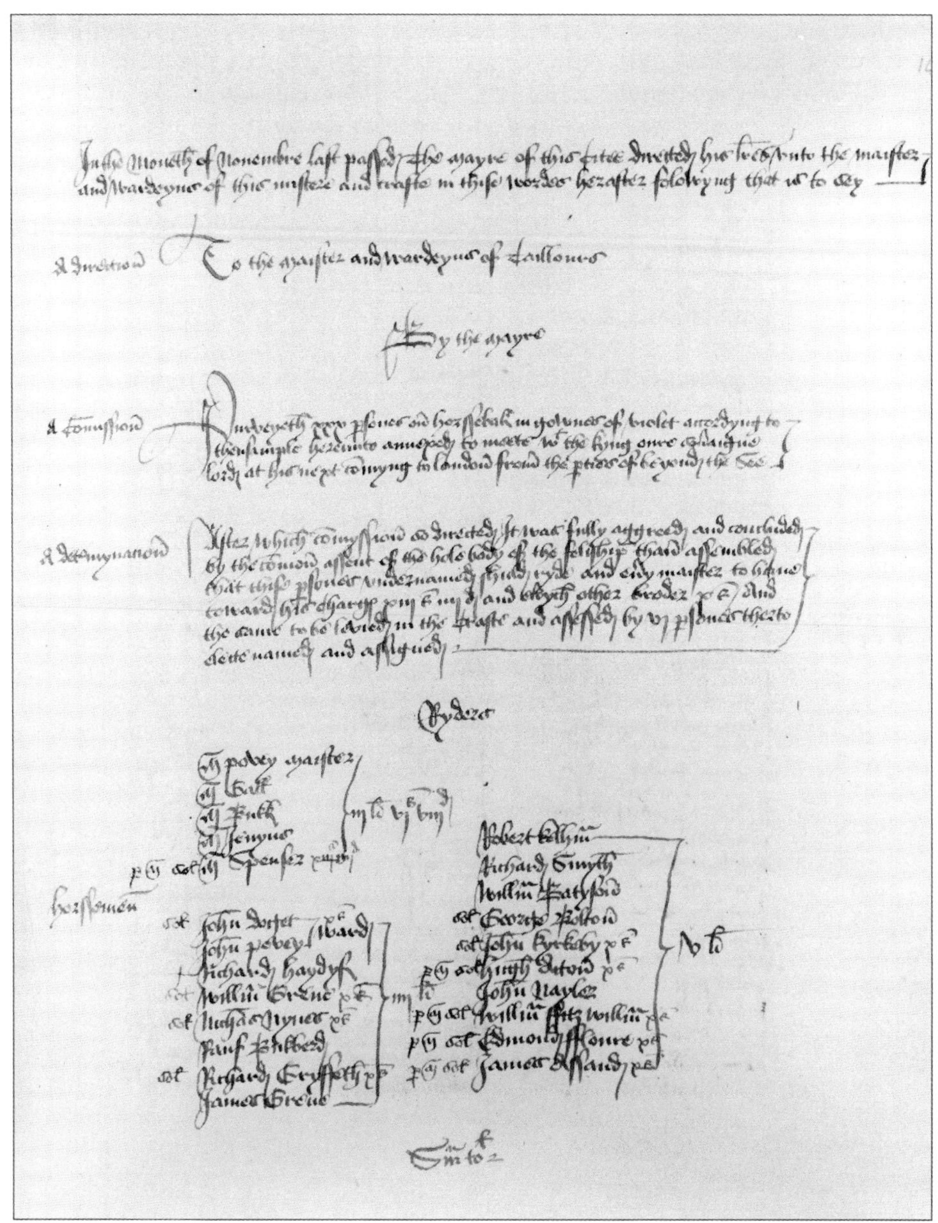

Expenses for men and equipment contributed by the Tailors' guild to the force being assembled in 1436 in order to relieve the town of Calais. (Merchant Taylors' Company, London, Accounts, vol. 1, f. 276. By permission of the Merchant Taylors' Company, London.)

apparent readiness of many tailors to engage in small-time trading in furs and to sew furs on to garments, specialized work traditionally done by skinners in more formal work environments, such as the Great Wardrobe. Moreover, by the late fifteenth century the structural similarities between these two crafts were striking: both were large, predominantly artisan crafts whose guilds had come to be headed by a small group of men with principally mercantile interests. In terms of the city's guild hierarchy, both the skinners and tailors could claim to be a cut above the majority of the artisan misteries, though not, of course, on a par with the ever-dominant merchants of the mercers, grocers and drapers. Matters came to a head in 1484 when the mayor, Robert Billesdon, was required to settle a 'variaunce and controversie' between the two crafts, which centred, once more, on the places occupied by the liverymen of these two guilds in civic processions. The settlement, which became known as the Billesdon Award, stipulated that the skinners were to take precedence over the tailors in alternate years in mayoral processions, except when a member of the craft was elected mayor in which case they would head the procession as was customary. The award also required each guild to invite the other to dinner, once again in alternate years, on the appropriate patronal feast day – Corpus Christi Day in the case of the skinners and the Nativity of St John the Baptist in the case of the tailors.[58] It is perhaps not surprising that some guilds tried to avoid the arbitration of the city government, particularly when there was an opportunity to extend their privileges by appealing to other sources of authority, most notably the Crown and Parliament. The presence of Drew Barantyn, a goldsmith, in the parliament of 1404 may have inspired his guild to petition for a new charter, which extended the rights of search of the wardens to the shops of the low-ranking cutlers. The cutlers' guild subsequently appealed against the provisions of these letters patent, but had clearly been out-manoeuvred by the well-connected goldsmiths.[59]

The Court of Aldermen was also the forum for the discussion of wider economic concerns, which often led to the formulation of an agreed policy to place before the Crown and before Parliament. An unprecedented number of petitions from the guilds in the later fifteenth century reveal widespread anxieties among London's artisans, of a kind which could not possibly be dealt with at the level of an individual craft. There were, of course, plenty of issues of city policy upon which the guilds could not agree, particularly when economic rivalries provoked defensiveness. The subject of provincial fairs, and the rights of citizens to attend them, was one which split the leading guilds and consequently the Court of Aldermen and the Common Council in the later fifteenth century. Debate centred on a controversial proposal to prevent citizens from taking their goods to fairs, on the grounds that the quality was often inferior and hence harmful to the reputation of the city. A ban would also help to encourage customers to come to London for their goods, and would thus further stimulate the retail trade in the capital. Much of the initial action was taken unilaterally, but in the reign of Edward IV efforts were made to achieve consensus among the crafts.[60] The mercers were at the forefront of this movement: in 1477 they sent a bill to the Common Council requesting that 'every freman and other dweller withyn this citie' should refrain from taking goods to be sold outside London.

Their concerns were not entirely altruistic, for it became clear that they were keen to prevent the upwardly mobile haberdashers from encroaching on their country business following their takeover of the hatters and cappers, which had left them with better access to the consumer goods they could sell in London and at fairs.[61] The concerned mercers sought to limit the activities of haberdashers to the London market, so that customers would continue to come to London where they might buy from mercers as well. The representatives of the crafts were split on the issues raised by the mercers' bill: seventeen guilds 'granted gladly to refrain' from such trading while eleven others 'in no wise would be thereto agreeable'. With no decision forthcoming the mercers decided to allow their members to continue to trade at fairs rather than see their business further eroded.[62] By the mid-1480s, however, opinion had shifted in their direction, and in February 1486 the Common Council agreed to a seven-year ban on freemen taking their goods to fairs, with the crafts seemingly prepared to put aside their disagreements for the sake of the city's reputation.[63] Yet any hopes that this would signal the end of the matter were to be dashed, for little more than a month after the Common Council's decision, the ban was suspended and was later 'annulled by autorite of Parliament'.[64] The Court of Assistants of the tailors' guild discussed the developments on two occasions in 1486. In April, as part of an agreement concerning the sale of cloth at Backwell Hall, they and the drapers decided to forbid their members to 'rede into the contre for to by any woollyn clothis' in an effort to guarantee the quality of cloth bought and sold in London. Later that year the tailors also forbade their craftsmen to take manufactured goods to sell at country fairs.[65]

Yet dialogue with the city, as well as with other guilds, could often achieve significant results in the shape of civic ordinances and even parliamentary legislation: the statute of 1463 which sought to ban the importation of a wide variety of consumer goods from abroad probably owed a great deal to earlier efforts by the cutlers, pewterers and other London guilds to protect the particular interests of their own artisans.[66] An important early example of the successful lobbying of the city by the crafts concerned was a statute of 1406, which prohibited parents from apprenticing their sons or daughters unless they were in possession of lands or rents that yielded at least £1 a year. The aim of the statute had been to release more young men into the rural labour market by restricting apprenticeship in this manner, thus reinforcing the fourteenth-century labour legislation.[67] As well as being viewed as an attack upon the customary practices of the city, the statute was also opposed for more practical reasons by many employers who were already concerned at the high price and poor supply of labour in the city at that time. Attempts to have the statute revoked began almost immediately: in 1408–9 the tailors paid 3*s* 8*d* in two instalments for annulling the ordinance for enrolling apprenticeship (*a les freres as ii foitz pur adnuller lordinaunce denrollement dapprentise*).[68] Rather than mount a concerted campaign against the Act, the city government's policy at this stage was simply to ignore it. This remained possible until 1428, when one of the king's clerks brought an action against a prominent London scrivener for breaching its provisions, prompting the city to draw up a petition seeking an exemption for London and its freemen.[69] Once more the tailors were active participants: the accounts for 1428–9 include £4 paid to the Mayor of London for persuading the king to repeal the statute (*paie a le meir de Loundrez pur dischargyng del statute des apprentises vers le Roy*). This may well have been their response to a general appeal to the guilds: the grocers' accounts record the payment of £2 'for costes of our parte off Repelyng off ye statut off prentyshodys'. Despite the rejection of a similar petition from the City of Oxford, the appeal of the citizens of the capital resulted in an amended statute which sought to preserve the city's liberties.[70] The sensitivity of Londoners and their guilds to external interference over the question of apprenticeship was not surprising, for by the fifteenth century the crafts had acquired a significant degree of freedom in this area, which was used to modify the existing legislative framework, established over many years by the Crown and the city. This laid down that apprentices had to be of free condition, of English birth and, following a statute of 1388, had to be at least twelve years old.[71] Within this framework the fifteenth-century guilds were often able to shape their apprenticeship regulations around such things as the physical requirements of particular occupations: the paviors, for example, required their apprentices to be at least eighteen years old because of the physical strength needed for their work.[72] More common, however, were attempts to respond to prevailing economic conditions by regulating access to the formal structures of the crafts. By the mid-fifteenth century, concern at the level of immigration into the capital prompted several guilds to control the numbers of apprentices who were taken on, in order to safeguard the opportunities for freemen. In 1453 the founders restricted their masters to two apprentices each because 'good mens children of the contrey have be gretely deceyved and this Cite disclaundered'.[73] Another approach to the same problem was enacted by the mercers and grocers, who raised their enrolment fees in the 1440s and 1450s in order to maximize opportunities for those who went on to become freemen.[74] Only rarely did guilds actually lengthen apprenticeships for this purpose; on the whole most artisans continued to enrol their apprentices for the minimum period of seven years. Terms longer than this were a matter for negotiation and might depend on the size of any payment a master could extract from the apprentice's parents: it was probably more than just an unfortunate surname which led Rowland Lytilskill, son of John Lytilskill of Hexham, to begin a twelve-year term as the apprentice of a tailor, William Huelette, in September 1486.[75]

A flexible approach to regulations governing formal access to the misteries was only one part of the strategy adopted in the fifteenth century to counter what was perceived by the guilds as a growing economic threat posed by the influx of immigrants, collectively known as 'foreigns', to the city. As well as craftsmen from elsewhere in England in search of employment, large numbers of 'aliens' from northern Europe, particularly from the Low Countries, came to live and work in London and the suburbs. Early in the century few guilds viewed such arrivals with concern: the widespread opposition to the 1406 statute had revealed the dependence of many masters upon immigrant labour at a time of continued stagnation in the city's population level. There was even a cautious welcome for some groups of immigrants, and in February 1420 foreign weavers were granted a dispensation to work in the city, despite the fact that many of them were too poor to afford the franchise.[76] Firm action at this time was demanded mainly in respect of the activities of some of the wealthier immigrants. In 1432–3, for instance, the Common Council agreed that a petition should be sent to the Court of Aldermen concerning traders who obtained the freedom by redemption but who promptly went to live outside the city, thus avoiding civic duties in their wards. They only ventured into the capital in order to sell goods of dubious quality at low prices, threatening the livelihoods of other citizens. The response of the mayor and aldermen was sympathetic: such 'outedwellers' were henceforth required to live with their wives and children in the city or else they would lose the franchise.[77] By the middle decades of the century, however, the guilds had shifted their attention to the increasing numbers of unenfranchised workers, especially aliens, who were arriving in London and whose activities were much harder to regulate. Shortly after the passage of the 1463 Act concerning imports, for instance, the bladesmiths complained to the Court of Aldermen about 'foreyns' who were selling inferior wares in the city, often using forged trademarks.[78] Meanwhile, a growing shortage of opportunities for freemen in the city prompted a hostile reaction against the employment of aliens as servants and apprentices by London citizens. In July 1451 the tailors and cordwainers petitioned the Court of Aldermen for restrictions to be placed on the hiring of such workers, including the payment of 5*s* for each one.[79] The employment of aliens was nothing new and had even been encouraged by some guilds in periods when there was plenty of work to go round. The tailors had themselves sanctioned it within the garment industry for many years and, moreover, had even allowed groups of aliens to become prominent within the thriving second-hand clothing market in the capital, where their activities led them to be known as 'bochers'. Fines were levied upon those who were found by the wardens producing 'nove werke', but otherwise these men and their families were left alone to meet the demand for such garments, despite their unfree status.[80] With an apparent rise in the immigrant population in the later fifteenth century, however, aliens and other unenfranchised workers were increasingly viewed as a threat to the opportunities for recently qualified artisans, many of whom often needed to work for fellow freemen for a while in order to raise the capital to open a shop. Legal obstacles were placed in the way of immigrants by some guilds: the goldsmiths, for instance, required craftsmen from the provinces to undertake an apprenticeship in London, regardless of the training they had already received, if they wished to become freemen. Next, servants from outside London were not to be enrolled for less than seven years. Finally, aliens were required to pay the huge sum of £20 for their freedoms.[81] Such ordinances were bound to be ineffective if no measures were taken to enforce them, and a step in this direction was taken by a statute of 1478, which explicitly rendered the workshops of alien goldsmiths living within 2 miles of the city liable to be searched by the London guild.[82] The cloth and clothing industry appears to have suffered more than most, perhaps, as Pamela Nightingale suggests, because of the flight of skilled workers from the provinces to the city and its suburbs. The decline of the Midland dyeing and finishing industries, for instance, may have increased the numbers of such workers in and around London. The dyers' charter, acquired in 1471, tried to respond to this by granting the wardens powers of search within an area of 20 miles of the capital.[83] A statute passed by the parliament of 1483 recognized the problems caused by skilled alien craftsmen arriving 'in greate noumbre and more than they have used to doo in daies passed'. Its harsh measures included a ban on the employment of aliens by fellow aliens, and on aliens exercising any craft unless they were in the employ of subjects of the king, but these were clearly almost impossible to enforce.[84] Indeed, a large number of the London guilds continued to submit petitions on this subject to the mayor and aldermen: the yeomen of the fullers and the painters successfully petitioned for a ban on the employment of foreigns within their crafts if there were freemen available to do the same work. By the end of the century the seriousness of the situation prompted several guilds, including the skinners and tailors, to call for an outright ban on the employment of foreigns: in April 1493 the tailors sent the master of the craft and three senior liverymen to see the mayor to propose a bill 'for the reformacion of all foreyns that they hereafter worke with no freman and citezein of this citee'.[85] Inevitably the second-hand market for clothing was also affected, and by 1518 the tailors were forced to act against the alien 'bochers' because of the threat posed to the livelihoods of older tailors who, perhaps because of failing eyesight or infirmity, were no longer capable of making new clothes and were 'fain to fall to the said feat of botching' in order to make a living.[86]

A related problem for the guilds was posed by the economic growth of Southwark, which for the most part lay outside the jurisdiction of the city authorities. Notwithstanding its growing alien population, many citizens were themselves accustomed to living there, out of the reach of most guild officials, and selling their goods in the city. One London saddler put his apprentice to work in Southwark as a 'fuster', making the saddle-bows which he would then turn into saddles in his own workshop in the city. This form of sub-contracting prompted the city government in 1456 to order all citizens living in Southwark to pay double the usual fee for enrolling an apprentice.[87] Even more serious were the activities of aliens and other unenfranchised workers living south of the Thames, and many crafts, including the fishmongers, acquired charters which gave their wardens rights of search there. For the goldsmiths the extent of the problem was revealed in a survey undertaken by the wardens in 1469 in which it was found that 98 out of 113 male alien craftsmen lived in Southwark and Westminster. The cloth industry, another flourishing trade in the suburb, was also subject to close attention by the drapers' wardens, who by the late fifteenth century had secured the right to search the fair held at St Mary Overey. The skinners too were increasingly aware of the need to send their wardens into the suburbs to search the houses of 'Dutchmen skinners'.[88] The problems posed by competition from across the Thames can be seen in the case of the glaziers who lived and worked in Southwark, and who, after 1500, monopolized the major glazing contracts, thus provoking a bitter dispute with the London guild.[89] On several occasions London artisans took matters into their own hands. Frustration as well as xenophobia doubtless played a part, especially when the city government could be annoyingly even-handed in its treatment of foreigns: in 1478, for instance, the brewers were alleged to have inflated their prices and so the city decided to allow alien brewers to compete openly with them. Unofficial action took a variety of forms: in December 1471 the Court of Aldermen was forced to act against some of the city's bakers who had been making false presentments against foreign bakers.[90] More severe action had been contemplated by a motley group of skinners, cordwainers, goldsmiths and tailors who in 1468 plotted to cross the Thames at night and cut off the thumbs or hands of the Flemings in Southwark so that they might never again take away 'the living of Englissh people'. The plot was foiled, but it is no coincidence that the crafts represented by the participants were precisely those which, according to the alien subsidy rolls, were most commonly practised by aliens in Southwark.[91]

These tensions graphically illustrate the limits which pertained to the authority of the city and its guilds in the later Middle Ages. The legislative response from the city government and from Parliament may have been helpful, but when it came to enforcement there was frequently little that the guilds and their officials could do. Suburbs such as Westminster and Southwark were ideal locations for the establishment of small-scale enterprises ready to serve the lucrative market for goods in the city, yet often out of reach of all but the most persistent guild officials. Similarly, the privilege of sanctuary within the precincts of churches such as St Martin le Grand and Westminster Abbey could often create 'islands of ungoverned commerce', adding to the problems faced by the guilds.[92] Within the city itself the manor of Blanch Appleton near Aldgate was a notorious haunt of criminals and unenfranchised craftsmen. Freemen were themselves reluctant to submit to guild authority, and in many instances their activities led to the introduction of new ordinances. In 1450 the tailors' guild expressed its concern at the difficulty in exercising 'due serche and correccion' upon the large numbers of newly qualified craftsmen who produced garments hidden away in rented attic rooms. In an attempt to remedy this the Court of Assistants ordered each 'chambur holder' to place himself as a servant with a more established freeman, or else to 'inhabite hym in the comons amonges other servauntes sowers of the seid mistiere under the good rewle and governaunce of the seid Maister and Wardeins' so that they could be employed by other freemen either by the day or by the garment.[93] This idea of a pool of skilled labour, though doubtless attractive to many masters, was clearly a difficult one to put into practice given the apparent tendency of many young freemen to set up in business as soon as possible. Such ordinances remind us of the essentially normative function of much guild legislation, which was designed to create an overall framework for the governance of the craft rather than a series of regulations that were always strictly enforced. This is not to say that craft wardens were powerless, merely that when it came to enforcement a selective approach, based on an intimate knowledge of the craft and prevailing economic conditions, often worked best.[94]

The surviving fifteenth-century records of the London guilds reveal the ways in which freemen and their families and servants could be subjected to internal disciplinary procedures, often following searches of their shops. The offences dealt with ranged from working on Sundays and feast days to serious disputes between masters and their apprentices, which were often submitted to the arbitration of senior guild members in the first instance or, as a last resort, to the scrutiny of the mayor.[95] Yet despite the broad spectrum of misdemeanours uncovered, it is clear that enforcement often reflected the prioritizing of certain issues over others, a flexible approach similar to that displayed in relation to apprenticeship. As the records of several guilds show, some economic problems were met with a more vigorous response than others. In the case of the tailors, the petitions submitted to the city concerning the activities of aliens and other immigrants were matched by firm action in the second half of the fifteenth century. In 1454–5, for instance, the wardens of the tailors discovered and fined a group of *forinseci* that 'practised this craft in the Dragon Inn beside the Great Wardrobe' (*occupavit istam artem in hospiceo de la dragon iuxta magnam garderobam*). The 'bochers' continued to be subject to regular spot-checks in order to make sure that they did not make new clothes, while those freemen who employed aliens were required to make regular payments to the common box of the craft.[96] Equally, there were some areas in which enforcement was not perceived as urgent or especially desirable, despite the strictures contained in many ordinances and statutes. An interesting example of this concerns the reactions of two guilds to the sumptuary legislation of 1463, which sought to regulate both the manufacture and wearing of various fashionable items of clothing. The cordwainers, for instance, were ordered not to manufacture shoes with 'pikes' more than two inches in length, but as Anne Sutton has shown, members of the guild were divided between those who wished to respond to public demand for these shoes and those who preferred to obey the statute.[97] The tailors may have been similarly doubtful about the benefits of another clause in the Act which controlled the wearing and manufacture of the increasingly fashionable short jackets of the time, unless these were 'of such length that the same may cover his privy members and buttocks'. Perhaps to show willing, the wardens fined four tailors a total of 7*s* 4*d* in 1463–4 for making such garments, although no reference was made to the Act, merely to breaches of unspecified ordinances of the craft.[98] No further fines were recorded, however, and it is likely that the wardens made little effort to enforce this part of the Act, in effect turning a blind eye so their freemen could continue to meet the buoyant demand for these garments. Partial vindication of their approach came in 1483 when a subsequent Act removed the penalties imposed on tailors, although it still sought to confine the wearing of such items to lords and above.[99]

This apparent reluctance to implement legislation of dubious benefit to many artisans was in keeping with the independence of mind that was shown by the guilds during the fifteenth century. During this period they developed into formidable organizations, already responsible for the regulation of the capital's trades, but now increasingly capable of articulating the concerns and aspirations of artisans and merchants to the city government and to the Crown.[100] As has been shown, a number of these concerns were common to many of the crafts and hence fostered a sense of common purpose, while others could create or perpetuate bitter divisions both between and within the livery companies, which necessitated a firm response from the mayor and aldermen. The hope that ceremonial occasions could transcend occupational rivalries may frequently have been a forlorn one, but the city authorities continued to make every effort to present a united front to the world. Following the treaty of Étaples, signed in November 1492, a lavish welcome was planned for Henry VII 'at his next comyng to London from the parties of beyond the see'. When the day drew near the mayor wrote a formal letter to the tailors' guild, asking it to provide 'xxx persones on horssebak in gownes of violet' to line the processional route. With his letter was enclosed a sample of the cloth from which the liveries were to be made, and while no reference to the events of 1477 was made, or even perhaps intended, this was a timely reminder of the significance of such occasions for the city's governors, and of the lengths to which they would go in order to ensure that the resources of the guilds were employed in the pursuit of civic rather than private goals.[101]

CHAPTER 8

London Parishes: Development in Context

CLIVE BURGESS

To write about the Church at any point in medieval history is a daunting assignment: it was an institution which played a role of central importance at all levels of life and experience. Indeed, the term 'the Church' is ultimately so broad in its range of reference that it can all too easily cease to be of particular use. The following will necessarily be selective, mentioning monasticism only in passing and neglecting mysticism, for instance (which is unfortunate, as discussion of each would be well worth while for the late medieval period); it will, moreover, hardly touch on the international Church or even the national hierarchy. Instead it examines life in a locality, drawing its examples in the main from London, then, as now, much the largest and wealthiest city in England. If not typical, London serves its purpose in that it affords a wealth of example and, despite the Great Fire and the Blitz, furnishes excellent records, factors which together permit an exceptionally well-focused glimpse of late medieval religion. By dwelling on an admittedly limited aspect of religious and Church life it is my intention to shed light both on what motivated fifteenth-century Christian men and women and on some of the more distinctive manifestations of contemporary spiritual practice. If narrow in many respects, in others this essay exceeds its obvious brief. In order to explain what was afoot in the century or more before the Reformation the essay will, as necessary, cast much farther back in time to isolate developments of moment for subsequent conditions and practice.

I will consider, first, the obligatory responses on which religion in the localities depended. While the late medieval Church was self-evidently a complex institution, highly organized and encompassing a wide variety of emphasis and behaviour, it must nevertheless always be borne in mind that it existed both to worship God and to teach and save fallen mankind. While popes and bishops naturally played a fundamental role in establishing doctrine and in organizing the cure of souls, for the majority of Christians the parish was the institution which played the most formative role in their lives. By the late Middle Ages the parochial structure of London was already many centuries old. Prompted by the

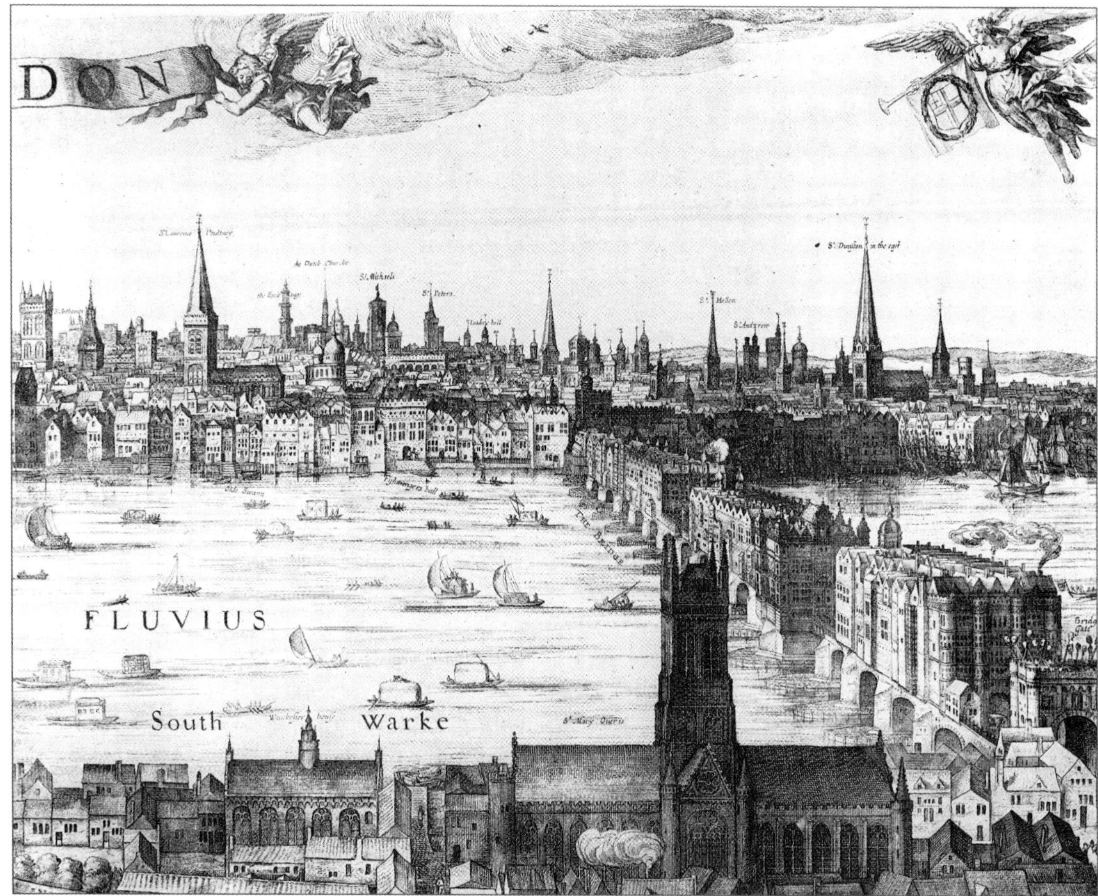

A detail from the Hollar panorama of London before the Great Fire showing Old London Bridge, the central sections of waterfront and the buildings in the city behind. The forest of church spires and towers is eloquent testimony to the presence of religion in the city, just as the density of housing speaks of the ease with which awareness of new developments might spread. Billingsgate is clearly visible to the right of the bridge.

Viking threat in the ninth century, London had relocated itself back inside the extant Roman walls and, while certainly flourishing in the tenth century, had established itself as the capital city of England following the Norman conquest. In the same period, apparently as the result of spontaneous 'organic' neighbourhood action and development, parishes had crystallized – small communities which came to number slightly in excess of one hundred within the city walls. It was here that sacred and secular intersected: teaching and the sacraments were ministered by the clergy and, in addition to a duty to attend regularly, the common obligations binding the laity to the Church were, in everyday terms, enforced through the parish.

Priests had to be supported and the laity was obliged to pay tithe on the fruits of the ground and on the profits of labour. Tithe was a complex system which had evolved to suit rural, agricultural conditions rather than the urban, commercial environment.[1] But while problems could and did arise – which, like all bad news, attract attention – it seems fair to conclude that tithe was for the most part collected efficiently. The laity generally discharged what was expected; disputes, even in a town like London, where reckoning tithe proved intrinsically difficult, were relatively rare.[2] In addition to supporting the personnel who might, by vocation and ordination, teach and administer the sacraments, the laity had obligations both towards the buildings in which the cure of souls was accomplished and towards providing the equipment necessary for the seemly discharge of parish services. In practical terms, as a result of synodal legislation passed in the thirteenth century in the wake of the Fourth Lateran Council, the maintenance of church buildings (or at least nave and tower) and provision of requisite equipment rested with the laity and, in time, specifically with churchwardens, pairs of laymen serving for a year or two at a time, who were responsible on behalf of all parishioners for the efficient discharge of agreed responsibilities.[3] Churchwardens managed certain aspects of the parish income, levying collections, rates and dues and managing property endowments devised by deceased parishioners. They also managed certain expenditures, for instance, overseeing building repairs, arranging cleaning, maintaining vestments and liturgical equipment and procuring new items when necessary. Finally, and depending on the parish, they might also have the responsibility for collecting and administering the revenues which supported auxiliary clergy, like the parish clerk. By the fifteenth century surviving documentation indicates that parishes were, on the whole, efficiently organized institutions, and that the laity and, more particularly, churchwardens were respectively forces to be reckoned with and agents of considerable competence. Laymen and women made a fulsome response to obligations laid upon them, and, contrary to the once-pervasive reputation for corruption and decline, the late medieval Church flourished at a local level, suggesting that the laity was obviously satisfied by what it derived from parish provision – one reason, at least, for this is that men and women were in a position, through parish procedures and personnel, to satisfy their needs simply by providing themselves with what they wanted.

If obligatory requirements were, in general, being efficiently fulfilled to facilitate the cure of souls, it is worth turning to another prominent aspect of late medieval church life which was voluntary and, rather than communal, more concerned with the actions of individuals, particularly the rich. A distinctive aspect of medieval piety which, to start with, was expressed outside the parish, was the foundation of intercessory institutions. London witnessed the endowment of a number of ambitious foundations of this type, like monasteries, nunneries and hospitals, both inside the walls and nearby. One might cite the Cluniac priory at Bermondsey, 'founded out of an unexplained alliance between William Rufus and a citizen of London called Alwin Cild, in 1089',[4] or Queen Matilda's foundation of the Augustinian priory of Holy Trinity, Aldgate in 1108, or, later (early in the thirteenth century), the Benedictine nunnery of St Helen's,

Bishopsgate, the individual founder of which cannot be identified. Mention could also be made of St Bartholomew, Smithfield, founded by Rahere in 1123, comprising both an Augustinian priory and hospital which, although founded together, developed separately. Other hospitals might be named: St Katherine by the Tower, founded by King Stephen's consort Matilda in 1148, and the 'New Hospital' of St Mary without Bishopsgate, founded in the 1190s by the London citizen Walter Brown and his wife Rosia, refounded in 1235. These are only a few of the many monastic and charitable institutions established in and around London by *c.* 1250.[5] Thereafter, although kings might still establish monasteries or hospitals, like Edward III's Cistercian foundation of the Abbey of St Mary Graces in 1349, or Henry VII's Savoy Hospital of St John the Baptist, established in 1505, it is fair to judge that in the later Middle Ages practice changed.[6] The emphasis shifted towards smaller, somewhat cheaper institutions, like colleges and almshouses, and particularly to a more personal foundation, ubiquitous in the later Middle Ages and differing from earlier foundations in that it could be dovetailed into parish life, the chantry. Founders, if still relatively eminent, might be drawn from farther down the social scale – although in London it is noteworthy that while mayors were notable founders they did not now establish monasteries. By 1332 John Pulteney had built a chapel of Corpus Christi and St John the Baptist, adjoining the church of St Laurence in Candlewick Street, for a college of a master and seven chaplains. In 1381 William Walworth founded a college of a master and nine priests in the church of St Michael Crooked Lane to replace chantries which had been founded in that church. In 1424 the executors of Richard Whittington founded a college attached to St Michael Paternoster Row, for five secular priests, two clerks and four choristers, and also an almshouse for thirteen poor men which was to be administered by the mercers' company.[7] And to pick but one perpetual chantry from the scores established in London in the two or three centuries preceding the Reformation, the foundation of another mayor, William Cambridge, will serve: he left instructions in 1431 that his chaplain was to celebrate divine service daily in the chapel of St Stephen the Martyr, which Cambridge himself had built on the north side of his parish church, St Mary at Hill.[8] There were many other chantries, both perpetual or celebrated for limited durations, which could have been chosen and which, if less ostentatious than Cambridge's, nevertheless invariably provided for a daily celebration of Mass for the repose of the founder's soul.

All the foundations mentioned were established voluntarily, either by Londoners, or those closely associated with them, and were very much a presence in the later medieval city. It must be remembered that in London, and, to a lesser extent, elsewhere, the existence and multiplication of such institutions layered the already complex developments of parish life with a prominent, varied and ambitious liturgical, intercessory and charitable provision. By the later fifteenth century these institutions had cumulatively harnessed considerable property, adding to the wealth and influence of the Church and profoundly affecting Christian society, both generally and in the parishes. These institutions were not established to achieve the universal cure of souls. They had, instead, a threefold purpose (each overlapping in practice with the others). First, all were institutions which observed the liturgy with some elaboration but which focused on the regular celebration of the Mass, to the worship of God and the benefit of society generally. Secondly, they were intended to cure social evils, reducing hardship and social tension by assisting the vulnerable: all were institutions which offered, to a greater or lesser extent, support and care for the old and infirm, teaching for the young, or provided alms for the poor.[9] Thirdly, they were of course to benefit the founders and their families and nominees, both as a result of the grace accruing from the liturgy and because the beneficiaries – the old, the infirm, the young and the honest poor – were intended to intercede for their benefactors. The number and prominence of institutions founded to provide worship, services to society and intercession proves the point that the rich, the penitentially challenged, took the teachings of Jesus and the Church on the problem of wealth very seriously indeed and responded very fulsomely, by foundation or by bolstering existing institutions.[10] Indeed, one of the most striking attributes of the late medieval Church in England is the success it achieved in persuading the rich to part with their wealth for their own spiritual advantage no less than for the physical advantage of the less well-off, and for the general benefit of the Church Militant.

If, as I argue, the results of the wealthy establishing intercessory institutions played so formative a role in creating the character of late medieval Christian life, it is permissible to investigate further the penitential purpose underpinning these manifestations. It is, therefore, with no apology at all that I turn to consider penance (although, of necessity, in simplified form): the tenor of Christian life in the late Middle Ages will never be properly appreciated without an adequate understanding of the ramifications that this sacrament had for the faithful.[11] The sacrament of penance bridges the chasm of sin separating God and fallen man and is pivotal in the practical pursuit of salvation. While theoretically stable in its operation, the sacrament moderated with time in terms of practical application. It should be emphasized that in the early centuries of Christianity in Europe the outlook for mankind was bleak because of the strictness of both penitential diagnosis and remedy. The early formal system, usually called canonical penance, held sway until the seventh century and was particularly rigorous. It excluded the penitent from the body of the faithful; the disavowal of sin, severe penances and formal reconciliation were all to be public actions which could be allowed once only for specific sins. A system which evolved in Ireland, spreading from there in the seventh century and later, used short manuals which classified sins and guided priests in the imposition of specified penances for particular offences. This system supplanted canonical penance and particularly introduced the idea of a set penitential tariff. It was considered preferable because it might operate in private, and was also reiterable for grave sins no less than minor misdemeanours. But, while these characteristics rendered it somewhat less daunting, it was still arduous and insisted that absolution had to be earned in this life. As a result, in the words of R.W. Southern, 'the recompenses which men were struggling to pay for their sins in the early Middle Ages were great, and for many quite hopeless'.[12] This situation nevertheless offers explanation, at least in part, for the foundation of the great Benedictine abbeys and the hospitals, many of which followed the Augustinian rule, established in London and elsewhere between the eleventh and the thirteenth centuries. For in founding these institutions the very rich were persuaded to part with huge landed endowments to provide the rents and renders necessary to maintain fabric and support the monks, or brethren, or almsmen and almswomen, all of whom were obliged to pray for founders and benefactors. Almost certainly unable to perform requisite penance in this life, the powerful sought to profit by harnessing substitutive penance performed in particular by monks, or by brethren and beneficiaries, and to share the benefits of the grace generated in those powerhouses of prayer, liturgy and largesse.[13]

While greatly enriching the Church, the proliferation of intercessory institutions inevitably increased the influence of the mighty; just as kings in practice appointed bishops who, in addition to any pastoral role, were to assist in regional and national government, so too founders and their descendants might benefit from the influence exercised in the localities by the great monastic houses and might, at the very least, have some say in the appointment of abbots or priors. Ultimately the Church sought to free itself from such control, but in doing so precipitated a crisis as the mighty fought to keep the eminence they had always enjoyed and which they saw as a proprietorial right; if never resolved (or resolvable) in favour of the Church, the struggle nevertheless had profound consequences in western Christendom.

Designations such as 'The Investiture Contest' and 'Gregorian Reform' infallibly suggest that the antics of popes and emperors, or kings and archbishops in the late eleventh and twelfth centuries and beyond have tended to monopolize historians' attention. Nevertheless, the attempts by the Church to gain more independence set up a groundswell which in many respects had more positive results than the high-profile clashes. If the Church sought freedom from the mighty, it had obviously to rely more on its rank and file, but, given the severity of the penitential system, how could 'ordinary' men and women be expected to support an institution which in practice often denied them a share in the benefits it existed to procure? Recasting financial and penitential imperatives had to proceed hand-in-hand. As the Church refined the system of tithe-giving, by which all paid to support the clergy, penitential emphases were adapted so that all might have a realistic chance to benefit from the ministry of the Church and be saved. Theologians and schoolmen overhauled the sacrament of penance. Two developments were of paramount importance. First and, most significantly, promulgated at the Fourth Lateran Council in 1215 was the duty incumbent on every Christian of either sex to confess sins at least once annually. Confession dealt with the all-important guilt (*culpa*) resulting from sin, and a properly penitent and shriven Christian could not be damned. But a problem remained: the penalty (*poena*) due to sin still had to be satisfied. Although strictly less important than the remedy for guilt, the development and definition of Purgatory, the third place or 'staging post' to Heaven (and remember, a soul in Purgatory was saved and could not go to Hell), the place where the *poena* due for sin might be expiated, was to have immensely important ramifications in the later Middle Ages. Rather than having to make amends before death, the important aspect of Purgatory was the idea that the whole process could take place after death if necessary, although it was possible and indeed desirable to start in the here and now, expediting the progress of the soul by performing and commissioning good works. The evolution of Purgatory (strictly, not fully defined until the Council of Florence in 1439, but certainly operative by the late twelfth or early thirteenth century) saw 'the creation of a workable system of religious discipline for everyone' and, as such, marked a liberation for western Christians. 'It played an important part in lifting the cloud of uncertainty and gloom about the after-life which lay over the early centuries of European history. It made possible a more relaxed attitude to this world and the next: it turned the straight and narrow way of salvation into a highway trodden by a multitude of feet.'[14] While the celebration of the Mass provided a focus for ritual life in the parish and elsewhere, penance, with the concomitant obligation of confession and emphasis on the proper preparation for Purgatory, did much to shape people's priorities and practice in Church and outside – indeed, if strictly only of subsidiary importance, Purgatory exercised a notably formative influence.

As suggested, one of the most important means of accumulating grace in this life, and in Purgatory, was by commissioning and performing good works, benefactions which were intrinsically meritorious and which would also oblige beneficiaries to pray for the souls of their benefactors. Indeed, the emphasis on good works and on reciprocal intercession became, if the testimony of wills counts for anything, one of the most pervasive ideas in popular religious culture in the later Middle Ages, and it was an idea that almost anyone could act upon. If a testator provided alms for the poor, he or she could expect their prayers in return. If a parishioner made donations, either of money or artefacts, to the parish clergy, he or she might expect prayers in return. If a parishioner made a donation to the parish church, either of vessels or vestments or of money for building work, he or she might expect prayers in return from the parishioners or clergy who profited. It is fascinating to see how various parishes had benefaction lists or bede rolls, recording who had given what and ensuring that they would be regularly remembered in prayer by living parishioners who were benefiting from their benefactions or whose financial obligations had, as a result, been lessened.[15] Moreover, many donations, be they vessels with names inscribed on them, or banners or hearse cloths with the names of the donors worked into them, or windows with the figures of the donors included in one of the depicted scenes, tell the same story: to benefit from intercession men and women wanted to be remembered. 'Of your charity, pray for the souls of . . .' becomes a litany for late medieval men and women, an exhortation endlessly repeated, found on or implied by church fabric, equipment and furniture, as the return the dead sought for benefactions showered on parish churches and their living parishioners. Men and women of all degree, save only the poor, gave generously – and the poor had their own role.

Two additional points should be made in passing. First, it is relevant and of interest to note that the friars, first recognized by Pope Innocent III at almost exactly the same time as the Fourth Lateran met to make its decisions, were the perfect transmitters of the new ideas concerning penance, particularly confession and Purgatory. Products of, and very often a sustained presence in, western Europe's burgeoning universities, friars were highly trained, mobile and expert

This drawing uses the crude analogy of water being drawn from a well to illustrate how souls are drawn out of Purgatory by alms and prayers. It is from a manuscript of the early fifteenth century and accompanies a poem about Purgatory that is equally direct:

The saules that to Purgatory wendes
May be relefyd thorow help of frendes.

(From British Library, Additional MS 37049, f. 24v. Photograph by courtesy of the Conway Library, the Courtauld Institute of Art.)

preachers, able to understand, take and spread the new imperatives into the localities and particularly the towns.[16] Moreover, they had an abiding interest in the practical implications of the doctrine: as mendicants, that is beggars, the friars were God's poor, dependent on almsgiving, and so possessed of a keen interest in spreading the message about the benefits of good works and charity to the poor. The second, related observation expands on earlier comments. The prayers of the honest poor were held to be especially efficacious: just as Christ and His disciples had been paupers, so the poor were close to God and were the spiritually rich.[17] The wealthy, whose status and possessions erected barriers between themselves and God, took this to heart and were notably generous in life and death, succouring the poor to stimulate and harness their intercession. However, if almsgiving was, if anything, the good work which generally absorbed most investment, there were obviously many other avenues to spiritual benefit, as men and women managed with extraordinary ingenuity to remind and oblige others to pray for the souls of their benefactors.[18]

Recasting penitential imperatives in the twelfth and thirteenth centuries explains the changes in emphasis in London noted earlier: rather than the obvious response being limited to those who might give much to establish ambitious institutions, by the later Middle Ages the less wealthy were encouraged to embark on foundation and provision. Their endeavours naturally tended to be on a smaller scale and were more 'atomized'. Rather than the great monasteries of the tenth and eleventh centuries, colleges, perhaps housing half a dozen or a dozen priests, were the more typical response; and rather than hospitals, almshouses were more commonly founded in the fourteenth and fifteenth centuries. London reflects this change well. Few monasteries were founded in and around the city in the later Middle Ages, and those that can be mentioned were generally for the more austere orders emphasizing individualistic rather than communal life, like the Carthusians[19] or the Bridgettines.[20] These were, however, high-status foundations, reflective essentially of the importance of the London region in national life.[21] Colleges and almshouses, founded by the likes of Walworth and Whittington, were indeed the more prevalent form of large-scale foundation, and it may be mentioned that just as Whittington entrusted his company, the mercers, with the supervision of his almshouse, so other companies, like the merchant taylors and vinters, established almshouses in the course of the fifteenth century to benefit their members.[22] But chantries were much the most commonly encountered foundation.[23]

While penitential developments played a part in prompting interest in smaller foundations, it should in fairness be admitted that there were additional factors militating against larger foundations in the later Middle Ages. Available land for endowments was generally in shorter supply; in the wake of the Black Death, which might have been expected to release property, tenurial upheaval in the countryside and depopulation in towns undoubtedly led to uncertainty about the buoyancy of long-term rents; moreover, after the mortmain statutes (intended to call a halt to land passing out of the king's influence and into the 'dead hand' of the Church), passed initially in 1279 and strengthened in 1391, founding ambitious institutions became dependent upon the king's good will in granting the requisite licence and, as a result of the fines that had to be paid, a more expensive process. In these circumstances it was wise to be less ambitious. The factors, then, of a shift in penitential emphasis and considerations of practicality combine to explain why the chantry became the most distinctive and certainly the most common intercessory foundation of the later Middle Ages, founded by nobility, gentry and bourgeoisie alike, in considerable numbers and with profound cumulative effect. It is, then, to a proper consideration of this service, and some of its related manifestations, that I now turn.

The chantry was in essence an arrangement which provided a priest to celebrate a daily Mass at a specified altar, usually an existing altar in a parish church, for the benefit of nominated individuals, sometimes in life, much more frequently in death, almost always including the soul or souls of the man, woman or family footing the priest's stipend. As a priest might, in ordinary circumstances, celebrate only one Mass daily, any serving a chantry was precluded from holding any other benefice or cure, and those who would benefit from a chantry had to be prepared to pay the celebrant's salary. While obviously far cheaper than a monastic foundation, it was still a serious undertaking. Those who sought a chantry in perpetuity invariably set aside real property, in towns usually tenements and shops, the rents from which would pay the stipend and provide sufficient to keep the endowment in good repair. But the more common form of the service was a foundation for a limited duration – a year or two being the most common, but ten-, fifteen- or even twenty-year durations being perfectly feasible. Temporary chantries could be paid for with a lump sum set aside in the founder's will, but were most commonly founded by heirs, who were obliged to set aside part of the income deriving from the inheritance they received from their progenitors, effectively paying a death duty on the estate to provide for the souls of their parents. While the chantry priest was undoubtedly bound to serve his founder, once he had celebrated the daily Mass he was available to assist in pastoral duties and other tasks in the parish. So, effectively, any chantry founder was providing his or her parish with a free auxiliary, able to swell the ranks of those assisting with the liturgy and serving parishioners generally. It was very often also the case that chantry celebrants were equipped with vestments and vessels to be used at the celebration of the founder's Mass, which equipment would undoubtedly add to the range and opulence of the parish liturgy and, in the case of temporary chantry foundations, would usually revert to the parish when the duration had been completed. This was an important way by which parishes gained liturgical equipment. Far from being a 'selfish' arrangement, a service intended to benefit only the souls of founders, the chantry is better regarded as part and parcel of a very generous benefaction – of a paid stipendiary and of equipment – to the parish.[24] Moreover, in the case of perpetual chantries, any surplus of income over expenditure on salary and endowment repair usually profited the parish. In addition, then, to the grace benefiting the founder's soul from the celebration of Masses, chantry foundation ensured that living parishioners would be bound to intercede for the founder who had provided stipendiary, equipment and perhaps even an income. All told, chantry foundation was a very effective way of benefiting the soul by procuring grace and intercession.

The basic idea of the chantry was very flexible, and two related arrangements should be briefly mentioned. First, the confraternities, or brotherhoods (and sisterhoods), which were a particularly distinctive aspect of late medieval pious life, were in essence simply corporate chantries. They sometimes represented trade guilds, but were more often simply voluntary associations with a shared devotional focus, honouring and petitioning a particular saint, often the Blessed Virgin, for instance, or her mother, St Anne, or a cult, like Corpus Christi. In practical terms, people, both rich but more frequently the less well off, might club together to support a priest who was to celebrate the fraternity Mass, daily or at specified intervals, and they might make additional payments to derive other benefits, like support in infirmity or care for their children were they to be orphaned, as well as invariably binding themselves to pray for deceased members. There were few parish churches in the century or more before the Reformation which did not house at least one fraternity, and these were organizations which added another layer of devotional practice and an additional focus of pious intensity to existing religious provision.[25]

Secondly, mention should be made of the anniversary or year's mind, which, K.L. Wood-Legh argues, was the prototype from which the chantry originated.[26] As the name suggests, this was an annual celebration of the Mass, usually on the anniversary of the founder's decease (although some were celebrated more frequently), and was in essence an exact repetition of the funeral rites. It comprised exequies on the eve and a Mass of Requiem on the day; a coffin was placed on the parish hearse, a pall was draped over the coffin and candles were lit (just as if the corpse of the commemorated were once again present), all of which was accompanied by generous doles to the poor, the tolling of parish bells and the town crier employed to broadcast the deceased's need for prayer in the locality. It was a concentrated and even a theatrical plea for intercession, which, because it could be provided relatively cheaply as compared to a chantry, was common in the centuries preceding the Reformation. And again, while procuring intercession, anniversaries also often profited parishes. The endowments supporting perpetual anniversaries were often generous, yielding appreciably more than the cost of the specified observance: the difference between income and cost frequently profited parish coffers, reducing the sums that had to be raised for present and pressing needs and obliging living parishioners, once more, to remember and pray for their dead predecessors and benefactors.[27]

Having outlined aspects of the obligatory and voluntary responses made by Christians in the Middle Ages, the first concerned with the parish and the second more with intercessory institutions and arrangements, I have been at pains to point out that, as emphases changed with time, the intercessory institutions that wealthier Christians established in the fourteenth and certainly in the fifteenth century tended to be relatively small-scale, with chantries, fraternities and anniversaries being the most commonly encountered arrangements. The two responses, obligatory and voluntary, increasingly intersected with time. Sited in parishes, smaller-scale intercessory arrangements had a profound impact, affecting local regimes by reducing or shaping the obligatory response incumbent on parishioners. They added to parish liturgies, providing extra services and equipment, devotions and observances. They increased the parish's role as a focus for and battery of intercession. Fraternities added considerably to the social role of the parish, attracting the attention and attendance of parishioners, very possibly, from elsewhere and engaging them in extra pious and self-help pursuits. More specifically, chantries added to the number of priests in the parish, bolstering the pastoral capacity of the parish and adding to the solemnity with which the liturgy might be celebrated; moreover, by the later fifteenth century, if not earlier, the presence of chantry priests had stimulated musical performance of some sophistication in many parishes, especially in towns. Chantries and perpetual anniversaries might also add to parish revenues, reducing the sums that parishioners were obliged to pay for services and repairs, or conversely enabling them to consider more ambitious outlay and provision. The responsibilities which accompanied services also affected parish life and government. Churchwardens and the parish clergy were invariably obliged to exercise a supervisory role, guaranteeing the proper and, if necessary, perpetual discharge of the services sited and endowed in their parishes. They had to select chantry priests when necessary and ascertain that they performed all that was expected and that they behaved with decorum; they had to ensure that endowments were properly maintained and that the requisite services were fully observed; depending on arrangements made by founders they might have to entrust (or strictly, enfeoff) other parishioners with the endowments that supported the services, repeating this exercise as generations passed; and, finally, they were frequently obliged to keep accounts of income and expenditure. The benefits that could accrue to the parish from intercessory arrangements and services were considerable, but founders were often at pains to stipulate that failure to ensure that all was being carried out as required would mean transfer to another parish. The duties accompanying intercessory services were therefore serious, demanding a regular investment of time and sustained effort. The benefits were such, though, to ensure that parishes took their duties very seriously. This had repercussions. Intercessory services acted as catalysts, prompting, among many other developments, both liturgical elaboration and managerial expertise, cumulatively changing parishes very considerably. This observation may best be illustrated by precise example.

Consideration, first, of the parish of St Mary at Hill in Billingsgate Ward, London, proves useful. It was a relatively wealthy parish,[28] home to many fishmongers and, in addition to numerous short-term or small-scale services which parishioners established in life and death, it housed seven perpetual chantries by the late fifteenth century.[29] This was, admittedly, an unusual concentration for any one parish, but it may be noted that there were some London parishes which housed more – in the south-eastern sector of the city which included Billingsgate, for instance, St Magnus the Martyr had perhaps as many as twelve chantries and St Dunstan in the East perhaps eight or nine.[30] However, possessed of fine surviving churchwardens' accounts, which permit a relatively close understanding of parish life, St Mary at Hill may be appraised in reasonable detail.[31] That the chantries were of importance to the parish is plain from the careful transcription of each founder's will in the parish records;[32] it is also worth noting that each was successfully maintained until the Reformation, bar the two whose rental income was lowest, which were amalgamated to form one very healthy institution.[33] Although it must always be borne in mind that the many smaller-scale benefactions and arrangements given to and sited in St Mary at Hill made a significant contribution to the opulence of its liturgy and the intensity of its intercessory battery, it proves convenient here to concentrate on the contribution made by the perpetual chantries. The churchwardens' accounts bear eloquent witness to the care lavished on each of them, and the chantry certificate, made at the dissolution in 1548, confirms the buoyancy of each arrangement.[34] Wrytell and Weston's combined arrangements produced an income in excess of £16 annually and the priest who served them was paid a salary of £8; the remaining five chantry priests were each paid a salary of £6 13*s* 4*d* in 1548, but Causton's endowments yielded an annual revenue in excess of £20, Nasyng and Bedham's each yielded in excess of £12 and Cambridge and Gosslyng's each in the region of £10. If, in some years, the demands on individual endowments were heavy – to pay for building repairs, for instance – in others, the parish, which was entitled to the surplus, did very well. Moreover, multiple chantry foundation meant that St Mary at Hill found itself the effective proprietor and landlord of property both inside and outside the parish. There was a tendency for the earlier foundations to be endowed with property in or near the parish. For instance, Rose Wrytell's endowment of a single tenement 'of old time called the Swan on the Hope' was situated in Thames Street in the parish, but, among the fifteenth-century foundations, while Cambridge's endowment was in the parish of St Christopher le Stocks, fairly near the parish, Gosslyng's consisted of various properties in Foster Lane in the parish of St Leonard, north of Cheapside, well towards the west of the city. Overall, somewhere in the region of half the endowments were in the parish, meaning that a good number of parishioners were also parish tenants. The multiple foundation of perpetual chantries meant that the parish of St Mary at Hill became the proprietor of a sizable holding of property spread through the city and managed by its parishioners.

The rents from these endowments augmented parish finances very considerably: with other revenues swelling receipts, annual income towards the end of the fifteenth century was in the region of £100 and, even if a good deal of this had to be spent on chantry priests and on property maintenance, much of the parish income came from *post obit* provision. A sustained administrative effort had to be devoted to maintaining the endowments and the services they supported, obliging both diligence and professionalism. These were responsibilities which galvanized parish government. They were also burdens which, in all probability, helped to confirm the successful men of affairs within the neighbourhood as the natural managers of the parish – too much was at stake for it to be entrusted to the inexperienced or inept. Close examination of the surviving archive certainly confirms that the parish élite were firmly in control of parish affairs by the late fifteenth and early sixteenth centuries.[35]

As suggested, the presence of six or seven perpetual chantries, in addition to whatever else was being provided by and commissioned in the parish, also had a profound effect upon the parish liturgy. It proves worthwhile, first, to examine the specific observances that were to comprise some of the services. John Bedham's celebrant, in addition to singing a Mass daily at the altar of St Katherine within the church, was to sing in the church at all the canonical hours and at all services, 'helping in all things to the best of his abilities', saying matins, prime and the other hours, evensong, compline, *placebo* and *dirige* and all other prayers and services 'by himself or with his fellow priests continually'. William Cambridge's demands were more elaborate. In addition to his requirement that a priest be provided to sing divine service in St Stephen's chapel in the church, and that his anniversary was to be perpetually kept 'by note' [i.e., with music], five wax tapers were to be found for the candlestick which Cambridge had bequeathed the church, and these were to burn at every feast of Our Lady and at every double feast[36] during the first and last evensong and also at matins and High Mass, but on low feasts at Mass only, all of which was to be done in honour of Christ, the blessed Virgin and all the saints. Cambridge also stipulated that every day, except at double feasts, his priest should say *placebo* and *dirige* with the Commendation of Souls, the Seven Psalms and the ferial litany. But the most revealing detail is to be found in a note added to Cambridge's will. This reveals that it was customary at the Magnificat during evensong on Christmas Day (which, note, is St Stephen's Eve) to distribute fifteen lighted candles, one to every surpliced priest, clerk and child providing the service; holding a lighted candle, all were to proceed to Cambridge's tomb, in the chapel of St Stephen which he had built, singing a respond of St Stephen with the prose, followed by a versicle with the collect of St Stephen, after which they were to proceed into the choir to sing an anthem of Our Lady. As well as adding to the liturgical elaboration of the parish, it is also abundantly apparent from these requirements that chantry founders could rely on, and were in fact building on, an already sophisticated round of observance within the parish; the chance survival of the appendix specifying the requirements on St Stephen's Eve reveals procedures that would never have been assumed. One is left, quite naturally, wondering what else was being provided in the parish. It is particularly striking that so many singers could be counted on as being so easily available and this, in turn, leads to a fruitful avenue of enquiry.

The more the parish archive is examined with music in mind, the more it discloses. Performance in St Mary at Hill was undeniably sophisticated by the late fifteenth and early sixteenth century, and the presence of six or seven chantry priests, who were to be able to sing and, apart from their own specific duties, were to assist with the parish's own musical repertory, must have stimulated standards in the parish. Indeed, it is worth mentioning that the mid-sixteenth-century chantry certificate reveals that almost all the chantry priests in St Mary at Hill were 'good singers', that one was a 'player on the organs' and that there were stipendiary priests in the church who were able 'to sing and help in the choir'.[37] The impressions derived from the detailed churchwardens' accounts, which survive in good series from the late 1470s, similarly suggest that music was already of importance. The parish, as a matter of course, purchased assistance from elsewhere to swell the numbers of musicians at particular feasts. For in addition to the chantry priests, the parish hired John Henly at times during the period 1477–9 to sing on Palm Sunday, Corpus Christi and St Barnabas' Day, in addition to four children from the neighbouring parish of St Magnus; Walter Pleasance was also paid for playing the organs. Within the years 1483–5 the parish paid 5*s* for wine bought at the tavern for 'singers within the choir' at feasts during the year, and another entry, now scored, reveals that the parish acquired a book of pricksong (vocal polyphony). Whether this was the first such book that the parish possessed is imponderable (although unlikely), but the indications are that polyphonic music was being performed in the parish by the mid-1480s at the latest. By the 1490s the parish had a considerable holding of music books. In 1496–7, for instance, the parish paid a stationer £1 13*s* 4*d* for setting all the new feasts into the books and Mass books that lacked them, and another 2*s* for setting the new feasts in the organ books. Musical standards and innovations were further encouraged by close association with musicians from the Chapel Royal, a number of whom lived in and regularly sang for the parish on a freelance basis, recruiting other colleagues from the Chapel as necessary.[38] Paving the way for stylish performance, the fact that professionals, like John Sidborough and John Kyte, even considered singing in the church implies high standards and achievement. In this context it is worth recalling the appendix to Cambridge's will: fifteen singers, priests, clerks and children were to be gathered on Christmas Day, with no difficulty apparently envisaged, to perform a sophisticated repertory both at his tomb and in the choir. There can be little doubt that in St Mary at Hill perpetual chantries provided both singers and money, which together helped to develop the remarkable musical and liturgical standards achieved in the parish by the later fifteenth century.

In sum, then, the presence of a number of perpetual chantries, in addition to whatever else had been sited in the parish, greatly increased St Mary at Hill's annual budget and obliged the parish to develop competence as a managerial and financial regime. The churchwardens' accounts confirm these impressions as well as disclosing that the chantry priests were consistently employed and that property endowments across the city were steadfastly maintained. Liturgically, too, all the indications are that the parish had become a force to be reckoned with. Generous penitential provision enlarged responsibilities and, because self-regulation had become a matter of importance to parishioners (with more to be lost should slipshod practices ever have been allowed to creep in), the parish may well have become more tightly knit and efficiently governed. The cumulative effects of multiple chantries went deep, fostering communal self-regard and producing a parish which, because of what it had and was achieving, mattered all the more in its own estimation. If St Mary at Hill was a parish fundamentally shaped by the penitential imperatives of the later Middle Ages, when smaller-scale institutions and benefactions were being sited in and lavished on parish churches, it is worthwhile pondering the wider implications of these developments. Shifting pastoral responses, centring now on the parish rather than on extra-parochial intercessory institutions, might spawn a well-developed local corporation which shared a surprising number of characteristics with a monastic house. Elaborate liturgy, a propertied endowment, a strong *ésprit de corps*, a well-articulated management and an emphatic intercessory function were characteristics which, by the later fifteenth century, applied just as strongly to

The beginning of the churchwardens' accounts for St Mary at Hill, London, for 1517–18. The account for the year is in two sections, of which the first (shown here) runs from Michaelmas 1517 until the following Midsummer. The prominence of chantries in the parish economy is immediately apparent, with 'the Renttes of John Nasynges Chauntry' being entered first, followed by the 'Quitrenttes and paymenttes of þe same Chauntry'.

some of London's parish communities as to monasteries. Penitential developments, and the response which the Church had elicited, recreated in some late medieval parishes many of the salient characteristics of a monastery in miniature. The laity as parishioners, moreover, exercised considerable influence as founders and control as managers, and by the later fifteenth century, as a result of generations of investment and effort, a parish like St Mary at Hill might both stimulate and satisfy the penitential aspirations and needs of a much wider social range of citizens than could a monastery. It is worth bearing in mind that the parishioners in question lived, not just in a parish, but in a city. The many large-scale intercessory institutions which functioned and flourished in London must have made some impression on their consciousness. At the very least they provided models. Changing penitential emphases, and the practical imperatives of these developments, afforded the laity with the opportunity, to a degree, to emulate, providing themselves with more sophisticated services and developing the managerial structures necessary to sustain these observances.

Unexpected conclusions emerge if, rather than treating intercessory institutions as axiomatically things apart, a late medieval parish is examined 'in the round'. At first glance, however, a parish like St Andrew Hubbard, Eastcheap, St Mary at Hill's immediate northern neighbour, which lacked perpetual intercessory arrangements, seems very much the poor relation. Its income was low and its standards appear comparatively mean. Close scrutiny of St Andrew Hubbard's churchwardens' accounts confirms, however, that although it lacked the property and revenues which came with ambitious intercessory foundations, it certainly employed many of the same basic managerial arrangements and procedures as its neighbour – as did any other urban parish. Sustained scrutiny reveals, more surprisingly, that the parish was far from being simply a poor relation.[39] Analysis of St Andrew Hubbard suggests that in the decades preceding the Reformation something very significant was afoot even in London's less affluent parishes, and that it was very probably a 'knock-on effect' in the city's neighbourhoods from the fillip which multiple intercessory foundations undeniably gave to some parishes.

No parishioner of St Andrew Hubbard ever managed to establish a perpetual chantry. Its parishioners were, on average, poorer, and those wealthy enough presumably had surviving heirs who had first claim on the family patrimony. Parishioners William and Juliana Fairhead attempted to establish a perpetual chantry in the parish in the 1440s, but their endowment proved insufficient. A priest was supported only intermittently in the 1450s and 1460s, and any pretence of celebrating daily Masses was abandoned by 1470; the service was pared down to provide only an elaborate anniversary for the Fairheads,[40] with surplus revenues being ploughed into parish funds. One or two sixteenth-century parishioners attempted to found perpetual chantries, but doctrinal change intervened. Throughout the late fifteenth and early sixteenth centuries St Andrew Hubbard's income stood in the region of £10 per annum. The income which the parish had diverted from the Fairheads' endowment accounted for something like a quarter of this, which, by comparison with the budget enjoyed by St Mary at Hill, serves to emphasize the limitations of the wardens' budget in

Not only are the accounts for St Andrew Hubbard less tidy; they show significant differences between the economy of this parish and that of its neighbour, St Mary at Hill. The account here, from Michaelmas 1517 to Michaelmas 1518, reveals that though Michael Everard paid £3 6s 8d for a year's rent, the bulk of St Andrew Hubbard's income came from small sums gathered in burial fees (known as knells), collections for the paschal light and the clerk's salary, and from bequests. Entries towards the foot of the page record many small donations. Bound toward the end of the first book of accounts, this is one of the 'rogue' accounts which reveal the parish regime in unusual detail.

this parish. Important as this inadvertent *post obit* income was for St Andrew Hubbard, the parish was obliged to depend in the main on collections and fees paid by living parishioners.[41] But, as suggested, the St Andrew Hubbard churchwardens' accounts disclose that the parish, while certainly poorer than its neighbour, should not be written off.

If sparser than those of St Mary at Hill, the St Andrew Hubbard accounts are easier to come to grips with and the lesson that emerges, and which can also then be applied to St Mary at Hill, is that a great deal might go on in a parish which usually finds no specific reference in the churchwardens' record of parish affairs. The decisions and machinations which paved the way to commuting the Fairheads' chantry in St Andrew Hubbard, for instance, although of obvious importance to the parish and to the churchwardens' budget, find no mention. Moreover, at roughly the same time as the vestiges of the chantry celebrations disappeared, the wardens seem to have taken on responsibility for the parish clerk – or at least the parish clerk begins to be mentioned regularly in the accounts as they have come down to us. The strong likelihood is that there had been a clerk or clerks in the parish before the 1470s but the wardens either bore no responsibility previously or accounted for him or them in other records not now surviving. These probabilities are disquieting. The churchwardens' accounts offer at best an imperfect impression of parish life: significant developments could occur without comment, or might reflect either change in the wardens' accounting procedures or else a simple redistribution of parish responsibilities.

Such impressions are further confirmed on close scrutiny of the accounts which have survived from *c.* 1515 to 1523. These fall at the end of the first volume of surviving accounts and, as well as being on different paper from all the earlier accounts in this volume, are much less tidy. It is a possibility that the earlier accounts (from 1454 to *c.* 1515) offer a tidied version of affairs compiled to extol the achievements of the churchwardens, whereas the last quire in the book reflects broader interests.[42] Certainly there is much more detail in the accounts for the years immediately following 1515. The two churchwardens are, for instance, revealed in one account as having had discrete responsibilites, each being in charge of different aspects of parish income and expenditure; this may very well represent a common practice normally summated in the accounts as they survive ordinarily. There are lists of parishioners who contributed to parish projects, like the names of those who gave towards the purchase of organs in *c.* 1518, a practice which finds no earlier parallel. There were, moreover, many more small collections of money entered into the parish income, including, for instance, a reference to a substantial Hock Monday collection in 1521–2, which similarly find no precedent.[43] The implications are clear: these accounts, which I have elsewhere referred to as 'rogue accounts', give a fuller than usual impression of parish life, emphasizing the limitations of most of the accounts which survive for St Andrew Hubbard. The Hock Monday collection may, for instance, have been a flash in the pan; it is much more likely that 'hocking' was a regular event in the parish, but that its revenues were not ordinarily the responsibility of the churchwardens. These conclusions from *c.* 1515 to 1523 affect the interpretation of churchwardens' accounts from other years, particularly those which survive from the mid-1520s onwards in the second volume of St Andrew Hubbard's accounts. It is evident that there were other officials in the parish besides the churchwardens. The auditors and assessors, for instance, were frequently mentioned and were men who had already served as wardens and who were of superior status: they seem to have been the real managers of the parish for whom the wardens acted as foremen, in charge of day-to-day affairs but not making important decisions. Agents other than churchwardens were obviously capable of directing additional affairs and could have kept additional records and accounts, now lost.

The material to clinch the argument, though, concerns music. It is striking that, while on first glance appearing to be a relatively poor parish, St Andrew Hubbard nevertheless had books of music, organs and an organist and singers, cumulatively indicative of an unexpected level of provision and performance. But the crux is that while there are sufficient references to suggest that provision was constant and of a reasonable standard, recorded payments are simply too sporadic to account for steady support. In 1485–6, for instance, the churchwardens record the payment of 2*s* 'to Thomas, stationer, for writing the visitation of the Mass of Our Lady and the Mass of the same', an entry followed almost immediately by a payment of 4*d* 'for an organ player at the Nativity of Our Lady'. Suggestive of an adventurous liturgy and seasoned performance, both references nevertheless come out of the blue, with the purchase or provision of more rudimentary music seemingly absent. Moreover in the early 1460s the churchwardens record the expenditure of £5 8*s* 8*d* 'for the organs and setting them up', but organists thereafter merit only the most cursory reference – 2*d* 'for a player on the organs' in 1465–6, or 1*s* 'paid to a man that played upon the organs one Christmas' in the years 1466–8. Singers, too, are often mentioned, but here the payments seem to be for special performances, like the sum of 1*s* 1*d* that was paid 'to clerks for drinking upon St Andrew's day [and] for singing' in the account for 1457–9, and in the same account the sum of 2*s* paid to 'Sir Harry for singing here all Easter week'. The entries in the churchwardens' accounts are clearly supplementary payments, for extra provision at certain times. The inescapable conclusion is that everyday provision and payment was coordinated by managers other than churchwardens.

The implications of these findings are of importance. While St Andrew Hubbard may not have had perpetual chantries, to condemn the parish out of hand as poor or backward is unhelpful. Its budget was clearly more extensive than its churchwardens' accounts suggest. If it was indeed a parish whose financial regime was heavily dependent on constant collection, there is at least a possibility that its management structure was rather more diversified than that in a parish like St Mary at Hill simply because eking sufficient revenue took more varied effort and depended more upon delegation and the division of labours to ensure manageable responsibilities. But it does not do to press the contrasts with St Mary at Hill too far, for on detailed appraisal a number of similarities between the two parishes emerge. It was certainly the case that by *c.* 1500 St Mary at Hill had an élite, a rank of managers superior to the churchwardens who directed parish policy; much the same was visible in St Andrew Hubbard from the 1520s onward, although probably in place much earlier. Furthermore, the considered findings about music in St Andrew Hubbard apply equally to St Mary at Hill: in the latter, while there are certainly sufficient references to suggest strikingly sophisticated provision, what we have in the accounts are supplementary payments – the day-to-day management of music in both parishes was not part of the wardens' brief. The similarities between the two parishes are greater than at first seems likely. Finally, with these precepts in mind, it is worth devoting attention to a chance survival in the St Mary at Hill accounts which sheds more light on the role that agents other than churchwardens might play in the parish, the implications of which confirm churchwardens' accounts as decidedly limited in their scope.

St Mary at Hill undertook an ambitious building programme in the final years of the fifteenth century, rebuilding the aisles and later the church tower. Thomas Colyns, who had served as churchwarden a few years previously, was in charge of the building initiative at the very end of the century, aided and abetted by the senior churchwarden, Harry Esmond. This much becomes clear in an appendix to the account for 1499–1500: at the parish audit, held on 18 January, the surplus on the year's account was £22 16*s* 1*d*, to which sum the said Thomas Colyns and another, William Smart, both parishioners who were part of the élite, respectively added £2 10*s* and pledged £1 10*s* 4*d*.[44] A total of £26 16*s* 5*d* was delivered to Colyns who, seemingly, had primed work on the tower with his own money and was still, after substantial repayments, owed in excess of £11 'for expenses upon the masons' workmanship and for stones for the steeple'. The sum of £15 or more which 'remained in Colyns' hands' was 'to be bestowed in time to come upon the works of the steeple'. The churchwardens' accounts mention work on the aisles and tower in, at best, a glancing manner. But if, on the one hand, substantial sums of money were involved in the building work (this much is plain from the material in the appendix summarized very briefly here), then, on the other, a member of the parish élite, previously a warden, was apparently in charge of the work and was certainly being entrusted with substantial sums of money, having previously made generous subventions from his own funds to continue the work. It was the churchwardens' responsibility, after all, to maintain the parish fabric; ambitious rebuilding appears to have exceeded their brief. Tried and tested men of affairs in the parish assumed the burden and were given considerable scope to act as they saw fit. Additional information in the appendix reveals, moreover, that Colyns kept his own record of the work he undertook, which could presumably be presented to the parish: 'paid in my reckoning that I laid out to the mason for stone and other things necessary, as it appears more plainly in my account'. Substantial works were done in addition to those managed by the churchwardens; additional records were being created. We know of such matters only by very good fortune. Parishes like St Mary at Hill and St Andrew Hubbard, while differing in many respects, must both be allowed as having been in possession of more extensive budgets and, if anything, as being capable of more, much more, be it in liturgical or administrative spheres, than at first sight seems plausible.

It is time for some conclusions. Intercessory institutions, particularly perpetual chantries, had done a great deal to stimulate both liturgical achievement and

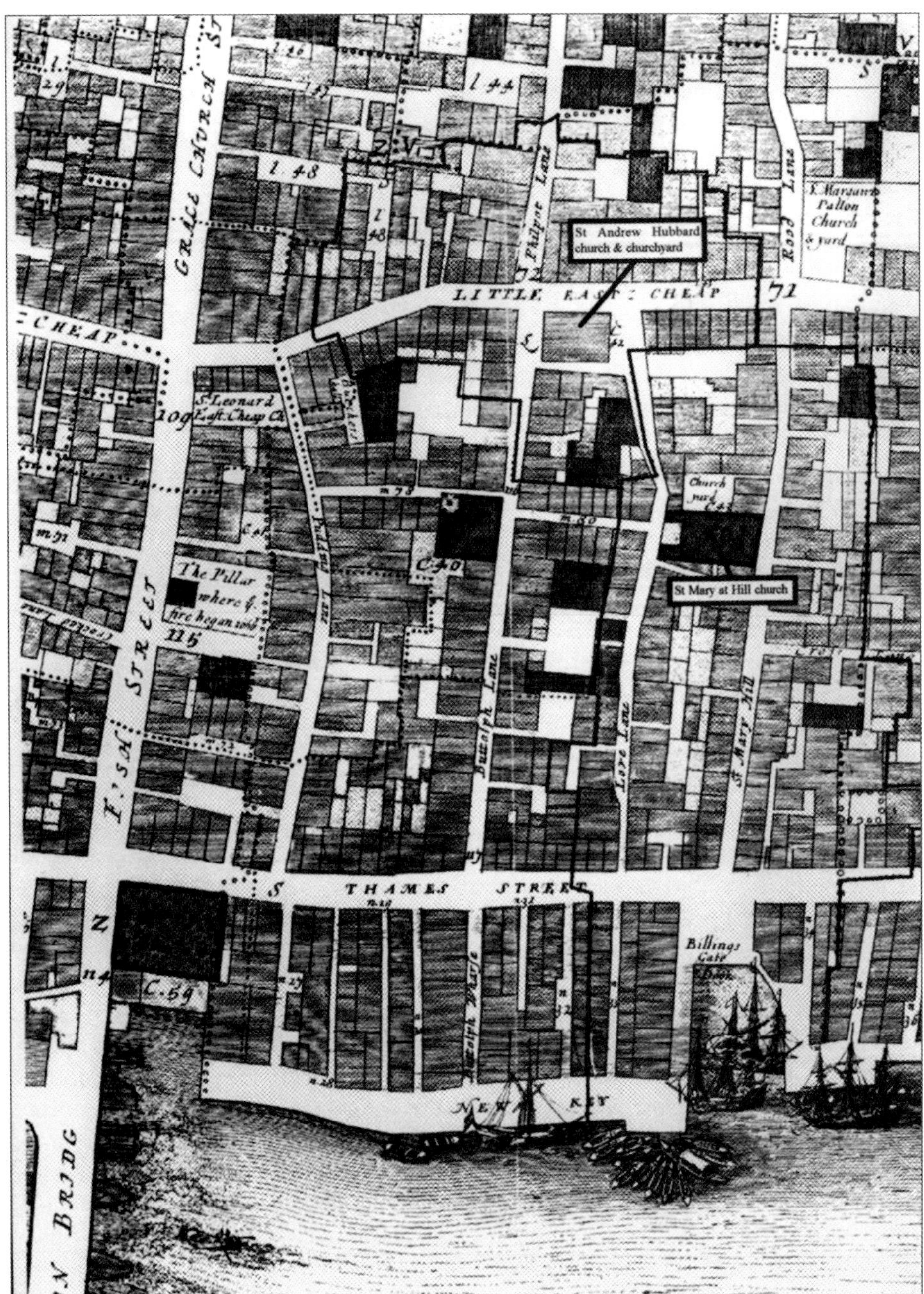

A detail from the parish map of London after the Great Fire of 1666, showing the area just to the north and east of London Bridge. The parish of St Mary at Hill runs north from Billingsgate Dock. Abutting it to the north and west, the parish of St Andrew Hubbard straddles Eastcheap. Both churches were burnt down in 1666, but only St Mary at Hill was rebuilt. St Andrew Hubbard retained its legal identity, with vestry and churchwardens, until the mid-twentieth century, but its parishioners worshipped in St Mary at Hill.

managerial competence in London's parishes by the later Middle Ages. St Mary at Hill had clearly been fundamentally shaped by the good fortune of having six or so perpetual chantries sited in its church. Strikingly, however, a parish like St Andrew Hubbard, while enjoying fewer revenues and being able to provide rather less overall, clearly shared many characteristics with St Mary at Hill. Indeed, lessons learned from the St Andrew Hubbard archive cast useful illumination on St Mary at Hill. More was afoot in each parish than respective accounts normally disclose, and it is striking that St Andrew Hubbard's government, by what must have been unstinting effort, seems to have been able to provide something at least of what was on offer in a much richer neighbouring parish. If intercessory responsibilities had shaped St Mary at Hill, which seems to be beyond dispute, then, in the close-packed environment of London, less fortunate parishes, far from abandoning a race they could never realistically hope to win, struggled to emulate the pacesetters. By their own lights they seem to have done so with some success. It is striking, for instance, when perusing the inventories of parish possessions compiled in 1552, made prior to the Edwardian government's confiscation of church goods, how much a parish like St Andrew had been able to amass, particularly in the way of vestments.[45] It had less than St Mary at Hill, but was by no means badly equipped. The generosity of parishioners, the careful and long-practised husbandry of parish leaders and, more generally, the determination of those in less well-endowed parishes simply to keep up might combine to render any late medieval parish an entity of quite remarkable competence. In the absence of perpetual chantries, the penitential regime might still encourage participation, generosity and hard work – all these were, in fact, good works, and any parish might benefit enormously from each or all of them. It is the lesson of St Andrew Hubbard, certainly, that 'poor' parishes should never be written off: parishioners worked all the more assiduously to keep up, which may, in fact, have been the most striking result of penitential priorities where such regimes were concerned. In an environment like London, with many layers of generous intercessory provison overlaying a basic pastoral structure of over a hundred parishes, the intermixing of obligatory and voluntary responses had by the later Middle Ages created an ecclesiastical establishment of marked range and formidable competence, wherein the laity, with many examples before them, played a noteworthy role in satisfying their own needs with considerable flair. It is tempting to conceive of parishes as small, inward-looking communities; it may be true that individuals concentrated on their own parish, but they did so aware of their neighbours and the city. In this broader context, penitential procedures and the accompanying imperatives and aspirations played a fundamental role in setting the standards and sustaining the effort which underpinned a widespread and surprising achievement in the late fifteenth and early sixteenth centuries. As a corollary, the changes wrought at the Reformation, radically recasting the intercessory response, must be accounted as all the more draconian, sweeping away a variety of institutions and slashing the budgets of those which survived, particularly a parish like St Mary at Hill. St Andrew Hubbard, used in any case to consistent effort to make ends meet, may not have been quite so seriously affected and doubtless had the expertise to manage in new, more straitened circumstances. St Mary at Hill, similarly possessed of formidable skills, could also adapt, even though losing more income. Later attempts at social provision, like the Poor Law, to be administered 'on the parish', were in many respects a recognition of the achievements in this sphere in the fourteenth, fifteenth and early sixteenth centuries, an achievement shaped in many of its fundamentals by intercessory imperatives.

CHAPTER 9

York under the Yorkists

RICHARD BRITNELL

York in the later fifteenth century was a stoutly built city in which its inhabitants could take pride, even if they had to bear heavy charges for its upkeep. Unusually for inland English towns, there were extensive town walls, with great gates, an encirclement that enabled the city authorities to close off the city centre at night for security; in November 1482 the council ordered that gates and posterns were all to be barred from 9 o'clock at night until 5 o'clock in the morning.[1] Near the centre of the city stood a stone bridge across the Ouse, on which stood the chapel of St William, together with a chamber used by the city council, the city exchequer and the civic prisons (the 'kidcotes'), at least six shops, forty-one tenements and a latrine for which the bridgemasters of the Ouse Bridge supplied lighting. There was also a *maison Dieu* for poor women.[2] There was another substantial stone bridge over the River Foss, upon which stood the chapel of St Anne, as well as other properties.[3] These bridges were each entrusted to two wardens, or bridgemasters, who accounted for annual receipts from rents and for expenditure on the upkeep both of the bridges and of the bridge chapels.[4] Between St Helen's Square and the river stood a larger common hall, the Guildhall (1445–59), which was unusual among the city's buildings in having walls constructed entirely of stone.[5] Much of the cost of maintaining these structures had to be borne collectively by the citizens.

Other major buildings, though their repair often depended directly on the wealth of the citizens of York, were the responsibility of separate or private interests rather than a corporate charge on all the citizens. Many of these were ecclesiastical. Within the walls there was the Minster, St Mary's Abbey, Holy Trinity Priory, four friaries and some thirty-nine parish churches.[6] St Leonard's Hospital, built within the walls between the Minster and St Mary's Abbey, was one of the largest in England.[7] The maintenance of parish churches was an ongoing commitment, even when major new construction was unnecessary. The one with the biggest problem was probably St Michael-le-Belfrey, next to the Minster, which was already reported to be needing expensive repairs in 1472, and apparently on the way to its eventual demolition. The church of St Mary Bishophill Junior was also lacking care and attention in 1481, when it was reported that because of broken windows 'byrdes cummys in and doth fyele [i.e. defile] all the church', and the roof leaked in five or six places.[8] Considering the number of

York churches, however, it is not surprising that some of them needed attention, and severe decay was exceptional. These examples of decay are offset by evidence of continuing new investment in church building elsewhere in the city. In 1466 the ancient church of St Olave's in Marygate received a new lease of life when the Archbishop of York redefined it as a parish church and allocated responsibility for maintaining it between its parishioners and St Mary's Abbey. The parishioners

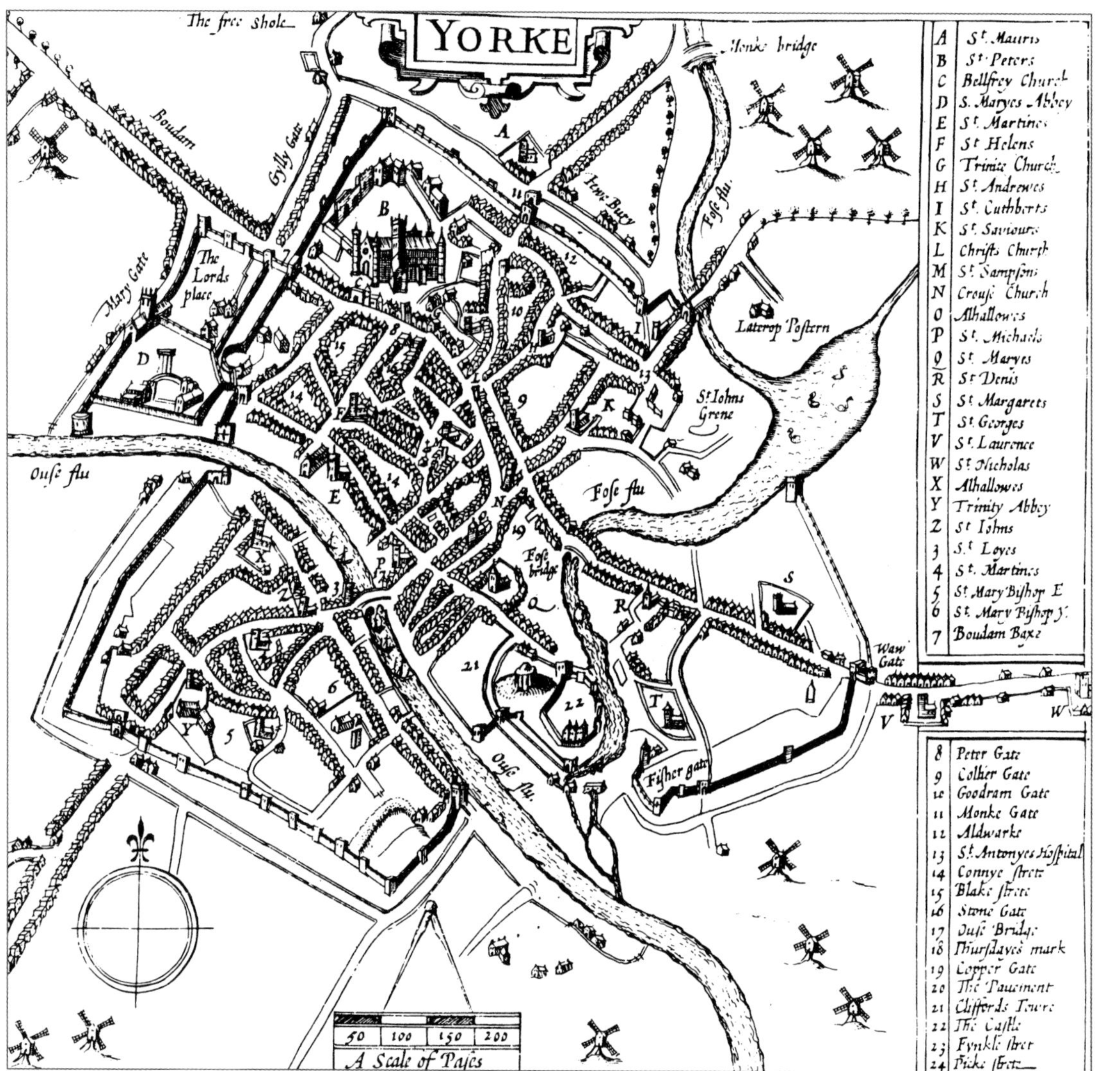

York in 1610, from the representation of the city attached to John Speed's map of the West Riding in his Theatre of the Empire of Great Britaine, *published in 1612. The picture map gives a useful impression of the medieval city, the chief change from the Yorkist period being the closure of the religious houses in the sixteenth century.*

found money for work on the nave, and a new tower was underway in the early 1480s.[9] Another reconstruction of the 1460s was the new chancel at Holy Trinity Micklegate, which depended upon a number of notable donations. Among others, Thomas Nelson, York merchant and former mayor, bore the cost of reglazing the new east window there.[10] At St Martin in Micklegate a new clerestory of good quality was added to the nave around the 1470s.[11]

Among the secular buildings of York outside the responsibility of the mayor and council, the grandest was the royal castle of York, an ancient bastion of royal authority in northern England which stood near the junction of the Ouse and the Foss. Two other notable York buildings, the Merchant Adventurers' Hall (built 1358–61), and the Merchant Tailors' Hall (built sometime between 1389 and 1415), belonged to wealthy misteries of the city. The principal guilds also had halls, or acquired them in the course of the period. St Anthony's Hall, stone below and timber-framed above, had stood since about 1446–53 at Peasholme Green. The St Christopher Guild had no separate hall, but shared the use of the Guildhall with the city officers, paying half the construction and maintenance costs.[12] York's leading religious guild, that of Corpus Christi, was combined with the Hospital of St Thomas in 1478 and immediately constructed a substantial new hall outside Micklegate Bar. For this construction the master and wardens bought 7,190 'thak' tiles and 50 ridge tiles, an indication of the normal roofing of city buildings and the large number of tiles required.[13] Some lesser crafts had their own premises; the butchers had their own hall in a yard on the south-east side of Little Shambles, and there may have been a Shoemakers Hall by the Carmelite Friary.[14]

Even among the private properties of the city streets, there was much in York to admire. The inns, facing the main streets, had distinctive names, such as the Bull and the George in Coney Street or the Crowned Lion in Micklegate. In Castlegate was the Boar, where Sir Roger Cotam, Henry Tudor's envoy, lurked after the battle of Bosworth, and 'durst not for fere of deth come thrugh the citie to speake with the maire and his brethre'.[15] Houses that served as inns would often have several chambers and often had more than one hall, and they also needed stables for visitors' horses and storage space for fodder. By an ordinance of 1477 all common inns in the city had to have signs over the door.[16] The larger alehouses likewise had names and signs. An aggrieved servant complained before the town council in 1484 that he had been robbed of a piece of gold when playing dice with the tapster of the Dragon in Lop Lane. He had gone to the doorway to relieve himself and when he came back his money had disappeared from the table where he left it.[17] Many of the principal merchants' private houses in the centre of the city were also impressive examples of the builder's craft, whether in stone or in timber and plaster. One of these in the centre of the city, off Stonegate, has been excavated and recorded by York Archaeological Trust and restored to the condition it may have had in 1483, when it belonged to William Snawsell, a goldsmith. Barley Hall, as it is now called, was a half-timbered building constructed round three sides of a courtyard, with a great hall in the central range flanked by two accommodation wings.[18] Meanwhile, interspersed between the finer buildings were many humbler constructions. Only the very poorest families were confined to a single room or a single-roomed cottage. Artisans commonly had houses containing at least three rooms – a hall for living, a chamber for sleeping and a kitchen – and many had in addition a storeroom or buttery and a brewhouse. Artisans' houses sometimes had a ground-floor room as a shop, meaning in effect a workshop where goods were both produced and sold.[19]

The concept of a 'residential area' was absent in a context where many people worked at least part of the time from their own homes, with workshops or other commercial premises integrated into their domestic arrangements. York was the greatest centre of trade and manufacturing in northern England. Not only were there larger numbers employed than elsewhere, but the range of specialization was exceptional. In the earlier fifteenth century eighty separate crafts had been charged with the production of pageants for the feast of Corpus Christi. Another list, of 1415, names fifty-seven crafts in the city.[20] These included not only the manufacturing of basic consumer goods, such as clothing and household utensils, but also highly skilled and specialized artistic activities, such as glass-making and wood-carving, that served a very wide region. The influence of York glaziers is to be traced all over northern England.[21] The evidence for all this activity would have been apparent to anyone visiting York, since manufacturing activities were located along the central streets; it was impossible to escape the sights, sounds and smells associated with the various crafts for long. Those in particular trades tended to group together, though such concentrations were loosely structured and unregulated. Dyers, for example, tended to reside in the parishes of St John and St Denys, Walmgate.[22] Industry inevitably meant noise and dirt, especially in the vicinity of metal trades, cloth-finishing and tanning.

Besides the open area known as the Pavement, most of the main streets of the city were paved, as in Micklegate, Skeldergate and Coney Street.[23] Other streets were cobbled. The owners of houses were expected to maintain the street immediately in front of them and were liable to be reported by their neighbours at wardmoot courts if they failed in this duty. If a house was leased, the landlord was responsible rather than the tenant.[24] In 1468–9 the bridgemasters of Ouse Bridge paid for paving on the bridge itself, at Walmgate Bar and 'at the end of Colliergate and the end of St Saviourgate, Hosiergate and Nessgate and in front of John Tanfield's door'. They purchased cobbles for the last of these repairs.[25]

The public spaces of the city were essential to its functioning and intrinsic to its character. A lot more activity went on in the open air in the fifteenth century than today, at least in the warmer months, because the permanent buildings were so often small and dark. However, access to public spaces, as well as water courses, was liable to be abused to resolve private problems of sewage and waste disposal. This is often recorded, since there were limits to what was tolerable, and the law of the land and civic pride combined to create some institutional guarantees of public hygiene. A city ordinance of 1475 imposed a fine of 1*s* on any tanner or other person who should pollute the Ouse by cleaning hides at the Pudding Hole, or jettisoning animal refuse there. The Pudding Hole was a public washing place on the River Ouse at the southern end of the King's Staith, and was so called because animal guts were cleaned there for the preparation of meat puddings.[26] Several butchers were fined in 1475–6 for slaughtering sheep in the high street, contrary to a bylaw. Another was fined for letting pigs run wild in the city. In the same year John Cooper was paid 1*s* for cleaning the Thursday Market when it was fouled with manure.[27]

Because York was a large city, its internal markets system was more complex than that of most English towns, many of which were served by a single, central market place. In York the number of trading areas had multiplied to the point that much of the central area of the city was taken up with buying and selling. The two principal markets for provisions were the Pavement and the Thursday Market. The former, surrounded by the premises of some of York's wealthy merchants, was a focal point of city life. The pillory was positioned there. The Thursday Market, so called from at least the early thirteenth century, was the modern St Sampson's Square. In the years 1462–3, 1468–9 and 1475–6, for which we have the details, its revenues were leased for £1 10*s* a year.[28] Outside these markets were specialized retail markets, for meat in the butchers' shops in the Flesh Shambles, and for fish on Foss Bridge. Only freemen of York were privileged to buy fish during the first two hours of trading; the city chamberlains made an annual payment to the chaplain of St Anne's Chapel for ringing the bell that signalled the opening of trade each day.[29] As in other English towns, the fish trade was strictly regulated, and citizens were prohibited from selling fresh sea fish from their own homes.[30] York also required specialist wholesale markets, particularly for livestock, much of which would be bought by the butchers for slaughter before the meat was available to the public in the Shambles. Cattle were sold, as were some horses, at Toft Green within the south-west angle of the city walls, and the market for pigs was in Swinegate.[31]

Another public space in the town, busy with commercial activity and with numerous installations to accommodate it, was the riverside. Here goods were loaded and unloaded and, in some circumstances, bought and sold. Goods coming down river would commonly dock at the landing places north of the Ouse Bridge, to which access was had along lanes leading off Coney Street. Stone for York Minster, having been quarried at Huddleston, was carried to Cawood and then shipped along the river to St Leonard's Landing, by the modern Lendal Bridge, and timber is recorded as being unloaded here after shipment from Selby and elsewhere.[32] Goods coming in from the sea, or from elsewhere downstream, were more likely to moor at the King's Staith south of the Ouse Bridge, where the stone quays and other apparatus were maintained by the mayor and citizens out of their hard-pressed annual budget.[33] The shipmen's ordinances of 1478 refer to the 'salte, granes, fuell, and all other thinges lying in ship at the said staith', and the porters' ordinances of 1482 envisage the need to carry from the Staith 'colls, turffys or odyr thyng'. Some trade took place, under regulated conditions, either aboard the moored ships or at markets on the quayside. The porter's regulations require them to carry each separate burden 'immediately to hys hows in whos name it was bowght at the stayth or at the shypp'.[34] A necessary installation at the riverside docks was a crane for unloading bulky cargoes. This was located in the Cranegarth, at the lower end of Skeldergate, and maintained by the mayor and citizens, who leased it and the fees to be derived from it for an annual rent. The Cranegarth was the place where imported goods were weighed for the assessment of customs duties and tolls.[35] In 1474 the city officers seized certain bails of woad belonging to Robert Briges of London in 'the house of the crane'.[36]

Amid the grandeur, domestic comfort and wealth that were undoubtedly to be seen in and around York, there were also signs of dereliction and dilapidation, especially among domestic properties. The general standard of housing had risen over the fifteenth century, but the number of houses had declined. The city's population is estimated to have fallen from perhaps between 12,000 and 15,000 around 1400 to about 8,000 in the early sixteenth century.[37] In the records of the bridgewardens, and those of the Vicars Choral at the Minster, there is direct evidence of declining property values in falling city rents in the later fifteenth century.[38] The revenue of the wardens of the Foss Bridge, derived from tenements by the bridge and in Fossgate and Walmgate at either end of it, were already recorded in 1469 as having been reduced because some rents had had to be lowered and some holdings were untenanted, but the properties rented then for £31 5*s* 0*d* brought in only £27 0*s* 2*d* in 1473, and the bridgemasters were spending a sizeable proportion of their income on repairs to property.[39] Changes in levels of rent were heavily influenced by location and type of property; the most likely buildings to be left derelict were small cottages in courtyards and alleys away from the main streets.[40]

Probably about one-tenth of the population of York was engaged in the building and furnishing crafts that were required to maintain and occasionally improve the city's material environment,[41] and they included some of the most highly paid of the city's workforce. Such, for example, was James Dam, the stone-carver, who worked with his servant on the fabric of York Minster for nine weeks in 1470 and thirteen weeks in 1479. Such, too, was David Dam, who carved bosses for the vault of the new central tower in 1471. The Yorkist period marked the culmination of a long phase of development at the Minster; the tower was completed in 1472. The fabric accounts show, however, that the end of that work, and the consecration of the building on 3 July 1472, did not imply the end of substantial building and furnishing at the Minster.[42]

Building workers operated under conditions unusual in medieval towns. Even the most distinguished of them, like James and David Dam, were employed by others rather than self-employed, frequently moved from workplace to workplace, and often had to work on large projects employing a dozen or more men. This did not mean that they were organized into large teams. A characteristic unit was one master craftsman and one or two assistants. Some worked in family groups, such as 'Robert Atkynson, carpenter, and his sons', employed by the master and wardens of Corpus Christi Guild in 1478–9 for work on their new hall. Others employed by the guild on the same occasion were more fluid groups. Thomas Braydryge, tiler, was taken on for five days for making a 'groundwall . . . with his assistants', but he was later employed for six days with a single assistant as a plasterer. Another characteristic sort of group was made up just of labourers: John Vynet and his mate were employed to dig earth for the construction of the new hall and for a new barn built by the guild in Baggergate.[43]

The manufacturing and food-processing operations that were carried out in private homes and small workshops might depend on help from family

*The tower crossing at York Minster, with a wooden vault constructed in 1471–3. The fabric rolls of the Minster record the carriage of the wood, the carving of bosses and the purchase of gold leaf and colouring. The master carpenter from 1457 to about 1472 was a York freeman called John Forster, but David Dam, who presumably worked under Forster's supervision, was an important figure in his own right. The fabric accounts name him as a carver of these bosses in 1471, and in addition to his wages the Chapter gave him a bonus of 10*s. *(A.F. Kersting.)*

members or servants, but were always characterized by small units of production.[44] William Coltman the brewer, who died in 1481, had a 'spinning house' as part of his property, but so far from this being a harbinger of the industrial revolution it contained no more than two old spinning wheels.[45] The size of enterprises was to some extent deliberately restricted by regulations that controlled many aspects of the city's industry. This was sometimes achieved by limiting the number of apprentices a master craftsman might take on, as in the case of the glaziers' regulations of 1464, or those of the plasterers and tilers of 1475, which ruled that apprenticeships should run for a minimum of seven years and that a master should maintain only one apprentice of under four years' standing at any one time. A comparable, but even more restrictive rule imposed on the makers of leather bags and bottles in 1471 allowed only one apprentice of under six years' standing; this meant that employers were allowed only one apprentice at a time, though there might be a year's overlap between the ending of one apprenticeship contract and the start of a new one.[46] The makers of woven covers and coverlets ('tapiters') were restricted to two apprentices at a time in 1473, and three years later agreed to restrict the number of looms a master might operate to no more than two.[47] Some apprentices went on to become freemen of York in their own right once their apprenticeship was finished. Evidence from the very end of the period shows that during the three years from 1482 to 1485 seventy-two apprentices were admitted as freemen and that they comprised 29 per cent of the total intake of new freemen during those years.[48] Within these small, domestic units, women often acquired craft skills, and sometimes continued to practise them after the death of their husbands. When Ellen Couper of York died in 1469 she bequeathed to another woman 'all the chests in my workshop'; her husband had been a pinner.[49] In 1485 Hugh Leyfeld, a smith, left all his anvils to his wife Alice.[50] Widows keeping a business together for the sake of under-age children might even engage in overseas trade, like Marion Kent in the early 1470s.[51] Some households engaged in more than one commercial activity; it was common for the wife to brew ale partly for household use and partly for sale. We know that there were about 247 brewers and tapsters in York in 1453–4, implying perhaps that ale was sold from about one household in every ten.[52]

Though many householders who engaged in manufacturing industry were independent artisans, this was not true of all. Some depended on being employed by others under the putting-out system – that is, the system whereby merchants supplied raw materials and paid workers to manufacture goods in their own homes. Spinning, a female occupation, was organized in this way, and so was some weaving, which employed men. In the making of gloves and the knitting of caps the practice was widespread, and in both cases the city council imposed rules against putting out work to households outside the city's jurisdiction, where normal surveillance could not be enforced.[53]

The amount and variety of economic activity in a household depended, of course, on its structure, and there was considerable variety. Many households were very small, since this was a period when adult couples were barely reproducing themselves, and when older children (from about the age of twelve) were often employed as apprentices and servants outside the parental home. Other families, headed by widows or widowers, had been reduced by the death of a marriage partner and the departure of children to households of their own. At the same time, some families of merchants and better-off artisans were extended by the addition of domestic servants and a few apprentices or additional workers. The numbers of servants that householders employed had more effect on the range of household sizes than did the numbers of their surviving offspring.[54]

As the evidence of falling rents suggests, the later fifteenth century was not a favourable period for the economy of York. Contemporaries were aware that the city had fallen on hard times, but because their problems were complex it required some discretion to see what they meant. Often they were thinking narrowly of the city's communal income, as handled by the city chamberlains, rather than in terms of any more sophisticated concept of their collective welfare. In 1460 the councillors lamented the city's decay, but had only the city treasury in mind, since they blamed the decay on the propensity of townsmen to evade tolls on trade.[55] In 1485, however, the corporation informed Henry VII that two-thirds of the city had become 'utterly prostrated, decayed and wasted', and this implies visible evidence of deterioration in the housing stock. The citizens ascribed this decay to Edward IV's reign, during which they said the city had decayed 'from day to day', though in fact, as we have seen, the problem was already there before Edward's accession.[56] The persuasiveness of the city's argument is evident from the success of its campaign for tax remission from 1482. Its case was endorsed in 1483 by Richard, Duke of Gloucester, who had first-hand evidence of 'the decay and the great poverty of the said city', and again three years later by Henry Tudor, who visited York in April 1486. Because of the 'great ruin and extreme decay' that he had seen there, Henry remitted most of the feefarm that the city owed to the crown.[57]

York's financial problems were only the political end of a widespread economic malaise that affected many of England's towns in the Yorkist period. One important aspect of the trouble was the decline of demand for the woollen cloths that had been important for the city's prosperity in the earlier part of the fifteenth century. The cloth industry had suffered severely from an export crisis in the mid-fifteenth century.[58] However, so far from recovering when English cloth exports grew in the 1470s, York's cloth industry had continued to contract.[59] The citizens of York were aware of other manufacturing centres experiencing much better fortunes and, in effect, growing at York's expense. Much of that development was in southern England and stemmed directly from advantages enjoyed by Londoners and other southerners that put all the northern towns at a disadvantage. This was to some extent the direct result of the power and political influence of London Merchant Venturers. York merchants tried to improve their situation in 1478 by petitioning Edward IV against practices of John Pykeryng, the current governor of English merchants to the Low Countries, which were allegedly detrimental to merchants from northern England, but the king merely referred the complaint to Pykeryng with instructions to treat the northerners more fairly in future.[60]

Table 9.1

Numbers of cloths paying ulnage to Edward IV in Yorkshire

	1468–9 (46 weeks)	*1471–3 (2½ years)*	*1473–5 (2 years)*
York	1569		2346½
Ripon	888	1897	1386½
Halifax	853	1518½	1493½
Wakefield	231	161	160
Leeds	176¾	355½	320
Almondbury	160	320	427
Hull	148	295	426½
Pontefract	106	108½	214½
Barnsley	88¾	177½	142½
Bradford	88½	125½	178½
Doncaster	35½	44½	35½
Selby	26½	26½	19

Source: H. Heaton, *The Yorkshire Woollen and Worsted Industry*, 2nd edn (Oxford, 1965), pp. 73–5.

However, the problems of the York merchants were deeper rooted than could be accounted for by mere unfair treatment by Londoners. Northerners were finding it more difficult to benefit from established patterns of trade credit, which increasingly favoured those with strong London connections.[61] One aspect of this was that, to circumvent the clothiers of York, London merchants were buying more cloth in smaller industrial centres, thereby stimulating the enterprise of the small farmers and others who were building up industry away from the city.[62] York's textile industry faced competition from smaller towns in the West Riding, notably Halifax.[63] Table 9.1 shows the extent to which, on the evidence of the ulnage duty payable to the king on sales of woollen cloth, the Yorkshire cloth industry had grown up by the Yorkist period. Even in York itself merchants were dealing extensively in cloth from elsewhere. When he died in 1485, John Carter, a wealthy York tailor, had a shop full of cloth from the West Riding, including 9½ ells of Halifax tawny, 7¼ ells of Halifax green, 7¼ ells of Halifax russet and 2 ells of black Halifax kersey.[64] York merchants were switching into the lead trade as one of their main interests, but this did more for employment in the Pennine leadfields than in the city.[65]

Economic difficulties had clear implications for employment in York and make it difficult to speak with any assurance about standards of living in the Yorkist period. By the standards of past centuries they were probably high, particularly in merchant households and even quite ordinary houses were usually comfortably furnished, with wooden tables, benches and beds and often a surprising amount of household utensils, bedclothes and other textiles.[66] When the goods of Richard Kirkeby, a tanner, were distrained in 1479 to compel him to answer a debt of £2, his domestic utensils included a pewter pot, a water can, a pair of tongues, a brass pot, a posnet, three kettles, a pan and a frying pan, and his bedding comprised a pillow, a mattress and a coverlet.[67]

Wage rates remained high by the standards of past generations. Throughout the period 1471–85 a York craftsman earned *6d* a day and a labourer *4d*, and since there were in theory about 270 work days in the year, allowing for holidays, this implies an annual income of £6 15*s* 0*d* and £4 10*s* 0*d* respectively, though it is unlikely that most men even wanted to work so much.[68] Often craftsmen were employed together with an assistant. In 1470, for example, James Dam the carver was paid for nine weeks' work at the Minster together with a servant, apparently working six days a week at 10*d* a day for the two of them.[69] The same rate of 10*d* a day was paid to Thomas Braydryge and assistants for walling, tiling and plastering over a period of twenty-five days in total in 1478–9 on behalf of the Corpus Christ Guild, and was presumably calculated as *6d* for the skilled man, together with 4*d* for an assistant.[70] Besides what was earned by men, allowance has to be made for the work of other household members, since wives and children were potential earners too. However, allowing for seasonal unemployment and structural unemployment arising from industrial decay, it is very unlikely that all men could do as well as the hypothetical maximum would suggest. In addition, economic problems also affected the role of women in the workforce so that it was more difficult for them to find employment. Jeremy Goldberg has suggested that as the urban economy of York ran into recession in the late fifteenth century the opportunities for female employment, in particular for independent employment, declined and women became increasingly marginalized in the labour force as poorly paid and highly dependent workers.[71]

The diet of the citizens of York, as of other English townsmen in this period, was cereal-based, in the form of either bread or ale. Much of the bread sold in the city came from outside, as we know from a complaint of 1479 to the effect that this country bread escaped the quality controls that were standard for bread baked in the city. However, the townsmen also ate large quantities of fish, and fishmongers are described by Heather Swanson as constituting 'the largest but possibly the most disorganized craft concerned with the sale of food'. A significant part of this trade was in freshwater fish, though in bulk the trade in sea fish was larger and attracted more interest from the merchants of York. The butchers of York remained prosperous through the fifteenth century, suggesting that the meat trade was more resistant to recession than some other aspects of the economy.[72] An undated list of butchers from about 1480–2 contains twenty-six names.[73]

The serious threat to health in the city was not shortage of supplies but disease, and especially epidemic disease, which, during the Yorkist period, struck with particular severity from the autumn of 1466 to early 1468, in the spring of 1471, 1474, 1477 and 1479, and again in 1483–4. It is not clear how much of this sickness was bubonic plague, but the epidemic of 1466–8 seems to have been of that nature.[74] Crisis mortality doubtless contributed directly to York's loss of population in the fifteenth century, though the evidence of economic contraction is needed to explain why such losses were not made good by immigration from the surrounding region or farther afield.

The supply of a large town like York involved a great deal of trade, and it could be that a quarter of urban employment was in the food trades, as in the period before the Black Death.[75] Besides the brewing and retailing of ale, women were often independently engaged in the marketing of foodstuffs, like Agnes Alan, bread seller, in 1476. A number of women leased stalls for this, as for other purposes.[76] The food trades were closely controlled by the city authorities, through regulation of markets, inspection of weights and measures, the assizes of bread, ale and wine administered by the city courts and through quality controls policed by the individual crafts.[77] A reformation of measures was a feature of the mayoralty of Richard of York in 1482, when the liquid measures of thirteen vintners and large numbers of bushel measures throughout the city were inspected and marked with a seal as evidence of their authentication.[78] Probably in York, as in other English towns, the mayor was responsible for controlling the prices of certain basic foodstuffs in the market place; in 1475–6 a salter from Sowerby was fined because he sold salt 'against the price given him by the mayor'.[79] A good deal of York's basic supplies of grain, meat and fish came in from outside the city, either overland or along the rivers, and a good deal of it passed by the King's Staith before either being sold directly to York householders or to the numerous bakers, brewers and other wholesale buyers who would pass it on to their customers.

York citizens nevertheless grew some of their own food. This side of city life is not well documented, but there were clearly widespread agricultural interests in York as in all other English towns. Even adjacent to the main streets the grass on the banks and ditches beside the city walls was let commercially for annual rents.[80] The city was surrounded by fields and pastures over which citizens had varying private and common rights. In 1479 there was a dispute between the citizens of York and Lord Lovell over pasture rights in Knavesmire, about a mile south of the city on the west bank of the Ouse, though the citizens modified their stand four years later.[81] To the north-west of the city, in 1484, the pastures of Clifton were the subject of another agreement, this time with the Abbot of St Mary.[82] A dispute resolved in 1480, again with the Abbot of St Mary, concerned rights of common in 'the feld of Fulford', which lay south of the river on the east bank of the Ouse, opposite Knavesmire. When a further agreement about the bounds of this field was required in 1483, York council agreed that the mayor should summon one or two commoners from every craft to go and inspect the newly marked divisions, and this implies that common rights were quite widely exercised among the townsmen.[83] In 1484 there was a riot in York about the enclosure of a piece of land belonging to the Hospital of St Nicholas on which the citizens had common rights. The council had agreed to a request by Richard III that the land should be permanently enclosed, but this led to a 'riotous assembly or insurrection' and the council had to backtrack, with the king's consent.[84] These events are a fitting reminder that land around the city contributed a significant part of the livelihood of many townsmen, and presumably the daily labours of many men and women of York involved tending animals and crops.

The government of royal boroughs like York in the late fifteenth century allowed scope for local initiative, since the officers of the town were elected by the townsmen rather than nominated by the king or his council. York was one of a select number of English towns whose government was formally incorporated by royal charter, so that it could own property as a corporation in law and engage in

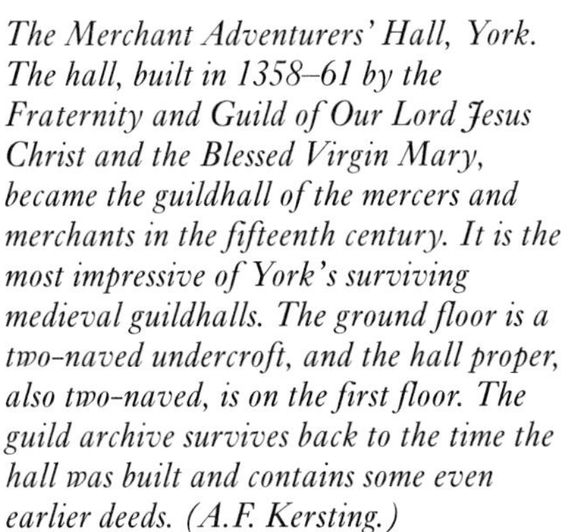

The Merchant Adventurers' Hall, York. The hall, built in 1358–61 by the Fraternity and Guild of Our Lord Jesus Christ and the Blessed Virgin Mary, became the guildhall of the mercers and merchants in the fifteenth century. It is the most impressive of York's surviving medieval guildhalls. The ground floor is a two-naved undercroft, and the hall proper, also two-naved, is on the first floor. The guild archive survives back to the time the hall was built and contains some even earlier deeds. (A.F. Kersting.)

legal actions. It had enjoyed this status since 1396. By virtue of having county status, York appointed its own two sheriffs. The lead in government was, of course, a matter for the wealthiest men. At the head of the city's government was the mayor, the twelve aldermen and the common council of twenty-four members, making a ruling group of about thirty-five or forty at any given moment. They were responsible for upholding both the king's government and the king's peace within the city, and also for the maintenance of bylaws specific to the needs of York. To this end they met quite frequently – perhaps about once a fortnight – and handled a wide range of business. The council met either in the Guildhall or in the council chamber on Ouse Bridge.[85]

The crafts were formally represented in York city government to an extent unusual among English towns. From the fourteenth century there was a body of forty-eight representatives, which seems to have been made up of craft representatives, though we do not know how they were chosen. The fact that this assembly was described as the *communitas* suggests that it was considered to represent all the burgesses. Unlike the council of twenty-four, however, it met only occasionally, and usually to attend to specific matters of a broadly political nature. The existence of this body probably reflects York's history of internal conflict, in which craftsmen had been prominently involved, as in 1381. The city's formal craft structure, together with its representation in a public body, and in the elaborate ritual of Corpus Christi pageants, may be seen as a way by which the city government attempted to harmonize the interests of these volatile groups and to preserve control over them.[86] From time to time the council intervened to resolve disputes between the crafts, as in *c.* 1472, when there were disagreements between the tapiters and the linen weavers, or in 1482, when the cutlers and bladesmiths were arguing with the blacksmiths.[87]

The city officers were charged with manning law courts both for basic policing of the city and for private pleas brought by and against the citizens. The aldermen and mayor served as justices of the peace for the city. Any three of them constituted the quorum for presiding over the city's quarter sessions, and much of the business of maintaining law and order was brought before them.[88] For police work, however, the city parishes were grouped into six wards, Monk, Walmgate, Bootham, Coney Street, Castlegate and Micklegate (or North Street), which stretched outside the city walls into the suburbs. Wardmoots were responsible for leet-court jurisdiction, a form of local policing in which teams of jurors from each parish were expected to report the misdemeanours of their neighbours. Some fragmentary wardmoot records from 1491 show that these courts dealt with public nuisances of all sorts, such as encroachments on public land and rights of way, overstinting common lands, health hazards arising from insanitary practices, disorderly houses and disorderly people, and uncontrolled dogs. They were presided over by a handful (three to five, in the few cases on record) of 'wardens and aldermen' or 'wardens of the wards'. At least three wardmoots met in friaries; in the spring of 1491 the court for North Street Ward was held in the Dominican Friary in North Street, the court for Castlegate Ward in the Franciscan Friary in Castlegate, and the Walmgate Ward court in the Carmelite Friary behind Fossgate.[89]

As these comments imply, the parish in York was as much a unit of city government as of ecclesiastical organization. Not only were townsmen represented by parishes at wardmoots, but fines for breach of the assize of ale were also assessed and recorded parish by parish.[90] In addition, the military obligations of citizens were coordinated by parishes, and each parish had a constable for this purpose. The wages needed to support soldiers in the king's service were raised in accordance with a standard parish rate and assessed by parish assessors, as for those with Richard, Duke of Gloucester, in Scotland in August 1482, or those to be sent to him in London in June 1483.[91] These various structures enabled the council to employ parochial organization for some unpredictable purposes, as on 9 October 1482, when it was resolved 'that every wardeyn in hys warde shall send for the constabyll[s] and caus tham to caus the parishoners of every parish to powl up the bumbylles, netyles and all odyr wedys that ar growyng abowt the walles of thys cite'.[92]

For private litigation, York had a court of civil pleas, presided over by the sheriffs, whose jurisdiction stretched outside the city to Ainsty. This met every week on Tuesdays, Thursdays and Saturdays, with brief interludes at the end of each legal term for the feasts of Christmas, Easter, Holy Trinity and Michaelmas. In termtime, courts were adjourned for significant saints' days and major civic events. A register of pleas surviving from 1478–9 shows that adjournments were imposed for the feasts of the Virgin Mary that fell on court days that year (Conception on 8 December, Purification on 2 February) as well as for the feasts of St Philip and St James (1 May), Rogation Day (18 May), Ascension Day (20 May), St William of York (8 June), Corpus Christi (10 June), the Nativity of

St John the Baptist (24 June), St Peter and St Paul (29 June), St Mary Magdalen (31 July), St Bartholomew (24 August) and the Exaltation of the Holy Cross (14 September). In addition business was halted on account of other official business of the sheriff on 1 December, 'for certain reasons' (unspecified) on 16 February, and 'on account of the liberty of L[awrence] archbishop of York' on 31 July. Even so, the court had 113 sessions during the year.[93] Most of the business was between citizens of York rather than outsiders, and to judge from its volume the courts were a most valuable resource for solving disputes. The number of pleas handled by this court was formidable. In addition (apparently) to at least 29 cases still actively being pursued at the beginning of the Michaelmas term, 856 new pleas were registered during the course of the year (575 for debt, 249 for various sorts of trespass, 27 for unlawful detention of goods, 2 for deception, 2 for unsettled accounts, and 1 for 'non-acquittance according to the custom of the City of York'). Even so, the business of the sheriff's courts did not exhaust the litigiousness of York citizens since there was another major city court, presided over by the mayor, that met on Mondays in the Guildhall. This court presumably heard pleas relating to the ownership and leasing of real estate, which are absent from the business of the sheriff's court, as well as disputes over wills, dower rights and other matters relating to property in the city.[94]

York's jurisdiction was not without challenges. There were powerful churchmen who claimed to have exclusive jurisdiction within parts of the city, including the Dean and Chapter of York, the Abbot of St Mary and the Warden of St Leonard's Hospital.[95] In addition there was a new secular challenge from the Council of the North, instituted in 1484. Though its permanent base was at Richard III's castle at Sandal near Wakefield, its public sessions were held at York.[96] Nevertheless, the city's own courts were the dominant ones for most citizens, and their accessibility meant that court activity, either as a litigant or as a juror, was much more a part of everyday experience than it is now. At the top end of the range, the sheriff's court registered pleas for some large debts, such as the £200 that John Sothyll, esquire, claimed against the Prior of Holy Trinity.[97] Most pleas that came before it concerned much smaller sums: William Barker sued for 8*d* and Henry Kent for 9*d*. The courts were also seemingly trusted by York's poorer and weaker inhabitants: John Clerk, labourer, sued John Norton for 1*s* 10*d*.[98] It was easy to sue neighbours for small debts and other minor offences, and use of the courts was a part of everyday life to an extent that the high cost of litigation makes impossible today.

One aspect of local government that is well illustrated in the surviving documentation is the responsibility of the mayor, aldermen and councillors for maintaining law and order and regulating the everyday urban environment through bylaws. Medieval towns were much more tightly regulated worlds than medieval villages – which is not to say that townsmen were less free, but just that the constraints on their activities were more formal. The text of a large number of craft ordinances survive from the Yorkist period.[99] Each of them, coming on top of a stream of earlier ones, created new obligations for the masters of the crafts concerned and increased the list of potentially punishable offences against the community. In each case the craft was expected to appoint searchers, who had the

St William's College, York. In spite of economic recession, there was new building in York in the Yorkist period. The college was founded c. *1455 to accommodate chantry priests at the Minster. The present building, begun about 1465, was built around a courtyard on the site of two older prebendal houses. It was extensively restored in 1906–11. (The Conway Library, the Courtauld Institute of Art.)*

power, often explicitly stated in craft ordinances, to summon the craft members to meetings where the affairs of the craft would be discussed.[100] Searchers were responsible for assessing bad work or inferior produce, either by inspecting it in the homes and workshops of craft members or by adjudicating in disputes.[101] They also had the duty of inspecting the work of newcomers who wanted to join the craft, to establish whether their work was of sufficient quality.[102] There were well-defined institutional limits to the independence of artisans, even if they were granted a considerable measure of self-regulation.

The famous York mystery plays provide an excellent illustration of the extent to which urban administration imposed upon urban culture. The pageants were not, of course, an everyday event, but preparing for them and storing the necessary equipment and stage properties represent a considerable commitment of time and space, far beyond the brief duration of the performances themselves. A schedule of 'the costes made of our pagyant' drawn up for the mercers in 1472 totals £1 10*s* 1*d*, equivalent to a single artisan's wages for ten weeks; the outlay included payments for timber, wheels, 'sarks' and 'a rope to the angels', and was recovered by contributions of 'pagyant silver' from members of the craft and others.[103] The organization of the plays required centralized direction, and the honour of the town required the pageants to be properly prepared, so there was often some coercion associated with the performance. In 1474, for example, it was ordered that anyone who sold gloves, purses or keybands called English ware in York should contribute to the glovers' pageant, and in 1475 makers of collars for draught horses were required to contribute to the girdlers' pageant. In 1477 the labourers of York, who cannot be supposed to have had any formal organization as a craft, were instructed to elect two of their number to collect the sum due to the masons' pageant.[104] Even the quality of acting was subject to control under a council ordinance of 1476.[105] These various requirements reflect the financial difficulties the crafts were under in this period. Many crafts applied to the council to be relieved of the responsibility of putting on their pageant, and in some cases they met with success, but this was clearly not a matter in which they could exercise free choice.[106]

The York plays illustrate well the extent to which civic and religious ritual and symbolism converged in the medieval town. They were one of the high spots of late medieval religious expression. This leads, finally, to the question of urban religious devotion, which to a greater or lesser degree must be regarded as a prominent part of everyday life for townsmen in the later fifteenth century. York was a principal centre of the ecclesiastical establishment in the North, so not surprisingly a major focus for the ritual celebrations of the Christian year, and most notably the feast of Corpus Christi when the York cycle of mystery plays was performed in the city streets. The commitment to orthodox practices that this implied seems to have fitted well with the inclinations of York citizens, and indeed with those of northerners generally, since there is no evidence of Lollard dissent in the diocese of York during this period.[107]

The citizens of York had quite exceptional opportunities to be well informed about the faith. The Corpus Christi play cycle was so extensive – there are forty-eight surviving plays – that it seems impossible they could all have been performed every year. A keen playgoer, watching year by year, would acquire a very considerable knowledge of both biblical and some extra-biblical narratives, and of their orthodox interpretation. Outside the Corpus Christi cycle, the guild of St Anthony was responsible for the annual performance of a Paternoster play, and the Corpus Christi guild for a decennial Creed play, both of which had an overt didactic purpose.[108] The inhabitants of York had the additional advantage of living in a city rich with paintings and stained glass, much of which was sufficiently low down and available to ordinary viewing to serve an educational purpose. The Prick of Conscience window in All Saints', North Street, represented fifteen signs of the end of the world, and another window in the same

St Anne teaching St Mary to read. This is the centre light of a three-light window in the church of All Saints, North Street, York. It was put in about 1440. It is impossible to know how many York families would have known such domestic instruction as part of everyday life; probably not many. However, female literacy was not merely a fantasy of glass-painters, since it was not uncommon in wealthier households. Children often took their first steps in reading and writing at home. (The Conway Library, the Courtauld Institute of Art.)

church illustrated the Acts of Corporal Mercy. Furthermore, some city-dwellers, both men and women, could instruct themselves from books. The York schools, of which that of St Michael-le-Belfrey is the best recorded, presumably managed to teach most of their pupils to read. The city may have had six schoolmasters, which is an exceptional number for English towns.[109] There was some formal instruction both in literacy and in matters of doctrine within the households of merchants and gentlemen of the city, and probably, too, in the households of many of the more serious-minded tradesmen. Some city families had books of hours at home to assist their prayers.[110] The iconography of the faith spread outside liturgical contexts to decorate items in daily use. Alice Langwath had a silver knife with a grey handle embossed with a representation of St Etheldreda, and six trenchers decorated (some might think gruesomely) with the head of St John the Baptist. Helen Couper had a maplewood bowl with the image of St Helen at the bottom, and Margaret Eropp had a gold ring with the image of St Katherine.[111] All told, there is good reason to believe that the inhabitants of York were well informed about the doctrinal tenets of their religion, its symbolic forms and its practical implications.

The evidence of surviving York wills strongly suggests that the principal focus for piety continued to be the parish church, and that is where most York townsmen and townswomen chose to be buried, often near other members of their families.[112] A sharp decline in the number of new chantries in York after 1450 is attributable to the deterioration of the city's economy rather than to any loss of confidence in the efficacy of prayers for the dead.[113] Townspeople continued to bequeath sums for prayers to be said for their souls, besides the money they specified for their funeral expenses. They also commonly left bequests for the benefit of the church, in the form of payments for candles on particular altars at particular times, as contributions to church fabric, or as personal gifts to parish clergy.[114] Wills clearly indicate the structure of parish organization. The rector, who was entitled to tithes and certain fees, was often recognized in bequests to settle the mortuary fee of the deceased, and to compensate for any tithes or other dues forgotten. The primary parish establishment that parishioners knew comprised the priest, vicar or parish chaplain, who was often made a personal gift, together with supplementary chaplains attached to the parish for the saying of Masses. In addition there was a parish clerk, and often a sub-clerk, both of whom were often recognized with small bequests of a few pence each.[115] Each church also had two lay churchwardens responsible for the fabric of the nave and nave aisles. These are less frequently mentioned in wills, but in 1467, for example, Robert Ase the tailor bequeathed a plot of land and a garden in Walmgate to Robert Appilby and Thomas Kilwik, 'wardens of the fabric of St Laurence's Church', and to their successors, for the future benefit of the parish.[116]

Wills also indicate the great scope for individual variety of choice within late medieval religious practice. A significant number of testators remembered more than one parish church, perhaps in recognition of previous residences and loyalties, and half of the York merchants whose wills survive from the later fifteenth century made bequests to at least one of the city friaries.[117] Gifts to almshouses and leper houses (or to each individual leper) were quite common, and many testators also left small sums to each prisoner in the civic prisons, in the castle prison or in the prison of the Archbishop of York.[118] Care of the poor was one of the characteristic concerns of Christian piety. It is difficult to find evidence relating to the normal charitable activity among the living, though it was probably a regular feature of parish life. However, gifts to the poor are well attested in wills of the period. Richard Parke of Bootham, who died in 1461, provided for a weekly dole of bread to the poor every Friday for a year. Richard Water (d. 1466) provided for the distribution of 100 gowns and 100 shirts, Margaret Bramhowe (d. 1471) instructed that her household utensils were to be given to needy newly-weds and Joan Johnson (d. 1474) left turfs and wood fuel 'to the poor of Christ'.[119]

Religious fraternities, or guilds, also attracted bequests, and these illustrate more than any other institution of fifteenth-century Christianity the freedom with which lay people created their own institutions under the general umbrella of the Church. In York in 1461 there were four large fraternities (of Corpus Christi, of St Anthony, of St Christopher and of St George), about ten smaller ones in parish churches and an additional one or two in religious houses.[120] The guilds of St Christopher and St George amalgamated sometime between 1463 and 1466.[121] A few guilds were associated with particular crafts, though most York crafts did not refer to themselves as fraternities or guilds and had none of the relevant organization.[122] Religious fraternities combined religious and social obligations; members were expected to attend each other's funerals, for example. They encouraged particular moral standards and encouraged members to participate in the devotional activities of the guild. After a low point in the 1460s, bequests to guilds increased during the 1470s and sixty-six known York testators made gifts to guilds between 1471 and 1480, some of them to more than one guild.[123] The most prestigious of all the religious gilds of the city was that of Corpus Christi, founded in 1408 and incorporated fifty years later, whose members were committed to organizing the Corpus Christi festival. This guild was at the height of its popularity around 1477, the year in which the Duke and Duchess of York became members. It adopted new ordinances in the same year.[124] Townsmen were exercising on a small scale a capacity for choice and variety, mostly within the bounds of orthodoxy, that princes and noblemen were able to exercise in a much more lavish and extravagant manner.

The more private forms of religion are inevitably more difficult to trace. The practice of prayer, for some people at least, is suggested by the sets of beads bequeathed in wills. Those mentioned tend to be the expensive ones, like Laurence Hobson's 'set of beads of silver with a crucifix', and his second 'set of beads of jet with a silver crucifix',[125] but there were surely many more ordinary sets of wood and bone in regular use. Wills are not very well suited to establishing the attitudes and practices of people with regard to prayer, meditation and confession while they were alive and well, and it would surely be wrong to represent daily life in York among the laity as a continuous round of pious thoughts and deeds. Nevertheless, for many families the matter of salvation was more than one of mere public obligation. In a world where epidemics were frequent, and mortality rates high, everyday life often came to an end suddenly.

Notes

Abbreviations

BI, York	Borthwick Institute, York
BL	British Library
CLRO	Corporation of London Records Office
DDCM	Durham Dean and Chapter Muniments
EETS	Early English Text Society
GL, London	Guildhall Library, London
OED	*Oxford English Dictionary*
PL	*Paston Letters*
PRO	Public Record Office
RO	Record(s) Office
Rot. Parl.	*Rotuli Parliamentorum*
VCH	*Victoria County History*
YCA	York City Archives

1. Dress and Fashion c. *1470*

1. *Partonopeu de Blois. A French Romance of the Twelfth Century*, ed. J. Gildea (3 vols, Villanova, 1967–70), vol. 1, pp. 198–200, ll. 4879–923. *The Middle-English Versions of Partonope of Blois*, ed. A.T. Büdtker, EETS, extra series, 109 (1912), pp. 237–8, ll. 6158–87 (spelling modernized).
2. The main English sources, that is the king's great wardrobe accounts, of which only the particular accounts are of real use to the historian of dress, are set out in the present author's 'Order and Fashion in Clothes: The King, his Household and the City of London at the End of the Fifteenth Century', *Textile History*, 22 (1991), pp. 253–76; the coverage of female dress is limited in these male accounts but there are no queens' accounts containing details of dress surviving for the Yorkist period, nor for the reigns of Henry VI and VII. For French sources, F. Piponnier, 'Le costume nobiliaire dans la France du bas moyen âge', in *Adelige Sachkultur des Spätmittelalters* (Vienna, 1982), pp. 343–67. And for the problems of medieval sources generally, F. Piponnier and P. Mane, *Se vêtir au moyen âge* (Paris, 1995), ch. 1.
3. The two great English pictorial sources are the Eton College Chapel wall-paintings, datable to the end of the 1470s onwards, and the Beauchamp Pageant of 1484.
4. *The Floure and the Leafe*, ed. D.A. Pearsall (London, 1962), p. 120, ll. 519–39; I cannot agree with the editor that this is describing fashionable dress of the 1470s.
5. For the use of studio-owned garments, compare the Master of the Tibertine Sibyl's *Marriage of the Virgin* (Philadelphia, Johnson Collection) and his *Augustus and the Tibertine Sibyl* (Frankfurt Staedelsches Kunstinstitut), both illustrated in A. Châtelet, *Early Dutch Painting* (Oxford, 1981), pp. 141–2.
6. F. Piponnier, *Costume et vie sociale: la cour d'Anjou aux xive et xve siècles* (Paris, 1970), p. 175, implies that the narrower range of activities open to women was the essential inhibition on

women's fashion, but it is arguable that the dictates of the Church and its rulings on 'modesty' were more powerful taboos and operated whether women were free to act independently or not.

7. Brussels, Bibliothèque Royale, MS 9066. G. Dogaer, *Flemish Miniature Painting in the Fifteenth and Sixteenth Centuries* (Amsterdam, 1987), pp. 71–6; P. Cockshaw, *Miniatures en grisaille* (Brussels, 1986), no. 10.
8. Piponnier, *Costume et vie sociale*, pp. 163–4. The best books for the history of medieval dress are usually French: aside from the works of Piponnier already cited, see C. Enlart, *Le Costume, Manuel d'Archéologie Française*, vol. 3 (Paris, 1916); M. Beaulieu and J. Baylé, *Le Costume en Bourgogne de Philippe le Hardi à Charles le Téméraire* (Paris, 1956).
9. A.F. Sutton, 'The Coronation Robes of Richard III and Anne Neville', *Costume*, 13 (1979), especially pp. 11–15: the king's final robe for the ceremony contained a kirtle, surcoat, tabard, mantle and train, hood and cap of estate; and the queen's a kirtle, surcoat royal, and mantle and train; Piponnier, *Costume et vie sociale*, p. 164.
10. Piponnier and Mane, *Se vêtir*, pp. 82–3, and see n. 36 below.
11. Up to the 1440s *gippon* could also be found: Piponnier, *Costume et vie sociale*, p. 167, who notes its earlier approximation to the *jacquette* and its later approximation to the *pourpoint*.
12. Piponnier, *Costume et vie sociale*, pp. 164–72 and plates; Piponnier and Mane, *Se vêtir*, pp. 80–8. For *chaperon* see the useful E.R. Lundquist, *La mode et son vocabulaire* (Göteborg, 1950), pp. 115–31, especially pp. 118–22. For *cornette* see also Lundquist, *Mode*, pp. 149–56; the *cornette* seems to have been called a tippet in England in the time of Cotgrave at least: ibid., p. 152. I have used mainly the evidence of the Great Wardrobe accounts to supply the English words.
13. Petticoats can also be found, e.g. inventory of Dame Elizabeth Wayte 3 Dec. 1488, PRO, PROB 2/18, m. 1, a petticoat of blanket.
14. Piponnier, *Costume et vie sociale*, pp. 175–8 and plates; and pp. 277–8, also for headdresses; she notes no use of *hénin* or *atour* in her Anjou accounts. And see also: Piponnier and Mane, *Se vêtir*, pp. 98–100; Beaulieu and Baylé, *Costume en Bourgogne*, pp. 70–89, especially 82–9 (headwear for women) and p. 83 (*atour*). Lundquist, *Mode*, pp. 56–64, is especially useful on the development of *atour*.
15. It is worth noting that Caxton translated *atour* as 'aray' in his *The Book of the Knight of the Tower*, ed. M.Y. Offord, EETS, supplement series, 2 (1970), p. 73, of which the French is given in Lundquist, *Mode*, p. 57. Whether he found it difficult to find a good English equivalent or was just working at his usual high speed is not evident. No medieval usage of the word for ladies' headdresses is recorded in H. Kurath and S.M. Kuhn, *Middle English Dictionary* (Michigan, 1956–in progress). 'Tire' is given in the *Vision of Edmund Leversedge* (1465) cited below (note 35), and used in the 1466 inventory of Lady Elizabeth Lewkenor cited below (note 17). See also *OED* under 'tire' (3).
16. Piponnier, *Costume et vie sociale*, pp. 277–8, 286.
17. PRO, PROB 2/3, m. 2; not complete; capitals modernized and ampersands extended. It presents a curious picture of decayed magnificence, with a few nice jewels and pieces of plate, worth in total just over £212. She owned an English book called *Gower*, worth 6*s* 8*d*, and a relic of St Katherine valued at 6*s* 8¾*d*. The word 'fillet' is unhelpfully given as a ribbon or band worn round the head, or a strip of material used for edging in the Kurath and Kuhn, *Medieval English Dictionary*.
18. *The Howard Household Books of John Howard, Duke of Norfolk, 1462–1471, 1481–1483*, introduction by A. Crawford (2 vols in 1, Stroud, 1992), vol. 2, p. 442.
19. The particular accounts of the royal Great Wardrobe are rarely in English before 1509, see note 2 above.
20. PRO, PROB 11/8, ff. 74v–76. For a glossary of cloths and furs see *The Coronation of Richard III*, ed. A.F. Sutton and P.W. Hammond (Gloucester, 1983).
21. Compare my analysis of the clothes in Margaret Bate's will of 1467, 'Order and Fashion', pp. 257–8.
22. *OED* under 'tucking' (5). For girdles in general, see G. Egan and F. Pritchard, *Dress Accessories c. 1150–c. 1450*, Medieval Finds from Excavations in London 3 (London, 1991), pp. 35–160.
23. PRO, PROB 11/10, ff.44v–45v.
24. *OED* under 'bonnet' (1d), and 'frontlet' (1a).

25. Not only the long tail or cornette of the hood, also a scarf, but increasingly at the end of the fifteenth century a garment worn round the neck and shoulders: *OED* under 'tippet' (1b). The word is frequently glossed incorrectly.
26. PRO, PROB 11/9, ff. 232v–33.
27. We must wait until someone photographs and records all the alabaster tombs in England before we have something like a database from which to work. At the moment the only long study is A. Gardner, *Alabaster Tombs* (Cambridge, 1940); and we have the Eton murals and the Beauchamp Pageant for the 1480s.
28. lettice = fur of snow weasel, a cheaper substitute for ermine.
29. *boureles* is untranslatable into English as a type of headwear; it means a stiffened or stuffed roll.
30. 'Bolsters' is the contemporary English term, see below.
31. *Chroniques d'Angleterre*, BL, Harl. MS 4424, f. 236v, corrected by Bibliothèque National, MS fr. 88, f. 224r–v. See also the version by Jacques Du Clerq, *Mémoires de 1446 à 1467* in *Choix de chroniques et mémoires sur l'histoire de France*, ed. J.A.C. Bouchon (Paris, 1838), p. 306. I am indebted for these references and comments on the translation to Livia Visser-Fuchs.
32. *Political Poems and Songs Relating to English History*, ed. T. Wright, Rolls Series (2 vols, London, 1861), vol. 2, p. 251. Exactly the same note is sounded in the *Chroniques de Saint-Denis*, cited Lundquist, *Mode*, p. 149: over-attention to fashion in France had caused the English invasions!
33. Pride as exemplified in clothes – the gallant was a standard scapegoat for every evil of this world, e.g. T. Davenport, 'Lusty fresche galaunts', in *Aspects of Early English Drama*, ed. P. Neuss (Woodbridge, 1983), pp. 110–28.
34. *Peter Idley's Instructions to His Son*, ed. C. D'Evelyn (Boston and London, 1935), pp. 55, 159–62, especially p. 159.
35. He was apparently the son of the Robert who had briefly served as deputy keeper of the king's Great Wardrobe *c.* 1417 (*Coronation of Richard III*, p. 58), a post which conceivably may have had a bearing on the interest of both the son and his father in clothes. For his identity (but not this fact), see *The Vision of Edmund Leversedge: A 15th-century account of a visit to the Otherworld edited from BL MS Additional 34,193, with an Introduction, Commentary and Glossary*, ed. W.F. Nijenhuis (Nijmegen, 1991), pp. 56–7, 136. For the similar vision of William Stranton/Staunton of Durham, ibid., pp. 3–4, 47. G.P. Krapp, *The Legend of Saint Patrick's Purgatory: Its Later Literary History* (Baltimore, 1900), includes an edition of the *Vision of William Staunton* of Durham, 1409; its references to dress are less detailed than those of Leversedge and suit the fashions of 1409, especially pp. 63, 70.
36. This appears to be a ban on skintight hose generally, but particularly on those which extended to the waist. If the gown was of a 'decent' length as specified, he could wear linen breeches above hose which only needed to reach to the top of his thigh. See e.g. Piponnier and Mane, *Se vêtir*, fig. 30. E. Birbari, *Dress in Italian Painting 1460–1500* (London, 1975), figs 18, 33–6. Knitted hose and stockings (length unspecified) were readily available in England and imported in large quantities, e.g., PRO, Sandwich Customs Accounts 1465, E122/128/6, f. 10v; ibid., 1479, E122/128/16, f. 4, 'knytt hosen'.
37. *Vision of Edmund Leversedge*, pp. 86, 89–90, 91–2, 93–4 (spelling modernized).
38. Ibid., p. 94; M. Erler, 'English Vowed Women at the End of the Middle Ages', *Medieval Studies*, 57 (1995), pp. 162–3; P.H. Cullum, 'Vowesses and Female Lay Piety in the Province of York, 1300–1530', *Northern History*, 32 (1996), p. 24. It is this modest headdress which is chosen by the pious donor of an hours to Queen Elizabeth Woodville: A.F. Sutton and L. Visser-Fuchs, 'The Cult of Angels in Late Fifteenth-Century England: An Hours of the Guardian Angel presented to Queen Elizabeth Woodville', in L. Smith and J.H.M Taylor (eds), *Women and the Book: Assessing the Visual Evidence* (London and Toronto, 1996), pp. 237–8 and pl. 8.
39. And see *Le Livre des Tournois du Roi René*, introduction by F. Avril (Paris, 1986), made for René d'Anjou 1459–60, which shows the new fashions well established.
40. CLRO, Journal of the Common Council 7, f. 17.
41. Women were not singled out in English sumptuary legislation, only their husbands. Compare the elaborate legislation aimed at women in the horizontally organized society of Italian towns, D.O. Hughes, 'Sumptuary law and social relations in Renaissance Italy', in *Disputes and Settlements. Laws and Human Relations in the West*, ed. J. Bossy (Cambridge, 1983), *passim*. The

single item of female dress that attracted vituperation on a similar scale to that levelled at short male clothes was the two-horned headdress worn at the beginning of the century, see Piponnier, *Costume et vie sociale*, pp. 177–8, and Piponnier and Mane, *Se vêtir*, p. 21. The latter explains the misuse of the word *hénin*, which should correctly be applied only to the early horned headdress and not to the later conical headdresses.

42. For all references, a general survey and some evidence of the English sumptuary acts being put into operation as regards the lower ranks, especially apprentices and young men in London, see Sutton, 'Order and Fashion', pp. 268–70.
43. BL, Royal MS 20 C ii, which also contains an *Apollonius of Tyre.* See G.F. Warner and J.P. Gilson, *Catalogue of the Western Manuscripts in the Old Royal and Kings' Collections* (4 vols, London, 1921), vol. 2, p. 371. It was certainly not made for Edward: no royal arms occur in it, and the arms of the original owner appear to have been erased from the first page. It was in the King's Library by 1535. Other works illustrated in the same workshop are BL, Royal MS 16 G ix, a *Cyropédie* with the royal arms and probably owned by Edward IV, and Harl. MSS 4379 and 4380, two volumes of Froissart's *Chronicle* owned by Philippe de Commynes. The latter are extensively (but rather crudely) reproduced in G.G. Coulton, *The Chronicler of European Chivalry* (London, 1930). All these manuscripts repeat a distinctive tapestry of trees and flying storks.
44. *Clériadus et Méliadice*, ed. M. Zink (Paris and Geneva, 1984), pp. ix–xii, xxi–xxii, xxxii–xxxv. Never translated into English. It is worth noting that this manuscript – superficially a luxurious one – is one of the poorest textually for this work, and that the picture sequence, when examined (see below), also confirms that this is a carelessly produced book.
45. Another, which would have been the fifth in the sequence, was apparently missed by the artist (f. 31).
46. Apart from the failure to reproduce the elaborate text in the plain pictures, lack of planning is evident, e.g. ff. 15, 19, both illustrated by very similar pictures of a messenger delivering a letter. It is difficult to relate them precisely to the text; certainly little care has been taken to vary the subjects of pictures so near to each other. The worst example occurs on the facing ff. 105v, 106. The vellum and the pictures make this a comparatively expensive book but with severe limitations.
47. *Clériadus et Méliadice,* p. 11, lines 63–7; p. 14, lines 124–30.
48. *Clériadus et Méliadice*, pp. 76–8; Clériadus also gives her a *braselet d'or* to wear on her arm in his absence.
49. *Clériadus et Méliadice*, pp. 207–8.
50. *de parvanche* = the *fleur de toute bonne*: see A. Tobler and E. Lommatzsch, *Altfranzösisches Wörterbuch* (Wiesbaden, 1925–in progress), and next note.
51. *Clériadus et Méliadice*, pp. 212–14, for all this episode; and Glossaire for *toute bonne*, the flower of *bonté*, probably sage, certainly an evergreen, see last note. The illustration of this episode (f. 56v) shows one damsel in updated dress with no sign of flowers.
52. *Clériadus et Méliadice*, pp. 252, 255–6, 265–6; the attire of Méliadice when she presents her gowns is described more fully as a very rich and beautiful *huque* and a hat of scarlet well dagged (*chapperon d'escarlate bien decoppé*).
53. *Clériadus et Méliadice*, pp. 302–3.
54. High-status *aumonières* are given to ladies, here the ordinary *bourse* is used.
55. *Clériadus et Méliadice*, p. 311. A *peleton* appears to be *peliçon*, a *pélisse*: F. Godefroy, *Dictionnaire de l'ancienne langue française* (Paris, 1883–1902).
56. *Clériadus et Méliadice*, pp. 315–16.
57. The exchange of news is illustrated by a pair of pictures on ff. 105v and 106 which underline the carelessness with which this manuscript was planned, and see comments on ff. 15, 19, above. The picture on f. 105v could conceivably show the Count of Asturies and Clériadus sending off the pursuivant. It is immediately followed by the almost identical picture on f. 106 of the same pursuivant being received by King Philippon. Warner and Gilson's interpretation of the picture on f. 106 as the King's examination of the prisoners is not tenable.
58. *Clériadus et Méliadice*: see the glossary under *chappeau*. She is not wearing a gold 'hat', but chaplet might be a better translation than coronet; a *chappeau d'or* occurs frequently as the headwear of Méliadice.

59. *Clériadus et Méliadice*, pp. 422–3, 426 (dress).
60. For such vows see G. Orgelfinger, 'Vows of the Pheasant and Late Chivalric Ritual', in H. Chickering and T.H. Seilor (eds), *The Study of Chivalry* (Kalamazoo, 1988), pp. 611–43, and *Le Banquet du Faisan*, ed. M.-T. Caron and D. Clauzel (Arras, 1997), passim.
61. *Clériadus et Méliadice*, p. 441–4 (peacock), p. 447–9 (dress): *sa teste estoit abillée à la guise de son paÿs, moult richement, et ung beau chappeau d'or dessus* (p. 448). The style of England is not explained.
62. *Clériadus et Méliadice*, p. 454.
63. *Clériadus et Méliadice*, p. 461–2.
64. *Clériadus et Méliadice*, pp. 470–5 (white gowns, etc.). *Floquart* is glossed by the editor as a *voile de tête*. Both V. Gay, *Glossaire archéologique du moyen age et de la renaissance* (2 vols, Paris 1887), and Godefroy, *Dictionnaire*, show that it was the name of an early fifteenth-century headdress. However, neither of these meanings seems to answer in this case. *Flochet/floquet* is glossed by Godefroy as *houppe, étoffe velue*, which might answer better.
65. *Clériadus et Méliadice*, p. 574, for the *corset* and chaplet of roses, the construction of which is obscure; *raye* is usually rendered as *résille*, hairnet, but this seems an unsuitable thing to confine a chaplet of roses. Ibid., p. 577, for the second ensemble: *si doree que à mille paine pouoit on veoir le velloux tant estoit riche et belle et avoit une sainture blance qu'elle avoit sainte par dessus et puis elle estoit atournee à templectes, une couronne par dessus son chief.* This is another description which is extremely difficult to understand and translate. For *atour* see above. Enlart, *Le Costume*, pp. 190–1, describes a headdress *à templettes* as having the hair dressed in circles over the ears and often with a crown above.
66. *crespies et tressonnee et, au bout de ses tressons avoit deux fermaulx d'or.*
67. *Clériadus et Méliadice*, pp. 592–3.

2. Townswomen and their Households

1. C. Phythian-Adams, *Desolation of a City: Coventry and the Urban Crisis of the Late Middle Ages* (Cambridge, 1979), pp. 97, 202–3, 239–41.
2. P.J.P. Goldberg, *Women, Work and Life Cycle in a Medieval Economy: Women in York and Yorkshire, c.1300–1520* (Oxford, 1992), pp. 7, 20; L.R. Poos, *A Rural Society after the Black Death: Essex 1350–1525* (Cambridge, 1991), p. 162.
3. Goldberg, *Women, Work and Life Cycle*, p. 7.
4. Phythian-Adams, *Desolation of a City*, p. 239.
5. P.J.P. Goldberg, 'Female Labour, Service and Marriage in Northern Towns during the Later Middle Ages', *Northern History*, 22 (1986), pp. 18–38; K.E. Lacey, 'Women and Work in Fourteenth- and Fifteenth-Century London', in L. Charles and L. Duffin (eds), *Women and Work in Pre-industrial England* (London, 1985), p. 46.
6. *Medieval English Verse*, ed. and trans. B. Stone (Harmondsworth, 1964), pp. 104–5.
7. *Records of the Borough of Nottingham*, ed. W.H. Stevenson (3 vols, London and Nottingham, 1883), vol. 2, pp. 24–5.
8. Ibid. vol. 2, pp. 64–5.
9. *Testamenta Eboracensia*, ed. J. Raine and others, Surtees Society, 4, 30, 45, 53, 79, 106 (6 vols, 1836–1902), vol. 4, p. 60.
10. Ibid. vol. 3, pp. 245–6.
11. GL, London, 9171/5, f. 52v.
12. Goldberg, 'Female Labour', p. 25.
13. S.L. Thrupp, *The Merchant Class of Medieval London* (Chicago, 1948), pp. 28–9.
14. GL, London, 9171/5, f. 127v.
15. A. Hanham, *The Celys and their World: An English Merchant Family of the Fifteenth Century* (Cambridge, 1985), pp. 309–11.
16. *English Historical Documents 1327–1485*, ed. A.R. Myers (London, 1969), p. 570.
17. *The Oath Book or Red Parchment Book of Colchester*, ed. and trans. W.G. Benham (Colchester, 1907), p. 97, concerned the surrender of a tenement by Hugh Coverour and his wife Christina, 'she being examined alone, as is fitting'.

18. R.E. Archer and B.E. Ferme, 'Testamentary Procedure with Special Reference to the Executrix', *Reading Medieval Studies*, 15 (1989), pp. 3–34.
19. GL, London, 9171/5, f. 127v.
20. Ibid., f. 134v.
21. GL, London, 9064/2, f. 179r.
22. Ibid. f. 170r–v. M.K. McIntosh, *Autonomy and Community: The Royal Manor of Havering, 1200–1500* (Cambridge,1986), p. 250, points out that in the late fifteenth century expulsion from the manor was the punishment used for sexual offences; the manor of Havering included Romford.
23. PRO, C1/17/210; C1/25/83–90.
24. *The Making of King's Lynn: A Documentary Survey*, ed. D.M. Owen, British Academy Records of Social and Economic History, new series, 9 (1984), p. 286.
25. *English Historical Documents 1327–1485*, p. 1059, gives the responsibilities of the *femme sole* at Worcester.
26. Lacey, 'Women and Work', pp. 36–7; C.M. Barron and A.F. Sutton (eds), *Medieval London Widows, 1300–1500* (London, 1994), pp. xvii, xxi.
27. PRO, Prob. 11, 40 Milles (8).
28. *Testamenta Eboracensia*, vol. 4, p. 24.
29. Barron and Sutton (eds.), *Medieval London Widows*, pp. xxiv–xxv.
30. PRO, C1/58/143; *Oath Book of Colchester*, p. 136.
31. *Testamenta Eboracensia*, vol. 4, p. 24.
32. *VCH Yorks., East Riding*, ed. K.J. Allison and C.R. Elrington (6 vols, Oxford, 1969-present), vol. 1, p. 84.
33. *The Book of Margery Kempe*, ed. S.B. Meech and H.E. Allen, EETS, original series, 212 (1940), pp. 6–9.
34. K. Lacey, 'Margaret Croke (d. 1491)', in Baron and Sutton (eds), *Medieval London Widows*, p. 151.
35. Thrupp, *Merchant Class*, pp. 198–200; S.L. Thrupp, 'The Problem of Replacement-Rates in Late Medieval English Population', *Economic History Review*, 2nd series, 18 (1965), pp. 114–15.
36. Lacey, 'Women and Work', pp. 46–8; *Women in England c.1275–1525*, ed. and trans. P.J.P. Goldberg (Manchester, 1995), p. 197.
37. GL, London, 9171/1, ff. 244r–245r, 344.
38. Such a bequest was made by Richard Manchestre, burgess of Gloucester, in 1454: *Calendar of the Records of the Corporation of Gloucester*, ed. W.H. Stevenson (Gloucester, 1893), pp. 399–402.
39. GL, London, 9171/5, f. 382r.
40. PRO, C1/57/200–201; C1/58/143; *Oath Book of Colchester*, pp. 133, 135–6, illustrates the property considerations underlying this case.
41. *St Albans Wills 1471–1500*, ed. S. Flood, Hertfordshire Record Publications, 9 (1993), p. 51.
42. *Testamenta Eboracensia*, vol. 4, pp. 182–3.
43. V. Parker, *The Making of King's Lynn: Secular Buildings from the Eleventh to the Seventeenth Century*, King's Lynn Archaeological Survey, 1 (Chichester, 1971), pp. 53–68.
44. L.F. Salzman, *Building in England down to 1540* (Oxford, 1967), pp. 483–5, 554–6.
45. M.O.H. Carver (ed.), *Medieval Worcester: An Archaeological Framework*, published as *Transactions of Worcester Archaeological Society*, 3rd series, 7 (1980), pp. 154–219.
46. *Testamenta Eboracensia*, vol. 4, pp. 16–17.
47. *Testamenta Eboracensia*, vol. 4, pp. 63–4. The three kings of Cologne were the three wise men who visited the infant Jesus according to the Gospel of St Matthew, and whose shrine was at Cologne.
48. *Le Menagier de Paris*, ed. J. Pichon (2 vols, Paris, 1846); a description of the Menagier's book is given by E. Power, *Medieval People* (Harmondsworth, 1937), pp. 92–115.
49. H. Swanson, 'The Illusion of Economic Structure: Craft Gilds in Late Medieval English Towns', *Past and Present*, 121 (1988), p. 29.
50. J. Laughton, 'Women in Court: Some Evidence from Fifteenth-Century Chester', in N. Rogers (ed.), *England in the Fifteenth Century* (Stamford, 1994), p. 99.
51. G. Rosser, *Medieval Westminster, 1200–1450* (Oxford, 1989), p. 128.

52. A.F. Sutton 'Alice Claver, Silkwoman (d. 1489)', in Barron and Sutton (eds), *Medieval London Widows*, pp. 129–42.
53. *Book of Margery Kempe*, pp. 9–10.
54. *St Albans Wills*, pp. 28–9; *Women in England*, p. 197.
55. *The Overseas Trade of Bristol in the Later Middle Ages*, ed. E.M. Carus-Wilson, Bristol Record Society, 7 (1937), pp. 154, 225, 227, 233.
56. T.P. Wadley, *Notes or Abstracts of Wills in the Great Orphan Book and Book of Wills in the Council House at Bristol* (Bristol, 1886), pp. 164–5.
57. Goldberg, *Women, Work and Life Cycle*, p. 125; H. Swanson, *Building Craftsmen in Late Medieval York*, Borthwick Papers, 63 (York, 1983), p. 29; *The Customs Accounts of Hull, 1453–90*, ed. W.R. Childs, Yorkshire Archaeological Society Record Series, 144 (1984), pp. 94, 116–19, 128, 132–3, 142, 148, 154, 158–61, 167, 170–2, 179; *The York Mercers and Merchant Adventurers, 1356–1917*, ed. M. Sellers, Surtees Society, 129 (1918), pp. 64, 67.
58. R.H. Hilton, 'Women Traders in Medieval England', in R.H. Hilton, *Class Conflict and the Crisis of Feudalism* (London, 1985), p. 212, stresses the multiplicity of occupations of the retail trader.
59. J. Laughton, 'Women in Court', in Rogers (ed.), *England in the Fifteenth Century*, p. 93.
60. M. Bonney, *Lordship and the Urban Community: Durham and its Overlords 1250–1540* (Cambridge, 1990), p. 222; *Records of the Borough of Nottingham*, vol. 2, pp. 268–9, 274.
61. *The Great Red Book of Bristol*, ed. E.W.W. Veale, Bristol Record Society, 2, 4, 8, 16, 18 (5 parts, 1931–53), Text, part 1, p. 133 and part 3, p. 90; *Records of the Borough of Nottingham*, vol. 2, pp. 42–3, 62–3, 102–6, 240–51; *Oath Book of Colchester*, p. 93.
62. *York City Chamberlains' Account Rolls 1396–1500*, ed. R.B. Dobson, Surtees Society, 192 (1980), pp. 105, 122, 146–7; *Register of the Freemen of the City of York, 1272–1558*, ed. F. Collins, Surtees Society, 96 (1896), pp. 182, 186, 194–5.
63. Rosser, *Medieval Westminster*, p. 198.
64. R.H. Britnell, *Growth and Decline in Colchester, 1300–1525* (Cambridge, 1986), pp. 89–90, 196–7.
65. *English Gilds*, ed. T. Smith, L.T. Smith and L. Brentano, EETS, original series, no. 40 (1870), p. 383.
66. *The Little Red Book of Bristol*, ed. F.B. Bickley (2 vols, Bristol, 1900), vol. 2, pp. 127–8. The prohibition was extended to non-Bristol inhabitants in the following year; ibid. pp. 128–9.
67. *York Memorandum Book BY*, ed. J.W. Percy, Surtees Society, 186 (1973), pp. 194–6, 216–18.
68. *English Historical Documents 1327–1485*, p. 1094.
69. GL, London, 9171/6, f.218; McIntosh, *Autonomy and Community*, p. 174. Margaret divided her goods among her daughters in her will.
70. *St Albans Wills 1471–1500*, p. 12.
71. M.C. Erler, 'Three Fifteenth-Century Vowesses', in Barron and Sutton (eds), *Medieval London Widows*, pp. 165–81. Examples of the vow are given in *Catholic England: Faith, Religion and Observance before the Reformation*, ed. and trans. R.N. Swanson (Manchester, 1993), pp. 173–4.
72. P.H. Cullum, '"And her name was Charite": Charitable Giving by and for Women in Late Medieval Yorkshire', in P.J.P. Goldberg (ed.), *Woman is a Worthy Wight: Women in English Society c.1200–1500* (Stroud, 1992), pp. 184, 197, 202–5.
73. GL, London, 9171/3, f. 246v.
74. T.P. Wadley, *Notes or Abstracts of Wills*, pp. 140–1; *The Pre-Reformation Records of All Saints' Bristol: Part 1*, ed. C. Burgess, Bristol Record Society, 46 (1995), pp. 7, 10, 25, 28, 48–9, 108.
75. *St Albans Wills 1471–1500*, p. 16.
76. Sutton, 'Alice Claver', in Barron and Sutton (eds), *Medieval London Widows*, pp. 139–40, 142.
77. *York City Chamberlains' Account Rolls*, pp. 107, 124, 150, 161. For Ouse Bridge, see R.H. Britnell, 'York under the Yorkists', p. 175.
78. *St Albans Wills 1471–1500*, pp. 70–3.
79. *The Coventry Leet Book*, ed. M.D. Harris, EETS, original series, nos. 134, 135, 138, 146 (4 parts, 1907–13), part 2, p. 545; *Records of the Borough of Leicester, 1103–1603*, ed. M. Bateson (3 vols, Cambridge, 1899–1905), vol. 2, p. 291; *The York House Books 1461–90*, ed. L.C. Attreed (2 vols, Stroud, 1991), vol. 1, p. 261.
80. M. Carlin, *Medieval Southwark* (London, 1996), pp. 212–16.

3. *Hospital Nurses and their Work*

1. R. Gilchrist, *Contemplation and Action: The Other Monasticism* (Leicester, 1995).
2. M. Candille, *Etude du "Livre de vie active de l'Hôtel Dieu de Paris" de Jehan Henry (xv siècle)* (Paris, 1964), pp. 3–9.
3. A. Saunier, *'Le pauvre malade' dans le cadre hospitalier médiéval: France du nord 1300–1500* (Paris, 1993), p. 100.
4. E. Coyecque, *L'Hôtel Dieu de Paris au Moyen Age* (2 vols, Paris, 1889–91), vol. 1, pp. 33–5, 46–51, 73, 79.
5. Candille, *Etude*, p. 13.
6. It was, however, noted by Henry, Duke of Lancaster, in his *Livre de Seyntz Médicines*, ed. E.J. Arnould (Oxford, 1940), pp. 207–33.
7. Candille, *Etude*, pp. 24, 26.
8. Jean Gerson, *Oeuvres complètes*, ed. P Glorieux (10 vols in 11, Paris, 1960–74), vol. 7(ii), pp. 714–17. This depiction of the nurse became a convention: C. Rawcliffe, *Medicine and Society in Later Medieval England* (Stroud, 1995), pp. 204–13.
9. C. Rawcliffe, *The Hospitals of Medieval Norwich*, Studies in East Anglian History, 2 (1995), pp. 13–18.
10. Ironically, more attention was paid to the medieval nurse in early, now largely forgotten, histories of the profession. The then classic study by M.A. Nutting and L.L. Dock, *A History of Nursing* (4 vols, London, 1907–12), vol. 1, devotes five chapters to the Middle Ages, relying heavily on A. Chevalier, *L'Hôtel Dieu et les soeurs Augustines de 650 AD à 1810* (Paris, 1901). Recent literature, with the exception of M. Wade Labarge, *Women in Medieval Life* (London, 1986), tends to concentrate on later periods: B. Bullough, V.N. Bullough and B. Elcano, *Nursing: A Historical Bibliography* (New York, 1981).
11. P. de Spiegler, *Les hôpitaux et l'assistance à Liège: aspects institutionnels et sociaux* (Paris, 1987), ch. 3, *passim*, provides a valuable illustration of the wide variety of institutions in one European city.
12. Background information may be found in M. Carlin, 'Medieval English Hospitals', in L. Granshaw and R. Porter (eds), *The Hospital in History* (London, 1989), pp. 21–39; and M. Rubin, 'Development and Change in English Hospitals, 1100–1500', ibid., pp. 41–59. Rubin's authoritative study, *Charity and Community in Medieval Cambridge* (Cambridge, 1987), chs 4–6, provides a case study of change. N. Orme and M. Webster, *The English Hospital, 1070–1570* (New Haven and London, 1995), offers an institutional history, but says little about nursing.
13. *The Will of King Henry VII*, ed. T. Astle (London, 1785), p. 15.
14. Coyecque, *L'Hôtel Dieu*, pp. 34–5; M.E. Wiesner, *Working Women in Renaissance Germany* (New Brunswick, N.J., 1986), pp. 40–1. The Corporal and Spiritual Works were listed, compared and contrasted by Thomas Aquinas, *Summa Theologica*, II, part 2, question 32, *passim*.
15. *The Register of Henry Chichele, Archbishop of Canterbury*, ed. E.F. Jacob (4 vols, Oxford, 1943–7), vol. 2, pp. 123–4; Jacobus de Voragine, *The Golden Legend*, ed. and trans. G. Ryan and H. Ripperger (New York, 1969), pp. 681, 685.
16. C.W. Bynum, *Holy Feast and Holy Fast: The Religious Significance of Food to Medieval Women* (Berkeley, 1987), pp. 22, 227.
17. BL, Cottonian MS Cleopatra C V, f. 11v (Statutes of the Savoy Hospital, 1524). This particular regulation relates to the hearing of confession, which was to be undertaken by two of the hospital priests, one visiting the patients in the morning, the other in the early evening, 'so that none of them will lack spiritual consolation or die without the sacraments'. See also C. Rawcliffe, 'Medicine for the Soul: The Medieval English Hospital and the Quest for Spiritual Health', in R. Porter and J. Hinnells (eds), *Religion, Health and Suffering* (forthcoming).
18. P.H. Cullum, *Cremetts and Corrodies: Care of the Poor and Sick at St Leonard's Hospital, York, in the Middle Ages*, Borthwick Papers, 79 (York, 1991), pp. 7, 15.
19. As, for example, at the London hospital of St Katherine by the Tower, where the sisters swore 'to live chastely and continently, and, according to their capacity, to serve in the presence of God with a pure heart and clean body'. They were also forbidden to wear brightly coloured or patterned clothing: C. Jamison, *The History of the Royal Hospital of St Katherine* (Oxford, 1952), p. 29.

20. M. Warner, *Alone of All Her Sex: The Myth and Cult of the Virgin Mary* (London, 1976), pp. 184–5 and pl. facing p. 201. On penitence, see R. Gilchrist, *Gender and Material Culture* (London, 1994), p. 191.
21. See note 6 above.
22. M. Carlin, *Medieval Southwark* (London, 1996), pp. 75–85; Rawcliffe, *Medicine and Society*, p. 208.
23. Gilchrist, *Gender and Material Culture*, pp. 18–19.
24. Norfolk RO, DCN 43/48; Rawcliffe, *Hospitals*, p. 102.
25. BL, Cottonian MS Cleopatra C V, ff. 30r–34v. They were paid £4 a year (ff. 20v–21r).
26. *VCH London*, ed. W. Page (1 vol., London, 1909), vol. 1, pp. 520–4.
27. P.H. Cullum, 'St Leonard's Hospital, York: The Spatial and Social Analysis of an Augustinian Hospital', in R. Gilchrist and H. Mytum (eds), *Advances in Monastic Archaeology*, British Archaeological Reports, British series, 227 (Oxford, 1993), p. 15; M. Aston, 'Segregation in Church', *Studies in Church History*, 27 (1990), pp. 237–94. For the disapproval voiced when nurses intruded into the sacred space of the chancel, see Rawcliffe, *Medicine and Society*, p. 207.
28. C.W. Bynum, *Fragmentation and Redemption: Essays on Gender and the Human Body in Medieval Religion* (New York, 1992), pp. 146–9.
29. See also, for example, a woodcut of the same date illustrating O. de Saint-Gelais, *Le Vergier d'Honneur* (Jehan Petit, Paris), Laon, Bibliothèque Municipale, 33 in-4o.
30. C. Gittings, *Death, Burial and the Individual in Early Modern England* (London, 1984), p. 112; P. Ariès, *The Hour of Our Death* (London, 1981), pp. 168–70, 205–6.
31. *The Canterbury Chantries and Hospitals in 1546*, ed. C. Cotton, Kent Archaeological Society, Records Branch, additional vol. (1934), pp. 5–6.
32. BL, Cottonian MS Cleopatra C V, f. 33r.
33. Thomas More, *Utopia*, ed. E. Surtz and J.H. Hexter (New Haven, 1965), pp. 139–41. The Savoy was closely modelled on the Hospital of Santa Maria Nuova, Florence, which had a large and highly-skilled nursing staff: K. Park and J. Henderson, '"The First Hospital among Christians": The Ospedale di Santa Maria Nuova in Early Sixteenth-Century Florence', *Medical History*, 35 (1991), pp. 164–88; E.P. de G. Chaney, '"Philanthropy in Italy": English Observations on Italian Hospitals', in T. Riis (ed.), *Aspects of Poverty in Early Modern Europe* (Florence, 1981), pp. 183–217.
34. BL, Cottonian MS Cleopatra C V, f. 33r.
35. C. Classen, D. Howes and A. Synnott, *The Cultural History of Smell* (London, 1994), pp. 61–3.
36. 'Vie de Saint Louis par le confesseur de la Reine Marguerite', in *Rerum Gallicarum et Francicarum Scriptores*, ed. M. Bouquet and others (23 vols, Paris, 1738–1876), vol. 20, pp. 97–8.
37. Carlin, 'Medieval English Hospitals', in Granshaw and Porter (eds), *Hospital in History*, p. 25; Rubin, 'Development and Change', ibid., p. 49.
38. BL, Cottonian MS Cleopatra C V, f. 24r, v; Wiesner, *Working Women*, pp. 38–9.
39. Candille, *Etude*, p. 23.
40. M.T. Lacroix, *L'Hôpital Saint-Nicolas du Bruille (Saint André) à Tournai de sa fondacion à sa mutation en cloître* (2 vols, Louvain, 1977), vol. 2, pp. 515–16.
41. *Aureum Opus de Veritate Contritionis* (Saluzzo, 1503), f. 3a. See also T.N. Tentler, *Sin and Confession on the Eve of the Reformation* (Princeton, 1977), p. 257.
42. Candille, *Etude*, p. 23.
43. P. Horton-Smith-Hartley and H.R. Aldridge, *Johannes de Mirfeld: His Life and Works* (Cambridge, 1936), p. 41.
44. It is, however, in Latin and may thus have been of limited use to the sisters. For the translation of learned medical texts into English by clergy for the benefit of the sick poor, see F.M. Getz, 'Charity, Translation and the Language of Medical Learning in Medieval England', *Bulletin of the History of Medicine*, 64 (1990), pp. 1–17.
45. Carlin, 'Medieval English Hospitals', in Granshaw and Porter (eds), *Hospital in History*, pp. 29–31.
46. T.S. Miller, *The Birth of the Hospital in the Byzantine Empire* (Baltimore, 1985), p. 6.
47. *The Historical Collections of a Citizen of London in the Fifteenth Century*, ed. J. Gairdner, Camden Society, new series, 17 (1876), pp. viii–ix. Pregnant women were often excluded from hospitals for moral as well as practical reasons.

48. P. Horden, 'A Discipline of Relevance: The Historiography of the Medieval Hospital', *Social History of Medicine*, 1 (1988), pp. 370–1.
49. Rawcliffe, *Medicine and Society*, pp. 182–90; M. Connor Versluysen, 'Old Wives' Tales? Women Healers in English History', in C. Davies (ed.), *Rewriting Nursing History* (London, 1980), pp. 175–99.
50. See note 31 above.
51. See, for example, John of Arderne, *Treatises of Fistula in Ano*, ed. D. Power, Early English Text Society, original series, 139 (1910), pp. 83–5.
52. Candille, *Etude*, p. 20.
53. Horton-Smith-Hartley and Aldridge, *Johannes de Mirfeld*, p. 91. See also *A Leechbook or Collection of Medical Recipes of the Fifteenth Century*, ed. W.R. Dawson (London, 1934).
54. P. Murray Jones, *Medieval Medical Miniatures* (London, 1984), ch. 6.
55. Rawcliffe, *Medicine and Society*, pp. 32–43; *The Medieval Health Handbook*, ed. L.C. Arno (New York, 1976), *passim*.
56. Horton-Smith-Hartley and Aldridge, *Johannes de Mirfeld*, pp. 30, 117.
57. The idea of a spiritual regimen, prescribed by the Divine Physician was a common late medieval *topos*: see, for instance, *Dives and Pauper*, ed. P. Heath Barnum, Early English Text Society, original series, 275, 280 (2 parts so far, 1976, 1980), vol. 1, part 1, p. 68.
58. B. Tierney, 'The Decretists and the "Deserving Poor"', *Comparative Studies in Society and History*, 1 (1958–9), p. 366.
59. J. Caille, *Hôpitaux et charité publique à Narbonne au Moyen Age* (Toulouse, 1978), pp. 97–8, 108.
60. 'Vie de Saint Louis', p. 98.
61. Lacroix, *L'Hôpital Saint-Nicolas du Bruille*, vol. 2, pp. 491–2.
62. Cullum, 'St Leonard's Hospital', in Gilchrist and Mytum (eds), *Advances*, pp. 14–15.
63. See, for example, P.H. Cullum, '"And Hir Name Was Charite": Charitable Giving by and for Women in Late Medieval Yorkshire', in P.J.P. Goldberg (ed.), *Woman is a Worthy Wight: Women in English Society c. 1200–1500* (Stroud, 1992), pp. 182–211.
64. See notes 14 and 26 above.
65. Lacroix, *L'Hôpital Saint-Nicolas du Bruille*, vol. 2, p. 473. Sisters who were sick were prescribed special food: ibid., pp. 481–2.
66. *Records of the Borough of Nottingham*, ed. W.H. Stevenson, (5 vols, London, 1882–1900), vol. 1, p. 33.
67. C. Harper-Bill, 'The Labourer is Worthy of His Hire? Complaints about Diet in Late Medieval English Monasteries', in C. Harper-Bill and C. Barron (eds), *The Church in Pre-Reformation Society* (Woodbridge, 1985), pp. 95–107; Page, *VCH London*, vol. 1, pp. 520–4; Carlin, *Medieval Southwark*, p. 79.
68. Cullum, *Cremetts and Corrodies*, pp. 15–18; Norfolk RO, press G, case 24, shelf A (Great Hospital general accounts), boxes 1306–98, 1465–1501, 1485–1508, 1509–27.
69. Gilchrist, *Contemplation and Action*, pp. 37–8.
70. BL, Cottonian MS Cleopatra C V, f. 35r, v.
71. Benefactors often supplied them and the money needed to provide the oil, as was the case at St Thomas' hospital, Southwark: BL, Stowe MS 942, ff. 99v, 106v.
72. J. Imbert (ed.), *Histoire des hôpitaux en France* (Toulouse, 1982), p. 57.
73. BL, Cottonian MS Cleopatra C V, f. 25r; Norfolk RO, DCN 43/48. In 1393–4 St Giles' had 1,460 bundles of faggots in store; in 1480–1 some 4,360 bundles of faggots, 600 bundles of firewood and 23 carts of brushwood were acquired for use in the precinct: Norfolk RO, press G, case 24, shelf A (Great Hospital general accounts), boxes 1306–98, 1465–1501.
74. PRO, C270/22.
75. *The Book of St Gilbert*, ed. R. Foreville and G. Keir (Oxford, 1987), p. 309.
76. BL, Cottonian MS Cleopatra C V, f. 49r, v. At St Giles' Hospital, Norwich, scented candles were regularly produced: Rawcliffe, *Hospitals*, p. 105.
77. Horton-Smith-Hartley and Aldridge, *Johannes de Mirfeld*, pp. 81–3, 117.
78. Gittings, *Death, Burial and the Individual*, p. 110.
79. 'Vie de Saint Louis', p. 90; Imbert, *Histoire des hôpitaux*, p. 120.
80. BL, Cottonian MS Cleopatra C V, ff. 33r, 36r.

81. Norfolk RO, press G, case 24, shelf A (Great Hospital general accounts), boxes 1306–98; accounts for Norwich properties, boxes 1415–60, 1465–1501, roll for 1485–1509, boxes 1510–28, *passim*. Archaeological evidence for the use of herbal medicine is discussed by Gilchrist, *Contemplation and Action*, pp. 35–6.
82. *On the Properties of Things: John Trevisa's Translation of Bartholomaeus Anglicus 'De Proprietatibus Rerum'* (2 vols, Oxford, 1975), vol. 2, pp. 720–1. See also, 'Norwich Cathedral Priory Gardeners' Accounts 1329–1530', ed. C. Noble, in *Farming and Gardening in Late Medieval Norfolk*, ed. C. Noble, C. Moreton and P. Rutledge, Norfolk Record Society, 61 (1997), pp. 6–9.
83. From 1364 onwards, the sister responsible for looking after the children at St Leonard's, York, was provided with one or two cows to supply milk: Cullum, 'St Leonard's Hospital', in Gilchrist and Mytum (eds), *Advances*, p. 16.
84. Classen, Howes and Synnott, *Cultural History of Smell*, pp. 61–2.
85. Rawcliffe, *Medicine and Society*, p. 43.
86. L.E. Voigts and R.P. Hudson, 'A Surgical Anaesthetic from Late Medieval England', in S. Campbell, B. Hall and D. Klausner (eds), *Health, Disease and Healing in Medieval Culture* (New York, 1992), pp. 34–56; *Sharp Practice, I. The Third Report on Researches into the Medieval Hospital at Soutra, Lothian* (Edinburgh, 1989), *passim*; Gilchrist, *Contemplation and Action*, p. 35; J. Harvey, *Mediaeval Gardens* (London, 1990), p. 130.
87. Gilchrist, *Contemplation and Action*, pp. 29–30.
88. PRO, C1/242/72. In 1287 the nurses of St Leonard's hospital, York, had made a similar complaint about the brothers who had sequestered their garden: Cullum, *Cremetts and Corrodies*, p. 15.
89. Jamison, *Royal Hospital of St Katherine*, pp. 59–60 and pl. II.
90. *Historical Manuscripts Commission, Ninth Report, I* (London, 1883), p. 220 (It is interesting to note the emphasis placed in these statutes on the avoidance of 'stenche or orrour' both moral and physical); K.J. Evans, 'The Maison Dieu, Arundel', *Sussex Archaeological Collections*, 107 (1969), pp. 68–70.
91. *Gesta Abbatum Monasterii S. Albani, a Thoma Walsingham*, ed. H.T. Riley, Rolls Series (3 vols, London, 1867–9), vol. 2, p. 506.
92. L. Demaitre, *Doctor Bernard de Gordon: Professor and Practitioner* (Toronto, 1980), pp. 47, 157.
93. A.H. Thompson, *The History of the Hospital and the New College of the Annunciation of St Mary in the Newarke, Leicester* (Leicester, 1937), pp. 156–7.
94. These included beer-brewing and glass-making at St Katherine's (*Letters and Papers Foreign and Domestic of the Reign of Henry VIII: Addenda* (London, 1929), nos 384, 1053), assorted artisans working noisily through the night at St Thomas's, Southwark (Carlin, *Medieval Southwark*, 79), and a tavern at St Mary Bethlehem (PRO, C270/22).
95. BL, Cottonian MS Cleopatra C V, f. 28r, v.
96. C. Rawcliffe, '"Gret Criynge and Joly Chauntynge": Life, Death and Liturgy at St Giles's Hospital, Norwich, in the Thirteenth and Fourteenth Centuries', in C. Rawcliffe, R. Virgoe and R. Wilson (eds), *Counties and Communities: Essays on East Anglian History Presented to Hassell Smith* (Norwich, 1996), pp. 37–55.
97. John of Arderne, *Treatises*, pp. 4–7.
98. Imbert, *Histoire des hôpitaux*, p. 117; Wiesner, *Working Women*, pp. 39–40; BL, Cottonian MS Cleopatra C V, ff. 24r, 33v.
99. Lacroix, *L'Hôpital Saint-Nicolas du Bruille*, vol. 2, p. 500.
100. P.H. Cullum, 'Hospitals and Charitable Provision in Medieval Yorkshire' (University of York, Ph.D. thesis, 1990), pp. 103–4; Chevalier, *L'Hôtel Dieu*, pp. 59–60.
101. As, for instance, Bodleian Library, Oxford, MS Bodley 270b, f. 79v.
102. Lambeth Palace Library, Reg. Arundel, 1, f. 256r, v.
103. *Register of Thomas Bekynton, Bishop of Bath and Wells, 1443–1465*, ed. H.C. Maxwell-Lyte and M.C.B. Dawes, Somerset Record Society, 49, 50 (2 vols, 1934–5), vol. 1, p. 289.
104. Carlin 'Medieval English Hospitals', in Granshaw and Porter (eds), *Hospital in History*, p. 32.
105. Rawcliffe, *Hospitals*, pp. 102–3.
106. D. Keene, *Survey of Medieval Winchester*, Winchester Studies, 2 (2 vols, Oxford, 1985), vol. 2, p. 816.

107. Caille, *Hôpitaux et charité publique*, p. 103; J. Henderson, 'The Hospitals of Late Medieval and Renaissance Florence: a Preliminary Survey', in Granshaw and Porter, *Hospital in History*, p. 81.
108. Rawcliffe, *Hospitals*, pp. 69–77.
109. Norfolk RO, Norwich Consistory Court, reg. Alpe, ff. 49v–50r (will of Richard Hawze).
110. As, for instance, *The Anatomie of the Bodie of Man*, ed. F.J. Furnivall and P. Furnivall, Early English Text Society, extra series, 53 (1888), pp. 303–15, and Norfolk RO, case 17, shelf B (Liber Ruber Civitatis), ff. 80v–84v.
111. Candille, *Etude*, pp. 21, 29. Jehan Henry's metaphor was not original. He was surely familiar with René of Anjou's chivalric romance, *Le livre du cuer d'amours espris*, in which three chief protagonists visit a hospital for wounded lovers, founded on an island by the God of Love. Dame Pity, the prioress, and Courtesy, the female infirmarer, preside over the house: *Oeuvres Complètes du Roi René*, ed. M. le Comte de Quatrebras (4 vols, Angers, 1846), vol. 3, pp. 97–100, and pl. facing p. 126.

4. Religion and the Paston Family

1. Roger Virgoe, 'Introduction', in *The Paston Letters, 1422–1509*, ed. J. Gairdner (Gloucester, 1983, reprinted from the 1904 edn), p. v. From now on this source will be cited as *PL*, ed. Gairdner.
2. H.S. Bennett, *The Pastons and their England* (2nd edn, Cambridge, 1932), pp. 119–20. On this point see further C.R. Cheney, *Handbook of Dates for Students of English History* (London, 1945), pp. 40–64; R. Hutton *The Rise and Fall of Merry England: The Ritual Year 1400–1700* (Oxford, 1996), pp. 5–48; D. Knowles, *The Monastic Order in England: A History of Its Development in England from the Times of Saint Dunstan to the Fourth Lateran Council, 943–1216* (corrected edn, Cambridge, 1949), pp. 448–51, 714–15.
3. Ibid., vol. 1, p. xxxv. Different scribes had no perceptible impact on the use of ecclesiastical dates.
4. *Paston Letters and Papers of the Fifteenth Century*, ed. N. Davis (2 vols, Oxford, 1971, 1976), vol. 1, pp. 27, 244, 443. From now on this source will be cited as *PL*, ed. Davis.
5. Ibid., vol. 2, p. 22.
6. For example, ibid., vol. 1, pp. 405, 412, 418, 426, 427, 429.
7. Ibid., vol. 2, p. 31.
8. Ibid., vol. 1, p. 241, vol. 2, p. 181.
9. Ibid., vol. 1, p. 34.
10. Ibid., vol. 2, p. 248.
11. Ibid., vol. 1, p. 486.
12. Ibid., vol. 1, pp. 148, 162, 199, 207, 364.
13. Ibid., vol. 1, pp. 138, 291.
14. Ibid., vol. 2, p. 344. See also, ibid., vol. 1, p. 307, vol. 2, p. 426.
15. Ibid., vol. 2, p. 426.
16. Ibid., vol. 2, p. 372. See also, ibid., vol. 1, p. 225, vol. 2, pp. 184, 529.
17. Ibid., vol. 2, p. 597.
18. Ibid., vol. 2, p. 426; E. Duffy, *The Stripping of the Altars: Traditional Religion in England c. 1400–c. 1580* (New Haven and London, 1992), p. 68. See, for example, the discussion of the Croxton Play of the Sacrament in G. M. Gibson, *The Theater of Devotion: East Anglian Drama and Society in the Later Middle Ages* (Chicago, 1989), pp. 34–41.
19. Ibid., vol. 1, p. 288.
20. C. Richmond, 'The English Gentry and Religion, *c.* 1500', in C. Harper-Bill (ed.), *Religious Belief and Ecclesiastical Careers in Late Medieval England* (Woodbridge, 1991), pp. 131–43.
21. *PL*, ed. Davis, vol. 1, pp. 43–4.
22. Ibid., vol. 1, p. 354 (cf. pp. 355, 515). For an extended examination of the way in which fear of death and judgement affected late medieval practices, see Duffy, *Stripping of the Altars*, pp. 301–76. For the impact of the Black Death, see (for example) P. Binski, *Medieval Death: Ritual and Representation* (London, 1996), pp. 126–34.

23. *PL*, ed. Davis, vol. 1, p. 639.
24. Ibid., vol. 1, p. 627.
25. Ibid., vol. 1, p. 315.
26. Ibid., vol. 1, p. 354 (cf. p. 355). See also, C. Richmond, *The Paston Family in the Fifteenth Century: Fastolf's Will* (Cambridge, 1996), p. 158.
27. Ibid., vol. 1, p. 243.
28. Ibid., vol. 1, p. 370.
29. Richmond, 'English Gentry and Religion', pp. 130 (note 20), 143–4; C. Richmond, *The Paston Family in the Fifteenth Century: The First Phase* (Cambridge, 1990), pp. 174–6; idem, *Paston Family: Fastolf's Will*, pp. 155–7.
30. *PL*, ed. Gairdner, vol. 6, p. 188.
31. *PL*, ed. Davis, vol. 1, p. liii.
32. Bennett, *Pastons*, pp. 197–8; Richmond, *Paston Family: Fastolf's Will*, pp. 154–7.
33. C. Carpenter, 'The Religion of the Gentry of Fifteenth-Century England', in D. Williams (ed.), *England in the Fifteenth Century* (Woodbridge, 1987), p. 61; K.B. McFarlane, *Lancastrian Kings and Lollard Knights* (Oxford, 1972), pp. 210–17; J.A.F. Thompson, 'Knightly Piety and the Margins of Lollardy', in M. Aston and C. Richmond (eds), *Lollardy and the Gentry in the Later Middle Ages* (Stroud, 1997), pp. 95–111.
34. For Lollard attitudes, see A. Hudson, *The Premature Reformation: Wycliffite Texts and Lollard History* (Oxford, 1988), pp. 290–4.
35. *PL*, ed. Davis, vol. 1, p. 585.
36. Ibid., vol. 1, p. 586.
37. Hamilton, *Religion*, p. 112; J. Bossy, *Christianity in the West, 1400–1700* (Oxford, 1985), p. 16.
38. For example, *PL*, ed. Davis, vol. 2, p. 108.
39. K. Dockray, 'Why Did Fifteenth-Century Gentry Marry?: The Pastons, Plumptons and Stonors Reconsidered', in M. Jones (ed.), *Gentry and Lesser Nobility in Late Medieval Europe* (Gloucester and New York, 1986), pp. 70–6.
40. *PL*, ed. Davis, p. 500.
41. Bennett, *Pastons*, pp. 42–6.
42. Hamilton, *Religion*, p. 114; Bossy, *Christianity*, pp. 22–3.
43. *PL*, ed. Davis, vol. 1, p. 342.
44. Ibid., vol. 1, p. 627.
45. B. Hamilton, *Religion and the Medieval West* (London, 1986), p. 115.
46. *PL*, ed. Davis, vol. 1, p. 225.
47. Ibid., vol. 2, p. 426. See also, ibid., vol. 2, p. 199.
48. Ibid., vol. 1, p. 34.
49. Ibid., vol. 1, p. 39.
50. Ibid., vol. 1, p. 36, vol. 2, pp. 108, 198.
51. Ibid., vol. 2, pp. 199, 205; Duffy, *Stripping of the Altars*, p. 93.
52. Ibid., vol. 1, p. 70.
53. Hamilton, *Religion*, pp. 22, 37.
54. *PL*, ed. Davis, vol. 1, p. 356.
55. Ibid., vol. 1, pp. 374, 585.
56. J.A.F. Thomson, '"The Well of Grace": Englishmen and Rome in the Fifteenth Century', in R.B. Dobson (ed.), *The Church, Politics and Patronage in the Fifteenth Century* (Gloucester, 1984), pp. 101, 109.
57. *PL*, ed. Davis, vol. 1, p. 375.
58. Ibid., vol. 1, p. 471.
59. Ibid., vol. 1, p. 501.
60. See R.H. Helmholz, *Roman Canon Law in Reformation England*, Cambridge Studies in English Legal History (Cambridge, 1990), for more information on the differences and disputes between the English and Roman courts.
61. W.A. Christian, Jnr., *Apparitions in Late Medieval and Renaissance Spain* (Princeton, 1981), p. 13.
62. Bossy, *Christianity*, p. 144; Duffy, *Stripping of the Altars*, p. 358.

63. *PL*, ed. Gairdner, vol. 3, p. 135.
64. Ibid., vol. 1, pp. 382–9.
65. Richmond, 'English Gentry and Religion', pp. 138–9; M. Rubin, *Charity and Community in Medieval Cambridge* (Cambridge, 1987), pp. 198–9.
66. *Records of the Gild of St George in Norwich, 1389–1547*, ed. M. Grace, Norfolk Record Society, 9 (1937), pp. 6–7.
67. Richmond, 'English Gentry and Religion', p. 137.
68. *PL*, ed. Davis, vol. 1, p. 640, vol. 2, pp. 320–1, 376; Bennett, *Pastons*, p. 210; Richmond, 'English Gentry and Religion', p. 130.
69. *PL*, ed. Davis, vol. 1, p. 443.
70. Ibid., vol. 1, pp. 440, 465, 511, 560, vol. 2, pp. 397, 487.
71. Duffy, *Stripping of the Altars*, pp. 190–200; Hamilton, *Religion*, p. 129; C. Rawcliffe, *Medicine and Society in Later Medieval England* (Stroud, 1995), pp. 21–4, 178–80.
72. *PL*, ed. Davis, vol. 1, p. 218. A noble was an English gold coin worth 6*s* 8*d*.
73. Ibid., vol. 1, p. 529.
74. Hudson, *Premature Reformation*, pp. 279, 307–9.
75. *PL*, ed. Davis, vol. 1, p. 517 and vol 2, p. 616. See also, vol. 1, p. 234.
76. *PL*, ed. Gairdner, vol. 6, pp. 202–3. See also, *PL*, ed. Davis, vol. 1, p. 217, vol. 2, pp. 360–3.
77. Bennett, *Pastons*, p. 206; *PL*, ed. Davis, vol. 1, pp. 27, 374, 375, 585.
78. See, for example, R.G.K.A. Mertes, 'The Household as a Religious Community', in J. Rosenthal and C. Richmond (eds), *People, Politics and Community in the Later Middle Ages* (Gloucester, 1987), p. 123; C. Richmond, 'Religion and the Fifteenth-Century Gentleman', in Dobson (ed.), *The Church, Politics and Patronage in the Fifteenth Century*, pp. 198–9. The argument is opposed by Carpenter, 'Religion of the Gentry', pp. 65–6.
79. *PL*, ed. Davis, vol. 1, p. 400.
80. Ibid., vol. 1, p. 321.
81. Ibid., vol. 1, pp. 178–9.
82. Ibid., vol. 1, pp. 179–80.
83. *PL*, ed. Gairdner, vol. 4, p. 230, n. 1.
84. *PL*, ed. Davis, vol. 1, pp. 315, 511.
85. Ibid., vol. 2, p. 7.
86. Bennett, *Pastons*, pp. 202–3.
87. *PL*, ed. Davis, vol. 1, p. 128; *PL*, ed. Gairdner, vol. 3, p. 135.
88. *PL*, ed. Gairdner, vol. 5, p. 82.
89. See *PL*, ed. Davis, vol. 2, p. 18.
90. Ibid., vol. 2, p. 296. See also, ibid., vol. 2, pp. 228–9, 265–6.
91. *PL*, ed. Gairdner, vol. 3, p. 135. See also, *PL*, ed. Davis, vol. 1, pp. 473–4, vol 2, p. 424.
92. *PL*, ed. Davis, vol. 1, p. 55.
93. Ibid., vol 1, pp. 233–4, vol. 2, pp. 184–5, 186, 210, 462, 522.
94. Carpenter, 'Religion of the Gentry', p. 58.
95. Richmond, 'Religion and the Fifteenth-Century Gentleman', p. 194.
96. *PL*, ed. Davis, vol. 1, p. 264. See also, for example, ibid., vol. 1, pp. 260–1, 265–6.
97. Virgoe, 'Introduction', in *PL*, ed. Gairdner, p. iv.
98. *PL*, ed. Davis, vol. 1, p. xxxvii.
99. Ibid., vol. 1, pp. 341–4.

5. *Peasants in Arden*

1. R.H. Hilton, *The English Peasantry in the Later Middle Ages* (Oxford, 1973), p. 161; M.M. Postan (ed.), *Essays on Medieval Agriculture and General Problems of the Medieval Economy* (Cambridge, 1973), pp. 41–8; J. Hatcher, 'The Great Slump of the Mid-Fifteenth Century', in R.H. Britnell and J. Hatcher (eds), *Problems and Progress in Medieval England: Essays in Honour of Edward Miller* (Cambridge, 1996), pp. 237–72; E. Miller, 'Introduction: Land and People', in E. Miller (ed.), *The Agrarian History of England and Wales, III: 1348–1500* (Cambridge, 1991),

pp. 1–33; R.H. Britnell, 'The Economic Context', in A.J. Pollard (ed.), *The Wars of the Roses* (London, 1995), pp. 41–64; J.M.W. Bean, 'Landlords', in Miller (ed.), *Agrarian History of England and Wales, III*, pp. 568–74; M.M. Postan, *The Medieval Economy and Society* (London, 1972), pp. 43, 74–6, 106, 116, 194–8.

2. D.L. Farmer, 'Prices and Wages, 1348-1500', in Miller (ed.), *Agrarian History of England and Wales, III*, pp. 443–67; N.S.B. Gras, *The Evolution of the English Corn Market* (Cambridge, Mass., 1926), pp. 12–49; R.H. Tawney, *The Agrarian Problem in the Sixteenth Century* (London, 1912), pp. 6–12; J. Thirsk, 'Enclosing and Engrossing', in J. Thirsk (ed.), *The Agrarian History of England and Wales, IV: 1500–1640* (Cambridge, 1967), pp. 200–51.
3. A.R. Bridbury, *Economic Growth: England in the Later Middle Ages* (London, 1962); F.R.H. Du Boulay, *An Age of Ambition* (London, 1970), pp. 13–14, 35, 50; Postan, *Medieval Economy and Society*, pp 156–8; R.H. Hilton, *The Decline of Serfdom in Medieval England* (London, 1969), pp. 44–7; W. Beveridge, 'Westminster Wages in the Manorial Era', *Economic History Review*, 2nd series, 8 (1955–6), pp. 18–35; C. Dyer, 'English Diet in the Later Middle Ages', in T.H. Aston, P.R. Coss, C. Dyer and J. Thirsk (eds), *Social Relations and Ideas: Essays in Honour of R.H. Hilton* (Cambridge, 1983), pp. 191–216; Britnell, 'Economic Context', pp. 41–64.
4. For the concept of margin and pays see M. Bailey, 'The Concept of the Margin in the Medieval English Economy', *Economic History Review*, 2nd series, 42 (1989), pp. 1–15; A. Everitt, 'Country, County, and Town: Patterns of Regional Evolution in England', *Transactions of the Royal Historical Society*, 5th series, 29 (1979), pp. 80–1. For the Arden's physical appearance see J.E.B. Gover, A. Mawer, and F.M. Stenton, *The Place-Names of Warwickshire*, English Place-Name Society, 13 (1936), pp. xiv–xv; G.T. Warwick, 'Relief and Physiographic Regions', in British Association for the Advancement of Science, *Birmingham and its Regional Setting* (Birmingham, 1950), pp. 11–14. For the later medieval economy of the area see, C. Dyer, 'A Small Landowner in the Fifteenth Century', *Midland History*, 1 (1972), pp. 1–14; C. Dyer, *Warwickshire Farming 1349–c. 1520: Preparation for Agricultural Revolution*, Dugdale Society Occasional Paper, 27 (Oxford, 1981), *passim*; C.C. Dyer, 'The Occupation of the Land: The West Midlands', 'Farming Practices and Techniques: The West Midlands', and 'Tenant Farming and Tenant Farmers: The West Midlands', in Miller (ed.), *Agrarian History of England and Wales, III*, pp. 77–91, 222–37, 636–47; A.D. Watkins, 'Cattle Grazing in the Forest of Arden in the Later Middle Ages', *Agricultural History Review*, 37 (1989), pp. 17–23; A.D. Watkins, 'Society and Economy in the Northern Part of the Forest of Arden, Warwickshire, 1350–1540' (unpublished Ph.D. thesis, University of Birmingham, 1989), pp. 124–68; A.D. Watkins, 'The Woodland Economy of the Forest of Arden in the Later Middle Ages', *Midland History*, 18 (1993), pp. 19–32; A.D. Watkins, 'Merevale Abbey in the Late 1490s', *Warwickshire History*, 9 (1994), pp. 87–104; A.D. Watkins, 'Landowners and their Estates in the Forest of Arden in the Fifteenth Century', *Agricultural History Review*, 45 (1997), pp. 18–33; A.D. Watkins, 'Maxstoke Priory in the Fifteenth Century: the Development of an Estate Economy in the Forest of Arden', *Warwickshire History*, 10 (1996), pp. 3–18.
5. M.J. Stanley, 'Medieval Tax Returns as Source Material', in T.R. Slater and P.J. Jarvis (eds), *Field and Forest* (Norwich, 1982), pp. 249–52; L. Proudfoot, 'The Extension of Parish Churches in Medieval Warwickshire', *Journal of Historical Geography*, 9 (1983), pp. 231–46; C.J. Bond, 'Deserted Medieval Villages in Warwickshire and Worcestershire', in Slater and Jarvis (eds), *Field and Forest*, pp. 163–4; M.W. Beresford, 'The Deserted Villages of Warwickshire', *Transactions of the Birmingham Archaeological Society*, 66 (1945–6), pp. 80–1.
6. Dyer, *Warwickshire Farming*, pp. 9–12; Watkins, 'Society and Economy', pp. 140–4; Watkins, 'Landowners and their Estates'.
7. Dyer, *Warwickshire Farming*, pp. 9–11; Watkins, 'Landowners and their Estates'; Dyer, 'West Midlands', p. 83; Watkins, 'Cattle Grazing', pp. 18–21; Warwick County RO, MR 1/11, MR 2/13, CR 440/1, 2, CR 284/8/9; Birmingham Reference Library, Norton MSS 106, 110; Nottingham University Manuscripts Department, MiL 5; BL, Additional Rolls 49650, 49651, 49654, 49661.
8. R.H. Hilton, *Social Structure of Rural Warwickshire in the Middle Ages*, Dugdale Society Occasional Paper, 9 (1950); *The Stoneleigh Ledger Book*, ed. R.H. Hilton, Dugdale Society, 24 (1960), pp. 100–8; PRO, SC6 1040/1-4; Warks. RO, MR 13/6; B. Harvey, *Westminster Abbey and its Estates in the Middle Ages* (Oxford, 1977), p. 271.

9. Postan, *Medieval Economy and Society*, pp. 150–8; Hilton, *English Peasantry*, pp. 40–8.
10. Dyer, *Warwickshire Farming*, pp. 7–9, 30–1; Watkins, 'Society and Economy', pp. 176–91; Watkins, 'Cattle Grazing', pp. 17–19.
11. F.R.H. Du Boulay, 'Who were Farming in the English Demesnes at the End of the Middle Ages?', *Economic History Review*, 2nd series, 17 (1965), pp. 443–55; Harvey, *Westminster Abbey*, pp. 151–2; J.W. Hare, 'The Demesne Lessees of Fifteenth-Century Wiltshire', *Agricultural History Review*, 29 (1981), pp. 1–15; Dyer, *Warwickshire Farming*, pp. 4–5; Watkins, 'Cattle Grazing', pp. 17–18.
12. Watkins, 'Cattle Grazing', pp. 18–19; Watkins, 'Society and Economy', pp. 267–77; Staffordshire RO, D986/13 D986/15.
13. *Leland's Itinerary in England and Wales*, ed. L.T. Smith (5 vols, London, 1907–10), vol. 2, p. 47; Hilton, *English Peasantry*, pp. 104–8; B.K. Roberts, 'Field Systems of the West Midlands', in A.R.H. Baker and R.A. Butlin (eds), *Studies of Field Systems in the British Isles* (Cambridge, 1973), pp. 188–231; V.H.T. Skipp, 'The Evolution of Settlement and Open Field Topography in the North Arden down to 1300', in T. Rowley (ed.), *The Origins of Open Field Agriculture* (Oxford, 1981), pp. 162–83.
14. Hilton, *English Peasantry*, pp. 134–8, Nottingham Univ. MSS Dept., MiM 131/25–52, MiM 175, 206, 207, 214; *Ministers Accounts of the Warwickshire Estates of the Duke of Clarence, 1479–80*, ed. R.H. Hilton, Dugdale Society, 21 (1952), pp. 31–4; Birmingham Ref. Lib., DV 329 347913; A.D. Watkins, 'The Development of Coleshill in the Middle Ages' (unpublished BA dissertation, University of Birmingham, 1982), pp. 7–28.
15. Warks. RO, MR1/15, 18 (Moxhull); Staffs. RO, D 641/1/2/275 (Maxstoke); Birmingham Ref. Lib., Norton MSS 94 (Lea Marston); Nottingham Univ. MSS Dept., MiL 5 (Kingsbury), MiM 131/33 (Middleton).
16. Dyer, *Warwickshire Farming*, p. 25; Nottingham Univ. MSS Dept., MiL, 5, MiM 131/32, 33; Birmingham Ref. Lib., Norton MSS 87, 91, 94.
17. *The Domesday of Inclosures*, ed. L.S. Leadam, Royal Historical Society (London, 1897), vol. 2, pp. 443, 448; Nottingham Univ. MSS Dept., MiM 131/37; Birmingham Ref. Lib., Norton MSS 71; Shakespeare's Birthplace Trust RO, DR 18/30/15/1.
18. BL, Add. Rolls 49564, 49578, 49587, 49596, 49598, 49611, 49612, 49637, 49651, 49653, 49655.
19. Birmingham Ref. Lib., DV 327 347863; *Warwickshire Estates of the Duke of Clarence*, p. 60; PRO, SC 2/207/97; BL, Additional Charters 48673, 48674.
20. C. Dyer, 'Power and Conflict in the Medieval Village', in D. Hooke (ed.), *Medieval Villages* (Oxford, 1984), pp. 27–32; Watkins, 'Society and Economy', pp. 101–12. For ordinances concerning communal cereal cultivation see, Warks. RO, MR1/5, 9,11, 16 (Moxhull), CR 1911/13 (Lyndon), CR 440/1 (Chilvers Coton); Birmingham Ref. Lib., DV 327 347863 (Erdington), Norton MSS 52, 76, 82, 94, 101, 103 (Lea Marston); Nottingham Univ. MSS Dept., MiL 5 (Kingsbury), 5/169b/9 (Maxstoke), MiM 131/29(3), 131/38(4) (Middleton), MiM 133/10 (Shustoke), MiM 134/13, 17 (Sutton Coldfield); Shakespeare's Birthplace Trust RO, DR 18/30/15/10 (Kenilworth); BL, Add. Rolls 49568, 49651 (Nuneaton).
21. For ringing pigs see Birmingham Ref. Lib., DV 327 347863 (Erdington); Nottingham Univ. MSS Dept., MiL 5 (Kingsbury), MiM 133/1 (Shustoke), MiM 134/3(a), MiM 134/13 (Sutton Coldfield); Shakespeare's Birthplace Trust RO, DR 18/30/15/16 (Kenilworth); Warks. RO, CR 254/8/9 (Claverton), CR 1911/12 (Lyndon); BL, Add. Rolls, 49633, 49661 (Nuneaton). For ordinances and by laws relating to folding and common grazing see Warks. RO, MR1/16, 18 (Moxhull); Birmingham Ref. Lib., Norton MSS 52 (Lea Marston); Nottingham Univ. MSS Dept., MiL5 (Kingsbury), MiM 133/10, 11 (Shustoke); Warks. RO, CR 1911/8 (Lyndon); BL, Add. Rolls, 49615, 49629, 49639 (Nuneaton).
22. BL, Add. Rolls 49653, 49656; Warks. RO, MR13/13; Nottingham Univ. MSS Dept., MiM 134/5. For blocked watercourses and unscoured ditches see the references in the two above footnotes. For Middleton specifically see Nottingham Univ. MSS Dept., MiM 131/34, 45.
23. *Leland's Itinery*, p.47; Watkins, 'Cattle Grazing', pp. 21–3; Dyer, *Warwickshire Farming*, pp. 22–4, 28–30.
24. Warks. RO, CR440/1 (Chilvers Coton), CR 1911/13 (Lyndon), MR1/5, 9, 11, 16 (Moxhull); Birmingham Ref. Lib., Norton MSS 52, 76, 82, 94, 101, 103 (Lea Marston); Nottingham Univ. MSS Dept., MiL 5 (Kingsbury), 5/169b/9 (Maxstoke), MiM 131/29(3), 131/38(4)

(Middleton), MiM 133/10 (Shustoke), MiM 134/13, 17, (Sutton Coldfield); BL, Add. Rolls 49568, 49651 (Nuneaton).

25. Dyer, *Warwickshire Farming*, p. 29.
26. Watkins, 'Cattle Grazing', p. 23; Dyer, *Warwickshire Farming*, pp. 29–30; Shakespeare's Birthplace Trust RO, DR37/73; Nottingham Univ. MSS Dept., 5/167/101(iii); Staffs. RO, D641/1/3/4/; Bodleian Library, MS Trinity 84, pp. 97, 101, 105.
27. Watkins, 'Cattle Grazing', pp. 20–1; Watkins, 'Society and Economy', p. 360; Warks. RO, MR13/2, 3, 4; PRO, Just 1/977.
28. Watkins 'Cattle Grazing', pp. 12–16; Dyer, 'Small Landowner', pp. 6–8; Dyer, *Warwickshire Farming*, p. 30.
29. Dyer, *Warwickshire Farming*, p. 30; Watkins, 'Cattle Grazing', pp. 19–20; Watkins, 'Merevale Abbey', pp. 96–7; Westminster Abbey, WAM 27721.
30. BL, Add. Roll 49640 (Astley); Nottingham Univ. MSS Dept., MiL 5 (Kingsbury), 5/169B/17 (Maxstoke); Birmingham Ref. Lib., Norton MSS 61 (Lea Marston); Warks. RO, CR 1911/12, CR 1911/13 (Lyndon), MR1/11 (Moxhull), CR 254/8/9 (Pinley); BL, Add. Rolls, 49612, 49615, 49629, 49650, 49661 (Nuneaton).
31. BL, Add. Rolls 49612, 49631; Warks. RO, MR1/11; Watkins, 'Society and Economy', pp. 223–4.
32. BL, Add. Rolls 49562, 49565; Shakespeare's Birthplace Trust RO, DR37/73.
33. C. Dyer, 'Gardens and Orchards in Medieval England', in C. Dyer, *Everyday Life in Medieval England* (London, 1994), pp. 113–32; Birmingham Ref. Lib., DV 327 347865, DV 327 347863, DV 327 347856; Watkins, 'Woodland Economy', pp. 26–8, 30–1; Dyer, *Warwickshire Farming*, p. 23.
34. C. Dyer, 'Were Peasants Self-Sufficient? English Villages and the Market, 1050–1350', in E. Mornet (ed.), *Campagnes médiévales: l'homme et son éspace* (Paris, 1995), pp. 653–66; Hilton, *English Peasantry*, pp. 45–6; Watkins, 'Society and Economy', pp. 328, 344–6; A.D. Watkins, 'William de Kellingworth and The George: an Early Reference to a Warwickshire Rural Inn', *Warwickshire History*, 7 (1989), pp. 130–4.
35. Westminster Abbey, WAM 27721; Birmingham Ref. Lib., DV 329 447939, 329 347943; B.K. Roberts, 'Medieval Fishponds', *Amateur Historian*, 7 (1966), pp. 122–3; Shakespeare's Birthplace Trust RO, DR 3/804; W. Dugdale, *The Antiquities of Warwickshire* (2nd edn, 2 vols, London, 1730), vol. 2, p. 914.
36. Watkins, 'Woodland Economy', pp. 27–8; Watkins, 'Merevale Abbey', p. 99; Watkins, 'Maxstoke Priory', pp. 14–15.
37. Watkins, 'Woodland Economy', p. 28; Watkins, 'Maxstoke Priory', pp. 14–15.
38. Watkins, 'Woodland Economy', pp. 19–25; Birmingham Ref. Lib., A 433, 629; Bod. Lib., MS Trinity 84, p. 121; Shakespeare's Birthplace Trust RO, DR 37/107/27, DR 37/978.
39. Watkins, 'Woodland Economy', pp. 29–30; BL, Add. Roll 17759; Gover, Mawer, and Stenton, *Place-Names of Warwickshire*, p. 12.
40. Watkins, 'Woodland Economy', p. 29; *VCH Warwickshire*, ed. H.A. Doubleday, W. Page, L.F. Salzman and W.B. Stephens (8 vols, London, 1904–in progress), vol. 2, pp. 219–20; Watkins, 'Merevale Abbey', p. 98.
41. Watkins, 'Woodland Economy', pp. 30–1, 25–7; Birmingham Ref. Lib., Norton MSS 65; Warks. RO, CR 1911/12.
42. T. Lloyd, *Aspects of the Building Industry in Medieval Stratford-upon-Avon*, Dugdale Society Occasional Paper, 14 (1961), p. 18; Watkins, 'Woodland Economy', pp. 28–9; Watkins, 'Merevale Abbey', p. 98; Watkins, 'Maxstoke Priory', p. 14; Dyer 'A Small Landowner', p. 9.
43. E.A. Gooder, 'Claymaking in the Nuneaton Area', in P. Mayes and K. Scott (eds), *Pottery Kilns at Chilvers Coton, Nuneaton*, Society of Medieval Archaeology, Monographs Series, 10 (1984), pp. 3–10; Watkins, 'Woodland Economy', p. 31; Lloyd, *Aspects of the Building Industry*, pp. 18–20; BL, Add. Rolls, 17759, 49653; Westminster Abbey, WAM 27724.
44. Lloyd, *Aspects of the Building Industry*, pp. 18–20; Watkins, 'Woodland Economy', p. 31; R.H. Hilton, *A Medieval Society: The West Midlands at the End of the Thirteenth Century* (2nd edn, Cambridge, 1983), p. 175; R.A. Pelham, 'The Establishment of the Willoughby Ironworks in North Warwickshire in the Sixteenth Century', *University of Birmingham Historical Journal*, 4 (1953–4), pp. 18–29; J. Hatcher, 'A Diversified Economy: Later Medieval Cornwall', *Economic*

History Review, 2nd series, 17 (1969), p. 227; Bailey, 'Concept of the Margin', pp. 10–13; H.S.A. Fox, 'Tenant Farming and Tenant Farmers: Devon and Cornwall', in Miller (ed.), *Agrarian History of England and Wales, III*, pp. 738–43; M. Kowaleski, *Local Markets and Regional Trade in Medieval Exeter* (Cambridge, 1995), pp. 16–17; E. Carus-Wilson, 'The Woollen Industry Before 1550', in *VCH Wiltshire*, ed. R.B. Pugh, E. Crittall and D.A. Crowley (16 vols, London, 1953–in progress), vol. 4, pp. 129–38.

45. Dyer, 'Small Landowner', pp. 12–14; Watkins, 'Society and Economy', pp. 294–99.
46. Nottingham Univ. MSS Dept., 5/167/101(i), 5/167/101(iii) 5/167/101(ii), MiDA 90; MiM 131/25–51, MiM 175, 214.
47. J. Thirsk (ed.), *The Agrarian History of England and Wales, V(1): 1640–1750, Regional Farming Systems* (Cambridge, 1984); J. Thirsk, *England's Agrarian Regions and Agricultural History* (London, 1987); E. Kerridge, *The Agricultural Revolution* (London, 1967), pp. 41–180; A.J. Pollard, 'The North-Eastern Economy and the Agrarian Crisis of 1438–1440', *Northern History*, 25 (1989), pp. 88–105; *The Duchy of Lancaster's Estates in Derbyshire, 1485–1540*, ed. I.S.W. Blanchard, Derbyshire Archaeological Society Record Series, 3 (1967), pp. 1–15.
48. Lack of awareness of medieval regional agricultural systems is articulated by J. Langdon, *Horses, Oxen and Technological Innovation* (Cambridge, 1986), pp. 273–6 and B.M.S. Campbell, 'Towards an Agricultural Geography of Medieval England', *Agricultural History Review*, 36 (1988), p. 88. Some pays are identified in Miller (ed.), *Agrarian History of England and Wales, III*, pp. 42–3 (Lancashire and Yorkshire), 53 (eastern England), 79 (the West Midlands), 119 (Kent and Sussex), 136–7 (other southern counties), 153–6 (Devon and Cornwall). Others are noted in Hilton, *Medieval Society*, pp. 7–22 and A.J. Pollard, *North-Eastern England during the Wars of the Roses* (Oxford, 1990), pp. 30–8. Studies which focus on a local *pays* include: D. Roden, 'Demesne Farming in the Chiltern Hills', *Agricultural History Review*, 17 (1969), pp. 9–24; M. Bailey, *A Marginal Economy? East Anglian Breckland in the Later Middle Ages* (Cambridge, 1989); R.H. Britnell, 'Agriculture in a Region of Ancient Enclosure, 1185–1506', *Nottingham Medieval Studies*, 27 (1983), pp. 37–55; P.F. Brandon, 'Demesne Arable Farming in Coastal Sussex during the Late Middle Ages', *Agricultural History Review*, 19 (1971), pp. 13–34; J.R. Birrell, 'The Forest Economy of the Honour of Tutbury in the Fourteenth and Fifteenth Centuries', *University of Birmingham Historical Journal*, 8 (1961), pp. 114–34.
49. Watkins, 'Cattle Grazing', pp. 24–5; Britnell, 'Economic Context', pp. 47–52; Farmer, 'Prices and Wages', pp. 508–12; Hatcher, 'Great Slump', pp. 248–55.

6. *A Priory and its Tenants*

1. M. McKisack, *The Fourteenth Century, 1307–1399* (Oxford, 1959), p. 341.
2. Other dates given in the form 1495/6 also signify the accounting year from the Michaelmas of the first year to the Michaelmas of the second.
3. *Durham Cathedral Priory Rentals Volume I: Bursar's Rentals*, ed. R.A. Lomas and A.J. Piper, Surtees Society, 198 (1989), pp. 129–97. The manuscript is in Durham Dean and Chapter Muniments (DDCM). All references to the bursar's rental of 1495/6 are to this edition.
4. The priory's financial year began after the previous year's accounts had been presented to the annual chapter which was held on the first Monday after Ascension Day.
5. R.B. Dobson, 'The Last English Monks on Scottish Soil', *Scottish Historical Review*, 46 (1967), pp. 1–25.
6. *The Priory of Coldingham*, ed. J. Raine, Surtees Society, 12 (1841), pp. lxxxv–civ.
7. R.B. Dobson, *Durham Priory 1400–1450* (Cambridge, 1973), p. 309.
8. In 1495/6 the bursar was William Hawkwell, who was to continue in office until 1506/7. The terrar, who at this time doubled as hostillar, was John Danby. The prior's steward was William Claxton. He had been in post at an annual fee of £5 since 1476 and was in his final year of service.
9. The workings of the priory's obedientiary system is the subject of R.A. Lomas, 'The Priory of Durham as a Landowner and a Landlord 1290–1540' (unpublished Ph.D. thesis, University of Durham, 1972).

10. *The Inventories and Account Rolls of Jarrow and Monkwearmouth*, ed. J. Raine, Surtees Society, 29 (1854), pp. 130–1, 223.
11. These developments are recorded in DDCM, Bursar's Account Rolls.
12. *Priory Rentals*, p. 226.
13. DDCM, Bursar's Account Rolls.
14. DDCM, Proctor of Norham's Accounts.
15. *Bursar's Rentals*, p. 225 (for Ellingham); K.H. Vickers, *A History of Northumberland*, vol. 11 (Newcastle upon Tyne, 1922), pp. 96–7 (for Branxton).
16. *Priory Rentals*, p. 226.
17. Ibid., p. 224; DDCM, Bursar's Account Rolls.
18. Ibid., pp. 222–4.
19. Ibid., pp. 206, 217, 221.
20. *Historiae Dunelmensis Scriptores Tres*, ed. J. Raine, Surtees Society, 9 (1839), p. ccxciv.
21. *Priory Rentals*, pp. 203, 207, 211, 215, 217.
22. R.A. Lomas, 'The Priory of Durham and its Demesnes in the Fourteenth and Fifteenth Centuries', *Economic History Review*, 2nd series, 31 (1978), pp. 339–53.
23. Dobson, *Durham Priory*, pp. 93–6.
24. M. Roberts, *Durham* (London, 1994), p. 70.
25. V.E. Watts, 'Some Northumbrian Fishery Names, I', *Transactions of the Architectural and Archaeological Society of Durham and Northumberland*, new series, 6 (1982), pp. 89–92.
26. R.A. Lomas, 'Developments in Land Tenure on the Prior of Durham's Estate in the Later Middle Ages', *Northern History*, 13 (1977), pp. 41–2.
27. R.A. Lomas, 'The Black Death in County Durham', *Journal of Medieval History*, 15 (1989), pp. 127–40.
28. Lomas, 'Developments in Land Tenure', p. 37.
29. DDCM, Halmote Court Rolls.
30. Lomas, 'Developments in Land Tenure', p. 36.
31. *Priory Rentals*, pp. 62–4, 217.
32. Ibid., p. 204.
33. Ibid., pp. 33, 39–40, 50–1, 54–5, 136–7, 150, 159–62, 172–5.
34. Lomas, 'Priory of Durham and its Demesnes', p. 344.
35. Lomas, 'Priory of Durham as a Landowner', pp. 132, 236.
36. DDCM, Cellarer's Accounts.
37. Lomas, 'Priory of Durham as a Landowner', p. 164.
38. *The Rites of Durham*, ed. J. Fowler, Surtees Society, 107 (1903), p. 99.
39. *Priory Rentals*, p. 145.
40. Ibid., p. 145.
41. M.E. Arvanagian, 'Free Rents in the Palatinate of Durham, and the Crisis of the Late 1430s', *Archaeologia Aeliana*, 5th. series, 24 (1996), pp. 99–108.
42. *Scriptores Tres*, pp. ccxciv–ccxcviii.
43. C.E. Challis, *The Tudor Coinage* (Manchester, 1978), p. 199.
44. *Priory Rentals*, p. 139.
45. DDCM, Bursar's Account Roll 1495/6, *garderoba* section.
46. Ibid., *Pensiones et Stipendia* section.
47. *Scriptores Tres*, pp. ccli–cclii.
48. *Priory Rentals*, pp. 154–5, 193.
49. DDCM, Proctor of Norham's Accounts.
50. Grey was the son of Sir Ralph Grey, one of the leaders of the Lancastrian cause in Northumberand, who was executed in 1464: M.H. Dodds, *A History of Northumberland*, vol. 14 (Newcastle upon Tyne, 1935), p. 212. Manners died in August 1495: J. Raine, *The History and Antiquities of North Durham* (London and Edinburgh, 1852), pedigree between pp. 328 and 329.
51. I am indebted to Dr C.M .Newman for identfying this man.
52. DDCM, Bursar's Account Roll, 1495/6.
53. C.E. Challis (ed.), *A New History of the Royal Mint* (Cambridge, 1992), pp. 190–7. I am also grateful to Dr Challis for his help in discussing this matter with me.
54. Lomas, 'Priory of Durham and its Demesnes', pp. 343–4.

7. *Artisans, Guilds and Government in London*

1. See C.L. Scofield, *The Life and Reign of Edward IV* (2 vols, London, 1923), vol. 2, p. 191.
2. *Acts of Court of the Mercers Company, 1453–1527*, ed. L.L. Lyell and F.D. Watney (Cambridge, 1936), p. 97. As on previous occasions it is likely that craft identity was confined to the 'dyvers dyvysyngs' worn on the robes and which allowed 'every crafte to be knowe from othyr'. *The Historical Collections of a Citizen of London in the Fifteenth Century*, ed. J. Gairdner, Camden Society, new series, 17 (1876), pp. 185–6.
3. See C. Phythian-Adams, 'Ceremony and the Citizen: The Communal Year at Coventry, 1450–1550', in R. Holt and G. Rosser (eds), *The Medieval Town: A Reader in English Urban History 1200–1540* (London, 1990), pp. 238–64; M. James, 'Ritual, Drama and the Social Body in the Late Medieval English Town', *Past and Present*, 98 (1983), pp. 3–29; M. Berlin, 'Civic Ceremony in Early Modern London', *Urban History Yearbook* (1986), pp. 15–28; S. Lindenbaum, 'Ceremony and Oligarchy: the London Midsummer Watch', in B.A. Hanawalt and K.L. Reyerson (eds), *City and Spectacle in Medieval Europe* (Minneapolis, 1994), pp. 171–88; B. McRee, 'Unity or Division? The Social Meaning of Guild Ceremony in Urban Communities', ibid., pp. 189–207.
4. *Acts of Court*, pp. 101–4; CLRO, Repertories, 3, ff. 64v–66.
5. G. Unwin, *The Guilds and Companies of London*, 4th edn (London, 1963), which supplies a bibliography of some older company histories on pp. 372–89. For some more recent, less 'institutional', studies see C.M. Barron, 'London in the Later Middle Ages, 1300–1550', *London Journal*, 20 (1995), pp. 25, 30.
6. E.M. Veale, 'The "Great Twelve": Mistery and Fraternity in Thirteenth-Century London', *Historical Research*, 64 (1991), pp. 237-63; eadem, *The English Fur Trade in the Later Middle Ages* (Oxford, 1966), p. 107.
7. M. Davies, 'The Tailors of London: Corporate Charity in the Late Medieval Town', in R.E. Archer (ed.), *Crown, Government and People in the Fifteenth Century* (Stroud, 1994), pp. 161–90; idem, 'The Tailors of London and their guild, *c.* 1300–1500' (unpublished D.Phil. thesis, University of Oxford, 1994), especially pp. 1–47.
8. Veale, 'The "Great Twelve"', pp. 240–2, 249–52, 256–60. For the origins of the Mercers' Company see A.F. Sutton, 'The Mercery Trade and the Mercers' Company of London from the 1130s to 1348' (unpublished Ph.D. thesis, University of London, 1995).
9. *Memorials of London and London Life in the XIIIth, XIVth and XVth Centuries*, ed. H.T. Riley (London, 1868), pp. 495–6, 542–4; *Calendar of Plea and Memoranda Rolls of the City of London*, ed. A.H. Thomas and P.E. Jones (6 vols, Cambridge, 1926–61), 1323–64, pp. 225–6, 231, 237; ibid., 1364–81, pp. 54–6, 291–4; Davies, 'Tailors of London and their Guild', pp. 147–56; C.M. Barron and L. Wright, 'The London Middle English Guild Certificates of 1388–9', *Nottingham Medieval Studies*, 39 (1995), pp. 114–15.
10. Merchant Taylors' Company, London, Accounts, vol. 1, f. 105; *Calendar of the Letter Books preserved among the Archives of the Corporation of the City of London*, ed. R.R. Sharpe (11 vols, London, 1899–1912), book K, pp. 263–6.
11. I.W. Archer, *The Pursuit of Stability: Social Relations in Elizabethan London* (Cambridge, 1991), pp. 108–12; S. Rappaport, *Worlds Within Worlds: Structures of Life in Sixteenth Century London* (Cambridge, 1989), pp. 219–32.
12. *Calendar of Letter Books*, book E, pp. 232–4.
13. Unwin, *Guilds and Companies*, pp. 218–19; Davies, 'The Tailors of London and their Guild', pp. 156–7.
14. GL, London, MS 5440, ff. 11v, 84; Unwin, *Guilds and Companies*, pp. 167, 181.
15. *Statutes of the Realm (1101–1713)*, ed. A. Luders, T.E. Tomlin, J. France, W.E. Taunton and J. Raithby (11 vols, Record Commission, London, 1810–28), vol. 2, pp. 298–9; *Rot. Parl.*, vol. 4, p. 507.
16. *Calendar of Letter Books*, book L, pp. 67, 73, 183–4.
17. Ibid., book L, pp. 199–203.
18. Unwin, *Guilds and Companies*, pp. 159–60, 163.
19. *Calendar of Letter Books*, book L, p. 138.

20. Ibid., pp. 168, 319.
21. I.W. Archer, *The History of the Haberdashers' Company of London* (Chichester, 1991), pp. 7–8, 18.
22. *Calendar of Letter Books*, book K, pp. 39, 224, 309. Davies, 'The Tailors of London and their Guild', pp. 121, 137–8.
23. *Calendar of Letter Books*, book L, pp. 73, 132.
24. S.H. Rigby, 'Urban "Oligarchy" in Late Medieval England', in J.A.F. Thomson (ed.), *Towns and Townpeople in the Fifteenth Century* (Gloucester, 1988), pp. 62–86.
25. *Records of the Borough of Leicester*, ed. M. Bateson (2 vols, London, 1899–1901), vol. 2, pp. 319, 326–30, 324–5.
26. S.L. Thrupp, *The Merchant Class of Medieval London* (Chicago, 1948), p. 60.
27. This definition was re-stated on a number of occasions, for instance in 1406 when apprentices and servants had caused disturbances at the election of the Mayor and Sheriffs: *Calendar of Letter Books*, book I, p. 34.
28. See C.M. Barron, 'Ralph Holland and the London Radicals, 1438–1444', in Holt and Rosser (eds), *The Medieval Town*, pp. 160–83, and Davies, 'The Tailors of London and their Guild', pp. 122–6.
29. Archer, *Pursuit of Stability*, pp. 18–30.
30. For this see R. Bird, *The Turbulent London of Richard II* (London, 1949), and P. Nightingale, 'Capitalists, Crafts and Constitutional Change in Late Fourteenth-Century London', *Past and Present*, 124 (1989), pp. 3–35.
31. See J. Schofield, *The Building of London from the Conquest to the Great Fire*, revised edn (London, 1993), pp. 115–18.
32. Merchant Taylors' Company, London, Accounts, vol. 1, ff. 387–87v.
33. Merchant Taylors' Company, London, Accounts, vol. 1, f. 214; J. Imray, '"Les Bones Gentes de la Mercerye de Londres": a Study of the Membership of the Medieval Mercers' Company', in A.E.J. Hollaender and W. Kellaway (eds), *Studies in London History presented to P.E. Jones* (London, 1969), pp. 175–6.
34. Davies, 'The Tailors of London and their Guild', pp. 141, 192–203.
35. Thrupp, *Merchant Class*, p. 110.
36. *Acts of Court*, p. 47.
37. Thrupp, *Merchant Class*, pp. 205–6.
38. Imray, '"Bones Gentes"', p. 160; *Calendar of Plea and Memoranda Rolls*, 1458–82, pp. xxvii–xxx.
39. The limited success of such policies can be seen in a case study of the barrel-makers of Bruges: J.-P. Sosson, 'La structure sociale de la corporation médiévale: l'example des tonneliers de Bruges de 1350 à 1500', *Revue Belge de philologie et d'histoire*, 44 (1966), pp. 457–78.
40. Merchant Taylors' Company, London, Accounts, vol. 1, f. 329; 2, ff. 124v, 189; 3, f. 6; *Calendar of Letter Books*, book L, p. 35; for Holland's career see Barron, 'Ralph Holland', pp. 160–3; Canterbury Dean and Chapter Library, Reg. F, f. 200.
41. P. Nightingale, *A Medieval Mercantile Community: The Grocers' Company and the Politics and Trade of London, 1000–1485* (New Haven, 1995), pp. 479–81, 540; Merchant Taylors' Company, London, Court Minutes, vol. 2, f. 21v.
42. Veale, *Fur Trade*, pp. 121–5.
43. Thrupp, *Merchant Class*, pp. 8–13.
44. For the role of guilds as 'agents' of town governments see H. Swanson, *Medieval Artisans: An Urban Class in Late Medieval England* (Oxford, 1989), pp. 110–18; H Swanson, 'The Illusion of Economic Structure: Craft Guilds in Late Medieval English Towns', *Past and Present*, 121 (1988), pp. 29–48.
45. Veale, '"Great Twelve"', pp. 237–63.
46. C.M. Barron, 'The Government of London and its Relations with the Crown, 1400–1450' (unpublished Ph.D. thesis, University of London, 1970), p. 194. The reaction may have been similar to that which followed the mortmain legislation of 1391, which itself followed on the heels of the governmental inquiry of 1388–9 and prompted many prominent guilds to seek new letters patent in the 1390s. See Davies, 'Tailors of London and their Guild', pp. 10–11.
47. CLRO, Journals, 4, f. 222 (1448); 5, ff. 40 (1450), 61v (1451), 116 (1453).
48. *The Chronicles of London*, ed. C.L. Kingsford (Oxford, 1905), p. 194.

49. Ibid., pp. 187–8.
50. CLRO, Journals, 9, ff. 81v–82, 85v. For the City's response to the events of these years see D.J. Guth, 'Richard III, Henry VII and the City: London Politics and the "Dun Cowe"', in R.A. Griffiths and J. Sherborne (eds), *Kings and Nobles in the Later Middle Ages: A Tribute to Charles Ross* (Gloucester, 1986), pp. 185–204.
51. *Calendar of Letter Books*, book K, p. 190.
52. Ibid., pp. 205–6. For the impact of this siege see J.A. Doig, 'Propaganda, Public Opinion and the Siege of Calais in 1436', in Archer (ed.), *Crown, Government and People*, pp. 79–106.
53. *Historical Collections*, p. 178; *Calendar of Letter Books*, book K, p. 206.
54. Merchant Taylors' Company, London, Accounts, vol. 1, ff. 271v, 276v. A levy of £28 11*s* was raised from 230 tailors who contributed between 4*d* and 6*s* 8*d* each: ibid., vol. 1, ff. 268–9v.
55. *Facsimile of the First Volume of the MS Archives of the Worshipful Company of Grocers of the City of London, AD 1345–1463*, ed. J.A. Kingdon, (2 vols, London, 1883–6), vol. 2, pp. 234, 236.
56. CLRO, Journals, 6, f. 138. C.M. Barron, 'London and the Crown, 1451–61', in J.R.L. Highfield and R. Jeffs (eds), *The Crown and Local Communities in England and France in the Fifteenth Century* (Gloucester, 1981), p. 95.
57. Barron, 'Government of London', p. 198; *Calendar of Letter Books*, book I, pp. 67, 71.
58. CLRO, Journals, 9, ff. 50v–51 and see *Calendar of Letter Books*, book L, p. 212. The dispute is indicative of the extent to which the constitution of the City was becoming more clearly defined and formalized in the later fifteenth century.
59. C.M. Barron, 'London and Parliament in the Lancastrian Period', *Parliamentary History*, 9 (1990), p. 359.
60. *Facsimile of the First Volume*, pp. 139, 185, 241, 262.
61. Unwin, *Gilds and Companies*, pp. 167–8.
62. CLRO, Journals, 8, f. 163; *Acts of Court*, pp. xvii, 115–16; Archer, *History of the Haberdashers' Company*, pp. 7–8, 18.
63. *Acts of Court*, pp. 138–9, 143; CLRO, Letter Book L, ff. 226-26v.
64. CLRO, Letter Book L, ff. 232, 236; *Statutes of the Realm*, vol. 2, pp. 518–19.
65. Merchant Taylors' Company, London, Court Minutes, vol. 1, ff. 3v, 9v.
66. *Rot. Parl.*, vol. 5, pp. 506–8; *Statutes of the Realm*, vol. 2, pp. 396–8; Barron, 'London and Parliament', pp. 360–1.
67. *Statutes of the Realm*, vol. 2, pp. 157–8.
68. Merchant Taylors' Company, London, Accounts, vol. 1, f. 47. The identity of the 'freres' is unclear.
69. Thrupp, *Merchant Class*, pp. 215–16; *Calendar of Letter Books*, book K, pp. 87, 105. For the City's petition see *Rot. Parl.*, vol. 4, p. 354.
70. Merchant Taylors' Company, London, Accounts, vol. 1, f. 207v; *Facsimile of the First Volume*, vol. 2, p. 204; *Statutes of the Realm*, vol. 2, p. 248.
71. *Calendar of Plea and Memoranda Rolls*, 1364–81, pp. xl–xli.
72. Davies, 'The Tailors of London and their Guild', pp. 183–92; Merchant Taylors' Company, London, Court Minutes, vol. 1, f. 6v; J.T. Ryan, 'Apprenticeship in Later Medieval London 1200–1500' (unpublished M.A. thesis, University of London, 1992), pp. 14–18.
73. *Calendar of Letter Books*, book K, p. 375.
74. This contrasts with the situation earlier in the century when guilds such as the goldsmiths and drapers were forced to lower their fees in order to attract more apprentices: Davies, 'The Tailors of London and their Guild', pp. 186–7; Ryan, 'Apprenticeship', p. 20.
75. Merchant Taylors' Company, London, Court Minutes, vol. 1, f. 6v.
76. CLRO, Journals, 1, f. 72.
77. *Calendar of Letter Books*, book K, pp. 161–6.
78. *Calendar of Letter Books*, book L, pp. 25–8.
79. *Calendar of Letter Books*, book K, pp. 335–8.
80. Davies, 'The Tailors of London and their Guild', pp. 171–2.
81. T.F. Reddaway and L.E.M. Walker, *The Early History of the Goldsmiths' Company* (London, 1975), pp. 231–4.
82. Ibid., pp. 231–4 (1478–83); *Statutes of the Realm*, vol. 2, pp. 457–8.
83. Nightingale, *Medieval Mercantile Community*, pp. 547–50.

84. *Statutes of the Realm*, vol. 2, pp. 489–93.
85. *Calendar of Letter Books*, book L, pp. 2, 10–11, 254, 256–7, 295, 302; Merchant Taylors' Company, London, Court Minutes, vol. 2, f. 64.
86. CLRO, Journals, 11, ff. 336–6v.
87. CLRO, Journals, 6, f. 109.
88. A.H. Johnson, *The History of the Worshipful Company of the Drapers of London* (6 vols, Oxford, 1914–22), vol. 1, p. 161; *The Records of the Skinners of London*, ed. J.J. Lambert (London, 1933), p. 131.
89. M. Carlin, *Medieval Southwark* (London, 1996), p. 163.
90. *Calendar of Letter Books*, book L, p. 100.
91. CLRO, Journals, 7, ff. 178–8v; Carlin, *Medieval Southwark*, p. 151.
92. G. Rosser, 'London and Westminster: the Suburb in the Urban Economy in the Later Middle Ages', in Thomson (ed.), *Towns and Townspeople*, pp. 56–7. See also Swanson, 'Craft Guilds', pp. 29–48.
93. Merchant Taylors' Company, London, Miscellaneous Docs. A.2, f. 10.
94. The nature of guild legislation is among the issues considered in G. Rosser, 'Crafts, Guilds and the Negotiation of Work in the Medieval Town', *Past and Present*, 154 (1997), pp. 3–31.
95. These issues will be discussed in *Court Minutes of the Merchant Taylors' Company, 1486–1493*, ed. M. Davies (forthcoming, Stroud).
96. Merchant Taylors' Company, London, Accounts, vol. 2, f. 33.
97. A.F. Sutton, 'Order and Fashion in Clothes: the King, his Household, and the City of London at the End of the Fifteenth Century', *Textile History*, 22 (1991), pp. 269–70.
98. *Statutes of the Realm*, vol. 2, p. 401.
99. Ibid., pp. 469–70.
100. For the development of the companies and their lobbying activities see I.W. Archer, 'The London Lobbies in the Later Sixteenth Century', *Historical Journal*, 31 (1988), pp. 17–44.
101. Merchant Taylors' Company, London, Court Minutes, vol. 2, f. 52.

8. London Parishes: Development in Context

1. A.G. Little, 'Personal Tithes', *English Historical Review*, 60 (1945), pp. 67–88.
2. Little, 'Personal Tithes', *passim.*; G. Constable, 'Resistance to Tithes in the Middle Ages', *Journal of Ecclesiastical History*, 13 (1962), pp. 172–5, 184–5. For more information specifically on London, however, see J.A.F. Thomson, 'Tithe Disputes in Later Medieval London', *English Historical Review*, 78 (1963), pp. 1–17.
3. C. Drew, *Early Parochial Organization in England: The Origin of the Office of Churchwarden*, St Anthony's Hall Publications, 7 (York, 1954), offers a very useful appraisal of the emergence and developing responsibilities of churchwardens. For a more recent discussion, see B. Kumin, *The Shaping of a Community. The rise and reformation of the English parish, c. 1400–1560* (Aldershot, 1996), and especially ch. 2.
4. C.N.L. Brooke and G. Keir, *London 800–1216: The Shaping of a City* (London, 1975), p. 313.
5. Brooke and Keir, *London 800–1216*, pp. 312–37; M.D. Lobel (ed.), *The City of London from Prehistoric Times to c. 1520*, The British Atlas of Historic Towns, 3 (Oxford, 1989), pp. 63–99; C. Rawcliffe, 'The Hospitals of Later Medieval London', *Medical History*, 28 (1984), pp. 1–21; *VCH London*, vol. 1, pp. 407–588.
6. Lobel (ed.), *City of London*, pp. 89, 93; *VCH London*, vol. 1, pp. 461–4 (St Mary Graces), 546–9 (Savoy).
7. Lobel (ed.), *City of London*, pp. 88, 90; *VCH London*, vol. 1, pp. 574–6 (Pulteney), pp. 577–8 (Walworth), and pp. 549, 578–80 (Whittington).
8. For references to William Cambridge, see S.L. Thrupp, *The Merchant Class of Medieval London* (Chicago, 1948), pp. 327–8. His foundation is discussed more fully below.
9. Perpetual chantry arrangements, which were very often made in conjunction with perpetual anniversaries, almost always made some provision of alms to the poor, or assisted the spiritual life of parishes to the benefit of parishioners. All chantries, whether perpetual or of limited

duration, specified that the priest was to celebrate for the benefit of all the faithful departed. A number of chantry priests may have offered instruction to the young. Schools might be attached to monasteries, hospitals and, of course, colleges, in addition to parish churches.

10. B.L. Manning, *The People's Faith in the Time of Wyclif*, 2nd edn (Hassocks, 1975), ch. 10; E. Duffy, *The Stripping of the Altars: Traditional Religion in England, c. 1400–1580* (New Haven and London, 1992), pp. 357–66; G.R. Owst, *Literature and Pulpit in Medieval England*, 2nd edn (Oxford, 1966), ch. 6.
11. Duffy, *Stripping of the Altars*, ch. 10 discusses Purgatory in some detail; see also C. Burgess, '"A Fond Thing Vainly Invented': An Essay on Purgatory and Pious Motive in Later Medieval England', in S.J. Wright (ed.), *Parish, Church and People: Local Studies in Lay Religion 1350–1750* (London, 1988), pp. 56–84.
12. R.W. Southern, *St Anselm and his Biographer* (Cambridge, 1963), p. 101.
13. On substitutive penance, see R.W. Southern, *Western Society and the Church in the Middle Ages* (Harmondsworth, 1970), pp. 225–8.
14. These quotations are taken from R.W. Southern's very useful and stimulating review of J. Le Goff, *La naissance du Purgatoire* (Paris, 1981) in *The Times Literary Supplement*, 18 June 1982, pp. 651–2.
15. There are references to bede rolls in many parish archives; one very full benefaction list survives for the church of All Saints, Bristol, and is available in print in *The Pre-Reformation Records of All Saints', Bristol: Part 1, The All Saints' Church Book*, ed. C. Burgess, Bristol Record Society, 46 (1995), pp. 4–30.
16. Southern, *Western Society and the Church*, pp. 272–99; C.H. Lawrence, *Medieval Monasticism* (London, 1984), ch. 12.
17. Manning, *People's Faith*, pp. 146ff.
18. For fuller discussion of charitable pursuits and their impact in a late medieval town, see P.H. Cullum and P.J.P. Goldberg, 'Charitable Provision in Late Medieval York: "To the Praise of God and the Use of the Poor"', *Northern History*, 29 (1993), pp. 24–39; and for a more general discussion, see M. Rubin, 'The Poor', in R. Horrox (ed.), *Fifteenth-Century Attitudes: Perceptions of Society in Late Medieval England* (Cambridge, 1994), pp. 169–82.
19. Sir Walter Manny founded a Charterhouse, the Priory of the Salutation, in 1371 near Smithfield, and Henry V founded another, the Priory of Jesus of Bethlehem, in fulfilment of his father's will at Sheen near Richmond. On the Carthusians generally, see Lawrence, *Medieval Monasticism*, pp. 133–7.
20. Henry V founded a Bridgettine abbey in 1415 as a sister house for Sheen; it was originally at Isleworth and moved to Syon in 1431. On the implications of the foundations to the west of London, see J. Catto, 'Religious Change under Henry V', in G.L. Harriss (ed.), *Henry V: The Practice of Kingship* (Oxford, 1985), pp. 109–11.
21. 'There was nothing random about these foundations; they were planned as a group, almost an Escorial, encapsulating the restored palace at Sheen': Catto, 'Religious Change', p. 110.
22. On the respective almshouses, see the references in the gazetteer in Lobel (ed.), *City of London*, pp. 63–99.
23. A. Kreider, *English Chantries: The Road to Dissolution* (Cambridge, Mass., 1979), ch. 1, hazards estimates of the numbers of perpetual chantries founded in some of the counties of England. He admits that these are far from being a reliable guide, and it should be emphasized that very many more chantries of temporary duration were being established. Even some flourishing perpetual chantries left surprisingly little trace in surviving documentation.
24. Cf. K.L. Wood-Legh, *Perpetual Chantries in Britain* (Cambridge, 1965), pp. 312–13. I explore some of the contributions that chantries in fact made to parish churches in C. Burgess, '"For the Increase of Divine Service": Chantries and the Parish in Late Medieval Bristol', *Journal of Ecclesiastical History*, 36 (1985), pp. 48–65.
25. On fraternities generally, see J.J. Scarisbrick, *The Reformation and the English People* (Oxford, 1984), ch. 2, and Duffy, *Stripping of the Altars*, ch. 4. For more particular studies, see C.M. Barron, 'The Parish Fraternities of Medieval London', in C. Barron and C. Harper-Bill (eds), *The Church in Pre-Reformation Society: Essays in Honour of F.R.H Du Boulay* (Woodbridge, 1985), pp. 13–37, which is of particular value in the present context; V. Bainbridge, *Gilds in the Medieval Countryside: Social*

and Religious Change in Cambridgeshire, c. 1350–1558 (Woodbridge, 1996); A.D. Brown, *Popular Piety in Late Medieval England: The Diocese of Salisbury, 1250–1550* (Oxford, 1995), ch. 6.
26. Wood-Legh, *Perpetual Chantries*, pp. 2–5.
27. I pursue these themes further in C. Burgess, 'A Service for the Dead: The Form and Function of the Anniversary in Late Medieval Bristol', *Transactions of the Bristol and Gloucestershire Archaeological Society*, 105 (1987), pp. 183–211.
28. For its relative place within Billingsgate ward, see *Two Tudor Subsidy Assessment Rolls for the City of London, 1541 and 1582*, ed. R.G. Lang, London Record Society, 29 (1993), pp. 22–8.
29. The perpetual chantries had been founded by the following parishioners: Rose Wrytell, 1323; John Causton, 1353; John Nasyng, 1361; John Weston, 1407; Richard Gosselyn, 1428; William Cambridge, 1431; John Bedham, 1472.
30. *London and Middlesex Chantry Certificate, 1548*, ed. C.J. Kitching, London Record Society, 16 (1980), nos. 21, 24, pp. 13–14, 15–16.
31. The material is to be found in the St Mary at Hill Book of Accounts and in a contemporary Miscellany Book, kept now in GL, London, respectively GL, London, MS 1239/1 (i–iii) and 1239/2. A good deal of the material is printed in *The Medieval Records of a London City Church, St Mary at Hill, 1420–1559*, ed. H. Littlehales, EETS, original series, 125 and 128 (1904–5).
32. *Medieval Records of a London City Church*, pp. 1–19. The original transcripts are to be found in the Miscellany Book.
33. Wrytell and Weston's chantries had been amalgamated.
34. *London and Middlesex Chantry Certificate*, no. 9, pp. 5–6.
35. I pursue such an enquiry in C. Burgess, 'Shaping the Parish: St Mary at Hill, London, in the Fifteenth Century', in J. Blair and B. Golding (eds), *The Cloister and the World: Studies in Medieval History in Honour of Barbara Harvey* (Oxford, 1996), pp. 246–86, where some of the other themes mentioned here are dealt with in more depth.
36. There are two fundamental liturgical categories for days: feast and feria. In an ordinary week Sunday is festal and the rest of the days ferial. By the later Middle Ages, however, the calendar in the contemporary Roman Missal was so crowded with saints' days that only six days were without festal observance; it was therefore essential to classify these in importance. There were two categories, simple and, for the most important, double. In practice, double feasts were further divided into as many as four separate ranks; see J. Harper, *The Forms and Orders of Western Liturgy from the Tenth to the Eighteenth Century* (Oxford, 1991), pp. 53–4.
37. *London and Middlesex Chantry Certificate*, no. 9, pp. 5–6.
38. Hugh Baillie makes much of this in his article, 'A London Church in Early Tudor Times', *Music and Letters*, 36 (1955), pp. 55–64.
39. St Andrew Hubbard's churchwardens' accounts, which survive from 1454 to 1621, are preserved in two volumes (GL, London, MS 1239/1 and 1239/2). I have edited these accounts from 1454 to 1570 for publication by the London Record Society. A number of the themes in the following discussion are pursued at greater length in the introduction to that volume.
40. Nevertheless, falling on what would appear to be the anniversary of Juliana Fairhead's death in late January, this celebration came to be one of the main social events in the parish's calendar, and possibly served as a celebration at the end of the financial year just after the audit of the churchwardens' accounts.
41. See C. Burgess and B. Kumin, 'Penitential Bequests and Parish Regimes in Late Medieval England', *Journal of Ecclesiastical History*, 44 (1993), pp. 610–30, for a further investigation of the differences between parish regimes with respect to income.
42. I discuss such practices further in *Pre-Reformation Records of All Saints', Bristol: Part 1*, pp. xxxviii–xli, and in the introduction to my forthcoming edition of the records of St Andrew Hubbard.
43. 'Hocking' occurred on the Monday and Tuesday of the second week of Easter, when bands of men and women held travellers of the opposite sex to ransom for fines; see Duffy, *Stripping of the Altars*, p. 13.
44. *Medieval Records of a London City Church*, p. 239.
45. H.B. Walters, *London Churches at the Reformation* (London, 1939), pp. 146–50.

9. *York under the Yorkists*

1. *York House Books, 1461–1490*, ed. L.C. Attreed (2 vols, Stroud, 1991), vol. 1, p. 270.
2. *York City Chamberlains' Account Rolls, 1396–1500*, ed. R.B. Dobson, Surtees Society, 192 (1980), p. 128; *York House Books*, vol. 1, pp. 139–40, 318; *VCH Yorks., City of York*, ed. P.M. Tillott (Oxford, 1961), pp. 515–16. Shops, tenements and *domus latrinarum* are recorded in the accounts of the bridgemasters of Ouse Bridge, e.g. YCA, C84.2 (for 1468–9). For the *maison Dieu*, see J. Ward, 'Townswomen and their Households', this volume, ch. 2.
3. *York City Chamberlains' Account Rolls*, p. 164.
4. *VCH Yorks., City of York*, pp. 516, 518.
5. D.M. Palliser, *Tudor York* (Oxford, 1979), p. 25; N. Pevsner, *Yorkshire: York and the East Riding, The Buildings of England* (Harmondsworth, 1972), p. 136; A. Raine, *Mediaeval York: A Topographical Survey Based on Original Sources* (London, 1955), pp. 135–8; H. Swanson, *Building Craftsmen in Late Medieval York*, Borthwick Papers, 63 (York, 1983), p. 3; *VCH Yorks., City of York*, p. 543; E. White, *The St Christopher and St George Guild of York*, Borthwick Papers, 72 (York, 1987), pp. 2–4.
6. There is a list of parish churches compiled in 1428 in *York Memorandum Book*, ed. M. Sellers, Surtees Society, 120, 125 (2 vols, 1912–15), vol. 2, pp. 131–3.
7. C. Rawcliffe, 'The Medieval Hospital', this volume, ch. 3.
8. *The Fabric Rolls of York Minster*, ed. J. Raine, Surtees Society, 25 (1859), pp. 253, 258; Raine, *Mediaeval York*, pp. 35–7, 233. St Michael-le-Belfrey was wholly rebuilt between 1525 and 1536: *VCH Yorks., City of York*, p. 396.
9. Raine, *Mediaeval York*, pp. 264–5.
10. R.B. Dobson, *Church and Society in the North of England* (London and Rio Grande, 1996), p. 272; Raine, *Mediaeval York*, p. 227.
11. Royal Commission on Historical Monuments, *An Inventory of Historical Monuments in the City of York, III: South-West of the Ouse* (London, 1972), pp. xlvi, 21.
12. J.S. Purvis, *St. Anthony's Hall, York: A History and a Prospect*, St Anthony's Hall Publications, 1 (York, 1951), pp. 3–5; Raine, *Mediaeval York*, pp. 53–4, 72–4; White, *St Christopher and St George Guild*, pp. 2–4.
13. YCA, C99.6; *VCH Yorks., City of York*, p. 482.
14. Raine, *Mediaeval York*, pp. 53–4, 65, 72–4, 186–7. A number of guilds had pageant houses to store what they needed for their Corpus Christi pageants: *Records of Early English Drama: York*, ed. A.F. Johnston and M. Rogerson (2 vols, Toronto, 1979), vol. 1, pp. 99, 102.
15. *York House Books*, vol. 1, pp. 52–3, vol. 2, p. 734; E. Miller, 'Medieval York', in *VCH Yorks., City of York*, p. 112; Raine, *Mediaeval York*, pp. 154–5, 193.
16. *York House Books*, vol. 1, p. 122; H. Swanson, *Medieval Artisans: An Urban Class in Late Medieval England* (Oxford, 1989), pp. 162–3.
17. *York House Books*, vol. 1, pp. 210–11. The manuscript text says that he 'went to the dore to make ware', but the circumstances of the episode seem to require inserting a letter t.
18. J. Goodall, 'Barley Hall, York', *Country Life* (8 December, 1994), pp. 28–31.
19. Swanson, *Medieval Artisans*, pp. 162–3.
20. Miller, 'Medieval York', in *VCH Yorks., City of York*, pp. 91, 481.
21. Swanson, *Building Craftsmen*, p. 22.
22. P.J.P. Goldberg, *Women, Work, and Life Cycle in a Medieval Economy: Women in York and Yorkshire, c. 1300–1520* (Oxford, 1992), p. 67.
23. YCA, CC.1a, ff. 136v, 137v.
24. For example 'Item dicunt quod pauementum iuxta domum Johannis Wyndryce in Skeldergate est disruptum et fractum in defectu domini dicti tenementi': YCA, CC.1a, f. 136v.
25. YCA, C84.2.
26. *York Memorandum Book*, vol. 2, p. 247; Raine, *Mediaeval York*, pp. 224–5.
27. *York City Chamberlains' Account Rolls*, pp. 144–6, 155.
28. Ibid., pp. 103, 120, 143; Raine, *Mediaeval York*, pp. 167–8, 177–8.
29. *York City Chamberlains' Account Rolls*, pp. 109, 125, 137.
30. Ibid., p. 86.

31. Raine, *Mediaeval York*, pp. 173–4, 243–4.
32. *Fabric Rolls*, pp. 72, 75, 81, 83, 85; Raine, *Mediaeval York*, pp. 146–8.
33. *York City Chamberlains' Account Rolls*, pp. 164–5; Raine, *Mediaeval York*, pp. 222–3.
34. *York Memorandum Book*, vol. 2, p. 216; *York Memorandum Book BY*, ed. J.W. Percy, Surtees Society, 186 (1973), p. 192.
35. *York City Chamberlains' Account Rolls*, pp. xxx, 103, 120, 143, and for repairs to the crane, see pp. 115–16, 131–2, 138, 156, 161–2; Raine, *Mediaeval York*, pp. 240–1.
36. YCA, E32, p. 57.
37. Palliser, *Tudor York*, pp. 201–2.
38. J.N. Bartlett, 'The Expansion and Decline of York in the Later Middle Ages', *Economic History Review*, 2nd series, 12 (1959–60), p. 30; S.R. Rees Jones, 'Property, Tenure and Rent: Some Aspects of the Topography and Economy of Medieval York' (unpublished Ph.D. thesis, 2 vols, University of York, 1987), vol. 1, p. 264.
39. YCA, C80.12, C80.14.
40. Rees Jones, 'Property, Tenure and Rent', vol. 1, pp. 218–19, 264.
41. Goldberg, *Women, Work, and Life Cycle*, p. 61; cf. p. 45.
42. J.H. Harvey, 'Architectural History from 1291 to 1558', in G.E. Aylmer and R. Cant (eds), *A History of York Minster* (Oxford, 1992), pp. 173, 186, 191.
43. YCA, C99.6.
44. Swanson, *Medieval Artisans*, pp. 127–8.
45. *Testamenta Eboracensia*, ed. J. Raine and others, Surtees Society, 4, 30, 45, 53, 79, 106 (6 vols, 1836–1902), vol. 3, p. 261.
46. *York Memorandum Book*, vol. 2, pp. 140, 209; *York Memorandum Book BY*, p. 183.
47. *York Memorandum Book*, vol. 2, pp. 196–7.
48. R.B. Dobson, 'Admissions to the Freedom of the City of York in the Later Middle Ages', *Economic History Review*, 2nd series, 26 (1973), p. 19.
49. Swanson, *Medieval Artisans*, p. 72.
50. Goldberg, *Women, Work, and Life Cycle*, p. 128.
51. J. Ward, 'Townswomen and their Households', this volume, ch. 2.
52. YCA, CC.1a, ff. 45r-47r.
53. *York Memorandum Book*, vol. 2, p. 235; *Memorandum Book XY*, p. 181.
54. Goldberg, *Women, Work, and Life Cycle*, pp. 168–9, 305–9; Swanson, *Medieval Artisans*, pp. 6–8.
55. *York Memorandum Book*, vol. 2, pp. 204–6.
56. Palliser, *Tudor York*, p. 203; Rees Jones, 'Property, Tenure and Rent', vol. 1, pp. 217–18.
57. R.B. Dobson, 'Urban Decline in Late Medieval England', *Transactions of the Royal Historical Society*, 5th series, 27 (1977), p. 12; D.M. Palliser, 'Richard III and York', in R. Horrox (ed.), *Richard III and the North* (Hull, 1986), p. 54; Palliser, *Tudor York*, p. 203.
58. J. Hatcher, 'The Great Slump of the Mid-Fifteenth Century', in R.H. Britnell and J. Hatcher (eds), *Progress and Problems in Medieval England: Essays in Honour of Edward Miller* (Cambridge, 1996), pp. 241–4, 268–9.
59. Bartlett, 'Expansion and Decline', pp. 29–30; Palliser, *Tudor York*, p. 209; Swanson, *Medieval Artisans*, p. 29.
60. *The York Mercers and Merchant Adventurers, 1356–1917*, ed. M. Sellers, Surtees Society, 129 (1918), pp. 75–80.
61. J. Kermode, 'Merchants, Overseas Trade, and Urban Decline: York, Beverley, and Hull, c. 1380–1500', *Northern History*, 23 (1987), pp. 70–2; J. Kermode, 'Money and Credit in the Fifteenth Century: Some Lessons from Yorkshire', *Business History Review*, 45 (1991), pp. 475–501.
62. A.J. Pollard, *North-Eastern England during the Wars of the Roses: Lay Society, War and Politics, 1450–1500* (Oxford, 1990), p. 73; Palliser, *Tudor York*, pp. 208–9; Swanson, *Medieval Artisans*, pp. 143–4.
63. H. Heaton, *The Yorkshire Woollen and Worsted Industry*, 2nd edn (Oxford, 1965), pp. 76, 146.
64. T.W. Hanson, *The Story of Old Halifax* (Halifax, 1920), pp. 82–3; Miller, 'Medieval York', in *VCH Yorks., The City of York*, p. 90; Swanson, *Medieval Artisans*, p. 144.
65. Palliser, *Tudor York*, pp. 8, 209–10.

66. Swanson, *Medieval Artisans*, pp. 162–3.
67. YCA, E25, p. 135 (cf. p. 147).
68. D. Woodward, *Men at Work: Labourers and Building Craftsmen in the Towns of Northern England, 1450–1750* (Cambridge, 1995), pp. 131–2, 274.
69. The payment for the nine weeks was £2 5*s*: *Fabric Rolls*, p. 72.
70. YCA, C99.6.
71. Goldberg, *Women, Work, and Life Cycle*, p. 337.
72. Swanson, *Medieval Artisans*, p. 12, 14, 18–19.
73. *York House Books*, vol. 1, p. 246.
74. P.J.P. Goldberg, 'Mortality and Economic Change in the Diocese of York, 1390–1515', *Northern History*, 24 (1988), pp. 46–7.
75. E. Miller and J. Hatcher, *Medieval England: Towns, Commerce and Crafts, 1086–1348* (London, 1995), p. 326.
76. *York City Chamberlains' Account Rolls*, pp. 105, 122, 147.
77. For example, *York City Chamberlains' Account Rolls*, pp. 144–6 (sale of bread against the assize, sale of diseased meat, sale of salt by false measure).
78. YCA, E32, pp. 45–8, 50–1.
79. *York City Chamberlains' Account Rolls*, p. 146.
80. For example, 'Et de herbagio crescenti super lez motez infra murum ex parte orientali de Walmegatebarr', nuper in tenura Willelmi Couper, iijs.':YCA, C80/12r. There are also numerous rents for such herbage in the accounts of the Ouse Bridgemasters, e.g. YCA, C84.2.
81. *York House Books*, vol. 1, pp. 193–4, 294.
82. *VCH Yorks., City of York*, p. 499.
83. *York House Books*, vol. 1, pp. 213–14, 266–7, 281.
84. A.S. Green, *Town Life in the Fifteenth Century* (2 vols, London, 1894), vol. 1, p. 137n.
85. For example, *York House Books*, vol. 1, p. 46.
86. Miller, 'Medieval York', in *VCH Yorks., City of York*, p. 78; Swanson, *Medieval Artisans*, p. 121.
87. *York Memorandum Book*, vol. 2, pp. 196–7, 242–5, 247–8.
88. Palliser, *Tudor York*, pp. 60–2, 78–9.
89. YCA, CC.1a, ff. 136r–9r. For the six wards see Miller, 'Medieval York', in *VCH Yorks., City of York*, pp. 314–15.
90. YCA, CC.1a, ff. 35r–37r, 45r–47r.
91. YCA, CC.1a, Chamberlains' Accounts 1480 (at the back of the volume), ff. 41v–42v; *York House Books*, vol. 1, pp. 262, 284.
92. *York House Books*, vol. 1, p. 268.
93. YCA, E25. The adjournment on 1 December *ob equitacionem vicecomitis* may have been to enable the sheriff to attend to business of Richard, Duke of Gloucester, who sent instructions to the mayor, aldermen and sheriffs from Raby on 30 November: *York House Books*, vol. 1, p. 171.
94. Miller, 'Medieval York', in *VCH Yorks., City of York*, pp. 75–7.
95. *VCH Yorks., City of York*, pp. 38–9, 68–9.
96. C. Ross, *Richard III* (London, 1981), p. 182.
97. Ibid., p. 71.
98. Ibid., pp. 17, 20, 40.
99. Makers of bags and leather bottles, 1471 (*York Memorandum Book*, vol. 2, pp. 139–42), carpenters, 1462 and 1482 (Ibid., pp. 193–4, 277–83), saddlers, 1473 (Ibid., pp. 194–5), tapiters, 1473 and 1478 (Ibid., pp. 195–6, 198), tanners, 1476 (Ibid., pp. 166–7), fullers, 1464 (Ibid., pp. 206–7), glaziers, 1464 (Ibid., pp. 208–10), dyers, *c.* 1472 (Ibid., pp. 210–12), shipmen, 1478 (Ibid., pp. 215–16), parchment-makers, 1474 (Ibid., pp. 237–8), vintners, 1482–3 (Ibid., pp. 275–7), cappers, 1482 (Ibid., pp. 283–6), pinners and wiredrawers, *c.* 1478 (Ibid., pp. 139–42), armourers (*York Memorandum Book BY*, pp. 176–8), glovers, 1475 (Ibid., pp. 179–81), millers, 1475 (Ibid., pp. 181–3), plasterers and tilers, 1475 (Ibid., pp. 183–4), fletchers, 1476 (Ibid., pp. 190–1), porters, 1476 and 1482 (Ibid., pp. 191–2), bookbinders, 1476 or 1484 (Ibid., p. 193), weavers, 1477 (YCA, A68), spurriers, *c.* 1470 (YCA, G25).

100. For example, *York Memorandum Book*, vol. 2, pp. 166, 194, 208, 216, 277; *York Memorandum Book BY*, pp. 177, 180, 182, 183, 193.
101. For example, *York Memorandum Book*, vol. 2, pp. 167, 181, 193, 196, 212, 276, 285; *York Memorandum Book BY*, pp. 181, 190, 193.
102. For example, *York Memorandum Book*, vol. 2, pp. 207, 210–11, 275, 284; *York Memorandum Book BY*, pp. 179, 182, 190, 193.
103. *York Mercers and Merchant Adventurers*, pp. 71–2.
104. Swanson, *Medieval Artisans*, pp. 60, 63, 96.
105. *York House Books*, vol. 1, pp. 29–30.
106. Swanson, *Medieval Artisans*, pp. 119–20.
107. J.A.F. Thomson, *The Later Lollards, 1414–1520* (Oxford, 1965), pp. 194, 197–8.
108. *VCH Yorks., City of York*, pp. 96–7, 482.
109. N. Orme, *Education and Society in Medieval and Renaissance England* (London, 1989), p. 50; Palliser, *Tudor York*, p. 174.
110. J. Hughes, '"True Ornaments to Know a Holy Man": Northern Religious Life and the Piety of Richard III', in A.J. Pollard (ed.), *The North of England in the Age of Richard III* (Stroud, 1996), p. 172.
111. BI, York, Prob. Reg. 4, ff. 43v (Alice Langwith, 1467), 135v (Helen Couper, 1469), 146v (Margaret Eropp, 1465).
112. For example, BI, York, Prob. Reg. 4, ff. 26r (Agnes Banke, 1471), 27r, v (William Hynde, 1471), 29r (John Huby, 1471), 30v (Thomas White, 1471), 31v (Nicholas Grenebank, 1471).
113. Dobson, *Church and Society*, pp. 259–64.
114. For example, BI, York, Prob. Reg. 4, ff. 9r (John Breerton, 1474), 10r (Joan Newall, 1474), 26r (Agnes Bane, 1474), 27r (Thomas Hudylston, 1471), 27r, v (William Hynde, 1471). Among the printed wills, see *Testamenta Eboracensia*, vol. 2, nos. 215, 219, 225, pp. 270, 273, 280; vol. 3, nos. 90, 92, pp. 243–4, 245–6.
115. BI, York, Prob. Reg. 4, ff. 86r (John Croft of St Sampson parish, 1472), 91r (Robert Sturwyn of St Helen's parish in Stonegate, 1475/1476), 102r (Henry Stoketon of Holy Cross parish, Fossgate, 1476), 115v–116v (Richard Wartere of St Saviour's parish, 1458/1465).
116. BI, York, Prob. Reg. 4, f. 39r. For the role of churchwardens see C. Burgess, 'Religion in London', this volume, ch. 8.
117. Information kindly made available by Dr. J. Kermode.
118. For example, BI, York, Prob. Reg. 4, ff. 26r (Agnes Banke, 1471), 27r, v (William Hynde, 1471), 30v (Thomas Whyte, 1471).
119. P.H. Cullum and P.J.P. Goldberg, 'Charitable Provision in Late Medieval York: "To the Praise of God and the Use of the Poor"', *Northern History*, 29 (1993), pp. 24–39.
120. *VCH Yorks., City of York*, pp. 482–3.
121. White, *St Christopher and St George Guild*, p. 5.
122. D.J.F. Crouch, 'Piety, Fraternity and Power: Religious Gilds in Late Medieval Yorkshire, 1389–1547' (unpublished Ph.D. thesis, University of York, 1995), pp. 211–12.
123. Crouch, 'Piety, Fraternity and Power', p. 188.
124. Crouch, 'Piety, Fraternity and Power', pp. 255–6, 268–71, 273, 290; *VCH Yorks., City of York*, pp. 111, 482.
125. BI, York, Prob. Reg. 4, f. 144r (Laurence Hobson, 1468).

Further Reading

H.S. Bennett, *The Pastons and their England*, 2nd edn (Cambridge, 1932).
P. Binski, *Medieval Death: Ritual and Representation* (London, 1996).
E. Duffy, *The Stripping of the Altars: Traditional Religion in England, 1400–1580* (New Haven and London, 1992).
C. Dyer, *Everyday Life in Medieval England* (London, 1994).
C. Dyer, *Standards of Living in the Later Middle Ages: Social Change in England, c. 1200–1520* (Cambridge, 1989).
B.A. Hanawalt, *The Ties that Bound: Peasant Families in Medieval England* (Oxford, 1986).
A. Hanham, *The Celys and their World: An English Merchant Family of the Fifteenth Century* (Cambridge, 1985).
B. Harvey, *Living and Dying in England, 1100–1540: The Monastic Experience* (Oxford, 1993).
R. Horrox (ed.), *Fifteenth-Century Attitudes: Perceptions of Society in Late Medieval England* (Cambridge, 1994).
C. Rawcliffe, *Medicine and Society in Later Medieval England* (Stroud, 1997).
H. Swanson, *Medieval Artisans: An Urban Class in Late Medieval England* (Oxford, 1989).
R.N. Swanson, *Church and Society in Late Medieval England* (Oxford, 1989).

Index